Advance Praise for

The Big Book of Nature Activities

From the beginning of time we have been connected to nature, but for the first time in history, that connection threatens to be broken for most of an entire generation and perhaps generations to come. When children play in nature — climb trees, build forts and dams in creeks and go exploring — here is what happens: they have less obesity, less likelihood of developing attention deficit disorder, lower rates of depression and suicide, less alcohol and drug abuse, less bullying, plus, they get higher marks. This book provides a wealth of ideas for adults to engage children and themselves in the wonders of the natural world with suggested activities for all seasons. Nature is magic. And nature is free.

—Robert Bateman, artist and naturalist

These are the understandings humans have passed down over hundreds of generations; now we need to make a conscious effort to insure our kids can understand and enjoy the gorgeous world around them.

—Bill McKibben, author, *Long Distance* and *Eaarth*

Today's children are growing up indoors. A lack of nearby access to nature, transportation, school budget cuts, and competing priorities are among the barriers that have left an entire generation inside. *The Big Book of Nature Activities* will be a great resource to all of us who work with children. As a former environmental educator, I know how it feels to see a child light up inside after a first nature experience. As I embark on a new phase of life, motherhood, I look forward to using activities in this book to help me share my love for the outdoors with my son.

—Jackie Ostfeld, Nearby Nature Director, Sierra Club

Nature is disappearing from our surroundings under the assault of human numbers, technology, consumption and an economic imperative. We will only fight to protect what we love but with most Canadians now living in large urban settings, nature has retreated before manicured lawns, concrete and glass so "weeds" and "pests" become remnants of what was once a world of rich biodiversity. *The Big Book of Nature Activities* is a welcome book that should be a bible for all adults and children eager to rediscover the very source of our health, joy and spiritual connection.

—David Suzuki, science broadcaster and environmental activist

The Big Book of Nature Activities

The Big Book of Nature Activities

A Year-Round Guide to Outdoor Learning

JACOB RODENBURG *and* DREW MONKMAN

To my grandchildren Anouk, Juniper and Oscar,
who I hope will enjoy a lifetime
discovering the wonders of the natural world.
DM

For my wonderful wife Jessica,
who appreciates the gifts of nature both great and small.
This book is also dedicated to my children Liam and Anna;
may nature ever be part of their Neighbourwood.
JR

Cover design by Diane McIntosh.
Cover images © iStock.

Printed in Canada. First printing May 2016.

Any other inquiries can be directed by mail to:
New Society Publishers P.O. Box 189, Gabriola Island, BC V0R 1X0, Canada
(250) 247-9737

LIBRARY AND ARCHIVES CANADA CATALOGUING IN PUBLICATION

Rodenburg, Jacob, 1960–, author
The big book of nature activities : a year-round guide to outdoor learning / Jacob Rodenburg and Drew Monkman.

Includes index.
Issued in print and electronic formats.
ISBN 978-0-86571-802-9 (paperback).—ISBN 978-1-55092-596-8 (ebook)

1. Nature study—Activity programs. 2. Natural history—Study and teaching—Activity programs. 3. Natural history—Outdoor books.
I. Monkman, Drew, 1952–, author II. Title.

QH54.5.R63 2016 508 C2016-902792-9
C2016-902793-7

New Society Publishers' mission is to publish books that contribute in fundamental ways to building an ecologically sustainable and just society, and to do so with the least possible impact on the environment, in a manner that models this vision. We are committed to doing this not just through education, but through action. The interior pages of our bound books are printed on Forest Stewardship Council®-registered acid-free paper that is 100% post-consumer recycled (100% old growth forest-free), processed chlorine-free, and printed with vegetable-based, low-VOC inks, with covers produced using FSC®-registered stock. New Society also works to reduce its carbon footprint, and purchases carbon offsets based on an annual audit to ensure a carbon neutral footprint. For further information, or to browse our full list of books and purchase securely, visit our website at: www.newsociety.com

Contents

Key Nature Concepts for Children to Learn 63

Fall: The Cooling Season 81

Winter: The Great Exhale 143

Spring: The Greening Season 197

Summer: The Crescendo 255

Appendix 313

Acknowledgments

A book of this sort would never have been possible without the assistance of many people. First and foremost, we wish to extend our sincere thanks to Judy Hyland, whose superb drawings illustrate much of the book. We are also grateful to Heather Watson for permission to use drawings by Doug Sadler, her late father, a well-known Ontario naturalist, writer and educator. Finally, we are fortunate to be able to include drawings by Jean-Paul Efford and Kim Caldwell as well as noted children's author and illustrator Kady MacDonald Denton.

The accuracy and completeness of this book was greatly enhanced by the following individuals who gave generously of their time to review sections of the manuscript and to share their expertise. Thanks are extended to Ken Abraham, Cathy Beach, Alan Berkowitz, Bob Boekelheide, Gary Burness (Trent University), Glenn Branch, Danielle Brigida (U.S. Fish and Wildlife Service), Glen Caradus, Terry Carpenter, Kim Dobson, Neil Fortin, Donald Fraser, Gord Harrison, Sandy Johnston, Erica Nol (Trent University), Anne Murray, Sheila Potter, Cathy Rowland and Laura Summerfeldt (Trent University).

While many have been supportive of this work, the responsibility for any errors remains with us. Any such reported to the publisher or us will be rectified in subsequent editions.

Introduction

Take one child. Place outdoors in nearby green spaces.
Leave for several hours at a time. Repeat daily.
Sprinkle in a dash of adventure.
Fold in a generous portion of exploration and discovery.
Top with wonder and awe. Let rise....

Connecting to Nature

Not long ago, we took a group of children out for a hike to a nearby wetland. Along the way we came across some northern leopard frogs. "Let's catch 'em," some of the boys yelled out, ready to pounce. "Why don't we watch first," we suggested. So we did. We hunkered down and stayed as still as we could. We observed how one frog hopped slowly against a backdrop of sedges and wildflowers, its wet, spotted skin glistening in the sun. We saw how, in less time than it takes for an eye to blink, a pink tongue lashed out and grabbed a grasshopper. "Did you see that?" a number of kids exclaimed with enthusiasm. "That was awesome!" And it most certainly was.

In an increasingly urbanized world, our children are having fewer encounters with the natural world. They are more likely to experience the flickering screen of a computer or the sounds of traffic than the rhythmic chorus of bird or insect song. And sadly, they are more likely to identify corporate logos or cartoon characters than even a few tree or bird species.

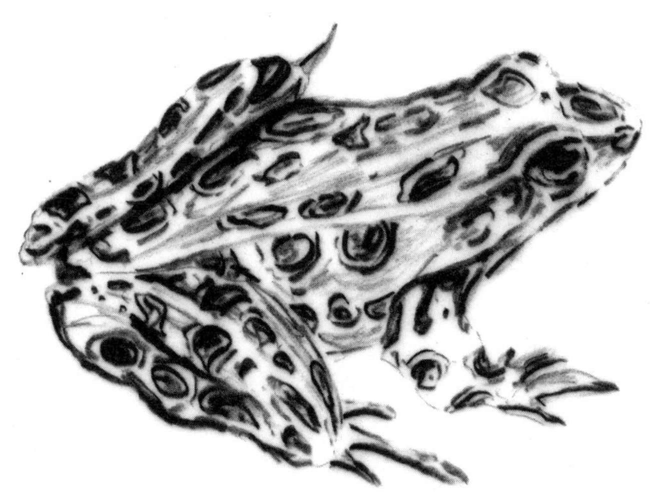

Leopard frog

This book calls on all of us to reclaim the natural world as an integral part of our own world. It also asks us to encourage our children to value nature-based experiences. The kinds of experiences in which we hear birds, feel the mud between our toes and stare skyward at northern lights.

In our families and our schools, a sense of belonging comes from laughing, sharing and learning together. Equally important is the sense of belonging that arises from being immersed in the natural world. All children should be given the chance to recognize that they are part of a larger community of other living things.

Building community is about creating long-term relationships, not only with each other but with the natural world. And like any relationship this involves commitment, time and effort.

Technology is the Answer, But What Was the Question?

Connected. Plugged in. These are today's new buzz words. And no doubt modern technology has opened up possibilities we could scarcely dream about a century ago. But as the architect Cedric Price once asked, "Technology is the answer, but what was the question?"

Nature Numbers for You to Ponder

2,500	The number of advertising messages a child encounters in one day
2,738	The number of hours the average North American child sits in front of a glowing screen, per year
183	The number of hours a child spends outdoors in unstructured play, per year
300	The percentage that obesity has increased over the past 20 years for children aged 6 to 11
300	The number of corporate logos the average child can identify
10	The number of native plants and animals the average child can identify

In this book, we'd like you to think about how to raise caring, responsible and engaged citizens—citizens who view their community as more than a collection of buildings, streets and people, but instead recognize that it includes the living systems that support and nurture us all. To reframe Price's question, "Nature has many answers—how can technology help?" While it is true that there are amazing technological tools—from smartphones to the Internet, from Kindles to iPods—we'd like you to think about selecting technologies that enhance outdoor learning rather than get in its way. As parents, educators, grandparents and community leaders, we all need to help kids—and, increasingly, ourselves—to see the value of connecting to nature, not just to screens.

As a society, we pay a huge price for being disconnected from nature. And nowhere is the price greater than when it comes to climate change. Now, more than ever, we need to pay attention to the many changes in the natural world—some subtle, some dramatic—that are occurring all around us right now. Yes, climate change is partly about disasters, but it's also about numerous "canary in the coal mine" events: early arrival of a migratory bird, early blossoming of a wildflower, late freeze-up of a lake. Noticing these small changes—and understanding that they represent a kind of climate-change early-warning system—requires a critical mass of citizens that know and care deeply for the natural world.

Nature Deficit Disorder

When we grew up (perhaps this sounds familiar to some of you of a certain age) both of us were allowed to play without supervision. Along with a gang of friends we tussled, climbed trees, built forts, rambled. From wading through cattail marshes and playing hide and seek among towering white pines, we came to feel a deep and abiding connection to our environment. We felt as though we belonged to a place, that the green spaces in and around our homes was an integral part of where we lived.

Plugging into nature

A growing body of research in environmental education has emerged called "significant life experiences." Researchers wanted to know what kinds of childhood experiences inspired people involved in conservation to want to protect the environment. Perhaps knowing this would help shape future environmental education curriculum. Not surprisingly, most of the respondents described rich encounters with the natural world while they were growing up. They lived on farms, they tramped through marshes, they visited cottages, they hiked, they canoed, they camped and they discovered. In short, they *engaged* with their natural surroundings. They felt that they were an integral part of their environment. As environmental educator Joy Palmer noted, "Childhood experiences in the outdoors is the single most important factor in developing personal concern for the environment."

In this book, we want to ask, Where will tomorrow's environmentalists come from? Who will advocate for shrinking habitat and the containment of urban sprawl? Who will speak for threatened and endangered species and for our own green spaces, when the formative experiences that make for caring stewards of our environment are removed from childhood?

In his popular book *Last Child in the Woods*, Richard Louv has a chilling term for those children who grow up in a world without nature. He coined the phrase "Nature Deficit Disorder" to describe some of the characteristics associated with a childhood spent indoors. He does not use the term in a medical sense. Rather, he wants us to consider what the long-term impacts might be for a child who grows up having little or no contact with the natural world. Here are some unexpected consequences of a childhood spent indoors:

- Because children are spending less time outside (and therefore are not getting regular exercise), rates of childhood obesity in North America have almost tripled over the past 20 years.
- Playing in nature promotes healthy development. Swedish scientists have found that children who explore and play in natural environments tend to be less competitive and more cooperative, and demonstrate fewer incidents of "interrupted play" (when adults have to intervene to prevent fights) than those who play in areas dominated by asphalt and play structures. Researchers

have discovered that playing in nature enhances creative thought, stimulates imaginative play and improves a child's ability to concentrate during school.

So, just what is stopping children from going outside? Here are a few factors:

- The natural world is perceived as dangerous. Louv calls this the "Bogeyman Syndrome." Studies have shown that the incidence of stranger abduction (stranger danger) is no more acute than it was 30 years ago, but he believes that the sheer amount of violence dramatized on the news and in TV shows and movies amplifies parents' fears.
- Liability concerns have put real pressure on school boards, city parks, daycares and other institutions to make sure children in their care stay "safe." Ironically, keeping children inside when the weather becomes cold, cutting down bushes near a school or getting rid of an untidy section of park land may just do the opposite. They prevent real opportunities for children to participate in natural play. Louv wants us to consider the opposite point of view; he believes it is unsafe *not* to take children outside.
- Nature has become the unknown. Not only do fewer and fewer children know the names of common plants and animals, but many people are honestly afraid that nature is out to get them. One common example is a generalized fear of spiders and insects. In reality there are just a few hazards, among them ticks, a few stinging insects, a handful of poisonous plants and snakes and the remote chance of getting lost. Serious dangers, such as an attack from a wild animal, are so rare as to be negligible. For example, there are about three bear-related fatalities per year in North America. Compare this with 115 deaths every single day from vehicle crashes in the United States—one every 13 minutes. Every ten minutes someone gets injured falling down stairs in North America. And yet none of us thinks twice about getting into an automobile or climbing stairs. But we're scared of camping in the wilderness!

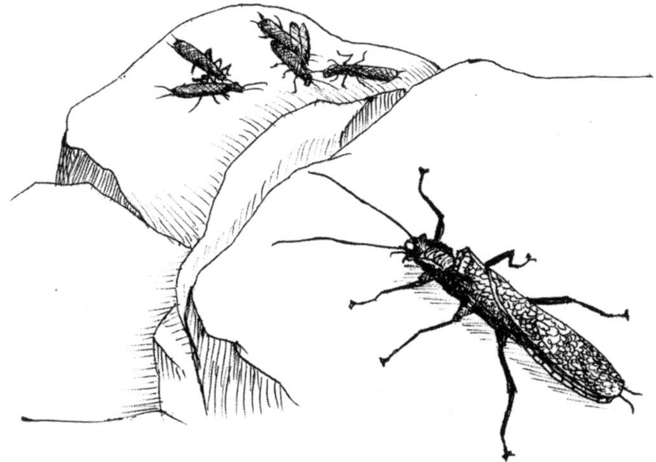

Winter stoneflies

- Unsupervised play is no longer socially acceptable. There is real social pressure to know where your children are for every moment of the day. Kids are "super" supervised. Yet Louv tells us that children learn important life skills by negotiating, problem solving and sharing during periods of unstructured play.

About *The Big Book of Nature Activities*

We hope that this book will inspire you with ideas, activities and information that will help foster a sense of place and, as importantly, a sense of belonging to your local environment. "Seeing" in nature means knowing what to look for and what to expect.

Nature is filled with rhythms, with cyclical change. This means being aware each and every day of signs that the seasons are changing; tuning in to the presence or absence of bird, frog and insect song; noticing the mix of tree species around us; appreciating how the smell of the air changes with each passing month; and being able to identify and describe the typical flora, fauna, landforms and climate of your region. Nature awareness is a feeling of comfort, integration and familiarity, a sense of being among friends, when you are out in the natural world. The upside for society is that by feeling this emotional connectedness, you automatically want to do your part to protect the natural environment.

We also want to make people more aware of evolution and how it is manifested in even the most common, backyard species. Armed with a little knowledge, we can learn to appreciate the wonder that resides in all species, not just the charismatic ones. The evolutionary story of the dandelion is every bit as compelling as that of the blue whale. Knowing a little bit about how evolution has shaped the behavior and appearance of a species enhances our appreciation of nature.

Who The Big Book of Nature Activities *is for*

This book is a resource guide for parents, grandparents, teachers, environmental educators, daycare providers, youth groups, camp leaders, park naturalists—anyone who wants to take children and

adolescents outside. Many kids become interested in nature if they witness adults showing a keen interest as well. In fact, though many of the activities are aimed at children, they often apply equally to adults.

What is inside The Big Book of Nature Activities?

We created this book to be a compendium of nature-based activities organized around seasonal change. Inside you'll find activity suggestions based on what is happening in nature during each season of the year.

Structure of season chapters

Introduction to season: An evocative description of the "mood" of the season and an overview of what is going on at that time of year.

Key Natural Events and Regional Highlights: A summary of some key events in fauna, flora, weather and the sky across North America but specific to each region. Keep a record: we suggest you check off and date each of these events as you observe them. We'll also suggest activities in the seasonal chapters that relate to the events.

Poems: Seasonal poems lending themselves well to memorization. Memorizing the poems also adds greatly to one's "sense of season," since the writing often captures the unique feeling of the time of year.

Collection Challenge: Suggestions for what to display or collect over the season for your nature table and collection box.

Art in the Park: Ideas for what to sketch and photograph—suggestions on interesting phenomena to draw or snap pictures of. The photographs can be used to make a nature journal, indicating where and when each picture was taken.

What is Wrong with the Scenario?: Nature Aware? Can you spot the mistakes made in a seasonal description?

Story of Black Cap, the Chickadee: A story that follows a black-capped chickadee and its interesting behaviors over the course of the year; includes suggested activities.

At Your Magic Spot: A suggested activity that children—or adults—can do at their "Magic Spot." This is a special, nature-rich area close to home that the child has chosen and visits regularly. It is a place to write and draw about sightings, feelings, questions, etc.

Exploring the season: Things to do. A selection of fun activities like games, exploration ideas, crafts and scavenger hunts is based on what is happening in nature during this season. We'll activate your senses, keep track of phenological events, and explore evolution and fascinating aspects of birds, mammals, reptiles and amphibians, fish, invertebrates, plants, fungi, weather and the sky. We also offer up suggestions on how to make nature part of seasonal celebrations.

Darwin: The father of modern biology will share facts, ideas and inspiration about evolution during each season. He'll even tell budding young scientists what still needs to be discovered!

Carl Sagan: Sagan was a famous American astronomer and science communicator. He will tell you about the wonder of the universe.

Neil deGrasse Tyson: Tyson is an America astrophysicist and director of the Hayden Planetarium in New York City. In 2014, he hosted the television series "Cosmos: A Spacetime Odyssey." Tyson and Sagan together will help to explain some of our current thinking about the universe"

Geographical Area Covered

The natural events described in the book cover an area extending from British Columbia in the northwest down to northern California in the southwest, and from Newfoundland in the northeast down to North Carolina in the southeast. This area includes six ecological regions, as identified by the U.S. Environmental Protection Agency (Western Ecology Division).

Ecological Zones of North America

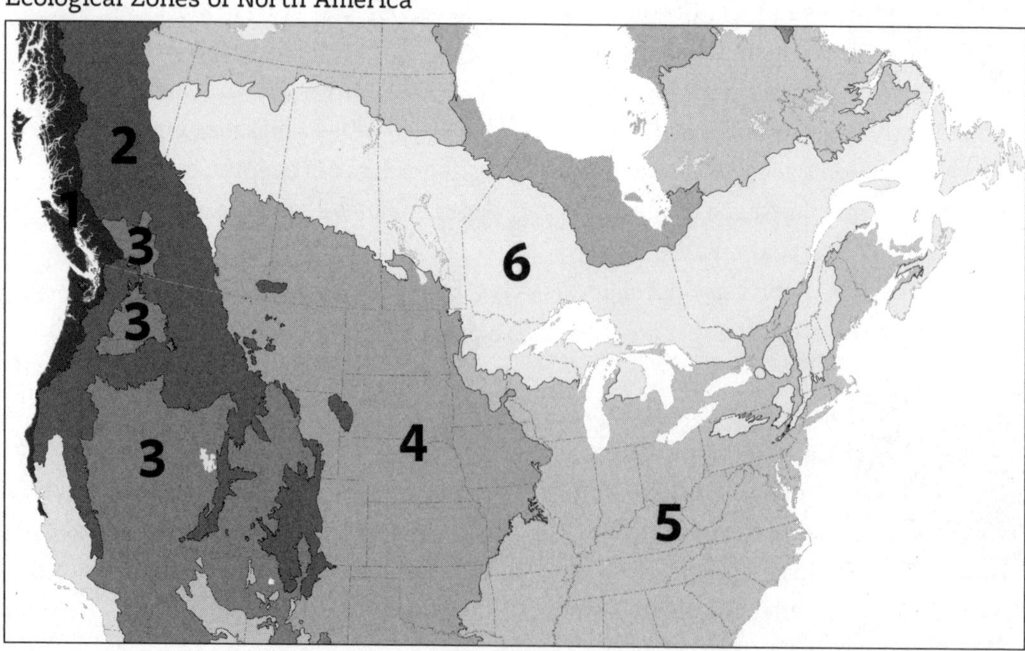

North American Ecological Zones

Region	Boundaries	Description
1. Marine West Coast	The Pacific Coast from Alaska south through northern California.	Characterized by mountains bordered by a coastal plain. Has the wettest climate of North America and contains large areas of temperate rain forest.
2. Northwestern Forested Mountains	The mountainous regions of the interior of British Columbia, Washington, Oregon, northern California, Idaho, Montana, Wyoming, Nevada, Utah and Colorado.	Contains four biological (life) zones: the Foothills Zone (transition from plains to mountains); the Montane Zone (lower slopes and valleys above the foothills, with the greatest variety of wildflowers, trees and shrubs); the Subalpine Zone (from the upper edge of the Montane to the treeline, with dense clumps of evergreens and wildflower meadows—most people's image of the western mountains); and the Alpine (Tundra) Zone (the area above the treeline, with bare rocks, glaciers and alpine meadows).
3. North American Deserts	Covers parts of south-central British Columbia, Washington, Idaho, Oregon, Nevada and northern California. Much of this area is also known as the Great Basin.	Distinguished from the adjacent forested mountain ecological region by its dryness, its unique shrubs and cacti (with a lack of trees) and generally lower relief. It has a desert and steppe climate, arid to semi-arid with marked seasonal temperature extremes.
4. Great Plains	From the prairies of southern Alberta, Saskatchewan and Manitoba, south through the Great Plains of the United States to Kansas, to western Indiana in the east and the foothills of the Rocky Mountains in the west.	The Great Plains is distinguished by mostly flat grassland with very few forests. The climate is semi-arid. Almost 95 percent of the prairies have been converted into farmland, with predictable effects on the original plant populations. Many native prairie vegetation types have been radically transformed.
5. Eastern Temperate Forests	Covers southern Minnesota in the northwest, New Brunswick in the northeast, Missouri in the southwest and North Carolina in the southeast.	This ecological region has a moderate to mildly humid climate with a relatively dense and diverse forest cover. There is a great diversity of species.
6. Northern Forests	From northern Alberta east to Newfoundland and Nova Scotia, and south through parts of New Hampshire, Vermont, Pennsylvania, Michigan, Wisconsin and Minnesota.	Distinguished by extensive boreal forests and a high density of lakes situated on the Canadian Shield. The climate is characterized by long, cold winters and short, warm summers.

100 Continent-wide Species to Learn

40 Birds: Canada goose, snow goose, mallard, bufflehead, common merganser, common loon, double-crested cormorant, great blue heron, turkey vulture, osprey, red-tailed hawk, bald eagle, sandhill crane, killdeer, herring gull, mourning dove, snowy owl, downy woodpecker, northern flicker, peregrine falcon, merlin, common raven, American crow, tree swallow, barn swallow, black-capped chickadee, white-breasted nuthatch, house wren, American robin, European starling, cedar waxwing, common yellowthroat, yellow-rumped warbler, chipping sparrow, song sparrow, dark-eyed junco, red-winged blackbird, brown-headed cowbird, house finch, American goldfinch

15 Mammals: Big brown bat, black bear, raccoon, mink, river otter, striped skunk, coyote, red fox, bobcat, beaver, muskrat, deer mouse, porcupine, snowshoe hare, white-tailed deer

21 Invertebrates: Canada tiger swallowtail, clouded sulphur, monarch, woolly bear (Isabella moth), tent caterpillar, common green darner, autumn meadowhawk, bluet damselfly, fall field cricket, snowy tree cricket, Carolina grasshopper (locust), dog-day cicada, honeybee, bumblebee, yellow jacket, firefly, whirligig beetles, crab spider, harvestman (daddy longlegs), wood tick, water strider

4 Amphibians and Reptiles: Bullfrog, painted turtle, leopard frog, garter snake

7 Trees and Shrubs: Tamarack, white spruce, quaking (trembling) aspen, white birch, weeping willow, chokecherry, poison ivy

13 Wildflowers, Ferns and Fungi: New England aster, black-eyed susan, Canada goldenrod, marsh marigold, oxeye daisy, Queen Anne's lace, jewelweed, wood fern, shaggy mane mushroom, morel, fly amanita, giant puffball, artist's conk

Some Key Regional Species to Learn

1. Marine West Coast

25 Birds: Tundra swan, harlequin duck, surf scoter, red-throated loon, western grebe, black oystercatcher, western sandpiper, dunlin, glaucous-winged gull, barn owl, Anna's hummingbird, red-breasted sapsucker, Steller's jay, western scrub jay, violet-green swallow, chestnut-backed chickadee, bushtit, Pacific wren, varied thrush, spotted towhee, fox (sooty) sparrow, white-crowned sparrow, western meadowlark, Brewer's blackbird, Bullock's oriole

10 Mammals: Columbian black-tailed deer, elk, Townsend's chipmunk, western gray squirrel, Douglas' squirrel, California sea lion, harbor seal, orca, gray whale, sea otter

4 Amphibians: Western toad, Pacific tree-frog, rough-skinned newt, western redback salamander

5 Fish: Chinook salmon, pink salmon, chum salmon, coho salmon, sockeye salmon

5 Invertebrates: Painted lady, sea stars, anemones, banana slug, almond-scented millipede

6 Trees and shrubs: Western red cedar, coastal Douglas fir, coast redwood, bigleaf maple, Pacific madrone (arbutus), salal

5 Wildflowers: Douglas aster, California goldfields, California buttercup, California poppy, western skunk cabbage

2. *Northwestern Forested Mountains*

15 Birds: Western grebe, golden eagle, rufous hummingbird, violet-green swallow, Steller's jay, Clark's nutcracker, black-billed magpie, mountain chickadee, American dipper, mountain bluebird, spotted towhee, western tanager, yellow-headed blackbird, Bullock's oriole, western meadowlark

10 Mammals: Mule deer, bighorn sheep, elk, cougar, American badger, American pika, yellow-bellied marmot, red squirrel, golden-mantled ground squirrel, least chipmunk

Western meadowlark

5 Amphibians and Reptiles: Western tiger salamander, western toad, Sierran treefrog, western skink, rubber boa

2 Fish: Cutthroat trout, rainbow trout

3 Invertebrates: Weidemeyer's admiral, anise swallowtail, eight-spotted skimmer dragonfly

10 Trees and Shrubs: Engelmann spruce, lodgepole pine, Douglas fir, ponderosa pine, Rocky Mountain juniper, Rocky Mountain maple, Saskatoon berry, rabbit-brush, thimbleberry, sagebrush

5 Wildflowers: Old man's whiskers, mariposa lily, yellow avalanche lily, alpine bistort, western showy aster

3. *North American Desert*

22 Birds: Cinnamon teal, California quail, greater sage-grouse, western grebe, Swainson's hawk, golden eagle, black-necked stilt, American avocet, barn owl, black-chinned hummingbird, red-naped sapsucker, prairie falcon, Bewick's wren, violet-green swallow, mountain chickadee, black-billed magpie, western bluebird, lark sparrow, black-throated sparrow, yellow-headed blackbird, western meadowlark, Bullock's oriole

6 Mammals: Golden-mantled ground squirrel, black-tailed jackrabbit, American badger, bighorn sheep, pronghorn, mule deer

5 Amphibians and Reptiles: Great Basin spadefoot toad, tiger salamander, short-horned lizard, sagebrush lizard, Great Basin gopher snake

7 Invertebrates: Western tiger swallowtail, Becker's white, eight-spotted skimmer, black meadowhawk, pallid-winged grasshopper, Jerusalem cricket, pale windscorpion

10 Shrubs, Grasses, Wildflowers and Fungi: sagebrushes (e.g., big sagebrush), rabbitbrush, fourwing saltbush, greasewood, bluebunch wheatgrass, cheatgrass, sulphur-flower buckwheat, plains pricklypear cactus, arrowleaf balsamroot, desert stalked puffball

4. Great Plains

17 Birds: Cinnamon teal, sharp-tailed grouse, western grebe, American white pelican, Swainson's hawk, black-necked stilt, American avocet, American woodcock, ruby-throated hummingbird, blue jay, black-billed magpie, dickcissel, vesper sparrow, northern cardinal, yellow-headed blackbird, western meadowlark, bobolink

10 Mammals: American bison, mule deer, pronghorn antelope, eastern gray squirrel, black-tailed prairie dog, white-tailed jackrabbit, Richardson's ground squirrel, Franklin's ground squirrel, American badger, black-footed ferret

6 Amphibians and Reptiles: Tiger salamanders, striped chorus frog, Great Plains toad, spiny softshell turtle, prairie rattlesnake, short-horned lizard

4 Fish: Walleye, largemouth bass, lake whitefish, orange-spotted sunfish

3 Invertebrates: Spring azure, eight-spotted skimmer, black meadowhawk

14 Trees, Shrubs, Grasses and Wildflowers: Eastern red cedar, eastern cottonwood, greasewood, sagebrush, blue grama grass, big bluestem, cheatgrass (invasive), white prairie aster, red swampfire, eastern pasqueflower, bitter root, Indian blanket, Wyoming Indian paintbrush, wood lily

5. Eastern Temperate Forest

19 Birds: Great egret, American woodcock, laughing gull, barred owl, chimney swift, ruby-throated hummingbird, red-bellied woodpecker, blue jay, purple martin, tufted titmouse, Carolina wren, eastern bluebird, northern mockingbird, white-throated sparrow, northern cardinal, rose-breasted grosbeak, common grackle, eastern meadowlark, Baltimore oriole

8 Mammals: Fox squirrel, eastern gray squirrel, red squirrel, southern flying squirrel, eastern cottontail, groundhog, Virginia opossum, humpback whale

17 Amphibians amd Reptiles: Spring peeper, chorus frog, gray treefrog, eastern cricket frog, green frog, American toad, eastern newt, eastern red-backed salamander, northern dusky salamander, spotted salamander, marbled salamander, common snapping turtle, box turtle, wood turtle, northern water snake, redbelly snake, eastern milksnake

7 Fish: American shad, channel catfish, pumpkinseed, bluegill, largemouth bass, smallmouth bass, yellow perch

10 Invertebrates: Butterflies: white admiral, viceroy; moths: Cecropia, luna, hummingbird clearwing moth; dragonflies: beaverpond baskettail; damselflies: river jewelwing, bluets; cicadas: Linnaeus's 17-year cicada; true katydids: common true katydid

18 Trees and Shrubs: Eastern white cedar, white pine, bald cypress, sugar maple, red maple, white oak, shagbark hickory, black cherry, tulip tree, white ash, black walnut, sassafras, sweetgum, American sycamore, flowering dogwood, staghorn sumac, Virginia creeper, pussy willow

12 Wildflowers and Ferns: Eastern skunk cabbage, Hepatica, white trillium, azure bluet, wild geranium, yellow lady's slipper, wild columbine, trailing arbutus, great laurel, common blue violet, ostrich fern, sensitive fern

6. Northern Forest

20 Birds: Ruffed grouse, American woodcock, barred owl, chimney swift, ruby-throated hummingbird, yellow-bellied sapsucker, pileated woodpecker, eastern phoebe, red-eyed vireo, blue jay, gray jay, gray catbird, ovenbird, white-throated sparrow, white-crowned sparrow, northern cardinal, common grackle, eastern meadowlark, bobolink, Baltimore oriole

8 Mammals: Moose, gray wolf, eastern chipmunk, eastern gray squirrel, red squirrel, woodchuck, harp seal, humpback whale

12 Amphibians and Reptiles: Spring peeper, gray treefrog, green frog, bullfrog, wood frog, American toad, blue-spotted salamander, spotted salamander, eastern

Ovenbird and young

newt, eastern red-backed salamander, common snapping turtle, northern water snake

10 Fish: Brook trout, lake trout, white sucker, northern pike, muskellunge, walleye, yellow perch, pumpkinseed, smallmouth bass, rock bass

10 Invertebrates: Butterflies: European skipper, white admiral, viceroy; moths: Cecropia, luna, hummingbird clearwing; dragonflies: beaverpond baskettail, Canada darner, familiar bluet; damselflies: river jewelwing

20 Plants: Balsam fir, white pine, jack pine, red maple, red oak, white ash, staghorn sumac, lilac, red-osier dogwood, Labrador tea, bunchberry, trailing arbutus, pink lady's slipper, blue flag lily, pitcher plant, yellow trout lily, white trillium, Hepatica, tall flat-topped aster, common milkweed

How to Raise a Naturalist

Eric Fromm coined the term *biophilic*, to describe the innate need all children have to connect with other species, what he called the desire to be "attracted to all that is alive and vital." In other words, children are born loving nature. It is a need that is deeply rooted in all our genes. Edith Cobb argues that there is a window of time lasting from early childhood until about 14 years of age when, if children are provided with rich and repeated experiences in nature, they are more likely to develop a life long love for the natural world. If we keep our children indoors, however, we run the risk that nature may simply become the backdrop for their daily lives, as inconsequential as the billboards, neon lights and telephone poles that decorate our cityscapes.

Children are active, curious, energetic and enthusiastic. They love to play, imagine, discover and explore. No wonder that a conventional hike through a park or the woods can be boring for a child. Take a few steps off the trail, however, and roll over a log, dip a butterfly net in a pond or romp along the edges of a rushing stream, and the experience suddenly becomes an adventure.

So, how can adults be effective mentors?

- Open doors but don't "push them through." Ultimately, loving nature should never be forced. Children will pick up and emulate your enthusiasm. Take time out of your personal life to get outdoors. If children see you making an effort to be out in nature, they'll want to come, too.

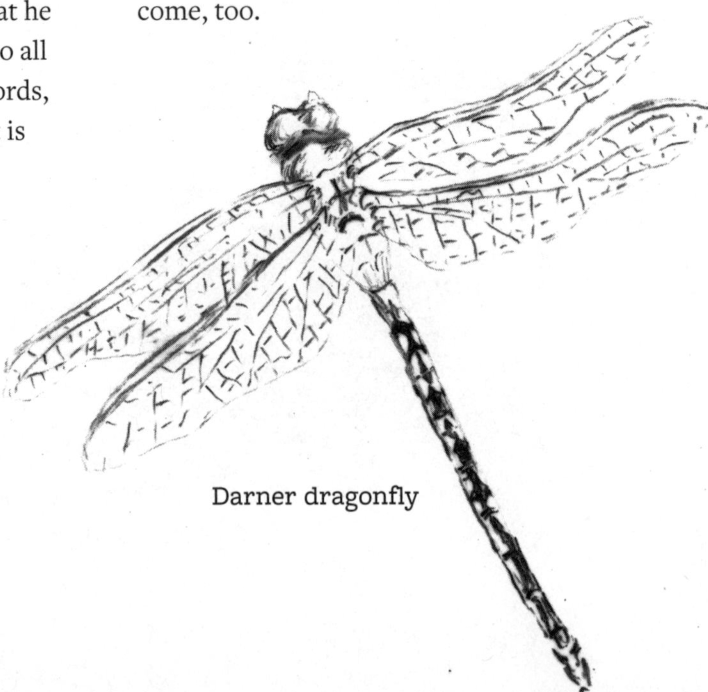

Darner dragonfly

- Go forth with explorer's eyes. Be amazed at what you see, but also allow your children the gift of discovery. For example, you might know where to find salamanders along a certain trail. You could simply say to your children, "Hey… do you want to find a salamander?" Or you might say, "I wonder what we'll find under these logs?" In the first instance, you have owned the discovery; in the second, the excitement and joy belongs to the child. There is nothing quite so thrilling as a child bellowing out in a lusty voice, "Look what I found!" Remember to give children the time and space for discovery. Revealing a small hint of that which is normally hidden from our sight is empowering, inspiring and, at times, simply unforgettable.
- Remember that play can be a powerful teacher. The natural landscape lends itself to creative play. A stick can become a magic wand, a sword or a tent pole; a copse of trees, a castle. It is through unstructured play that children cultivate and enhance their imaginations. Being creative means creating—letting your children make forts, mud pies and flower crowns. Never doubt the value of exploring and playing in the natural environment—these experiences are at the very heart of developing young naturalists.
- Buy your child a good hand lens (10×), a small compound microscope and, when they are ten or so, a good pair of binoculars. Teach them to delight in the very small, from the cells of leaves enlarged by a microscope to the feathery antennae of a moth revealed by a hand lens. A close-up view gives you an entirely different perspective on the natural world. Learn to use binoculars to view birds, the Moon or even a distant galaxy (see page 27).
- Encourage building in nature. One of our most memorable childhood experiences was building a fort or tree house. Children have a yearning to create dens, nests and hiding places. The process of building involves problem solving, understanding the properties of natural materials and lots of exercise! Together, build a survival debris hut (see page 134).
- Set up a terrarium in your house. A terrarium is basically an aquarium that is filled with plants, soil and rocks suitable for terrestrial or land-based creatures. Allow your children to bring home "pets" for a few days: caterpillars, frogs, insects. Don't forget to release each critter in the same place you found it! (see page 132).

Ash seeds make a nice addition to the collection table

- Create a collection table and let your children display their discoveries—perhaps a collection of shells, feathers, plant material, living invertebrates. When they find something new, put something else back from where it came—in this way the table changes over time.
- Encourage your child to join up with a local group of birders on outings. This can be a particularly powerful experience when some of the birders are teenagers—they make excellent role models. See if there are any Junior Field Naturalist Clubs in your area.
- Take your child to the zoo, the aquarium and the botanical garden. Pick a particular animal or plant (orchids for example) for close-up study and focused observation instead of just wandering passively through the exhibits.
- Take your child camping. Being outside for 24 hours a day allows you to see and hear things you might otherwise miss. Positive camping memories will make it much more likely that your child will want to camp as an adult.
- Speak positively about nature. We forget as adults how powerful language can be. Be careful how you speak about nature—we communicate values through our words and expressions. Seeing a bug may elicit the response "Yuck—is that ever creepy!" or "It's dirty—you don't know where it's been." To cultivate a sense of wonder, you need to use the language of wonder: "Wow—is that ever cool"—"Did you see that?" Show surprise, curiosity and joy in everyday observations of the natural world: the movements of an ant, the wagging of a dog's tail, the stealth of a cat, the smell of a flower, the myriad shapes of leaves. In other words, take notice, show respect and, more than anything, display *enthusiasm*, because kids will see that you truly value and love the natural world.
- Huh? Consider the art of questioning. A question can either inspire curiosity or shut it down completely. The engine of learning is curiosity. A name or a label is merely a beginning point, the start of a story—it is up to you to keep the story going! A good question should invite other questions. Think about your questions as ways to encourage kids to ask why, to wonder, to marvel at the natural world and to want to explore further. Let's think about the bird called a white-breasted nuthatch. A good beginning question

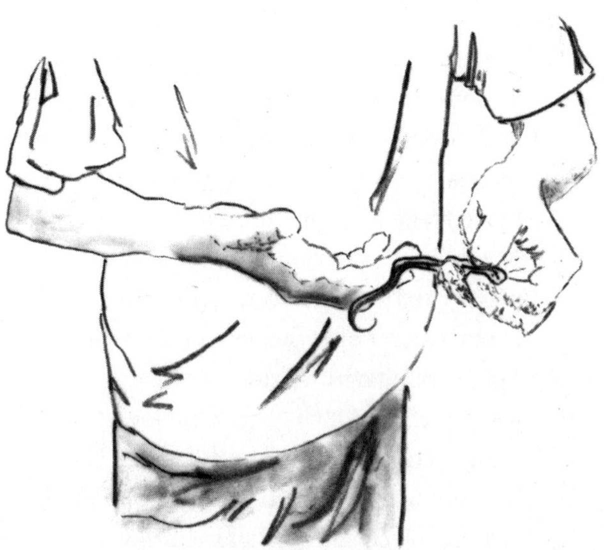

Child holding a garter snake

might be, "Why is she upside down on the tree?" (Scientists think she can spot insects that right-side birds miss). How does she fly? (Like a rollercoaster, with an up-and-down pattern). Why is she called a nuthatch? (From her ability to jam large nuts into tree bark, then whack them with her sharp bill to "hatch" out the seed from the inside.) Don't be afraid to say "I don't know!" when a child asks you a question. Think of this as an opportunity to find out together. Look it up. And if you still don't know, isn't it wonderful that there are still so many things that science does not yet understand? You might suggest that this is a question that they, as curious young people, may be able to find the answer to when they grow up.

White-breasted nuthatch

How Do We Get Kids Outside?

(and more or less on their own)

Despite a decrease in violence against children in recent years, parental *fear* is still real. This should be respected and not dismissed. Not many parents feel comfortable letting their kids roam free, so we need ways to reduce perceived risk, manage fear and still get our kids outside.

1. Take your kids outdoors yourself but be a "hummingbird parent": If we want our children or grandchildren to experience nature, we'll need to be more proactive than parents of past generations. Just try to stay out of your kids' way much of the time, so they can explore and play in nature on their own. You can always "zoom in" like a hummingbird, when safety may be an issue (which thankfully, isn't very often). Slowly increase this distance and their autonomy as time goes by. Kids crave and thrive on autonomy, so don't be afraid to "let them loose" sometimes—with a minimum of rules!

2. Organize family nature clubs: An increasingly popular way to get kids engaged with nature is for families to get together and create their own informal nature clubs. The benefits are many: family ties are strengthened, a sense of community is enhanced and kids often become passionate about nature by experiencing it with their peers. To get started, all you need is a group of people with an interest in connecting children with the natural world. Start by inviting your friends and their families to gather once or twice a month in a nearby park, preferably with trails. You will be surprised how interesting your local parks can be. Later, you may wish to advertise at your school or community organization, should you want to expand the group. And don't worry if you lack nature skills. All that really matters is being enthusiastic about getting your family outdoors. Consider asking a local naturalist to come along on some of your hikes to help with species identification. Groups usually gather before or after the hike for a potluck meal, after which the kids play on their own in a nearby woods or field, while the adults relax and socialize.

Characteristics of Kids and Nature: Ages and Stages

We've found that children of different ages respond to nature in different ways. Use the hints below to help you approach nature with preschoolers, teens and in-betweens.

Younger children

1. Nature playscapes: Kids aged three to eight love to pretend, imagine and, especially, play. Never underestimate the power of creative play in natural landscapes. The space under the fragrant branches of a spruce can magically transform into a castle or a spaceship. A fallen log might morph into a canoe or pirate ship.

2. Micro-environments: I remember taking my two young children to a wonderful overlook. We hiked the better part of two hours to get there. The view was breathtaking, with lakes and hills glistening in the afternoon sun. And there were my children hunched at their feet—staring at a caterpillar crawling along the ground. Young children have a contracted view of the environment; they respond to what is immediately in front of them. Spend time with your younger children soaking in the details of your surroundings.

3. Tending: Young children yearn to belong and crave connections to other living things. They want to nurture and care. Provide your children with the chance to tend a garden, raise monarchs, look after a lizard. Even growing herbs in planter boxes and harvesting the fragrant leaves connect children to the natural world and to local food. Don't forget that children learn by imitating. When I was shoveling in the garden, so was my three-year-old daughter, right alongside me—with her own tiny shovel. After we went for a nature walk, she would set up her own nature walk, right there in the backyard. Children are more likely to love nature when they see you making a genuine effort to love it yourself.

Middle childhood (In betweens)

Eight to 12 is an evocative age—an age ripe for discovery and immersion in natural landscapes. Flipping over logs, climbing trees, wading in wetlands, jumping in puddles, catching bugs in ponds and staring upward into the deep beyond of the night sky are all activities that children of this age love to engage in.

1. Exploration and discovery: Our children are born explorers, full of unbridled enthusiasm and energy for the world around them. Sadly, this is also the time that many children are holed up inside, trapped behind a glowing screen. If we don't connect them to the wonder and mystery that resides in nearby green spaces now, they may grow into teens that experience the outdoors as a place that is uncomfortable, foreign and, at worst, irrelevant to their daily lives.

2. Action projects: Kids need to feel a sense of agency, need to believe that they can and will make a difference. Encourage kids to participate in activities that enhance nature in their own neighborhood, perhaps by naturalizing a backyard or a school ground—building nesting boxes, planting trees, creating pollinator gardens—or by helping to protect local green spaces.

Older children

As kids get older (ages 12 to 17), they crave adventure! They want to prove that they are tough, strong and resilient (which of course, they are!). They often yearn for activities with an element of competition such as birding.

1. Recreational exploration: Ah, the pendulum teenager: one moment sitting sullen, arms folded on the couch, angry at the world; the next moment, jumping around the living room, coursing with energy—enough to power a small town. One way to deal with these mood swings is to introduce your teenagers to the outdoor skills that help them connect to nature. Take them on an overnight camping trip. Make sure that your itinerary is robust enough to be challenging but that they have the food, clothing and equipment to be comfortable, even in inclement weather. Competitive activities such as geo-caching are also popular with teenagers and still have a modicum of nature appreciation.

2. Traditional skills: Have your children experiment with bow-drill fire-making, shelter-building, basic tool-making or cordage. There is something immensely satisfying about creating your own fire—by rubbing wood against wood. Some of

Child rolling over a log

our most popular children's programming has involved teaching traditional skills. We've included traditional games and activities in this book.

Build Nature Skills: For teenagers who really show an interest in nature, encourage them to:

3. Contact a local naturalist club: They may know of teenagers in your community who are active birders. Your son or daughter may be able to join them in their outings.

4. High schools often have environmental or outdoor clubs: Many schools also take part in "envirothons," environmentally themed academic competitions. Contact the science department at your high school.

5. Find a local cause and encourage your kids to get involved: There is always a wetland to save, a park to protect or habitats to enhance. Kids need to feel like they can make a difference. Participating in local action empowers children and helps them recognize what it means to be part of a larger community.

Making a fire with a bow drill

Adults and Nature: How Knowledge and Appreciation Enhance Our Lives

From the joy of encountering a brand new season to the sense of wonder as a loon's call echoes across a starlit lake, adults find pleasure from nature in so many ways. Spending time in nature makes us not only physically fitter but also psychologically healthier. We also gain a more balanced perspective on the world's problems, and this in turn makes us less inclined to believe in the myth of human dominance of—and separateness from—nature. Many of us who develop a deep relationship with the natural world come to understand that we are as much a part of the biosphere as any other species. Our physical, mental and spiritual well-being depend not only on clean air, clean water, healthy soil and a stable climate but also on the company of other species.

Almost everyone has an intuitive sense of the restorative power of natural environments. As Trent University psychologist Dr. Lisa Nisbet writes: "We may not think of nature contact as a health practice, but in other parts of the world scientists have been studying nature's benefits for several decades. Forest medicine researchers in Japan, Korea, and Finland are untangling the nature-specific mechanisms responsible for stress reduction. Our built environments are often full of traffic, technology, and noise. This detracts from the limited attentional resources we have, making us tired and unable to concentrate. Natural environments seem to replenish these resources as well as improve our mood. Medical researchers and environmental psychologists have been testing how nature contact can improve human physical and mental health, to buffer the stress of modern living" (*Peterborough Examiner*, March 5, 2015).

Having some basic knowledge of the natural world in our own bioregion connects us intimately to the particularities of place and serves as an antidote to the many forces of homogenization at work in the world today. Knowing the plants and animals of where you live, be it a cottage community, a local park or a suburban backyard, makes any outing—or simply just going outside—infinitely more interesting. There is also a strong emotional dimension in knowing and identifying with a specific location, landscape and mix of species. This "sense of place" roots us and helps us to know who and where we are. It also helps to promote an ethic of stewardship and conservation. This is why so many cottagers, for example, are

> Everybody needs beauty as well as bread, places to play in and pray in, where nature may heal and give strength to body and soul.
>
> — JOHN MUIR

Common loon in winter plumage

also engaged environmentalists and care deeply about the health of their lakes and surrounding areas.

Paying attention to the night sky, too, eventually leads to curiosity about the origin and history of the universe. We soon learn that nearly all of the elements that make up the atoms in our bodies were created in exploding stars billions of years ago. So, yes, we are literally made of stardust. Humans are, therefore, "of the universe" much more than "in the universe." From the flowers and insects in the garden to the stars and galaxies looming above us in the night sky, knowing and appreciating the natural world helps to cultivate a deeply satisfying sense that human beings are part of something much bigger. We are intimately related not only to all other species but also to the universe as a whole. There is both awe and comfort in this knowledge.

Species Identification and Naming

The importance of being able to identify and name species has always been a subject of much debate in environmental education. Granted, too great a focus on naming can become boring and frustrating. However, that's not because people somehow lack the ability or the force of memory to learn the names. People may need a naturalist to help them put names to species in a forest, but these same people would never need such assistance when wandering through stores in a mall. They would instantly recognize and be able to name hundreds of products, based mostly on the company logos. Even crows can recognize the McDonald's logo and go to a McDonald's bag first when scavenging in a parking lot.

We feel that it is important to be able to identify and name at least the common species. The process of identification involved in naming forces the observer to look for specific field marks and to notice important differences between species. This, in turn, makes us more aware of the natural order of living things and the incredible diversity of the natural world—and appreciating biodiversity is hugely satisfying. To walk in the woods and not recognize the common trees, wildflowers and birds is not to see them.

> A rose by any other name may smell as sweet, but without a name it is simply a flower.
>
> — JIM WRIGHT and JERRY BARRACK, *In the Presence of Nature*

Plants, for example, become nothing less than a green blur. When we can put names to the plant and animals that we see during a walk, we are suddenly among friends—friends whose names we know. Remember, though, that a name is simply the beginning. The real magic comes from finding out more about each and every living thing—from how it is adapted to its environment to the part it plays in its vibrant living system.

For each region, we have prepared a list of common plants and animals to try to see, identify and name (see pages 10–14). Along with an understanding of basic concepts such as evolution, pollination and photosynthesis, being able to put a name to these common species and phenomena is part and parcel of "nature literacy."

One more thing...

We hope that you will find small and simple ways to enrich yourself, your children, your grandchildren or your students through a closer relationship to the natural world. And to help us recognize that whatever actions we undertake should be not just for our own benefit but also for those millions and millions of living creatures yet to be born. By bestowing on our children—and ourselves as adults—the gift of nature, we are fostering both conservation and conservationists. In the end, we will only be inspired to protect what we know and love.

Smelling a sunflower

Basic Skills for Connecting to Nature

Do you ever wonder why some of your friends come back from a hike with colorful stories of close encounters with the natural world yet when you return, all you've seen are mosquitoes, trees and the odd crow? Why are some people so lucky?

Seeing nature is partially knowing where to look and partially knowing what to look for. Think about being in the natural world with the right kind of attitude, your senses activated and your patience primed. Nature awareness starts by looking for wonder both in the very small, the very large and everything in between. Mostly, however, it means venturing forth with a healthy curiosity and a willingness to discover. In this section, we'll provide you with some skills and techniques to help you locate and identify a little of the vast diversity of life found in nearby nature.

Hints for Paying Attention

- Be patient. Nature is rarely like you see on TV—animals instantly appearing, up and close and in focus. Sometimes, all you'll find are signs that an animal has passed through. Remember, nature needs time to reveal her secrets.
- Concentrate. Paying attention requires looking and listening with complete concentration. As the black-capped chickadee suggests in its two-note, slurred springtime song... be still! Take the time to stand motionless in a forest for a minute or two until the bird you thought you heard finally sings again.
- Shhhh! To activate all of your senses, try to be as quiet as you can. If your

Children playing in a stream

goal is to see birds or mammals, move as silently as you can. Be aware, too, of where and how you are walking. Choose carefully where to place your feet so that you don't step on that brittle branch or walk through a bed of crunchy leaves (see Predator Stalking, page 225).

→ Avoid abrupt movements. Sudden, jerky movements will scare animals away as quickly as loud noises. Move slowly, smoothly and deliberately, even when bringing binoculars up to your eyes.

Engaging All of Your Senses

In today's age, it is easy to be seduced by modern technology: the latest TV, computer game or home theatre system. We tend to forget that nature has endowed us with some amazing sensory equipment that technology just can't duplicate!

Humans have stereoscopic vision that helps us to gauge both depth and position—at the same time. We can also hear sounds from different locations simultaneously—one could even say that we hear in three dimensions. With every breath in and out, we pick up odors—more than 10,000 of them. We are enveloped in skin—the barrier between us and the world—and special receptors called Meissner's corpuscles respond to the slightest pressure, a gentle caress or the sweep of a cool breeze. Crammed in our mouth like tiny volcanoes, our thousands of taste buds help us to detect the faintest of flavors—our tongue, for example, can detect bitterness in as little as one part per two million. Our inner ear helps us to locate our body's position in space.

So here is our advice. We all need to take the time to unplug technology and "plug in" to nature through the wonder of our senses. This is our green conduit—the most basic and most powerful way to connect our children to nature. To soak the natural world up through our senses takes practice. Included in each of the seasons will be ideas on how to practice sensory awareness. Here are few ideas to get you started:

Sight

Humans are visual animals that have evolved to use sight more than any of our other senses.

→ Use "splatter vision." When we walk in a natural setting, chances are our eyes are cast down. Makes sense, for our inclination is not to stumble. However, by focusing only on our feet as we move through nature, we are missing so much of what is going on behind, above and beside us. Practice being an "all-around watcher" by using what naturalists call "splatter vision." This means not keeping your eyes in one place for too long. Try to get in the habit of looking in all directions and distances. For example, occasionally look ahead of where you are walking, such as a good distance down the road or path; scan the sky from time to time; when you arrive at a body of water, look for any dark objects (e.g., possible ducks, loons or beavers) swimming or floating on the surface;

and check out the crowns of trees, dead branches and telephone wires. Be as aware as possible, too, of your peripheral vision; this helps you tune into movement at the edges of your field of vision. You can practice extending your peripheral vision by looking straight forward but placing your fingers on either side of your head. Waggle your index fingers and slowly move both of your fingers back until you can't see them anymore. Keep practicing and you can extend your range of vision. Some of your most amazing discoveries can be out of the corner of your eye.

Splatter vision

⟵ Use binoculars. The sense of sight can be greatly enhanced by learning to use binoculars properly. Many bird watchers find 8 × 40 or 8 × 42 binoculars the best choice. They provide good magnification but also offer a wider field of vision. Most serious birders purchase a roof prism design because it is the lightest, most durable and most waterproof. Good birding binoculars should also have "close focus," meaning they will focus on objects as close as three or four feet (one meter). Not only will you be able to study birds up close, but when birds aren't your focus, you can watch butterflies and dragonflies.

⟵ Always remember, too, to hold your binoculars with both hands. It can also help if you brace yourself against a tree trunk, car roof or building. When you see a bird that you want to check out, begin by locking your eyes on it. Then slowly raise your binoculars to your eyes. If you have done this correctly, the animal should be right in the middle of your field of vision. Don't make the mistake of simply scanning randomly with your binoculars in the general vicinity of the bird in the hope of stumbling upon it!

⟵ Use a hand lens. A good hand lens can open up an entire new world when used properly. Hold the lens as close to your eye as possible. Bring the object you are looking at towards the lens until it is in focus. Give yourself extra support by

Binoculars

holding it with the back of your thumb across your cheek. For most nature study purposes such as examining insects, plant parts and rocks, 10× is an excellent magnification. Bring the lens to the eye you wish to look with.

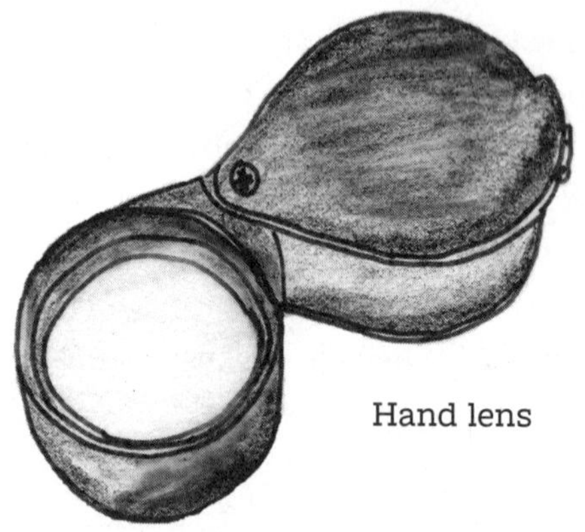

Hand lens

Sound

From the buzzing of bees and the trilling of toads to the symphony of birds warbling from the tree tops, every natural area is characterized by a unique soundscape. With practice, you can identify nearly all animal species by their vocalizations. This book will help you to get to know the sounds of your local frogs, insects and birds.

Taste

The healthiest food, argues the poet, Wendell Berry, is the shortest distance from the earth to your mouth. Introduce kids to the edible wild and the wonder of tasting gifts from the landscape. Some plants with edible leaves (generally the young leaves taste best) and flowers include chickory, dandelion, fireweed, wood sorrel and all of the different violets. You should also try the fruit of blackberries, raspberries, blueberries, strawberries and even bunchberry. A delightful breath freshener can be had by chewing on a leaf or berry of wintergreen. Warning! As always, be sure you absolutely know for certain what you are tasting before you put anything in anyone's mouth!

Smell

Each season has its signature scent. Think about the musty, earthy smell of damp soil in spring, or the spicy fragrance of fallen leaves in autumn. When you are out for a walk or a hike, get into the habit of smelling flowers, buds, green leaves and needles, fallen leaves on the forest floor, conifer sap and even mushrooms. Gently rubbing plant parts such as leaves and buds releases additional chemicals, which greatly enhance their smell.

Take the time to think about how certain smells make you feel. The nerves that sense smell are directly connected to the emotional part of your brain, making smell a strong trigger for emotions. The smells of wintergreen and plants from the mint family such as wild bergamot are said to improve concentration and may decrease irritability, while the citrus-like smell of northern prickly ash may promote clear thinking. Studies suggest that our sense of smell is sharper after exercise, so here's yet another reason to get out walking in nature!

Finally, try taking short, shallow sniffs—just like a dog does! This has proven to be more effective for smelling than taking one long sniff.

Touch

When you're out on a walk, or just in the backyard, take a moment to think about what you are feeling—not just with your hands, but with your entire body. You might want to rub the object against your cheek to further enhance your sense of touch. Some things to feel: temperature—compare the hot sun on your shoulders with the coolness of the shade. Can you feel a breeze? Feel the bark of different trees. Can you identify the species by the feel of its bark alone?

Leading a Walk or Hike: Some Pointers

Getting past the barriers to outdoor learning

1. Dress well: One of the biggest barriers for kids to enjoying the outdoors is discomfort. Nothing makes an excursion more miserable than wet feet, mosquito bites or a bad case of poison ivy! Make sure you dress your kids well. In winter this means a sturdy pair of insulated boots, two pairs of socks, snow pants, a sweater, a good winter jacket, a hat that covers the ears and insulated gloves and mittens. In summer it means a peaked sun hat, sunscreen, bug repellent (if necessary) and long pants with closed-toed shoes. In spring and fall, dress in layers and always have a waterproof rain jacket to pull on—just in case. Learn to recognize poison ivy and, in some areas,

Warm woolies

poison oak (see page 5) and be aware of the potential for biting insects. And don't forget to visit the bathroom before you head out! Give yourself the challenge of exploring the natural world even if the weather isn't at its best. Some of the most wonderful discoveries are revealed in the midst of a soaking rain!

2. What to bring: Depending on how long you're going to be out, bring along a backpack with some or all of the following: wax crayons, a good supply of regular pencils, colored pencils and erasers for drawing, several pencil sharpeners, nature journal, blank cards or notebooks, a digital camera and/or smartphone (for recording sound and video, taking photographs, taking notes and accessing nature apps), some good-quality magnifying glasses (at least 10×), ziplock bags and small plastic jars for collecting samples, bug repellent, sunscreen, Band-Aids, lots of water and a snack. Make use of backpacks. We find children enjoy the experience more if their hands are free.

3. Hush mode: At times, you may want total silence. This is the only way to see and hear many kinds of animals. Explain to the children that when you say, "We are now in hush mode," all talking stops and walking is done as quietly as possible.

4. Halfway past: If you are leading a large group of people, keep on walking until about half the group has passed an object you want to point out (e.g., a bird nest high in a tree). Stop and step back to the middle of the group to discuss the object, so all can see it.

5. Kid containment: If you have a large group, be sure to designate a leader and a sweep. Kids naturally move at different speeds and before long it is easy to become strung out over a great distance.

6. Getting back together: Have a prearranged signal like a bell, a whistle, a loon call or a special word to bring everyone back to the meeting spot.

7. Transitions: Give children a task as you walk. For example, cup your ears with your hands and ask, "How many natural noises can you hear between now and our next stop?" (See Focused Hearing page 270.) Use the scavenger hunts or the suggestions outlined in the night hike section as transitional activities.

8. Informal walks: If your walk is an informal "romp through the woods," encourage kids to explore up ahead or off to the sides of the path. However, insist that they stay within sight of you. Joyful, unstructured play in nature is a delight in and of itself. Tie a bandana around a tree. Tell the kids they can explore as far as they like, as long as they can see the bandana.

Some "Back-pocket" Activities

However, just in case the kids get bored, it's not a bad idea to have a few "good to go" activities in your back pocket, even for an informal walk. We sometimes forget that the best teacher of all is the very landscape we are standing on. As Bert Horwood, professor of outdoor education, puts it, the land "affords" opportunities for learning. When an American toad hops by or a red-tailed hawk soars overhead, these are "affordances"—chances to get to know your natural neighbors. Don't let them pass you by! Stop what you are doing and enjoy what the Earth is teaching you. This moment may not come again.

- Stop every once in a while and do a Hand Lens Hike (at least a 10× power) along a fallen tree trunk or under a log or stone. Areas where there are different kinds of moss are especially good. Closely investigate leaf veins, flower parts, seeds, tree bark, the wings of a dead butterfly, etc.
- Have everyone lie down on their backs and watch the clouds pass over and the leaves wave with the wind.
- Periodically, simply sit and listen for several minutes—in complete silence—and then compare notes on what you heard. What were the natural sounds? Listen for the different sounds the wind makes as it passes through different trees. Some people can identify the tree by the sound the wind makes in its canopy. Can you?
- Pay attention to the wind as you walk along. Try to tell what direction it is blowing from. What do you see moving?
- Take note of where the Sun is in the sky. Use it to tell direction and to approximate the time of day.
- Collect natural objects such as rocks, leaves, seeds and bark of different shapes and colors. Stop and take the time to do a bark rubbing or a sketch. If there are flowers in bloom in large numbers, collect some of the blossoms.
- Play Basement Windows. Gently roll over a log or a rock. Peer underneath. Use a hand lens to take a closer look. Can you find a salamander, a centipede, a beetle, a millipede, an ant colony? (See color section, figure 5.)
- Scan the area for signs of birds, including holes in trees, feathers, nests and droppings.
- Do the same for signs of mammals, such as tracks, scat, half-eaten cones, fur, browse marks, bark gnawed off shrubs or trees felled by beavers.
- Encourage the kids to feel and smell a leaf or bud or even a piece of mushroom. Rub it gently between their fingers. How does it smell? You might want to share the smell with others.
- Play Exploration Dice. Get two large wooden blocks (6 in./15 cm by 6 in./15 cm cubes). On one, place a direction on each face—N, S, E, W, NW, SE. On the other place six numbers: 4, 8, 12, 16, 20, 24. While walking, roll the dice. Using the compass, walk in the direction for the number of paces indicated, for example, NW for 12 paces. Then say "hunker down." Ask kids to find something interesting near where they are crouching. The dice will bounce you around the landscape to places you might never have gotten to. And there is always something interesting to discover: a spider, a browse mark, a hole, a flower, an animal track. (See color section, figure 4.)
- Follow a bearing. Using a compass, strike out in one direction, then crouch down every ten paces and find out what

is living there. This is the way biologists conduct a biophysical inventory of an area. You'll be amazed at how life changes along this transect.

Birding

So just who is that LBJ (Little Brown Job) visiting my feeder? How can I figure out who she is? By learning a few birding tricks, you'll soon find out!

By any measure, birds have never been more popular. Bird-watching, or birding as it is often called, combines skills such as quiet stalking, observation and analysis. It is all about the thrill of using one's knowledge of season, range, habitat, field marks, song and behavior to identify and appreciate the birds we see. Birding can also become a window on environmental issues. Many environmentalists started out as birders, perhaps because it helps you recognize how vulnerable bird populations are to pressures like urban sprawl, habitat destruction and climate change. Birders are acutely aware of how quickly species can decline. (See color section, figure 3.)

White-crowned sparrow

Birding 101: The basics of bird identification

Bird identification is really about three things:

1. Paying attention
2. Being patient
3. Knowing what to expect

Paying attention means looking and listening with complete concentration. Being patient can mean standing motionless in a forest for several minutes until the bird you just heard sing eventually calls again and lets you know where it is lurking. In fact, one can often see more birds by standing in one good spot than by always moving. Finally, knowing what to expect means having a good idea of what species should be present in a given time of year and habitat. Experienced birders have a 95 percent idea of what they'll probably see in a given day and place. Birds are found at predictable times and locations.

When you come across a bird you can't immediately identify, try following these steps:

1. Take note of the bird's general shape. Many birds can be identified by shape alone, often at considerable distances.

2. Turn your attention to the bird's size by comparing it to a common benchmark species. Ask yourself if its size is closest to that of a hummingbird, house sparrow, American robin, American crow, or Canada goose.

3. Examine the plumage and field marks. Take a careful look at the wings, underparts, rump, tail and head (if you find *mnemonics* [memory aid] useful, think WURTH). Start with the part of the bird you can see best, but look at its entire body before it flies away. Try to see if it has bars on the wing or if its chest, belly and sides have spots, stripes or a special coloration. Is there anything special about the tail or rump? Pay special attention to the head. Many small songbirds such as warblers and sparrows can be identified by characteristics of the head alone. Does the eye have a circle around it? Does the crown or throat have special markings such as stripes or a contrasting color? Take particular note of the size and shape of the bill.

4. Take note of what the bird is doing. Is it feeding on the ground, perched at the very top of a tree, moving head-first down the trunk, standing motionless in shallow water or soaring high overhead? Is it alone or with others of the same species? Some common feeder birds, for example, almost always feed on the ground in small flocks (e.g., white-throated sparrow), while others are nearly always seen on feeders (e.g., black-capped chickadee). If the bird is flying, how would you describe its flight pattern? Some hawks, for example, soar in circles on motionless wings, while others have a "flap, flap and glide" style of flying.

5. Consult your field guide or app. Don't forget to look at the range maps, relative abundance of the species, whether it is migratory or resident, its preferred habitat and typical behavior. The guide will also point out the most important field marks and how the bird compares to any similar species.

Red-tailed hawk

Shapes of different raptors

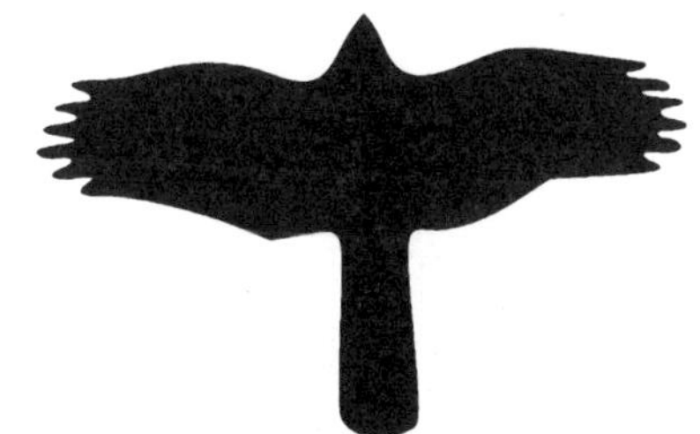

Goshawk

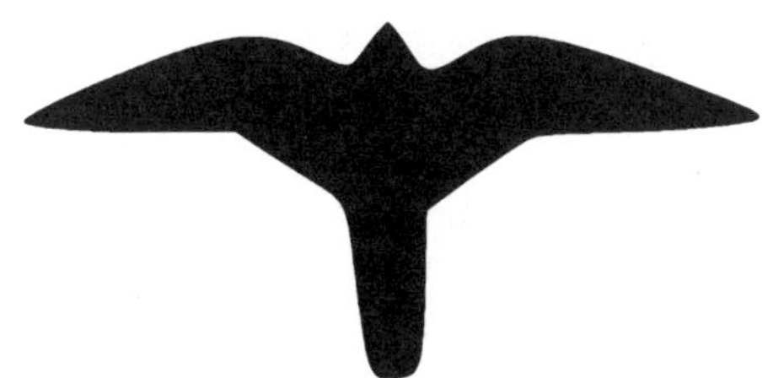

Peregrine

Bohemian and cedar waxwings

Other things to keep in mind...

- Bird identification is not an exact science and at times it's difficult to be completely certain of what species you have seen. Being "reasonably certain" is sometimes the best you can do.
- When you are looking at an unidentified bird, remember that it could be a female or an immature. Although the male and female are quite similar in most species, there are birds—such as the red-winged blackbird—where the differences are striking. Ducks, too, show a big difference between the sexes. When identifying eagles, hawks and gulls, remember that you might be looking at a juvenile or immature bird.
- The bird in your binoculars may not be in its breeding plumage. In a small number of species (fortunately!), the plumage can vary considerably between spring and fall. These birds tend to be colorful in the breeding season but drabber in fall and winter. American goldfinches are an example of this challenging characteristic.
- Many songbirds respond well to pishing (explained on page 46) and will come in quite close so that you can take a closer look.
- The habitat in which you see the bird can also help you identify it. Some species are almost never seen outside of their preferred habitat—except maybe during migration—while others are generalists and can turn up in many different habitats.
- Many birds are found along edges such as the edge of a woodlot, a road or even a lawn.
- Learn common bird sounds. Identification by songs and calls will really boost your birding skills and provide a great deal of satisfaction. With practice, nearly all birds can be identified by song. Start by learning the songs of the common species you see and hear around your house. Listen to recordings of their songs—in the car, for example—and learn the associated

mnemonic (memory aid) for the species you're interested in. There are many bird identification apps that include songs and calls.

- Purchase a pair of good binoculars (see page 27). As your interest in birding grows, you may wish to invest in a spotting scope. This is a compact telescope used in situations that require magnifications beyond the range of typical binoculars.
- Choose a field guide with paintings of the birds rather than photographs, and a range map right beside the illustrations. Most birders use one (or more) of the following: *The Sibley Field Guide to the Birds of Eastern North America*, *The National Geographic Field Guide to the Birds of North America*, and *The Peterson Birds of Eastern and Central North America*. We recommend the *Sibley* for its convenient size and weight and the multiple plumages it shows of each bird.
- Check out seasonal abundance charts for your area. These show how the numbers of a given species change over the course of the year. With time, you will start to develop a mental checklist of what species are most likely, given the time of year. The eBird website (ebird.org) provides these charts in the "Explore Data" section.
- Keep track of your sightings—and share them with others—by using eBird. Register at ebird.org. Subscribers also receive alerts of rare birds in your area as well as birds you have not yet seen during this year.

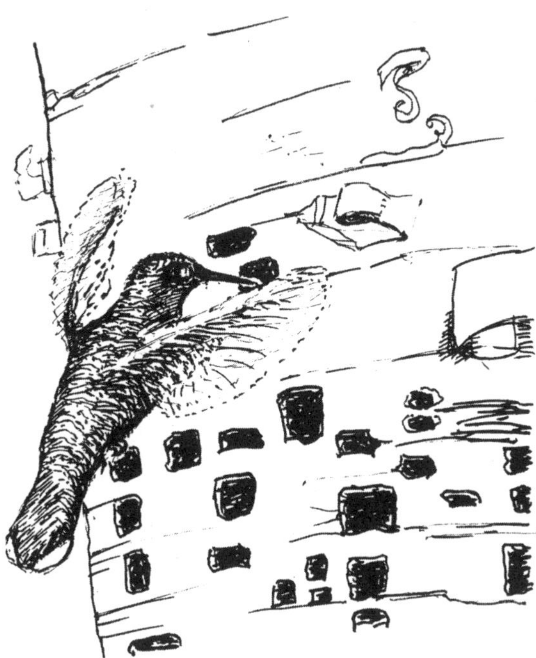

Hummingbird feeding at a sapsucker hole

Invertebrate-watching: Butterflies, Moths and Dragonflies

In our experience, kids are captivated by insects. Here are some hints to help you find out more about the many insects that live in your area. Most parts of the U.S. and southern Canada are home to 100 or more species of butterflies, 150 or more types of dragonflies and damselflies and thousands of kinds of moths.

Butterflies

Who has not been enchanted by the delicate, fluttering, colorful wind dancers known as butterflies? They are the hallmark of any warm summer's day. Butterflies are easy to observe and turn up almost everywhere, from suburban backyards to country roadsides and woodland trails. We encourage you to try out butterfly-watching, also known as butterflying.

Compared to birding, which often involves getting up at the crack of dawn in less than perfect weather, butterflying is a much more civilized affair. These gentle insects are rarely on the wing before 8 AM and fly only on warm, sunny days.

Viewing and identifying butterflies is easier and more enjoyable with binoculars (especially those that focus to within 3–6 ft./1–2 m). A digital camera with a zoom lens also comes in handy, especially for identification purposes. Lots of excellent field guide books and apps are available. Serious butterfly watchers will sometimes use a butterfly net and plastic jar for catching and viewing hard-to-identify species like some of the skippers. The butterfly can then be released.

Mourning cloak

Hints for viewing butterflies

- To find a given species, keep in mind the time of year it flies and the kind of habitat it prefers. Roadsides and wetland edges can be particularly productive, as long as there are sufficient flowers such as milkweeds in bloom.
- Learn to identify the plants that attract butterflies, either for nectar or to lay eggs on their stems and leaves. Among the most important are the milkweeds.
- Watch for butterflies basking on gravel roads, tree trunks or animal dung, or visiting puddles.
- Approach a butterfly from behind, being careful not to make any sudden movements. You should also avoid casting a shadow on the insect, since this will usually cause it to fly away.
- As with birds, pay attention to the butterfly's size, shape, color and patterning. The pattern on the underside of the wing, easily visible as the butterfly feeds, is often useful in identifying the species.
- If you have time, take a picture of the butterfly, including the underside of the wings.

Moths

If you aren't the most energetic person, then moth-watching (or mothing) may be just for you. It often requires no more effort than leaving the porch light on in the evening and checking periodically to see what is clinging to the screen door!

With more than 10,000 species in North America, moths offer endless options for study, photography and fun. A good starting point is learning to distinguish between moths and butterflies. Butterflies have club-like knobs on the ends of their antennae and usually perch with their wings held upwards. Moths, on the other hand, perch with their wings outspread and have antennae that closely resemble bird feathers. Unlike butterflies, most moths are nocturnal.

To really bring moths in, purchase a bulb that projects light in the UV spectrum such as a black light CFL. You will also need a spring-clamp light bracket and a white cotton sheet. Clamp the bracket and bulb onto a tripod or stepladder and set them up in front of the sheet, which can be hung from a wall or suspended from a clothesline. Make sure the bulb is upright or it will burn out quickly.

Not all moths, however, are interested in lights. Some are nectar-feeders and will come to a sugar bait such as over-ripe bananas. A slightly more complicated way to entice moths is with a syrupy "goop." One mixture calls for one over-ripe banana, a dollop of molasses, a scoop of brown sugar and a glug or two of beer. Mix the ingredients in a blender and spread the concoction on a tree trunk or a hanging rope, then check regularly to see what has been attracted. With any luck, species such as underwing moths will show up.

A lot of the fun in mothing comes from photographing and identifying the insects. Be aware, however, that using a flash may create washed-out images. A way to get around this is to carefully catch the moth in a small container, put it in the fridge overnight and take a picture of it the following morning using natural light and a pleasing background such as a leaf or a piece of bark. You should have at least 30 seconds before the moth warms up and flies away. You may wish to place a ruler beside the moth for one of the shots, for size reference.

Unfortunately, moth identification is not always easy. Start by focusing your efforts on the larger moths, the species you see the most on a given night and those that stand out from the rest because of their distinctive colors or markings (e.g., silk moths). Time spent flipping through your field guide is helpful, too.

Sphinx moth and caterpillar

Hints for identifying moths

- How large is it? Size is very important in identification.
- How does it hold its wings when at rest? Are they spread out to the side or tent-like over its back? The former is probably a moth in the family Geometridae while the latter likely belongs to the family Noctuidae.
- Once you have a rough idea of what family the moth might belong to, look more closely at the patterns on its wings and try to compare these to the photographs on a website or in a field guide.
- Consider the time of year. Like butterflies, the moths you see change with the seasons. Knowing the flight period will help to further narrow down what species or genus you are dealing with.
- If you have a guide such as *The Peterson Field Guide to Moths*, look at the range maps and make sure the species occurs in your area. Be aware, however, that these maps are "guesstimates" in some cases.
- Check the type of host plant (larval food plant) the moth requires. If, for example, the species lays its eggs on tamarack trees and there is none in your area, you might be able to discount it.

Dragonflies

Some of the most acrobatic of all flying insects, dragonflies are capable of bursts of speed of more than 30 mph (50 km/h). Almost everything that applies to butterfly-watching also applies to the observation and enjoyment of dragonflies and their close cousins, damselflies. Collectively, these two groups of insects are known as the Odonata or simply "odonates." Like butterflies and moths there is a great deal of species diversity, and they, too, make great subjects for photography.

Hints for identifying odonates

- On warm, sunny days, dragonflies and damselflies can be found in just about any wetland, lake or river. Many species are also attracted to meadows, roadsides and backyard gardens.
- The same equipment you use for butterflying can be used for odonate-watching.
- For identification purposes, it is sometimes necessary to catch the insect in a butterfly net. If you wish, you can hold a dragonfly in your hand by placing your thumb and index finger on either side of the thorax. Then gently move your

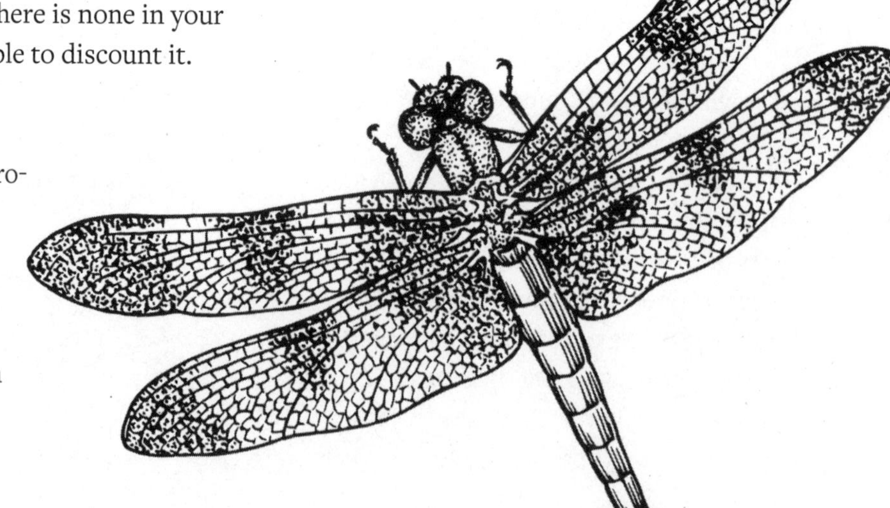

fingers upwards and pinch all four wings together over the body. If you prefer, you can also transfer the insect to a transparent jar or plastic bag. Despite what many people think, dragonflies cannot sting or bite you!

- The best way to catch an odonate with a net is from behind, since its view is blocked directly to the rear. Capturing a dragonfly or damselfly is easiest on a cool morning while the insect is perched.
- Learn the different Odonata families. Knowing the family will greatly narrow down the choice of possible species.
- For dragonflies, take special note of eye position, body shape and coloration, resting position and wing venation.
- Remember that the male and female in many species can be quite different.
- As with common moths, butterflies and beetles, you may want to start collecting odonates and form a small reference collection. Doing so will not have any impact on the population. Guidelines for proper collecting (e.g., using glassine envelopes) can be found online.

Botanizing: The Art of Plant Identification

A green blur. For many of us, that is what a forest or field looks like. Because we don't have the knowledge to identify individual plants, everything green simply blends together and we turn our attention elsewhere. However, with a bit of patience and practice you will begin to find familiar plant species everywhere you go. You will probably discover that you've been surrounded by hugely interesting species—maybe even some that are edible or have medicinal qualities—without even knowing it.

When you head out into the field, bring one or more field guides (or apps) with you, depending on what plant group you are interested in (e.g., ferns, grasses, trees or wildflowers). You may want to collect plants and identify them when you get home. Collect the entire plant if possible, since features such as basal leaves can be important in the identification process. Take along a large plastic bag (just tie it to a belt loop) to carry the plants home safely and conveniently. Stash the bag in a cooler or the back of the fridge until you're ready to identify the plants. Do not collect rare plants or any plants in parks or other public areas. Although not as reliable as actual specimens, digital photos of the leaves, leaf arrangement, flowers, flower arrangement, etc. can also be used for identification purposes.

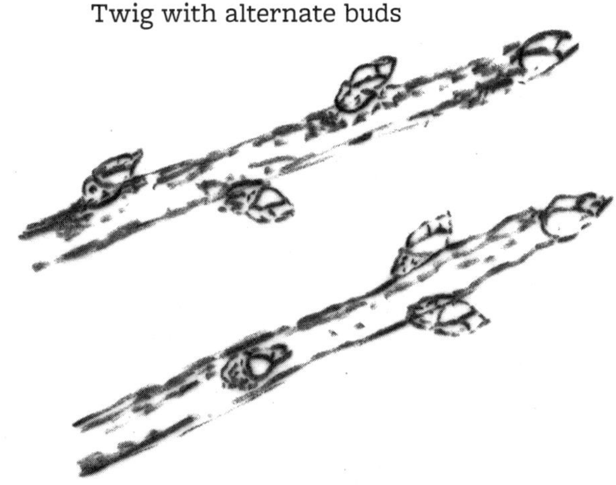

Twig with alternate buds

Twig with opposite buds

Hints for identifying wildflowers, shrubs and trees

- Learn the most common terms used to describe plants and their parts, such as conifer, stamen and simple leaf.
- Learn the most common families, such as the rose, orchid and pine families.
- When you find a plant you want to identify, take note of your surroundings. Are you in the woods, a meadow, a disturbed roadside or by a stream?
- Is the plant woody like a tree or shrub, or herbaceous like a dandelion?
- Look at the arrangement of the leaves (or buds) on the stem or twig. Are they opposite each other or alternate to each other, simple or compound, furry or smooth, with toothed margins or even margins?
- Does the leaf or bud have a unique smell when crushed?
- Look to see if there is a specimen with flowers or seeds. How are the flowers arranged? Are they regular (radially symmetrical like a daisy) or irregular (like a snapdragon)? Are the flower parts easily distinguishable or indistinguishable? How many sepals, petals, stamens are there? (See page 241 to learn more about the parts of a flower.) What color are the flower parts? What color and shape are the seeds or fruit?
- Refer to a field guide or app. Alternatively, if you have a hunch as to what it might be, go to Google Images and enter the plant's name. You may also wish to visit a plant identification website.
- Be sure to look at the range map to make sure the species occurs in your area.
- A folding 10× hand lens can be very useful to help you to see features such as flower parts or hairs on leaves.

Mushroom-hunting

Mushrooms—the spore-producing, above-ground "fruits" of fungi—come in an amazing variety of shapes, colors and sizes. They are a delight to photograph and knowing at least the common species adds a great deal to any nature walk. Like so much else in nature, mushrooms soon become old friends.

The main mushroom groups are the gilled fungi or "true mushrooms," which have the typical flat or rounded cap; the coral fungi, which are highly branched; the polypores, which look like wooden shelves or brackets protruding from a tree trunk; the jelly fungi, which are rubbery to the touch and extremely colorful; and the

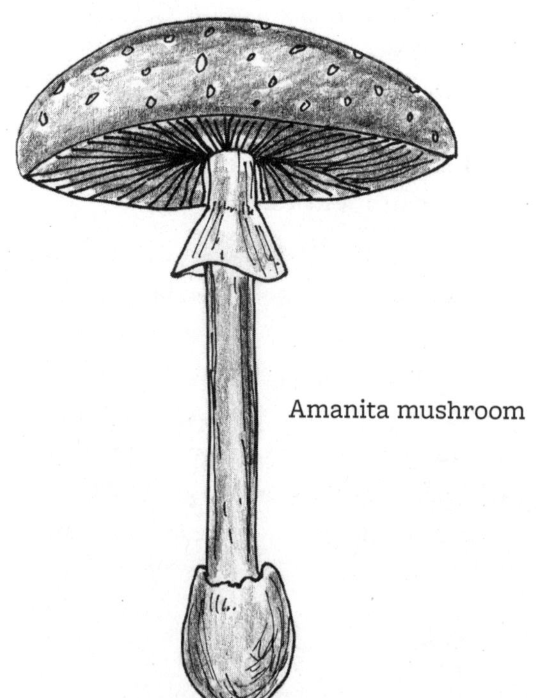
Amanita mushroom

puffballs, which release their spores in a plume of "smoke" from a small opening in the top of the mushroom.

Identifying mushrooms is, above all else, an exercise in paying attention to detail. For example, two mushrooms may appear indistinguishable unless you take careful note of the characteristics discussed below. *Never eat an unfamiliar mushroom without first getting someone with the required knowledge to confirm its identity and edibility.*

Hints for getting started at identifying mushrooms

- Lots of mushrooms grow in urban areas. Look on lawns, on stumps, on live and dead trees, under trees, in gardens, etc.
- Generally speaking, coniferous and mixed woodlands are richer in fungi than deciduous forests. However, stands of oak, beech, birch and poplar are often exceptions to this rule.
- Keep in mind that many species are season-specific. Morels grow in the spring; boletes are primarily a summer mushroom; and shaggy manes (*Coprinus comatus*) appear in the fall.
- Mushrooms need moisture to fruit. A heavy rain triggers the most fruitings.
- It is often easiest to do your identification at home. Dig the mushroom out of the ground (right down to the base of the stem), put it in a paper bag and take note of where you found it. This should include the habitat type and the kind of tree it was growing under, if any.
- Crush a small piece of the mushroom's cap between your fingers and smell it. Many mushrooms have amazing smells. Agaricus mushrooms smell like almonds, while Inocybes are reminiscent of corn silk.
- Check whether the stem of the mushroom bears a ring, or annulus, and whether the stem arises from a cup, or volva.
- Look at the shape of the cap (e.g., cylindrical, knobbed), whether any special markings or "warts" are present, and the color(s). Take note, too, of the shape of the stem (e.g., with cup, bulbous) and any unique features.
- Check whether the underside of the mushroom has gills radiating from the center or a sponge-like surface.
- Because different species produce different-colored spores, spore color can be very useful in identification. To check this, remove the cap, place it on a sheet of white paper and wait a few hours. You'll soon have a spore print! See page 133 for hints on making spore prints.
- Refer to a good field guide, app or website. If you have an idea of the family or genus the mushroom belongs to, Google Image the name and compare with the photos posted.
- Remember that most mushrooms have both a common name (e.g., shaggy mane) and a scientific name (*Coprinus comatus*). Even amateur mushroom hunters usually refer to the scientific name because the common names are unreliable and can change from one book to another.

Enjoying the Sky

(*Don't forget to look up!*)

There is nothing quite so humbling and breathtaking as looking into the vault of the night and bearing witness to a glistening canopy of stars overhead. You are literally staring back through time. Light from even the visible stars has taken thousands of years to reach your eyes.

Day or night, the sky offers an endless source of interesting phenomena. From planets, constellations and the phases of the Moon to clouds, rainbows and sunsets, knowing what to look for in the sky adds richness to any outing. Paying attention to the night also reconnects us with the countless generations of our ancestors for whom watching the comings and goings of the celestial bodies was an integral part of life.

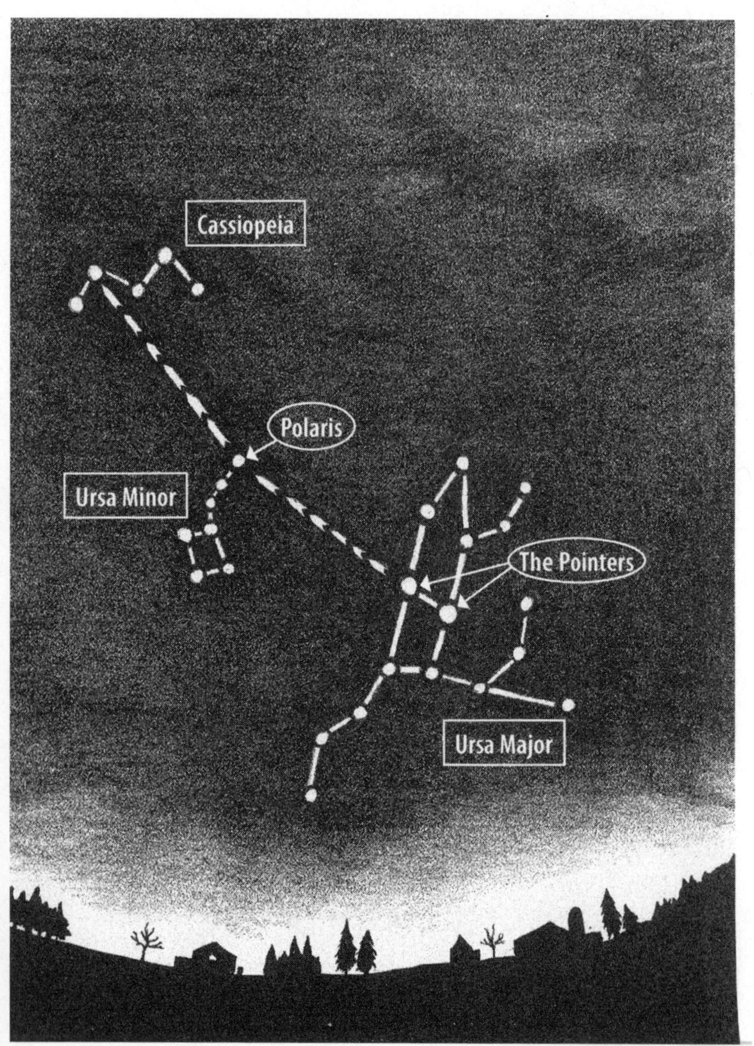

The north sky in January

Constellations

It comes as a surprise to many people that the night sky changes from one season to the next. The various stars and constellations come and go in much the same way as the hummingbirds fly south in the fall and the trilliums bloom in the spring. Getting to know the most typical, easy-to-see and interesting constellations adds a great deal to your sense of season and enjoyment of the night. Night skies soon become "friendly skies" and this positive feeling for the constellations and the night can last a lifetime.

Exactly where in the sky you will see a given constellation, however, depends not only on the time of year but also on the hour of the night. The first step in learning the main stars and constellations is to become familiar with Ursa Major (Big Bear) and its asterism, the Big Dipper. An asterism is a prominent pattern or group of stars, typically having a popular name but usually smaller than a constellation. Ursa Major, Ursa Minor (Little Dipper) and Cassiopeia (the "W") are known as circumpolar constellations because they appear to rotate around the North Star (Polaris), which is almost exactly at true north. They will guide you to other constellations because they are visible above the horizon all year long. Most other constellations disappear below the horizon for part of the year; there is no use looking for Orion in late spring or Leo in November.

Ursa Major and the Big Dipper can always be found in the northern sector of the sky. The Dipper consists of seven stars and forms the tail and body of the Bear. To "see" the rest of the bear, look for two curves of stars. The curve in front of the Dipper's bowl forms the head and forepaw of the Bear, while the curve below the rear of the bowl forms the hind leg. The handle of the Dipper is the Bear's tail. The front two stars of the Dipper's bowl are known as the Pointers because they point directly toward Polaris, the North Star. Starting at the Pointer star at the bottom of the bowl, imagine a line running up to the upper Pointer. Project this line five times and you will find Polaris. There are no other bright stars near Polaris. This technique works at any time of the night and at any season of the year.

Although Polaris is not particularly bright, it is unique. When you are facing Polaris, you are facing almost due north. South is, therefore, directly behind you, east is to your right and west is to your left. Polaris is approximately half-way up in the sky and appears to remain stationary while Ursa Major and the other constellations seem to rotate around it. Polaris is also the first star in the Little Dipper's handle. This is helpful to know because the Little Dipper is a rather dim asterism.

The other well-known circumpolar constellation is Cassiopeia. Its five bright stars form an easy-to-recognize "M" or "W" shape. To find Cassiopeia, extend the line from the Pointers to Polaris and curve slightly to the right (see diagram). The Inuit imagined this constellation as a pattern of stairs sculpted in the snow.

A few tips for better star-gazing

- Don't worry about not having a telescope. The brighter constellations can be seen quite easily with the naked eye. You may, however, wish to have a pair of binoculars for gazing at objects such as the Milky Way. Any size will do, as long as you know how to focus them properly.
- Be sure to bring along an all-sky star chart or app. If you do not have a good guide book to the night sky, you can print off a chart from skyandtelescope.com.
- Bring along a flashlight. It should be dimmed down, either with a layer of red tissue paper over the glass or with a coating of dark red nail polish. The red coloring will help your eyes to retain night vision. You may even wish to buy an inexpensive penlight for this purpose.
- Try to get as far away as possible from light interference. Generally speaking, the farther you can get out of built-up areas, the darker the skies.
- If at all possible, avoid the four days before and after a full moon. The moon washes out many of the dimmer stars.

- Be sure to take advantage of nights with low humidity. You can gauge the humidity by looking at the Milky Way. If it is extra clear, you have a great night for star-gazing.
- Don't stand and bend your neck—you will be much more comfortable sitting on a lawn chair or, better still, lying on your back with your head propped up on a pillow or life jacket. A recliner chair is ideal. This will help avoid a bad case of "astronomer's neck" the following morning.

When you can't be outside...

Nature-viewing from a Car or School Bus

Most of us spend a great deal of our lives in vehicles. We can turn on the radio and shut the world out, or discover a little

Barn swallows perched on wires

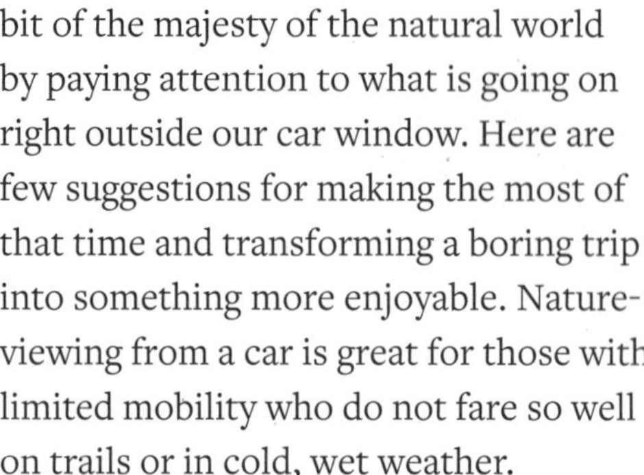

bit of the majesty of the natural world by paying attention to what is going on right outside our car window. Here are few suggestions for making the most of that time and transforming a boring trip into something more enjoyable. Nature-viewing from a car is great for those with limited mobility who do not fare so well on trails or in cold, wet weather.

If you see a bird or mammal along the road and decide to stop, try to view the animal from inside the car. Cars are effective blinds and animals will often allow you to get quite close, as long as you don't get out. Lower your windows before the car comes to a stop, since the noise can spook some birds. Be sure to leave a pair of binoculars in the car and maybe an old digital camera and field guide or two. You never know when they might come in handy.

You will find season-specific ideas for what to watch for in the Fall, Winter, Spring and Summer chapters.

1. Watch for birds perched on wires, fence posts, telephone poles, dead trees, street lamps and signs.
2. Watch the sky for soaring raptors, vultures, gulls and ravens.
3. Practice identifying distant conifers and some hardwoods by shape alone.
4. Look at the Moon. What phase is it in? Is it waxing or waning? Is there a halo around it?
5. Identify the cloud formations and try to forecast what kind of weather they might be bringing.
6. Check fields at dawn and dusk for deer and maybe even a coyote.

7. Pay attention to the ever-changing parade of different flowers along the roadside.
8. Look for different types of rock (e.g., limestone, granite) and different kinds of landforms, such as plains, mountains and glacial features (e.g., drumlins, moraines).
9. At night, scan the sky for constellations, planets, the Moon and maybe even the northern lights.
10. When you're traveling at low speeds, keep the window partly down. It is amazing what you can hear in the way of bird, frog and insect sounds.

Traveling games and activities

- Try to spot ten different species of birds or other species over the course of your trip. As an alternative, try to find birds in different locations, such as perched in a tree, or showing different behaviors, such as flying in a flock (see Fall, page 81).
- Have a family scavenger hunt of nature-related things you can spot from the car. These might include a dog, horse, cow, bird on wire, bird soaring, leaves of different colors, fake animals in people's yards, etc.
- The Alphabet Challenge: First person starts with something they see from the car in nature that starts with the letter "A," next person the letter "B," and so on. Can you get through the entire alphabet? Variation: Taking turns, look for the letters of the alphabet (in order) on signs, license plates, etc. and name a local plant or animal that begins by that letter.
- Take along a nature journal and quickly sketch out plants, animals, objects or landscapes you pass on the highway. Label with time and location.
- When traveling by bus with a class, look for some of the things listed on the seasonal scavenger hunts (see Appendix, page 313), or make your own list tailored to a specific route and distribute it to the class. You could also arrange with the bus driver to stop if you spot something of interest (for example, a large hawk perched in a tree).

Time of Year and Time of Day

With experience, you will come to know what animals to expect depending on the time of day and year and the habitat you are visiting.

With a few notable exceptions, animals are most active in the early morning from first light to two or three hours after sunrise. This tends to be true all year around. On the other hand, animal activity is usually at its lowest from about 10 AM to 4 PM. Quite often, activity will increase once again as evening approaches, with many mammals being active at dusk. Some of the animals that are most active in midday include nearly all insects (for example, butterflies and dragonflies) and many birds of prey, such as hawks and eagles, which take advantage of thermals that form once the Sun is high in the sky. Shorebirds (e.g., sandpipers, plovers) and water birds (ducks, geese, loons, herons) are often active all day long.

An outing at night can be a special experience, too. Not only can you see or hear species that are generally inconspicuous during the day—owls, whip-poor-wills, fireflies and more—but nighttime adventures create powerful memories for the whole family. They are also great moments to promote sensory awareness.

Where to go

Remember: nature is close at hand. You don't need to travel far to provide your children with rich experiences in nature. Go to a nearby municipal park, an abandoned field, an untended fence line or even your own backyard to discover the species that thrive near your home—any public green space can provide rich and repeated interactions with the natural world. Help your children to pick a "Magic Spot" that is rich in nature and a comfortable location to sit and observe. Encourage them to visit this same spot—alone or with others—over and over again, throughout the seasons and in varying weather conditions. You want your children to feel a sense of belonging to a specific patch of nature. As with the plants and animals, it can become their home, too. The book provides Magic Spot activities for each season.

In every area there are pockets of unique green that local naturalists are aware of. Call your local naturalist club and they'll let you into their unique green space.

Red-winged blackbird

Increasing Your Chances of Seeing Wildlife

1. Pishing: Unfortunately, birds are not always easy to see. They may be high in the leafy crown of a tree, concealed by cattails or hopping about in a dense stand of conifers. There is a way, however, to coax them into view. Known as "pishing," it is a human imitation of the scolding calls of chickadees and titmice. It works best with forest birds and is most useful in or at the edge of a forest, though it can also be used to coax birds out of a cattail marsh, a heavy tangle of vines or a dense hedgerow. With a bit of practice, you can usually draw in chickadees, titmice, nuthatches, bushtits, woodpeckers, vireos, warblers and sparrows—sometimes to within arm's reach.

Before you begin to pish, place yourself within five to ten feet (two to three meters) of trees, shrubs or cattails where the birds you wish to attract can land. Pucker your lips and make a loud, forceful "shhhh" sound, while tacking a "p" on at the beginning: Pshhhh, Pshhhh, Pshhhh. Make sure it sounds shrill and strident. You might want to try adding an inflection at the end, as in PshhhhEE. Do it in a sequence of three, repeating the sequence two or three times. At first, you'll probably need to pish fairly loudly, but you can lower the volume once the birds get closer. Continue pishing for at least a couple of minutes after the first birds appear, to give all of the species present a chance to make their way towards you. Chickadees and nuthatches are especially receptive to this sound, but other species will almost always approach as well, especially if you are patient. Mammals like weasels, squirrels and even foxes will sometimes appear as well!

2. The Big Sit: Try sitting or standing still in one place—the more comfortable, the better—for 5, 10 or 15 minutes. Soon, you'll become aware of all of the other beings that surround you. Who knows what you might see—a pileated woodpecker landing on a nearby tree? Or perhaps a weasel emerging from a brush pile? By being still and remaining calm, the natural world begins to move at its own pace—the longer you stay, the more you become a part of this unfolding story and less of an intruder. By returning to the same spot again and again, you begin to attune yourself to its rhythm. The animals will sense this, too, and become less suspicious and more conspicuous. Don't be surprised if you come nose-to-nose with a curious squirrel or rabbit!

3. Get up close: Any patch of vegetation—even a clump of moss—will transform into a universe of its own if you get down on your hands and knees and get really close. You'll see things you never noticed before, such as ornate color patterns on flower petals and maybe even battles between insects. A hand lens makes your close-up look even more exciting and rewarding.

Bringing Nature Inside

Set up a display area for natural objects. The "nature table" is an ever-changing exhibit that can involve the entire family or class. A table with a sheet of pegboard or a bulletin board behind it works best. Think about natural objects that reflect the passing seasons. Add new items as they are discovered and remove older ones. Consider giving responsibility for the table to a different family member or group of children each month. We suggest having tags or stickers available to identify your discoveries. The table can also house an aquarium or terrarium, seedlings or bulbs growing in a flower pot, several good-quality hand lenses and a bag of assorted containers. You might even want to purchase a special microphone and speakers to bring the bird song happening outside right into your home. You will find suggestions of typical items you can collect for each season in this book.

More ideas for permanent items for the nature table

- A photo of where the Sun rises and sets at the equinoxes and solstices
- A poster of the night sky of each season
- Several rocks typical of your region (e.g., granite, limestone)
- A vase for the common wildflowers (including roadside species) of each season
- A laptop computer
- Small plastic bottles to hold any dead insects the children bring in
- Nature specimens. If someone finds a dead bird or insect in good condition, don't forget that this can be an amazing learning opportunity. Bring it in for a day. Ask the children to examine its body markings, shape and other distinctive features, and have them try to identify the species. Sketch and label your find in your nature journal.
- Different fossils. Indicate which modern animals are their closest relatives. Fossils are time machines and help children begin to grasp the Earth's long evolutionary past.
- Hand lenses and a microscope
- A poster of the tree of life
- An evolution timeline

Sketching and Journaling

Nature is replete with beautiful vistas, vibrant colors, poetic moments, discoveries in the very small and the very large, hidden treasurers and—always, always—the unexpected. It is wonderful to be able to capture some of our impressions, to ponder what we've discovered and to write about what we think and feel, as ways to consolidate our experiences in

Nature table

the natural world. Journaling is a skill that will help children retain their memories and impressions for decades to come. (See color section, figure 1.)

- Nature journaling and sketching is the act of using words and sketches to record your observations, feelings and thoughts about an aspect of the natural world that has caught your attention.
- A journal can include questions, philosophical ramblings, notes on what you are observing, favorite quotes or lines of poetry and any other reflections you may have.
- Drawing helps you to focus your observations and, in the process, see more detail. Your journal soon becomes a much-loved companion to all of your outings. Even years later, clear memories of a species or event in nature will come flooding back as you leaf through its pages.
- You may wish to make detailed field notes, or simple, point-form notes scattered around a drawing.
- Drawing like an artist can be intimidating, so it may be better to think of yourself as a scribe or reporter, simply recording what you see. This is not an art exercise, but something you are doing for enjoyment. Think of a nature journal as a treasure hunt.
- You don't even have to be outside. Seniors who cannot easily get outdoors can record the observations they make through their windows as the seasons pass. You can also collect items on a walk (for example, a variety of leaves) and draw them at your desk when you get home.
- Families can use journals to record activities and observations on trips or at the cottage. This results in a "memory record" that you can go back to in the future.

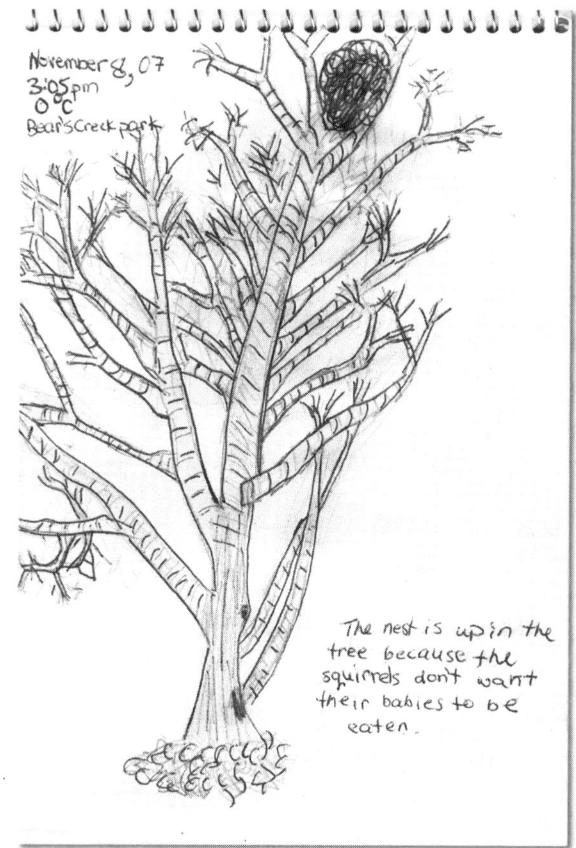

Entry from a child's nature journal

Keeping a nature journal

- Some basics: Include the date, time (clock time or "early afternoon"), location, weather, approximate temperature and any other environmental conditions of note (e.g., birds singing, smell of balsam poplar in the air); take no more than a few minutes per drawing; include short notes about what you've drawn. Include the species name, if you know it.

- Materials: a small, hard-covered sketchbook with unlined paper; a 2B pencil (softer graphite for plants and birds), although any pen or pencil will do; good-quality colored pencils and/or watercolor pencils; a small pocket knife to sharpen your pencil; an eraser.
- What to draw: ground observations such as things you can draw life-size (e.g., a maple key); eye-level observations (entire plants); overhead observations (an entire tree, a soaring bird, clouds); whole landscape observations (be sure to label the main elements).

Sample title page of a nature journal

- Where to draw: your own backyard, gardens, bird feeders, a wetland or any body of water, a meadow or roadside, a hedgerow.
- A seasonal journal: A wonderful focus for your journal can be seasonal change. Try choosing subjects or places that change with the seasons. This can be as simple as a tree in your neighborhood or as complex as an entire landscape.
- What to write: Try writing down a question about each subject you draw; include a measurement if it's important (know your thumb and forearm lengths for reference!); include your impressions, thoughts and feelings about your experiences in nature.
- Inspiration: Don't worry about recording rare species or rare landscapes—focus on the commonplace and the nearby. Start in your own backyard or Magic Spot. Nature journaling is a wonderful way to really get to know where you live and the creatures that inhabit that space over the different seasons. Focus on the stories of your natural neighbors.
- When time or weather doesn't work: When you don't have time to make a field sketch, you can always take a picture and draw the subject later on at home.
- What else to add: newspaper clippings, photographs (e.g., printed out on photocopy paper), maps, images printed off the Internet.

Nature Photography

It is amazing how a good picture anchors your memory and conjures up the intimacy and beauty of a natural experience.

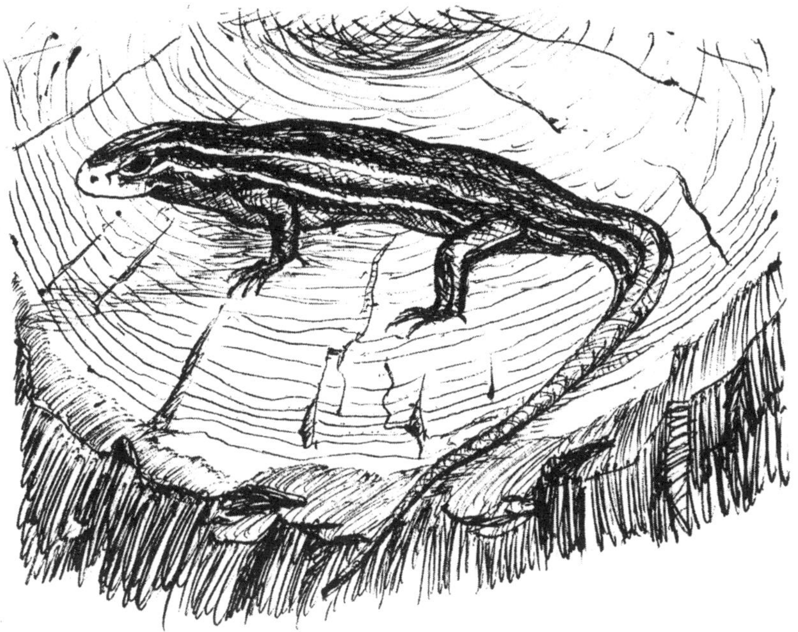

Five-lined skink

Here are a few hints for taking effective photographs. *NOTE: they don't just apply to children—many are for adults*:

1. Never cause stress to your subjects for the sake of a picture. Try not to damage plant life. Leave your subjects just the way you found them.

2. Persevere and learn to be patient. Nature photography is often a waiting game.

3. Try to get close enough to have eye-to-eye contact with your subjects for certain shots (e.g., a frog whose head is just above the water).

4. When taking pictures of flowers, get down low rather than shoot from directly above.

5. Get out early in the morning when the light is at its best and animals are usually most active. Late afternoon, too, can often be good.

6. Remember to use the "rule of thirds." This states that an image is most pleasing when its principal subject is situated along imaginary lines that divide the image into thirds, both vertically and horizontally.

7. Adding a point of interest to the foreground makes landscape shots more visually pleasing. Include an overhanging branch in the upper section of a shot, for instance.

8. Spend some time photographing the most common species around your home such as squirrels, gulls and pigeons. It's a great way to improve your skills.

9. You can get wonderful bird pictures from your car. Simply steady your camera on the half-down window or, better still, buy a window mount.

10. Don't hesitate to use the video function on your camera; it can be especially good for recording sound.

11. Don't forget to put yourself in some of your photos, especially as seen from the side or behind. (e.g., sitting in a chair on a dock on a foggy morning). Simply use the 10-second timer.

12. Make the most of the camera on your smartphone. Quite often, it will be the only camera you have with you, so learn how to use it properly. It can also be a great tool for children—for proving what they find during a scavenger hunt, for instance.

13. Teach your kids about taking pictures: Teach your child how to shoot from different perspectives—up high, down low and especially in close. Teach your children how to use the zoom on the camera—or simply their legs—to get in close. Be sure they hold the camera straight and use two hands to keep it steady. Tell them to take a breath and hold it before they take a shot, then exhale after shooting.

Geo-caching

Geo-caching. A Tool for Nature Appreciation

Who doesn't like a treasure hunt? That is what the sport of geo-caching is. With some planning, it can be an enticing way to encourage young people to get outdoors—we all know how much they like gadgetry. Think of geo-caching as a hi-tech marriage between orienteering and treasure-hunting. Participants use a GPS (global positioning system) receiver and other navigational techniques to hide and find containers, known as "geo-caches" or "caches." Because today's smartphones contain GPS technology and geo-caching apps are readily available, the tools of the sport are literally at everyone's fingertips.

Typically, a "cache" is a small container which contains a logbook. Geo-cachers sign the book with their code name, enter the date and then place the cache back exactly where they found it. Large caches such as military-style ammunition boxes may contain items for trading such as buttons. Geo-cachers also share their experiences online. The largest geo-caching website, geocaching.com, lists countless caches and has members in more than 200 countries. It provides them with access to coordinates of where caches are located, plus descriptions and logs for many of the caches.

With careful planning, knowledge about the environment and nature observation skills can be taught by means of a geo-caching route. For example, a route can allow for the exploration of different habitat types and ecological processes.

A few suggested activities

1. Bring along a tree or wildflower guide or app. You never know what interesting plants you might find along the route to a geo-cache.

2. Expand the "treasure hunt" aspect of geo-caching beyond the cache itself. Challenge kids to find (and maybe sketch or photograph) a given number of wildflowers, fungi, tree leaves, insects, birds, animal scat, etc. You might even want to take along your phone and use the voice recorder app to record the calls or songs of different birds, frogs or insects.

3. Geo-caching routes/hides can be designed to highlight one habitat type or natural feature (e.g., a creek bed, a deciduous forest). Each cache can be located at a different point of ecological or species significance—such as an unusual type of tree, a decomposing log or a den tree—to highlight a given lesson about nature.

4. Children or young adults can design their own route together so that it focuses on different species or points of interest. This can even be done in an urban environment and cover some of the typical species of suburbs and cities. According to Dr. Stefani Zecha of Catholic University of Eichstatt, "The best and most effective method with regards to environmental education is when pupils create their own geo-caching route. This allows for the routes to be incorporated into their daily lives. They look for the special locations to install the cache. They develop the task of the cache themselves. An extension of this is that you upload the created geo-caching route onto the Internet so that other people can use the route themselves. In an Internet forum, they discuss the results of some caches and look for further information. This is a very important step in integrating student participation."

5. The caches can contain questions or information about natural history. They can also include a task that appeals to the senses, such as observing vital details of a leaf or of tree bark. Others could include touching, smelling or listening. A task might be to take a picture of a specific species of tree near the cache. To do this, you would have to be able to identify the tree.

6. Participants could also note their findings using a smartphone or recorder, and then upload them to a website where they can discuss them with others. This approach improves their reflections on their own experiences of nature.

7. Take care where you install the cache. Many natural areas are sensitive, and if a lot of people go there to find the cache, these areas could be destroyed or compromised.

Citizen Science

Yes—you, too, can become a scientist. How? By getting involved in the rapidly expanding field of "citizen science." This is scientific research conducted in whole or in part by volunteers, usually with no formal background or experience in the area. A huge variety of projects give people of all ages and backgrounds the opportunity to participate in important research and, in the process, learn more about nature, science and conservation. Citizen science projects make you really pay attention to all that surrounds you. Participants can become the "eyes" and "ears" for professional scientists. Fields such as conservation biology now have a huge need for citizen scientists to do their work properly. Dentists are becoming lepidopterists, plumbers are contributing to our knowledge of lizards and grade-three students are tracking monarch butterflies. In the process, people feel more engaged with the scientific process and the natural world in general. They also develop a new sense of what a specific plant or animal is going through as human impact on the environment increases.

The Christmas Bird Count, which began in 1900 and continues today, is one of the oldest examples of citizen science. The data gathered is analyzed by researchers and shows how bird populations are changing. This is especially important in light of the increasing effects of climate change.

Citizen science networks often observe the cyclical events of nature (phenology), such as the effects of climate change on plant emergence in the spring. An example of this is PlantWatch, in which citizen scientists record flowering times for selected plant species and report them to researchers through the Internet or by mail. The data is added instantly to web maps showing bloom dates across Canada.

There are projects for people at all levels. You can almost always choose your own level of involvement and a project that interests you. Nature centers, schools, museums, community groups and other organizations often become involved in citizen science projects, too. A great way to start is by visiting scistarter.com, where you can search through hundreds of projects based on different criteria, including suitability for children. You'll find everything from monitoring fireflies to reporting on roadkill! Some of the most popular projects include Nature's Notebook, iNaturalist, Project Squirrel, Bat Detective and the Great Backyard Bird Count.

There is still so much yet to discover about the natural world. There are countless species of insects, for example, about which science knows next to nothing. Just about anyone can become involved in this voyage of discovery and develop a whole new appreciation for nature in the process. This is an uplifting message, especially in today's world where there is so much negative news about the environment.

Connecting with Nature in the Digital Age

If you are anything like us, you probably appreciate both technology and the natural world. Although it might seem counter-intuitive, there are actually many ways in which digital technology can inspire people of all ages to get moving, exploring and enjoying nature. Sharing through social media, and the feedback from others that often follows, can keep the outdoor

Evening grosbeak feeding on maple keys

experience alive for days or weeks. And while digital technology can help us to enjoy nature, it shouldn't replace it. Take the time to unplug and savor the natural world, with no filter for your senses. As someone once noted, "There may not be any Wi-Fi in the forest but I promise you'll find a better connection."

Finding the right balance

- Consider a system in which your children receive screen-time in exchange for time spent playing outdoors or simply sitting in their "magic spot," where they can open their senses and experience nature all around them (e.g., 30 minutes of video games for every hour spent playing outside).
- Set up an outdoor reading or homework station with Wi-Fi access.
- Use digital resources before heading out on a nature walk. For example, the children can research a new nature activity by visiting a website such as Activity Finder from National Wildlife Federation (nwf.org/Activity-Finder.aspx).
- Use technology in outdoor nature games, such as camera scavenger hunts or geo-caching events.
- Go on a tech fast for a few days. Fill the void by simply playing outside—with very few rules!
- As much as possible, model healthy media habits yourself. Have a designated time each day for checking Facebook or e-mail, texting, etc. Ideally, this should be when your kids aren't around.

Making the most of your smartphone

- Thousands of nature apps are now available for smartphones. Apps are much lighter than field guides!

- Use your phone as a camera for both photographs and video. You can even buy a digiscoping adapter to take pictures with your phone directly through your binoculars or spotting scope. (See color section, figure 2.)
- Use the video function and/or voice recorder to record nature sounds (e.g., a frog chorus) and to take field notes.
- Use voice recognition to dictate notes, using an app such as "Notes" on iPhone.
- Purchase a small, portable Bluetooth speaker to amplify bird songs played from an app. Remember to follow ethical guidelines when broadcasting bird calls, such as never playing a call for more than 30 seconds (including pauses).
- Use the built-in flashlight in your phone to illuminate small or darkened objects.
- Have fun! Take selfies beside your favorite plant, animal or habitat.

Nature apps

Like websites, nature apps are constantly changing and improving. Two of the very best apps are iNaturalist and Project Noah. iNaturalist helps you keep track of your own observations with journals, life lists, etc. It also allows you to get help from the naturalist community in identifying what you have observed. You'll have fun participating in projects that other people on iNaturalist are running. Project Noah is also an online community of naturalists, where you can post pictures of species for identification by others and participate in ongoing citizen science research projects. It can also be used as a location-based field guide.

Other recommendations

1. Birds: Merlin Bird ID (walks you through ID process & free)*, Audubon Birds*, iBird Pro, National Geographic Birds*, Peterson Birds and Sibley eGuide to Birds, BirdsEye Bird Finding Guide.
* = best for novice birders

2. Mammals: MyNature Animal Tracks, Audubon Mammals, iTrack Wildlife

3. Amphibians and reptiles: Audubon Reptiles & Amphibians

4. Trees and plants: Audubon Trees, MyNature Tree Guide, LeafSnap, TreeBook (beginners), Florafolio, Audubon Wildflowers, Arbor Day Tree Identification Guide, Botany Buddy, BeeSmart (native plants for pollinators)

5. Invertebrates: Audubon Insects & Spiders, Audubon Butterflies

6. Fish: Audubon Fish, Find-A-Fish

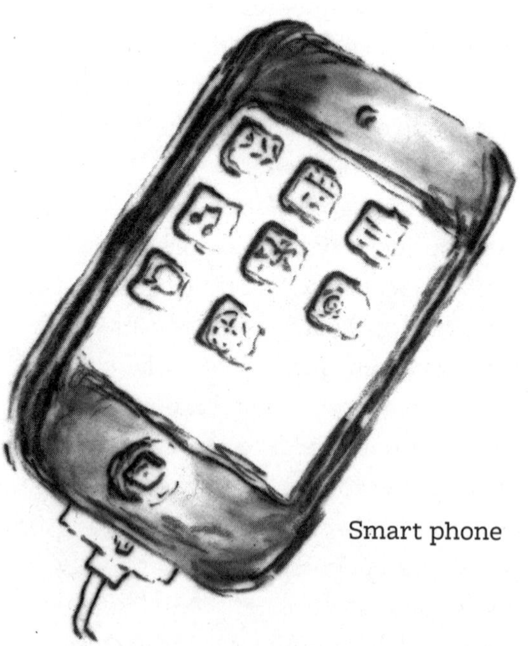

Smart phone

7. Fungi: Audubon Mushrooms
8. Astronomy: Star Walk, SkyView, Google Sky Map
9. Geology: Rockhound
10. Recording sightings: iNaturalist, Project Noah, Journey North, SciSpy, WildObs Observer
11. Where to go: Parkfinder, EveryTrail, Trailhead
12. Evolution: NHM Evolution
13. Social networking: iNaturalist, Project Noah
14. For kids only: NatureTap, Hippo Seasons, Backyard Scat & Tracks, Parts of Plants, Parts of Animals

Using social media

There are host of ways to share your experiences using social media. Here are brief descriptions of some of the more popular platforms and how they can be used. When posting to social media, remember to keep your comments short and to the point; on Facebook, for example, don't go beyond five or six sentences. Remember to use one or two hashtags each time you post and to include interesting visuals. Finally, make a point of sharing other people's content. This is a great way to post on days when you don't have any of your own content ready. Maybe just add a few comments of your own!

- **Instagram:** This is a photo- and video-sharing site. Kids love taking pictures and will love posting them online. Use that love to help them pay attention to nature. When you take pictures, upload them to Instagram, add a filter (hashtag) and share them with your friends. Some common filters include #Nature, #Wildlife, #Naturelovers and #Wildlifephotography. Use filters, too, to search for the thousands of photos other people have submitted. You can also search for your favorite places. It's inspiring to see the different views of your favorite parks or natural places!
- **Google+:** Google+ is a social network. Its "Circles" feature enables users to organize people into groups or lists for sharing across Google products. Google+ also has a lot of features of interest to photographers, such as an online photo editor.
- **Flickr:** This well-known site is for photo-sharing, commenting and photography-related networking. There is a very active and passionate wildlife photography community on Flickr. By joining local or wildlife-specific groups, you can meet others with similar interests and get help with identification.
- **Facebook:** This is a general social media site for sharing pictures, videos, blogs, apps, etc. You might want to create Facebook Interest Lists, a collection of pages or profiles (e.g., of people with special expertise in "gardening for wildlife") that are wonderful for managing your content. This is a great place to go to share your outside experience and ask experts questions about what you saw.
- **Twitter:** This "micro-blogging" site is wonderful for sharing sightings, photos, videos, opinions, news stories, etc, and for finding like-minded individuals. Search for wildlife watchers with hashtags such as #wildlife, #birding or #enviroed. If you are a teacher, Twitter is also the best

tool for making connections with other environmental educators.

- **YouTube:** Upload your videos to YouTube and share them with the world.
- **Pinterest:** Pinterest is a "virtual pinboard" where you can organize and share most anything you find. You can browse other people's pinboards for inspiration and make your own board on any nature-related topic you wish.
- **Padlet:** Padlet is a virtual wall where people can collaborate and share information and thoughts on a common topic. It works like an online sheet of paper where people can post any kind of content (e.g., text, images, videos, links) anywhere on the page, from any device. You and your children could create a free "Padlet" and invite others to share—such as wildlife pictures from a group hike, sightings of monarch butterflies in your area or things to see and do in a local park.

Blogging

One of the greatest joys of nature is sharing your experiences with others. A great way to do this is through a family nature blog. WordPress, Tumblr and Blogger are all excellent, easy-to-use platforms. You can find information on setting up blogs for your children at "How to: Help Your Child Set Up A Blog" (mashable.com/2010/10/03/help-children-blog/).

Deciding what to blog about shouldn't be a problem—nature is all around you, including right in your own backyard. Be sure to include photographs. If you don't have a photo for a given topic, go to the Wikimedia Commons website, a database of freely usable media files including video, audio and photos. Involve younger children in your blogging by using a speech-to-text program—not only does this save time, it also gives your blog a

Sibley bird app

conversational feel. Each family member can describe a different part or aspect of an experience. Even if your "public diary" doesn't attract a lot of readers, it will still serve as a family record of memorable experiences with the natural world. In fact, you don't have to share your blog with the public—it's still a great place to post pictures and stories, like a modern and much improved photo album!

Making videos and slideshows

Video is "the" way to share for youth today, so helping your children to create a video or slideshow of images they've taken outdoors is a great way to use technology to build a love of nature.

- ShadowPuppetEdu is a free iPad app that allows children to create great audio slideshows using pictures from their camera or from websites like NASA or the Creative Commons section of Flickr. They can also add their own narration and share the slideshow with others.
- Stupeflix is a slick and easy-to-use FREE video creation website that allows kids to create professional-looking audio slideshows from their pictures and the ready-made themes, transitions and music provided.

Live wildlife webcams

Wildlife cams (for example, of a loon nest, an underwater scene) are a great way to sow the seeds of interest and concern for wildlife in children. They can provide hours of captivating observations, which would be very difficult to experience in person. Three live webcam sites to get you started are:

- Explore (explore.org/search/more/live %20cams/feed/).
- Minnesota Bound Live Loon Cam (mnbound.com/live-loon-cam/.
- All About Birds (allaboutbirds.org/).

Websites for species identification and more

The number of nature sites on the web is staggering. Here are some of the ones we find most useful.

General

- Google Images: a great site for pictures of the same animal or plant species taken by different people. Often helpful in identification.
- YouTube: great nature videos, both amateur and professional. If you are not sure what a species sounds like, do a YouTube search (e.g., "American robin singing").
- eNature (enature.com): the web's premier destination for information about the wild animals and plants of North America. Includes excellent guides to the night sky.
- Wikimedia Commons (wikimedia .com): copyright-free nature pictures to use, for example, on your blog or to accompany a tweet.
- Animal Diversity Web (animaldiversity .org): an online database of the natural history of thousands of species, from invertebrates to mammals. Includes videos and recordings of sounds.

- Discover Life (discoverlife.org): free online tools to identify species and contribute to and learn from a growing, interactive encyclopedia of life.
- Children & Nature Network (children andnature.org): founded by Richard Louv and others, CNN is leading the movement to connect children and their families to nature through innovative ideas.
- The Net Naturalist (netnaturalist.com): Danielle Brigida's blog provides a host of ideas for using social media to share and enhance the experience of nature.

Evolution and Biodiversity

- Encyclopedia of Life (EOL) (eol.org): a free collaborative encyclopedia and database for every one of the planet's 1.8 million named and known species.
- Understanding Evolution (evolution .berkeley.edu/evolibrary/article/evo_01): a one-stop source for information on evolution, including teaching materials.

Birds

- All About Birds (allaboutbirds.org/): the premier site for online bird identification, including songs. Includes bird cams, a beginner's guide to the bird identification process, bird photography and much more.
- eBird (ebird.org/): make checklists of the birds you see, share your sightings, check the seasonal abundance of birds in your area and much more. eBird will also notify you each day of interesting species being seen in your area.
- 10,000 Birds (10000birds.com): one of the top ten birding blogs on the web; hosts some of the best writers and photographers in the birding world.

Mammals

- North American Mammals (mnh.si .edu/mna/main.cfm): an excellent site sponsored by the Smithsonian Institute.
- Nature Tracking (naturetracking. com): guides to animal tracks and signs, such as scat.

Reptiles and Amphibians

- Frog Watch Canada (frogwatch.ca): learn to identify the calls of frogs and toads in your province.
- Frog Watch USA (aza.org/states-and -territories/): learn to identify the calls of frogs and toads in your state.
- Snakes of North America (pitt.edu /~mcs2/herp/SoNA.html): names and pictures of the continent's snakes.

Social media

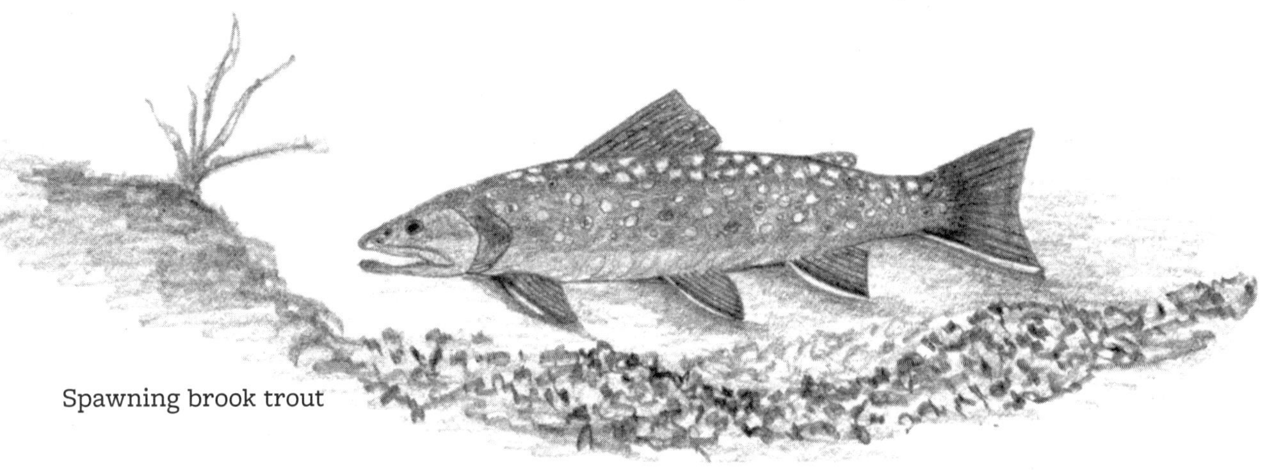
Spawning brook trout

Fish

- Fishes of Canada (aquatic.uoguelph.ca/fish/fish.htm): a treasure-trove of information on Canada's fishes including descriptions, distribution and reproduction.
- eNature: Fishes (enature.com/fieldguides/intermediate.asp?curGroupID=3): a site that covers both fresh and saltwater fishes of North America.

Invertebrates

- BugGuide (bugguide.net/node/view/15740): an online community of naturalists who enjoy learning about and sharing photographs and other observations of insects, spiders and other invertebrates. Use the clickable guide to identify most any insect-like creature and submit photos of mystery insects for identification.
- Odonata Central (odonatacentral.org): all you need to know about the distribution and identification of Odonata (dragonflies and damselflies). The checklist provides a list of species found in your state or province.
- eButterfly (e-butterfly.org): an online checklist and photo storage program where butterfly enthusiasts can report, organize and access information about butterflies in North America.

Plants

- What tree is that? (arborday.org/trees/): this Arbor Day Foundation site provides an easy, step-by-step guide to tree identification.
- Identify That Plant (realtimerendering.com/flowers/flowers.html): an identification program for wildflowers in the northeastern and north-central U.S. and adjacent Canada. If you live on the West Coast, try Reny's Wildflowers (renyswildflowers.com).

Fungi

- Mushroom Expert (mushroomexpert.com): everything you'll need to study and identify mushrooms.

Astronomy

- Earth Sky (earthsky.org/tonight): shows you the most interesting and noteworthy planets, stars and constellations that are visible on any given night.

Phenology

- Nature's Notebook (usanpn.org/natures_notebook): a national online program where amateur and professional naturalists record regular observations of plants and animals to generate long-term data sets used for scientific discovery and decision-making.
- Journey North (learner.org/jnorth/): an outstanding children's "citizen science" website where youth can record and share their observations of the changes in flora and fauna as the seasons progress.
- Step Outside (r4r.ca/en/step-outside/nature-guides): a compilation of events in nature (e.g., migrants arriving, flowers blooming) in south-central Ontario but applicable to most of northeastern North America. Lots of activities of particular interest to teachers.

Conservation

- Environmental News Network: Wildlife (enn.com/topics/wildlife): provides the latest news in wildlife conservation issues.
- Living Alongside Wildlife: (livingalongsidewildlife.com/): David Steen's blog provides outreach about wildlife ecology and conservation, as well as an appreciation for animals with a bad reputation.

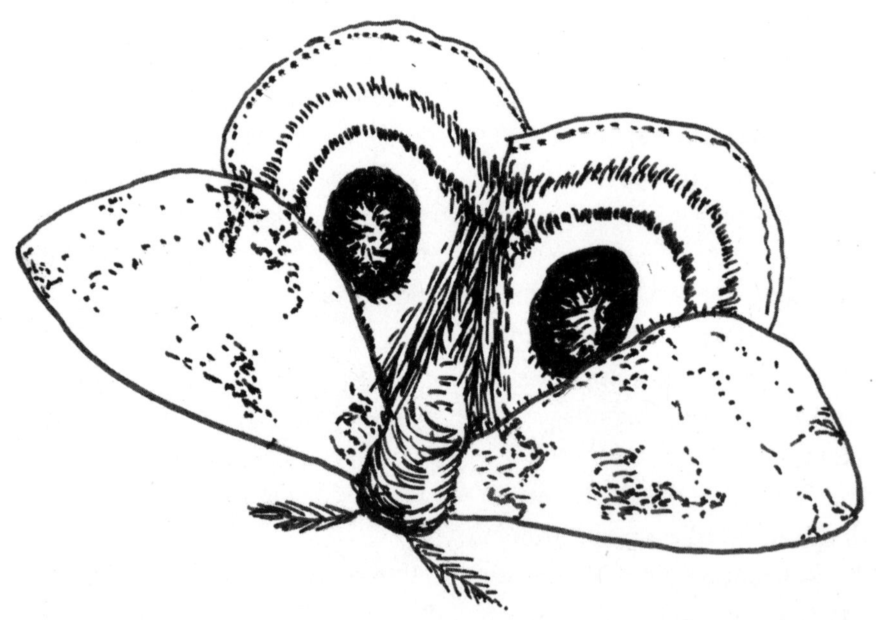

Io moth

Key Nature Concepts for Children to Learn

Why Do We Have Seasons?

Lean over to one side. Just a bit. Even a gentle lean, if you are a planet called Earth, creates big changes. To help you imagine this, think about a globe on a teacher's desk. You'll notice that it is not straight up and down. In other words, the imaginary line between the Earth's north and south poles (the axis) is on an angle (23.5 degrees). Because the Earth rotates on this axis, the northern hemisphere ends up being *tilted toward the Sun* for part of the year—our spring and summer—*and away from the Sun* for part of the year—our fall and winter. This tilt causes a huge difference in the amount of heating the Earth's surface receives from one season to the next.

In summer, sunlight strikes our part of the globe much more directly (perpendicularly) than during other times of the year, and the Earth receives more heat. The solar radiation also takes a shorter path through the energy-absorbing atmosphere before striking the Earth.

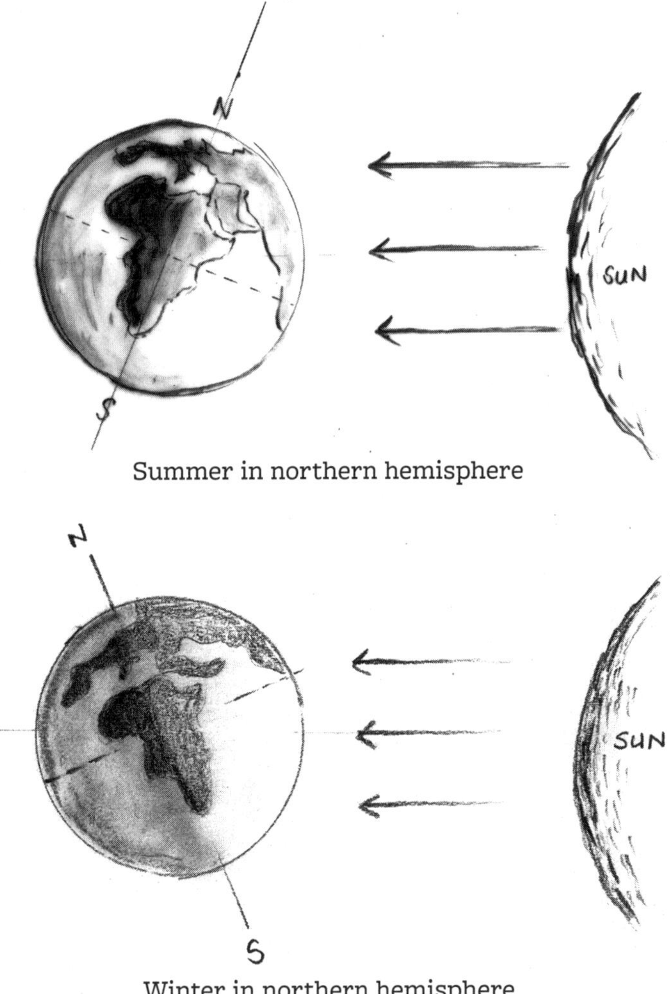

Winter in northern hemisphere

In winter, on the other hand, the Sun casts a weaker, angled light from its lower position in the southern sky, and the sunlight must travel through more of the atmosphere, so the Earth's surface receives far less heat.

The difference in heating between the summer and winter can also be shown by pointing a flashlight at a tabletop. Shine the flashlight directly over the tabletop so the beam is vertical. You'll notice that the light shines over a small, round area. The tabletop will soon feel warm to the touch. This is what happens in summer, when the Sun is higher overhead in the sky. To simulate winter, angle your flashlight beam to the side so that the light scatters over a larger area. You'll feel less heat, because the same amount of light covers a larger area. The difference in the angle of the light between summer and winter creates the profound differences in temperature and available sunlight. All life responds, from the rich plant growth and bird song of a solar-soaked June day to the dormant plants and silent birds of a dim day in December. The tilted axis is also the reason shadows are at their longest at the winter solstice and at their shortest on the first day of summer.

The tilting also creates more hours of daylight in the summer and fewer in winter. This, too, makes a huge difference in the lives of plants and animals. One of the main reasons birds migrate north in the spring—instead of staying in the tropics, for example—is to take advantage of the longer days of the temperate summer. These mean more time for birds to gather food to feed their young, leading to greater reproductive success.

Tree swallows in flight

Phenology

Phenology is the science of observing and recording the annual cycle of "first events"—such as spring's first tree swallow, lilac bloom or frog song. Many of the "citizen science" projects described in this book are phenological in nature.

Keeping track of these dates of first happenings from year to year not only enhances our pleasure at witnessing them but also provides a measure of order and predictability to the cycles of nature. These dates also tell us a great deal about how nature is responding to climate change. For example, studies have shown that some native plants in the eastern United States are flowering as much as a month earlier in response to a warming climate. The dates were compared to

> To be interested in the changing seasons is a happier state of mind than to be hopelessly in love with spring.
>
> —GEORGE SANTAYANA

more recent phenological data by using the records of two iconic American naturalists, Henry David Thoreau and Aldo Leopold.

Phenology is also a great way to heighten our awareness of the living systems that surrounds us. It helps us to see the land as a whole. It allows us to compare any given event to others that usually happen at the same time. For example, when spring peepers are calling in Ontario in late April, American woodcock are displaying, walleye are spawning, American elms are in flower, the ice has probably just gone out of the lakes, the Sun is setting shortly after 8 PM and Orion is low in the western sky.

The chart below shows seasonal occurrences of some events in nature that attract particular attention. The activity levels apply most accurately to the northeast.

Climate Change

Climate change is one of the most serious issues of our time. This is the elephant in the room for all of us who care deeply about the future of the natural world. For many, the sheer magnitude and scope of this issue is so overwhelming that a normal response is to simply try not to think about it. However, climate change is hard to ignore. As we write this book, California is in the midst of an unprecedented drought. The state's ecology seems to be changing and becoming more like Arizona's. In the Sierra Nevada mountains, many older, giant trees are dying. The majestic sequoias are even at risk.

Seasonal Occurrences of Natural Events of Special Interest

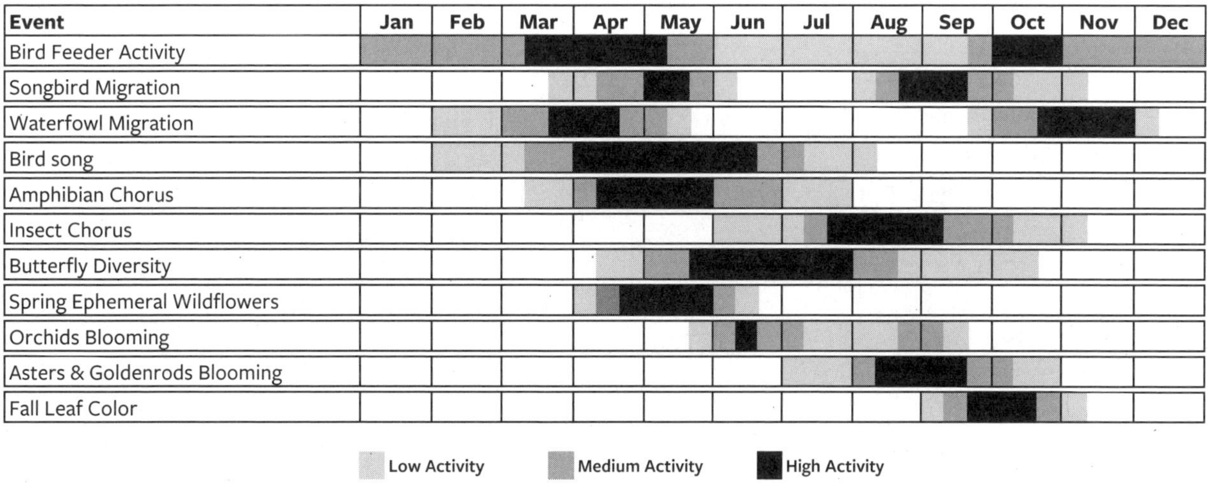

Event	Jan	Feb	Mar	Apr	May	Jun	Jul	Aug	Sep	Oct	Nov	Dec
Bird Feeder Activity												
Songbird Migration												
Waterfowl Migration												
Bird song												
Amphibian Chorus												
Insect Chorus												
Butterfly Diversity												
Spring Ephemeral Wildflowers												
Orchids Blooming												
Asters & Goldenrods Blooming												
Fall Leaf Color												

Low Activity Medium Activity High Activity

Yet we sometimes forget that nature is extraordinarily resilient. There are still wonderfully diverse natural habitats to enjoy, be they parks, the nearby countryside or your own neighborhood or backyard. And even though some species are now absent or reduced in number, children don't necessarily feel the sense of loss; how many of us mourn the passenger pigeon? Today's young people probably won't be saddened by the loss of once-common species such as the piping plover or the woodland caribou because they will never have known them. Kids simply accept nature the way it is now.

Gnarled old tree

There is, however, one thing we can do: help our children be amazed at the wonder and beauty of the existing natural world, even as it changes over time. We can give our children rich and repeated exposure to nature, and show them practical ways to conserve, protect and enhance natural areas. And we can teach them about the very real impacts of climate change. Clearly, the importance of nature connectedness is greater today than ever before.

Among the impacts of climate change in North America, we are already seeing some migrant birds returning earlier in the spring and in many cases, lingering later into the fall. Warmer early spring temperatures are also linked to an earlier start to the nesting season, the spring frog chorus, the flowering and leaf-out of trees and wildflowers and the emergence of insects. These events may not appear alarming in themselves, but they are almost certainly the "canary in the coal mine" for things to come—and things that have already started to happen.

1. Shoreline erosion: This is expected to become much worse because of rising sea levels and increased flooding and storm surges. It will have a major effect on coastal ecosystems like salt marshes.

2. More wildfires: Drought conditions and hotter temperatures in many areas, especially western Canada and the United States, are contributing to an increased

Ragweed, the bane of hayfever sufferers

number of wildfires and longer fire seasons.

3. Forced migrations: Plants and animals are migrating to higher altitudes and latitudes. In some cases, humans may need to assist in this process. Plant-hardiness zones are shifting northward and to higher elevations. Many bird species are already extending their range northward. Plants and animals living in extreme habitats such as tundra and alpine regions may become extinct because they literally have no place to go.

4. Decreased bird diversity: The Audubon Birds and Climate Report (Sept. 2014) stated that "314 of the 588 North American species studied will lose more than 50 percent of their current climatic range by 2080." With earlier springs, resident birds like mourning doves and black-capped chickadees will be able to breed earlier and raise more young. However, increased resident bird populations could reduce the food and other resources available to tropical migrants that arrive later in the spring.

5. Mammals: Species such as raccoons and skunks will probably benefit from milder winters. The already prolific white-tailed deer should also fare well, since it is not really adapted to snow and cold to begin with. Moose, on the other hand, could be negatively affected, not only by the warmth but also by increased levels of parasites such as winter tick and brain worm.

6. Increase in insect pests: Milder winters are contributing to widespread infestations of species such as pine bark beetles, which now complete more reproductive cycles than in the past.

7. Desynchronization of life-cycle events: For instance, abnormally mild late-winter weather may cause trees to flower early, leaving the flowers vulnerable to late frosts. Birds returning from the tropics may reach breeding grounds after insect numbers have peaked, resulting in less nesting success.

8. Changing forests: Forests are under pressure from more frequent droughts, forest fires, severe windstorms, insect pests, invasive plant species and fungal diseases. Many of these impacts are linked to climate change.

9. An Increase in allergens and noxious plants: As CO_2 levels rise, plants such as poison ivy and ragweed are thriving, growing bigger and spreading more rapidly. People who suffer from hay fever or are allergic to poison ivy (about 80 percent of the population) will need to take special precautions. Many invasive, non-native species such as common reed and dog-strangling vine also appear to thrive in higher atmospheric CO_2 levels.

> The future of mankind is dependent on every human being intimately associated with a half-acre of ground.
>
> —FRANK LLOYD WRIGHT (American architect, 1867–1959)

10. Changing lakes and rivers: With warmer temperatures, streams and lakes are likely to become unsuitable for cold-water fish. Native fish communities could change drastically. A changing climate may favor non-native invasive species with generalized habitat and feeding requirements over native species with more specialized needs. Changes in precipitation such as more droughts and floods may make reproduction difficult for some species. Salmon appear to be especially vulnerable.

> Knowledge without love will not stick. But if love comes first, knowledge is sure to follow.
>
> —JOHN BURROUGHS

11. Ocean chemistry: The world's oceans are becoming more acidic as more and more CO_2 from the atmosphere dissolves into seawater. This impairs the ability of shelled organisms and coral reefs to form skeletons and shells.

If we are to avoid the worst-case scenarios of a changing climate, we must all do our utmost to convince politicians—starting with our families, friends and neighbors who elect them—to take aggressive action on cutting greenhouse gas emissions and building a carbon-free economy. Despite what advertisers tell us, we are not just consumers. Instead, let's think of ourselves and our children as enablers: difference-makers and stewards for the natural environment.

Evolution

Anyone who observes the natural world inevitably starts to ask the question "Why?" Why do monarch butterflies migrate? Why do trees shed their leaves in winter? Charles Darwin, the father of modern biology and the theory of evolution, was the first person to make "Why are plants and animals the way they are?" a sensible question—and one demanding a reasonable answer. Thanks to the theory of evolution, we now realize that almost every aspect of a plant or animal—from its physical appearance to its behavior—

represents a solution to the problems posed by the environment in which it lives. Every organism has its own fascinating evolutionary history. This means that nature provides all of us with many lifetimes' worth of knowledge to acquire—and gives scientists amazing discoveries yet to be made. Prior to Darwin, we simply had to accept organisms the way they are. End of story.

We have highlighted the wonder of evolution throughout this book by providing examples of the amazing adaptations of even the most "ordinary" plants and animals. Almost every characteristic of an organism, whether it is the flat tail of a beaver or the ethereal song of a hermit thrush, is the culmination of a complex story of adaptation to the pressures of the environment. And the good news for eager, young scientists-to-be is that science is just beginning to unravel many of these stories. There is so much more to discover!

Consider this: for every living thing that exists today, there are countless thousands of species that went extinct. The very fact that you are alive today means that you have an unbroken chain of ancestors stretching back to the beginning of life. Think about that. Even one premature death of a potential ancient mother or father would have ended the possibility of you being you. You come from a long line of survivors!

As we develop a deeper appreciation of the theory of evolution, we inevitably consider our own origins and adaptations as a species. We are connected to every other living organism on Earth in much more intimate ways than we might think. For instance, we still share many basic housekeeping genes (the blueprint of an organism) with all living, cell-based organisms—even algae and bacteria. We may believe we are special, but humans share almost all the same genetic material as chimpanzees. We differ only slightly, by about 1.2 percent. Yet these differences, small though they may be, have spurred humans on to create complex civilizations, build rocket ships capable of visiting the Moon and figure out how to split the atom!

Charles Darwin

Even though a full understanding of the mechanisms of evolution—natural selection, for example—is challenging for children, they should be able to grasp the essential components by age seven or eight, even without any understanding of genetics. These components are variation (all life forms in a population vary), inheritance (traits are inherited from parents and passed on to offspring), selection (life forms with traits that help them to survive and reproduce are most likely to pass on these traits to the next generation) and time (major change usually takes thousands of generations).

A quick primer

1. About 150 years ago, Charles Darwin, an English scientist, figured out how nature produces new species of living things and why we have—and have had in the past—so many different kinds. He proved that new species of living things develop from older forms of life through a process called *evolution*.

2. The theory of evolution is the most important idea in the study and appreciation of living things. It is the foundation of modern biology. In science, the word *theory* refers to an idea or set of ideas that is widely accepted by the scientific community and has been proven in many different ways to explain facts or events (e.g., the theory of gravity). This is the opposite of the everyday meaning of *theory*: a "hunch" with little evidence to back it up.

3. Darwin noticed that new traits (e.g., a slightly bigger bill, a more aggressive behavior, a longer stem) show up in plants and animals from time to time. He realized that some of these traits would give an individual an advantage over its brothers and sisters and, therefore, improve its chances of surviving and reproducing. On the other hand, some traits (e.g., reckless behavior) would make survival more challenging.

4. From his work in breeding pigeons, Darwin also observed that survivors who were able to reproduce would pass this new trait on to their offspring. He called this process "selection." When it happens naturally (i.e., in the wild) he called it "natural selection." When it happens because humans do the selecting (e.g., breeding pigeons), he called it "artificial selection."

5. What Darwin didn't know at the time was that new traits occur because of changes in genes. Genes act like a recipe for growing a living thing. They determine how it will look and behave. There are genes for everything from eye color to whether your hair is straight or curly. Plants and animals can have thousands of genes; we humans have about 20,000. Our entire set of genes is located in the nucleus of each of the trillions of cells in our body. Cells are organized into tissues, such as skin, muscle and bone, and each cell uses only the instructions from some of the genes. For example, a muscle cell uses only the genes related to making and using muscles. It is as if each cell reads only that part of the recipe that it needs.

6. A gene is made up of a stretch or section of deoxyribonucleic acid (DNA), a long, chain-like molecule that is tightly wound in a little "package" known as a chromosome. Humans have two sets of 23 chromosomes in every cell, one set inherited from each parent. Genes provide instructions to the cell for making proteins. Some proteins like lactase help us digest milk. Other proteins do everything from forming muscle to helping us see colors.

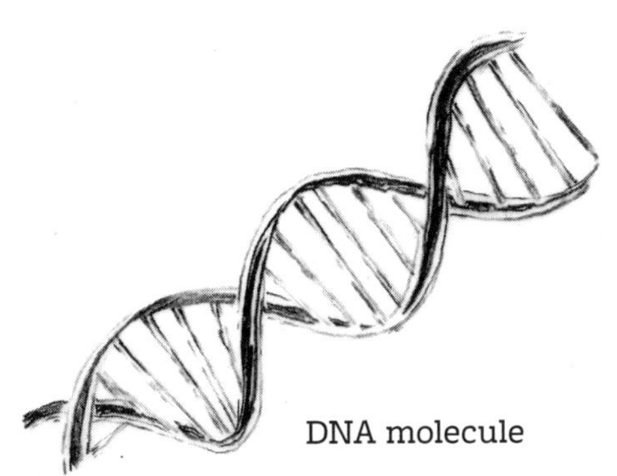

7. When cells divide, the chromosomes are copied. Change (i.e., a new trait) happens when something goes wrong with the copying, and there is an error (mutation) in the DNA that makes up a gene. The error can have a big effect, a small effect or no effect. It was a mutation in the lactase gene that allows most people of European ancestry to properly digest milk for their entire life. People without this mutated gene—99 percent of Chinese people, for example—can only digest milk as babies.

8. New species resulting from evolution are usually just updates, not radical redesigns. For instance, the same basic body plan (e.g., four legs) usually remains. A good example is the similarity in the skeletons of humans, horses, dogs and even frogs. Some species are so well adapted to their habitat and lifestyle that they have hardly changed since the time of the dinosaurs (e.g., crocodiles, dragonflies).

9. In a kind of natural selection known as "sexual selection," some traits in animals (especially males) such as bright feathers, large antlers or an attractive song have evolved because they lead to greater success in mating. These traits make the animal more attractive to the opposite sex because they are interpreted as signs of good health and strength. Animals with these traits, therefore, get to mate more often.

10. Natural selection, however, is not perfect. Many traits are "trade-offs"—changing one feature for the better may mean changing another for the worse. For instance, the drumming of the ruffed grouse may be attractive to the opposite sex, but it also makes the bird vulnerable to predators who are also attracted to the sound.

11. It's false to assume that *everything* about a living thing is an adaptation. Some traits are just accidents. For instance, the fact that blood is red is not an adaptation. It is a result of blood's chemistry.

12. Evolution does not tell us how life began in the first place. The term for this mystery is *abiogenesis* and scientists are working on several hypotheses to explain it.
13. It's very important to understand the word "species." One definition of species is a group of creatures that can only successfully reproduce among themselves. For example, blue jays can only breed with blue jays and snapping turtles with snapping turtles. If you try breeding a blue jay with a snapping turtle, you won't get a snapping jay. You will be out of luck.
14. Another key term is "common ancestor." It refers to a single species that two or more descendant species share as an ancestor. For example, your grandfather is the common ancestor of both you and your cousin, and the wolf is the common ancestor of all dogs. In terms of language, Latin is the common ancestor of Spanish and French. All humans have a common ancestor with chimpanzees, which means that if you and a chimpanzee at the local zoo were able to trace back all of your ancestors (father, grandfather, great-grandfather, great-great-grandfather, etc.), you would eventually arrive at the same individual ancestor. We didn't evolve *from* chimpanzees, however; we just have a common ancestor. Going back further in time, we also have a common ancestor with monkeys, dogs, birds, algae and the first life to appear on Earth!

Effective questioning to reveal the wonder of evolution

Children—and adults, for that matter—should remember that almost everything about an organism—its size, color, behavior, etc.—is an adaptation to help it survive. In other words, these traits help the organism to live in this place, at this time and under these conditions. Thoughtful questioning will not only make this clear, but also help to elicit a sense of wonder, curiosity and deeper appreciation for the process of evolution and for nature itself.
1. Start by encouraging children to look in detail at the organism or behavior in question. Ask them to describe what they see and why they think the plant or animal looks or behaves that way.
2. Ask open-ended questions such as those beginning with "Why?" or "What do you think?" These types of questions elicit more thinking than yes or no questions. Encourage children to ask the same questions of you.

Evolution in a nutshell

1. All creatures struggle to survive and reproduce, but many fail.
2. Creatures born with a helpful trait are more likely to survive and reproduce.
3. Parents pass on the useful trait(s) to their young.
4. Over time (sometimes short, but usually very long periods of time, such as thousands or millions of years), these new traits lead to a new species.

3. Encourage critical thinking. If they don't know the answer, ask the children to come up with a reasonable hypothesis—an educated guess, in other words. Do the same yourself. When you get back home, follow up with an Internet search.

4. Try to get a sense of where the children's interest in an organism's appearance or behavior lies and steer them in that direction.

5. Use the language of wonder, beauty and awe: Isn't it amazing that...? Think how incredible it is that...? Think of yourself trying to live this way (e.g., like a tree, a woodpecker, a frog).

Lewis's woodpecker

What's bugging you? A story about bugs to help younger kids understand the concept of evolution

Let's say I release 100 bugs onto a green lawn. Fifty are green and 50 are brown. Now, which bugs do you think will best be able to hide from enemies like bug-eating birds? (Most kids will say green ones.) So, if I go back in a few years, would I find more green or more brown bugs? (green again). And what color will the babies of the green bugs be? (green). That's right. Just as your mom or dad passed on a certain trait like blue eyes, red hair or a big nose to you, the parent green bugs will pass on the green color to their babies.

(Now comes the tricky part.) Let's say some green bugs that usually live on green lawns—we'll call them green lawn bugs—get blown in a storm to an island where there is mostly brown sand. Life will be hard, won't it? But once in a rare while, a pair of these green lawn bugs might produce a brown baby. This is because little mistakes sometimes happen in how an animal's body makes a baby. Do you think those rare brown babies would have an advantage over their green brothers and sisters? (Most kids will say yes or probably.) And, if the rare brown bugs live a little longer because they can better hide from enemies, do you think they may have more babies than the green bugs? (Most kids will agree.) What color would the babies be?

Brown sand bug

(Most kids will say brown.) As the years go by, do you think the brown bugs will become more and more common? (Most kids will agree.)

Color isn't the only thing that might change. Because a sandy habitat offers fewer places to hide, the babies that are born with other good traits for hiding—once again because of a mistake in how the parents' body makes a baby—would end up surviving more easily. Such a trait might be bigger, stronger front legs that are good for digging hiding spots in the sand.

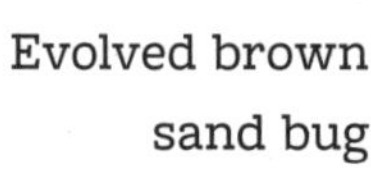
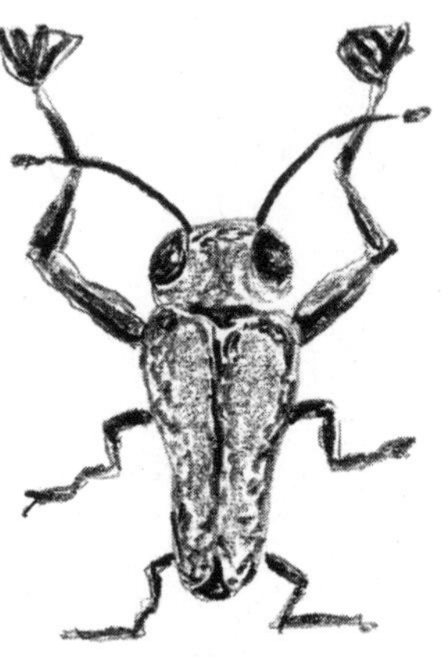
Evolved brown sand bug

Now, let's say that hundreds of years later, there is another huge storm. Some of the brown bugs—let's call them brown sand bugs—get blown off the island and end up on the grassy lawns where their ancestors came from. Would they have trouble surviving? (Kids should say, yes.) Well, that's not the only problem they would have. Other than eating, what else do all animals do? (Prompt someone to say, "have babies.") Well, imagine a male brown sand bug meets a female green lawn bug. She might just chase him away or completely ignore him. She won't want to make babies with him because, being brown and having huge front legs, he looks so different. The same thing would happen when female brown sand bugs come across male green lawn bugs. At this point, we can say that the green lawn bugs and the brown sand bugs have evolved into two different species.

Here is a true story illustrating how evolution works. In England, there is a species of moth that is pale with dark, pepper-like specks. It is called a pepper moth. This species hides well on trees with light-colored bark. A very few of these moths are dark all over. During the Industrial Revolution (1760 to 1840), the burning of coal blackened many of England's trees with dark soot. Light-colored moths, therefore, lost their camouflage and were gobbled up by birds. Suddenly, dark moths had a better chance of surviving and breeding. Within 100 years, almost all the moths were dark. Only now, with pollution levels way down, are they reverting to their original pale color. This story shows that evolution is still happening all around us. We just don't tend to notice it because the changes take place over many years.

Imagining your ancestors

Just how far back do your ancestors go? We might think about our parents, our grandparents or maybe even our great grandparents. After that, we tend to lose track and our ancestors disappear into the mists of time.

It is important to remember that for you to be here now, today, you have to have unbroken chain of ancestors stretching back to the very beginnings of life. If even one of your direct ancestors had passed away before finding a mate and having children, you wouldn't be here. Here is a thought experiment to help you imagine your unbroken link to the ancient past. You will see that there never was a "first" human. Let's start by imaging the following.

Begin with a printed picture of yourself. Now, find a photo of your father (or mother—it makes no difference which side of the family you choose) and place it on top. Do the same with a picture of your grandfather, your great-grandfather and maybe even your great-great-grandfather. Continue to pile on the photos of each of your ancestors going further back in time. Remember, this is a thought experiment, so the fact that you don't actually *have* photographs is not a problem.

To do this activity you will need to go back 185 million generations in time. That is going to make for one really big

Imagine your ancestors

pile of photographs (about 10 mi./16 km tall, depending on how thick the pictures are). So instead of making a vertical pile, let's tilt our pile sideways and place all those pictures beside one another along an extremely long imaginary bookshelf. At the beginning of the shelf is a picture of you, while at the far end is the picture of your 185-million-greats-grandfather. Fossils give us a pretty good idea of what he or she would have looked like. No, he was not a cave dweller wrapped in animal skins. Surprisingly enough, he was a FISH! So was your 185-million-greats-grandmother.

Now, let's go for a long walk—and later a bike ride. We'll occasionally stop to pull pictures from the shelf and look at them as we go. You'll see pictures of animals that look like apes, others that look like monkeys and others that look like shrews (mouse-like mammals). Keep in mind, however, that every picture in the line will look almost identical to the picture right before and after it—or at least as similar as you look like your father, mother, brother or sister. This is because evolutionary change is very, very gradual. Think of yourself. There was never a day when you went to bed as a baby and woke up as a toddler. However, if you pick any two pictures far enough apart in the bookshelf, they will be very different.

Our first stop is just 4 in. (10 cm) down the shelf at picture number 400. This is from 10,000 years or 400 generations ago, when your 400-greats-grandfather lived. You won't notice much difference. Once he had a shave and a haircut, he would look very similar to a modern human. Let's keep going.

Now, stop one big step (40 in./1 m) from the start. Let's study this picture from 100,000 years ago, where we find your 4,000-greats-grandfather. Now there has been a noticeable change! His skull appears a little bit thicker, especially under the eyebrows.

Walking 12 steps or so will take us to a million years ago—the 40,000th picture and your 40,000-greats-grandfather. At this point, you are looking at someone different enough to count as another species, the one we call *Homo erectus* or "upright man." He was, however, about the same size as modern humans and used both fire and tools.

Let's resume our journey. We are now going to stop at six million years ago—80 steps (200 ft. or 60 m) down the line, where we will find a picture of your

Homo erectus

Lemur

240,000-greats-grandfather. Had you met him, he probably would have looked a bit like a chimpanzee. However, he wouldn't actually have been a chimpanzee. He would have been the common ancestor we share with modern chimpanzees—in other words, the 250,000-greats-grandfather of a chimp living today.

Now, let's see what the picture looks like if we stop at 63 million years ago, another 840 steps (2100 ft./640 m) down the shelf. Here we'll see a photo of your 7-million-greats-grandfather. He will look something like a lemur and be the ancestor of all modern lemurs, monkeys and apes, including us. He would, of course, have a tail.

Well, now it's time to hop on our bikes. At 2.5 mi. (4 km) from the start, we will find a picture of your 45-million-greats-grandfather. He is also the ancestor of all modern mammals, except marsupials like kangaroos and monotremes like the platypus. He looks like a mouse with a long nose. At card 170 million, 9 mi. (15 km) from the beginning or 310 million years ago, you will see a picture of an ancestor that looks like a big lizard. He or she is the ancestor of all modern mammals, reptiles and birds, and all of the dinosaurs. You'll be surprised to learn that many reptiles haven't changed all that much since that time.

We'll now ride another 1000 ft. (300 m) back—almost to the end of the shelf—where we'll see your 175-million-greats-grandfather. He will probably look a bit like a salamander, and be the ancestor of all modern amphibians as well as all the other land vertebrates.

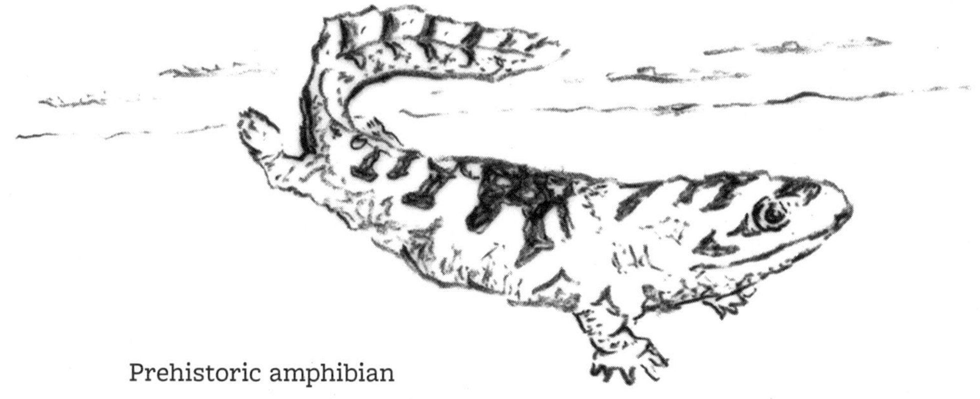

Prehistoric amphibian

Finally, riding just a half-mile more (just under one kilometer) will take us to the end of the shelf, where we'll finally meet your 185-million-greats-grandfather. This fellow was essentially a fish! From there we could go back in further in time, meeting more and more distant great-grandparents, including various kinds of fishes with jaws, then fishes without jaws. At about this point, however, we start to run out of fossils, so we can't be sure just what your oldest great-grandparents looked like. We do know, however, that boarding a plane and traveling several thousand miles further would take us to a picture of the very first life form to exist on our planet—possibly something like blue-green algae, and your oldest ancestor.

It is a long and perhaps a strange journey—but remember, you are a part of this story of creation. So are each and every one of your ancestors. You are one more photo along the shelf. So let's make sure you leave your mark! Do something special to make planet Earth an even better place to live for the sake of your descendants yet to come.
(Adapted from *The Magic of Reality* by Richard Dawkins)

Big History

It is a big universe out there. Bigger than we can possibly imagine. And when we look up into the deepness and vastness of space, we begin to ask many of the same questions our ancestors asked. How did this all begin? When did it begin? There is nothing more human than to ponder our origins. Cultures around the world have always had their own creation stories. And we, in this modern age, certainly have ours.

Big History is the most current theory of who we are and how we came to be. It uses modern science and the best and latest evidence-based information to tell a single, coherent story of the origin of all that exists. Big History explains the creation of the universe, the stars, our planet Earth, life itself and, of course, our very own species, *Homo sapiens*. It helps us realize the depth and richness of our connectedness to everything that is and ever was.

Our story is a never-ending and creative unfolding. Scientists believe that it began with the Big Bang, a great burst of radiant energy that occurred some

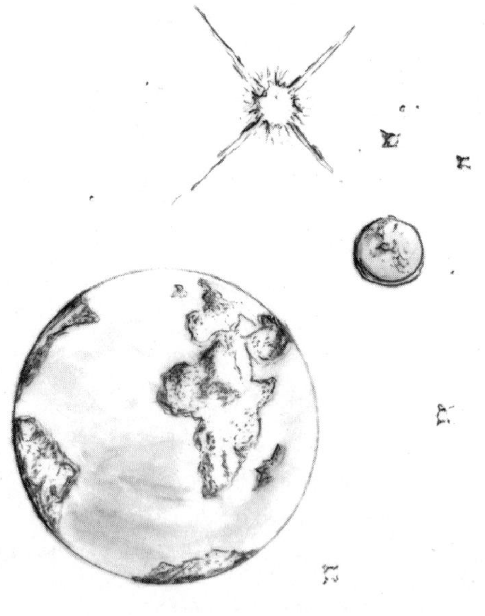

Big History

13.7 billion years ago. Just stop for a moment and think about how long ago that is. If you were to count at a rate of one number per second—1,2,3...—it would take you more than 400 years to count to 13.7 billion!

Flaring forth from an infinitesimally small point, the universe expanded and then cooled. As the elementary particles stabilized, hydrogen and helium atoms were formed and eventually came together to form stars. When these stars died in fantastic stellar explosions known as supernovae, the helium and hydrogen atoms were transformed into new atoms that had not existed before, creating atoms such as carbon, oxygen, phosphorous and iron.

This creative emergence continued as planets such our Earth came into being. Next came a blossoming of unparalleled ingenuity in the universe—something we are not yet certain exists anywhere else but here on this Earth. From deep within a frothing sea, punctuated by lightning and earthquakes and the chaotic energy of a newly formed world, a spark of life was coaxed into existence some four billion years ago. We don't yet know exactly how life began, but we do know that over many eons, simple cells became more complex. Through the process of evolution, life began packaging itself into a variety of different forms. Some forms captured the Sun's energy through photosynthesis. Other forms became predators. The predator-prey relationship encouraged more, ever-novel ways to survive, eat and move. Eventually, everything from eyesight to sexual reproduction evolved, finding expression in millions upon millions of new forms of life. Everything that ever lived is part of this story, including humans and including you!

Oxygen atom

The human brain is by far the most sophisticated and remarkable organ to have arisen through evolution. Scientists believe that about seven million years ago in Africa, something happened to hugely accelerate brain development. Perhaps it was early hominids, crouched

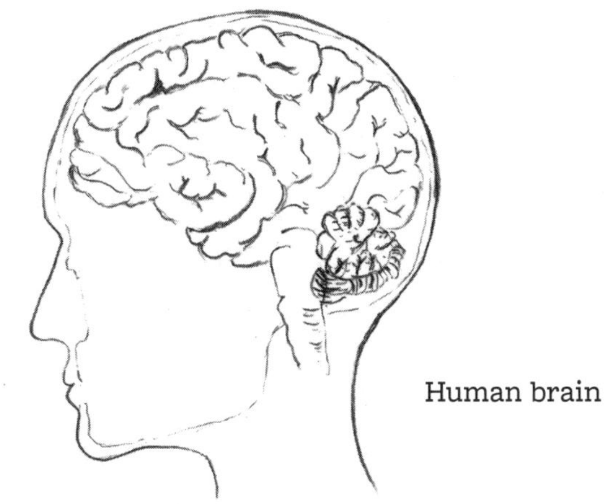

Human brain

on the savannah, using a stick to dig for roots and then using that same stick as a weapon. This may have inspired them to experiment more and discover new uses for tools, which in turn led their brains to develop. There is no clear consensus. We do know, however, that a new line of apes slowly emerged. Species such as *Homo naledi*, *Homo habilis*, *Homo rhudolfensis* and *Homo erectus* acquired larger brains than their primate cousins. Eventually they developed the ability to dream, ponder, show compassion and anticipate.

Whatever the exact mechanism, consciousness arose in humans, thanks largely to our ability to advance our thinking through oral and written language. This, in turn, led to astonishing cultural and scientific accomplishments. So, just who are we human beings? In the words of Carl Sagan, "We are the local embodiment of a Cosmos grown to self-awareness. We have begun to contemplate our origins: star stuff pondering stars...." Like every other living thing, humans have emerged from the elements created in supernovae and the interplay of sunlight, water, atmosphere and, especially, time. (See color section, figure 6.)

Fall

the cooling season

Of all the seasons, we might consider fall as the true start of the new year. It is a time of new beginnings and sad endings as we say goodbye to the warmth and freedom of summer. Cup your ears and you'll notice that the early fall soundscape resonates with the rhythmic drone of crickets, katydids and cicadas. On or about September 21, the Sun marches across the equator on its annual southward course, marking the official beginning of this season. By this time, northern forests will already be approaching peak color. As trees shed their cloak of leaves and birds wing their way southward, many mammals, insects, amphibians and reptiles are getting ready to face the coming cold and shortage of food. With the shortening days, there is a noticeable hush, almost as if the land were exhaling as it prepares for a long winter's rest.

Some Key Events in Nature in Fall

The "early fall" period runs from early September through mid-October; "late fall" covers mid-October through November. Timing of events will vary depending on latitude, elevation and the vagaries of the weather. Climate change, too, is accelerating some events and delaying others. The sequence of events, however, is always the same. The references point to an activity based on a given event.

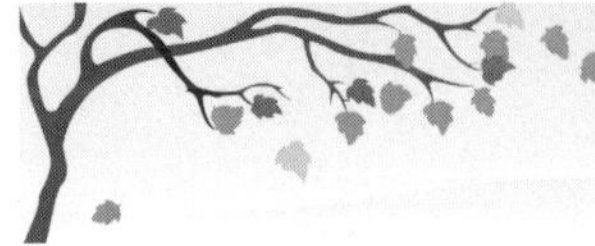

Continent-wide Overview

Birds

General

- Migration is underway and for some species will last into December. Most birds are migratory, including many birds of prey. Those that don't migrate (e.g., grouse, cardinals) are called *residents*. With just a little effort, you will find birds all around you. (See Activity 11, page 104.)
- Fall migrants usually move in large numbers just after a cold front has passed through. Birds have many adaptations to make these long flights possible. (See Activity 12, page 105.)
- Only a few birds sing in the fall; however, contact calls are common. In many areas, the calls of blue jays and crows are familiar sounds.
- Birds face numerous dangers during migration, the most serious of which are window collisions and cats. Please keep your cat indoors and make sure at least some of your windows are bird-safe.

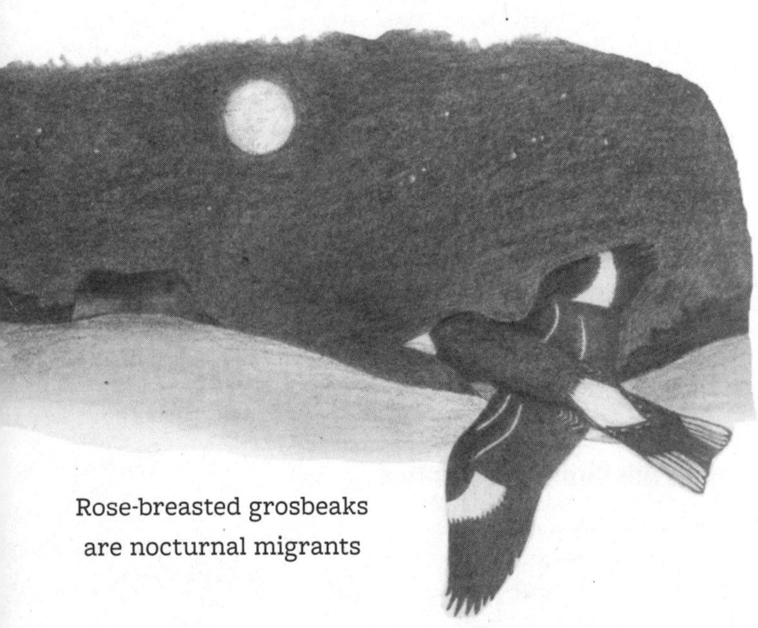

Rose-breasted grosbeaks are nocturnal migrants

Early fall

- Numerous shorebirds (e.g., sandpipers, plovers) and songbirds (e.g., warblers, orioles, swallows) migrate south, many to the tropics. Warblers and vireos are often found during the day in mixed-species flocks with chickadees and can be “pished” into view. (See Activity 13, page 107.)

- In October, hardier migrants such as sparrows and juncos pass through and often visit backyard feeders. Some will stay all winter. In many areas, the variety of birds at feeders hits its annual peak at this time. (See Activity 14, page 108.)

Purple sandpiper

Late fall

- Waterfowl migration increases in late fall as diving ducks (e.g., mergansers, goldeneye, scaup) start arriving on larger lakes and both coasts. Flocks of gulls, robins, blackbirds, crows and both Canada and snow geese are widespread.
- Migrants from the Arctic arrive (e.g., northern shrikes, snow buntings, American tree sparrows, rough-legged hawks) and overwinter in many regions. Some years, nomadic northern finches (e.g., redpolls, pine siskins, pine grosbeaks, crossbills) and snowy owls also show up, although influxes of these species are difficult to predict.

Northern shrike

Mammals

General

- Mammals are feeding heavily in preparation for winter. Black bears are gorging themselves on acorns and berries, and squirrels are caching food items for future consumption. (See Activity 15, page 110 and Activity 16, page 110.)

- All the members of the deer family (e.g., elk, moose, white-tailed deer, mule deer) mate in the fall. Some species, like moose and elk, are very vocal.
- Carnivores like red foxes are active at dawn and dusk and can often be observed hunting at these times of day. (See Activity 17, page 113.)

Early fall

- In preparation for the rut and to advertise their presence to does, buck white-tailed deer make scrapes in the leaf litter and urinate on them. They also rub their antlers on trees to deposit scent. You may find bark rubs on small trees or scrapes on the ground.
- Bats either migrate south or head to hibernation sites in caves and abandoned mines. White nose syndrome disease is decimating many bat populations.

Late fall

- Snowshoe hares and weasels acquire their white winter coats.
- Sensing the shorter days, beavers begin cutting down trees for winter food. Aspens are the preferred species in many areas.
- In marshes, watch for muskrats building cone-shaped homes and feeding platforms of mud and vegetation.
- Once the leaves fall, the "leaf-ball" nests (dreys) of gray squirrels are very visible.
- Some species, such as bears, go into hibernation and will remain in their shelters until spring.

Amphibians and Reptiles

General

- Salamanders are easily found in fall, often under flat rocks, boards and logs. (See Activity 18, page 114.)

Early fall

- Frogs feed heavily and can be quite common in fields near wetlands. (See Activity 19, page 115.)
- Some frog species (e.g., spring peeper, gray treefrog) will call sporadically during the day, but never in a full chorus.
- Baby turtles are hatching.

Late fall

- As colder weather arrives, nearly all species move to hibernation sites in leaf litter (e.g., treefrogs), at the bottoms of lakes and ponds (e.g., turtles, bullfrogs) or under the ground below the frost line (e.g., snakes, most salamanders, toads).

Fishes

General

- Many kinds of fishes feed heavily in the fall (e.g., walleye, northern pike) and fishing can be good.
- Brook trout, lake trout and most species of salmon are spawning. (See Activity 20, page 115.)

Invertebrates

Early fall

- Monarch butterflies are migrating south. Monarchs east of the Rockies head to the Sierra Madre mountains in the Michoacán region of west-central Mexico, while populations on the Pacific coast winter in central and southern California in sites such as Pacific Grove. (See Activity 22, pages 120.)
- Goldenrods, asters and other fall wildflowers attract huge numbers of insects and provide excellent opportunities for close-up observation. (See Activity 23, page 121.)
- The mating calls of crickets, katydids and cicadas continue to fill the air, both day and night. (See Activity 24, page 123.)
- Woolly bear caterpillars are on the move, searching out spots to spend the winter. (See Activity 25, page 125.)
- Spiderwebs are everywhere. They are especially visible in the early morning on shrubs and grasses near wetlands. (See Activity 26, page 125 and Activity 27, page 126.)
- Large mating swarms of ants are a common late-summer phenomenon, especially on warm, humid afternoons. Watch for them even in the city. (See Activity 28, page 126.)
- Small, red or yellow meadowhawk dragonflies are abundant in many areas.

Late fall

- Ball-like galls of the goldenrod gall fly stand out on goldenrod stems.
- With cooler weather, most insects die or enter an inactive state called diapause. Some will overwinter as eggs (e.g., most mosquitoes), larvae (e.g., woolly bear caterpillar), pupae (e.g., swallowtail butterfly), nymphs (e.g., dragonfly) or adults (e.g., queen wasps, queen bumblebees, mourning cloak butterfly). Honeybees remain relatively active inside the hive throughout the winter.

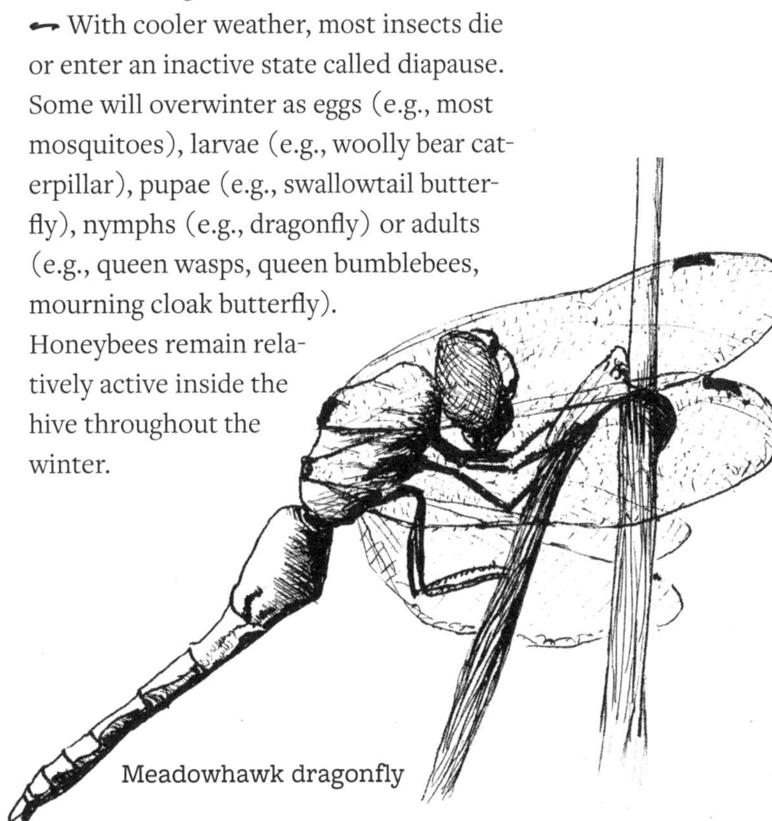

Meadowhawk dragonfly

Plants

General

- Seeds in their various forms (e.g., berries, acorns, keys, fruit) can be very visible on trees, shrubs and other plants. The amount of fruit and seed present varies considerably from year to year. Intriguing methods have evolved to disperse the seed. (See Activity 29, page 127.)

- Most deciduous trees and shrubs change color as their chlorophyll breaks down. In some species, color change may begin in late summer (e.g., chokecherry). As a rule, ashes and maples turn first, followed by aspens, birches and oaks.
- Conifers such as pines and cedars shed many of their needles in the fall.

Early fall

- The leaves of many of our native trees and shrubs are changing color. The dates on which this reaches its climax depends on the species, latitude, altitude and weather, but in many areas, fall foliage peaks in late September through mid-October. (See Activity 31, page 130.)
- Goldenrods and asters turn fields into a riot of yellow, purple and white in much of North America.

Late fall

- The last of the wildflowers—asters, in many areas—bring the year's wildflower parade to a close.
- Most native deciduous trees have shed their leaves by late October, when the smoky gold of tamarack lights up wetlands. Some non-native trees and shrubs (e.g., Norway maple, weeping willow) remain green and fully leaved into early November.
- On the forest floor, mosses, club mosses, evergreen ferns and evergreen wildflowers stand out against the leaf litter. (See Activity 34, page 132.)

Fungi

General

- A rich variety of mushrooms can usually be found, especially if the weather has been damp. It takes rain and several days of high humidity to make mushrooms appear. Generally speaking, coniferous and mixed woodlands are richer in fungi than deciduous forests. (See Activity 35, page 133.)
- Many edible (E) varieties appear in the fall. However, because of the risk of poisoning, only pick the easily recognizable species. Some common species found across the continent include giant puffballs (*Calvatia gigantea*) E, pear-shaped puffball (*Lycoperdon pyriforme*) E, fly agaric (*Amanita muscaria*) poisonous!, shaggy mane (*Coprinus comatus*) E, and turkey tail (*Trametes versicolor*).
- Two varieties that appear in late fall are waxcaps (Hygrophorus) and oyster mushrooms (Pleurotus). Bracket fungi and jelly fungi are also easy to find in late fall.

Weather

General

- With quickly shortening days and less direct sunlight, temperatures slowly decrease.

- We lose about an hour of daylight over September, about 90 minutes in October and another 60 minutes in November.
- By late fall, the first heavy frost occurs in many areas (depending on elevation and proximity to large bodies of water) and sometimes the first heavy snowfall. (See Activity 36, page 134.)
- With climate change, mild fall weather is lasting later into the season.

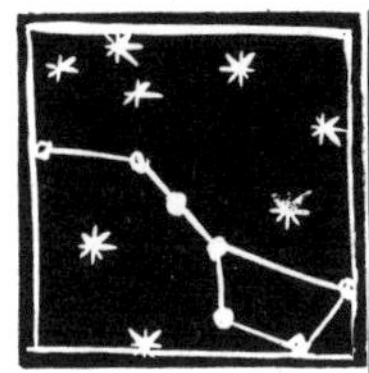

The Sky

General

- At the equinox, the Sun rises due east and sets due west. Day and night are nearly equal in duration. (See Activity 37, page 135 and Activity 38, page 135.)
- The Great Square of Pegasus rules the Fall sky. Using the Great Square as a guide, you can locate the Andromeda constellation and the adjacent Andromeda Galaxy. (See Activity 39, page 136.)
- In the evening, Ursa Major, which includes the Big Dipper, is low in the north, while above you can see Ursa Minor with Polaris, the North Star. The Milky Way is directly overhead.
- The Harvest Moon—the full moon closest to the fall equinox—usually occurs in September. It bathes the evening in moonlight. For several days the Moon rises close to the same time early every evening. (See Activity 40, page 137.)
- Every 29½ days, the Moon goes through the full cycle of eight distinct phases. Knowing the phases and why they occur adds one more dimension to appreciating the rhythms of the natural world. (See Activity 41, page 138 and Activity 42, page 140.)

Fall Nature Highlights by Region

1. Marine West Coast

- Fall is a great time to see large numbers of ducks, geese, swans, loons, grebes and shorebirds (e.g., western sandpipers, dunlins, black-bellied plovers) along the coast and at many inland locations. Hawk and eagle watching can be excellent, too.
- Dabbling ducks (e.g., mallards, northern pintails, American wigeons, green-winged teals) and lesser snow geese arrive in early fall. Late fall sees the arrival of

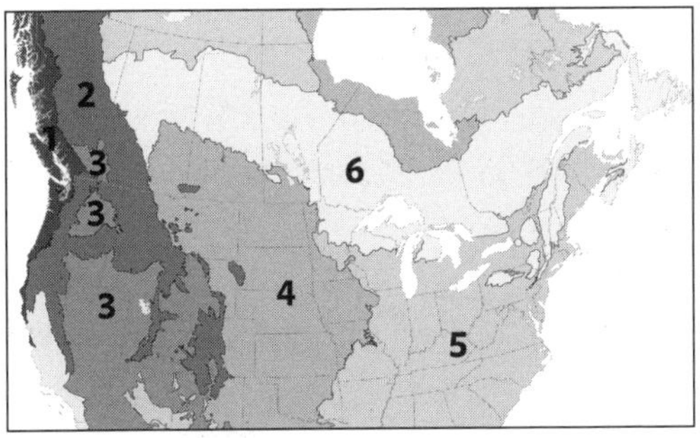

Ecological Zones of North America

diving ducks (e.g., scoters, goldeneye), brant geese and, in some parts of the region, both tundra and trumpeter swans. Many will remain for the winter. Bald eagles prey on waterfowl during the winter.

- Gull-watching is excellent in many areas, including the Olympic Peninsula and southern British Columbia. Large numbers of California, mew, and western gulls and other species arrive after the breeding season and join resident glaucous-winged gulls. Bonaparte's gulls migrate south in October.
- In late fall, varied thrushes migrate down from the mountains into the lowlands. Listen for their whistled notes.
- Salmon are spawning throughout the region. Typical dates are sockeye (Aug–Nov), chinook (Sept–Dec), pink (June–Oct), chum (Nov–Jan) and coho (Nov–Dec). There is, however, a great deal of regional variability, and dominant runs occur only in some years. Salmon die after spawning and provide food for more than 100 species of microbes, stream invertebrates, mammals and birds, including bald eagles.
- In suburban backyards, watch for the abundant webs of the common European garden (or cross) spider.
- Slugs and snails are active and noticeable. Many species mate in the fall, including the Oregon forest snail and the banana slug, which can grow up to 8 in. (20 cm) long!
- Small variegated meadowhawk dragonflies migrate south throughout September and can be abundant along the coast.
- Early fall-blooming wildflowers include asters, Canada goldenrod, pearly everlasting, explorer's gentian, fireweed and Indian paintbrush.
- Fall leaf colors can be impressive. Peak color usually occurs from mid- to late October.
- Fungi love the cool, damp climate of the region. Thousands of species fruit in the fall, with the first "bloom" occurring after the first good rain—usually in early fall. A few fall edible species include golden chanterelle (*Cantharellus formosus*), king bolete (*Boletus edulis*), and spreading hedgehog (*Hydnum repandum*).
- Fall weather is often rainy and cool. The sweet, earthy smell of the Pacific Northwest permeates the air.

Male common goldeneye

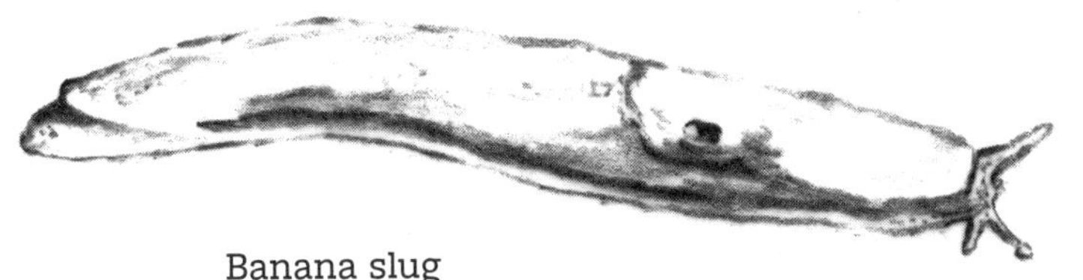
Banana slug

2. Northwestern Forested Mountains

- In October, large numbers of golden eagles move south.
- Early fall is the breeding season for elk. Bulls fill the air with their "bugling" calls at dawn and dusk, and will also clash antlers with challengers.
- In late fall, bighorn sheep are in rut and engage in head-butting contests.
- Color change in aspens—sometimes known as the "Aspen Gold Rush"—starts in late August at high elevations. Aspen forests turn a shimmering gold, a vibrant color that often remains until early October, depending on elevation and latitude.
- The seeds and feathery, rose-colored styles of long-plumed avens are a lovely sight in forest meadows. Arctic gentian blooms well into September in the alpine zone.
- Clear blue skies brighten most days. However, there is occasional snow and frost at night starting in September.

3. North American Deserts

- Waterfowl migration begins in early September with the arrival of northern pintails and white-fronted geese. Large numbers of vocal sandhill cranes arrive and feast in grain fields.
- In some areas, tundra swans begin to arrive in mid-October and stay into January. Duck migration peaks in mid-November. Bald eagles arrive en masse at wintering grounds such as Klamath Basin in Oregon and California.
- In early fall, elk are bugling in many areas.
- Mule deer rut begins in late fall. Bucks compete for groups of females, often engaging in violent battles of clashing antlers and kicking hooves. Mule deer move from higher elevations down to sagebrush-dominated sites for the winter.

Sandhill cranes

- Dense clusters of yellow flowers on rabbitbrush are the iconic harbinger that fall has arrived. The cottonwoods also turn brilliant yellow in the fall.

4. Great Plains

- In early fall, migration brings thousands of waterfowl to the region. They are mostly ducks, Canada and white-fronted geese, and tundra swans. Sandhill cranes also pass through in large numbers.
- This is also the season of the rut for American bison. Dominant bulls engage in a lot of jousting and posturing.
- In early fall, white prairie asters blanket roadsides and fields. Violet and purple species like the sky blue and aromatic asters bloom well into October. In dried-up wetlands, look for bright red carpets of red swampfire.
- A wide variety of grasses flowers in fall, including little bluestem, Indiangrass and sideoats grama.

Indiangrass

- The leaves of the cottonwood turn a bright yellow and stand out from other trees. Chokecherry shrubs add splashes of orange and red to the landscape.
- In late fall, prairie grasses turn to shades of gold as winter snows threaten.

5. Eastern Temperate Forests

- Thousands of raptors—hawks, falcons, vultures and eagles—soar and glide southward, providing an amazing spectacle for hawk watchers along the Great Lakes, the Appalachians and the Atlantic coast. The migration begins in early September with ospreys, sharp-shinned hawks and tens of thousands of broad-winged hawks moving through.
- Depending on the state of the population, large numbers of Mexico-bound monarchs can sometimes be seen along the north shores of Lake Ontario and Lake Erie in early fall. The highest concentrations, however, usually occur at Cape May, New Jersey.
- Chinook salmon, coho salmon and brown trout leave the Great Lakes in early fall to spawn in upland streams.
- In early fall, a sea of yellow, gold, purple, pink and white covers roadsides and fields as a huge variety of goldenrods and asters—more than 50 species of each—come into bloom. The New England aster is the showiest species.
- In woodlands, birds and mammals alike gorge on acorns and beechnuts, the burr-like fruits of the American beech. No fewer than 18 species of oak can be found in the region.

Turkey vulture

⟶ Eastern forests undergo an electrifying transformation as green gives way to reds, oranges, yellows, pinks, purples, browns and everything in between. Nowhere else in the world is the fall color spectacle more dazzling. "Leaf peekers" travel by the thousands to rural landscapes to see the show. Peak color varies by elevation, latitude and species: in the northeast mountains it generally occurs during the first week of October, for example, while in Virginia, the display does not peak until mid- to late October.

6. Northern Forests

⟶ Flocks of dark-eyed juncos migrate southward through the north woods in mid-fall, scavenging along roadsides for seeds. White-throated, white-crowned and American tree sparrows are often mixed in with the juncos. In October, kinglets move south."

⟶ Large, high-altitude flocks of Canada geese that nested along James Bay fly over as they make their way to wintering grounds in the Tennessee Valley. Snow geese, too, move south, often stopping in grain fields in areas such as southeastern Ontario.

⟶ Each fall, migrating raptors coming down from breeding areas as far north as the Arctic concentrate in impressive numbers at the western tip of Lake Superior.

⟶ Brook trout feed heavily and start moving upstream in preparation for spawning. Males acquire a deep orange to red color, to the delight of fish watchers.

⟶ Red maples growing along the edges of lakes and wetlands reach peak color by mid-September or earlier. By late September, sugar maples on the Canadian Shield are usually at or close to peak color. Soon after, the yellows of aspens, birch and tamarack take over.

⟶ Sun-warmed sweetfern leaves and fallen pine needles scent the air, especially on granite outcroppings.

Golden-crowned and ruby-crowned kinglets

Close-up of
purple and yellow
New England
aster blossom

September

The goldenrod is yellow;
The corn is turning brown;
The trees in apple orchards
With fruit are bending down.

The gentian's bluest fringes
Are curling in the sun;
In dusty pods the milkweed
Its hidden silk has spun.

The sedges flaunt their harvest,
In every meadow nook;
And asters by the brook-side
Make asters in the brook,

From dewy lanes at morning
The grapes' sweet odors rise;
At noon the roads all flutter
With yellow butterflies.

By all these lovely tokens
September days are here,
With summer's best of weather,
And autumn's best of cheer.

— Helen Hunt Jackson

Collection Challenge

Fall items for your collection box and/or nature table (see also page 54 in "Connecting with Nature"):

- Monarch caterpillars (for raising) and a poster of the monarch life cycle
- Various tree and wildflower seeds, including milkweed pods, acorns and burdock
- A collection of colorful fall leaves, some of which should be labeled
- A sumac twig (with fruit) or fruit-bearing twig of another tree or shrub. Anchor in modeling clay.
- Seed heads of grasses, sedges and/or rushes
- Different mosses and club mosses
- Smells of fall: ziplock bag with fallen leaves
- Terrarium: woolly bear caterpillar to keep for a day or two
- Laptop: highlight websites with insect calls and monarch videos
- Evolution display: theme of natural selection—Put out an assortment of different plant adaptations (e.g., thorns, downy leaves). (See Fall: Evolution.)

Leaf of red maple

Art in the Park

Ideas for what to sketch and photograph in fall:

- The same tree and/or landscape at regular intervals to show progression of color change. Begin when all is green and continue until all of the leaves have fallen.
- Fall wildflowers (e.g., asters, pearly everlasting, goldenrods)
- Vines such as Virginia creeper growing on a cedar rail fence or dead tree
- Close-ups of different kinds of grasses, sedges, seeds, berries, moss and fungi
- Insects on goldenrod blossoms
- The rising Harvest Moon
- Morning mist over a road, lake, wetland or meadow
- Fallen leaves on the ground or floating on water
- Tree canopy as seen when lying on one's back
- Shapes of branches of leafless trees

What's Wrong with the Scenario?

How many mistakes can you find?

It is a beautiful fall morning. As the Sun climbs higher in the western sky, its rays shine brightly on the red leaves of the birch trees. White apple blossoms, too, sparkle in the sunlight. High overhead, a flock of geese is flying northward, whistling their cheery song as they go. Most of the bird sound, however, is coming from robins as they pour their hearts out in song. In the distance, a black bear is catching fish in a stream, a newborn cub clinging to its back.

Turn to the Appendix, page 342, to see how you did!

The Story of Night Cap, the Chickadee

Night Cap is an energetic black-capped chickadee. Throughout each of the seasons, follow her story to find out what she is doing as the year unfolds. We'll provide some hints on what you can do to learn more about chickadee natural history and behavior.

It is early September. Night Cap's head is constantly moving. Her eyes dart above, behind each shoulder, always scanning, always looking, always wary for any sign of danger. With flashing wings, she flies to a nearby feeder, grabs a black-oil sunflower seed in her beak and flits to a nearby branch. She places the seed between her toes and uses a quick and precise pecking motion to remove the husk. Then she eats the tasty seed within. Night Cap doesn't

Black-capped chickadee and tufted titmouse

Darwin: Watch how chickadees feed one at a time at your feeder. In chickadee flocks, evolution has created a hierarchy — a kind of ranking system — that allows the most dominant bird to feed first. This is usually an older male. Dominant chickadees usually get the best mates, food, nesting sites and even the warmest and safest sleeping sites. Without this system, the birds would spend most of their time fighting! Juncos show a similar pecking order. Scientists don't understand, however, why some common feeder birds like American goldfinches and pine siskins feed in large flocks at feeders together.

have a strong bill and can't crunch her seed open—that's why she carries her seed to a safe perching spot among the branches of a tree. Night Cap returns to the feeder one more time and snatches another seed. This time, she finds a long crack in a nearby tree and places the seed carefully in the folds of the bark. Night Cap may be small, but she has a great memory for where she hides thousands of her seeds. She'll be back when the cold winter winds blow and food is much harder to find.

What you can do:

- Watch how chickadees peck open seeds. Do they fly to a nearby branch and place the seed between their toes as the story suggests?
- Can you spot where the chickadees have hidden their seeds? If you can, remember where and keep an eye out to see if the chickadee remembers, too! They'll be back sometime in the late fall or winter to retrieve their cache of food.

At Your Magic Spot

Finger Frame View: Sometimes we gain a new appreciation for what surrounds us when we take the time to isolate features. Here is a technique used by photographers to create an instant and portable frame. Take each hand and extend your finger and thumb to make an "L." Flip one hand so your palm is facing you, and you are viewing the back of your other hand. Join your fingers and thumbs together (see picture). In your magic spot, look through your homemade finger frame. Do you see any images that are particularly striking? If so, use a real camera and see if you can replicate this view. Variation—you can also use an empty cardboard frame with several clothespins. Hang the empty frame in front of a beautiful view. Share your discovery!

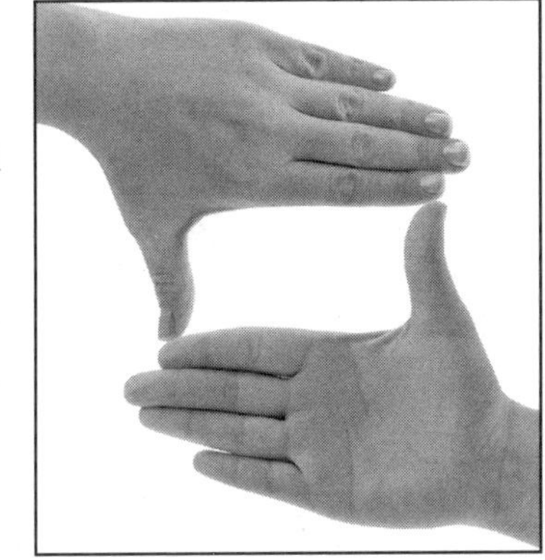

Here are few other suggestions for things to do at your magic spot:

- Don't forget to take your nature journal! Sketch and write about the place.
- Breathe in deeply. How does your spot smell this season? Does the smell change each time you visit?
- Notice the nearby plants. How are they changing as the temperature begins to fall?
- Look down, around your feet. Do you notice any insect activity? If so, what do you think the insects are doing? Where are they going?
- Do you see any chew marks, a munched leaf, bark beetle etchings or any other evidence that something has been eating?
- Do you notice any small holes, cavities or places where a small animal might hide? Do you see any signs of animals passing through, such as tracks, worn-away places or tunnels?
- How does your magic spot make you feel? Jot down your feelings and impressions in your nature journal.

Exploring Fall: Things to Do

Fall looks like...

- The intense reds, yellows, oranges, purples and browns of the leaves
- The gentle mist over water and lowlands in the early morning
- A delicate spider's web covered in droplets of water
- Ice crystals of the first frost and your own breath crystallizing in the cold air
- The monotonous browns and grays of a late fall roadside or woodland

Rainbow Connection

Cut up a variety of paint color samples—especially reds, oranges, yellows, purples and greens—into smaller pieces. Hand out five to ten pieces to each member of the group. Ask them to try to find leaves along the trail that exactly match the color of each paint sample. Once you start looking closely, you will be amazed at the variety of fall colors. What other natural objects (e.g., grasses, rocks, flowers, bark) match your paint cards? After a time, switch colors. To make the game even more challenging, look for different shades of each color.

Fall sounds like...

- The rich insect chorus of an early fall afternoon
- The calls of crows, jays, gulls and geese
- The rustle of fallen leaves and leaves still clinging to branches
- The "whisper songs" (much softer than spring songs) of robins and sparrows
- The near-total hush that falls upon the land in late fall

Activity 2 Silent Walk

At dawn or dusk, take a 5- to 15-minute walk along a park trail in total silence, stepping so you make little or no noise. Dress in clothes that make the least noise possible; avoid synthetic jackets. Stay close together and if you see or hear something of interest, stop and point, tapping a companion's shoulder if necessary. Observe and/or listen without saying a word. Afterwards, share your experiences.

Activity 3 Make an Acorn Whistle

We know that oaks produce acorns. What you may not know is that every five or six years, oaks produce a massive number of acorns—as many as ten times the number they produce in a typical year. This is called a "mast" year. Scientists believe that this abundance of nuts helps to ensure that at least some of the acorns will grow into trees. Is this a mast year?

Visit a local park or forest where oaks are growing. Most oak leaves have rounded or pointy lobes. Hunt for an acorn and remove the cap. Take the cap and place your thumbs over the hollow in a V shape (see color section, figure 7). Blow across your knuckles and over the hollow. You should hear a sharp whistling sound. If you don't, shift your thumbs around and try again. Watch out for incoming dogs!

Autumn leaves

Fall tastes like...

- A fresh, crisp apple, maybe from a farmers' market
- The edible roots of wild onion, cattail and dandelion, all of which become sweeter in the fall
- Late-season berries such as salal, blackberry, currants, huckleberries and Oregon grape
- Late-season greens like watercress, sheep sorrel, violets, mint and fireweed
- Wild mushrooms such as boletes (e.g., *Boletus edulis*), chanterelles (e.g., *Cantharellus cibarius*), shaggy manes (*Coprinus comatus*) and puffballs (e.g., *Calvatia gigantea*)

Activity 4 Dine on Puffballs

The giant puffball is an edible species that grows in fields and open woods. It is easy to identify because of its giant size, smooth white skin with shallow indentations, mostly spherical shape and the absence of a stem. Some puffballs look like big loaves of white bread.

Cut the puffball in half to make sure the inside is uniformly white. If it is yellowish or brown, it will have an off-flavor. Without washing the puffball with water—which it will soak up like a sponge—cut a few firm white specimens into thick slices. Sauté on both sides in butter with some sliced onions. You can also try dipping the slices in a beaten egg and coating them with breadcrumbs before cooking. Like tomatoes, giant puffballs don't all taste the same, so try several different ones. Puffballs can be stored several days in the fridge without any loss of quality.

Giant puffball

Fall smells like...

- The spicy fragrance of fallen leaves
- A leaf fire
- Pickling spices, nutmeg and cinnamon
- Fallen apples on the ground under a tree
- Smoke from a wood stove on a cool morning

Activity 5 Scratch and Sniff

Next time you go for a walk, take along some small pieces of sponge and some water. Dab a moistened sponge under everyone's nose; just a little moisture on the upper lip will suffice. The wetness under your nose helps you to distinguish more odors. Try a little "scratch and sniff." Gently rub the leaves of different trees and shrubs between your fingers. Evergreens work especially well. The act of rubbing releases chemicals that your nose will quickly register as a series of distinctive smells.

Scents of the Season

Mix a few spoonfuls of cloves, cinnamon and nutmeg together and pour onto a square of aluminum foil. Stir in a few drops of water and close the foil, making sure to leave a small opening at the top. Place in the oven at 300°F (150°C). As the mixture warms up, the wonderful harvest aroma will fill the house.

Fall feels like...

- The welcome relief of cooler temperatures
- The coolness of a wet, dew-covered lawn in the early morning
- The dry, spiky texture of hay and straw bales
- The bumpy surface of a gourd or pumpkin
- The sticky seeds of burdock
- The icy bite of frost that you scrape from a car windshield
- The fragility of dry, fallen leaves

Barefoot Walk

Take off your shoes and socks and, wearing a blindfold, have a friend guide you as you walk across a lawn with patches of sun and shade, or through shallow water with a sandy bottom. If there are a number of people, try holding onto a rope. Explore the edge of a marsh, too, where the wet soil squelches underfoot—anywhere that is safe and free of sharp objects. Change roles. What did you feel? Did the temperature change? As an additional challenge, could you retrace the route you took by remembering the various textures under the soles of your feet? (See color section, figure 16.)

Phenology

Fall Phenology: Tracking Seasonal Change

• **You'll learn:** How the local climate changes through the seasons and how plants and animals take their cues from these changes.

• **You'll need:** Blackline master on page 326, access to Internet.

• **Background:** Plants and animals have events in their lives that seem to occur like clockwork every year: leaves changing color, birds migrating south, etc. They take their cues from day length and the

Citizen Science Suggestions

Journey North: Follow Journey North in tracking the migration of wildlife across North America. This is a wonderful citizen science project for children of all ages. Children can share their observations about the migration of birds and mammals, the leaf-out of trees and other phenological data with classrooms from around the continent. Go to **learner.org/jnorth/**.

Nature's Notebook: This is an online phenology observation program of the USA National Phenology Network. Amateur and professional naturalists regularly record observations of plants and animals to generate long-term data sets used for scientific discovery and decision-making. There are many ways classrooms can become involved. Go to **usanpn.org/natures_notebook**.

local climate. The study of how nature times these events is called phenology. Phenological observations are very important as the climate changes (also see page 65).

• **Procedure:** In this season-long activity, you will track day length, shadow length, temperature, precipitation, and plant and animal activity. You will also compare your data to long-term averages. As a class, family or individual, complete the Phenology Chart for each season. At the end of the season, discuss how typical the season was compared to the long-term average. What really stands out?

Oak leaf

Evolution

Look at Leaves like Darwin

• **You'll Need:** Scavenger Hunt Sheets (see Appendix). A variety of leaves (including needles) with marked differences in size, edge shape, texture, thickness and color; scavenger hunt sheets; pencils; clipboards; plastic baggies for collecting leaves.

• **Background:** In fall, our attention is drawn to trees and their colorful leaves. We shouldn't take leaves for granted, though. They are highly advanced structures that respond to their environments in complex ways. This can be a hard concept for humans to grasp, especially since leaves just seem to "be there" doing nothing. Through natural selection, however, leaves have evolved some amazing adaptations.

• **What to do:** Copy the Leaf Scavenger Hunt Sheet (one for each pair of children) found in the Appendix, page 315. Go to an area with a variety of tree leaves. Establish clear boundaries. Hand out sheets. Give 20 minutes or so for participants to collect as many leaves as they can. When they return, ask participants to pile the leaves in front of them. Ask the following questions. As you do so, ask each child to have a leaf in hand that best matches what you are describing.

⟶ Why do trees have leaves? (To make food for the tree so that it can grow. This happens through a process called photosynthesis. "Photo" is the Greek word for "light," and "synthesis" is the Greek word for "putting together." That's exactly what's happening. The plant is harnessing the energy of sunlight to make food in the form of sugar from two ingredients: carbon dioxide and water. At the same time, the leaf produces oxygen, which it releases into the atmosphere. Plants breathe in the carbon dioxide, an invisible gas, through tiny holes in the leaves. They use their roots to suck up water. Some water is released back into the atmosphere through the leaves.)

⟶ Why are leaves green? (Leaves contain an amazing chemical called chlorophyll. It is green and made out of rare and precious "minerals" or "nutrients" like magnesium from the soil. Chlorophyll captures the Sun's energy and, through photosynthesis, uses it to combine carbon dioxide and water to make sugars. These sugars are used to produce cellulose and all the other materials that make up a tree.)

⟶ Why have so many trees evolved to be tall? (So they won't get shaded out by their neighbor and die from lack of sunlight.)

⟶ What are some of the challenges or problems a leaf faces? (Answers include, getting eaten, over-heating and drying out, getting blown off the twig, getting enough sunlight.)

⟶ Ask the children to rub and smell some of the leaves. Why might some leaves

Hobblebush

have evolved a bad taste or be poisonous? (To discourage herbivores like caterpillars, deer.)

⟶ What else might evolve in leaves to make them hard to eat? (Spines, hairs)

⟶ Why do you think pine needles have evolved to be waxy and thick? (To reduce water loss, especially in winter.)

⟶ Show a large simple leaf like a maple and a compound leaf with small leaflets like an ash or a walnut. Explain how to tell the difference between a simple leaf and a compound leaf. Ask: Why have so many different sizes and forms of leaves evolved? (Compound leaves with leaflets don't heat up so much in the sun because air circulates around them; large leaves gather more light and are, therefore, necessary in shady areas and on the lower, more shaded branches of trees, e.g., hosta.)

⟶ Ask the children to pick up a few leaves of very different shapes. Why have leaves evolved so many different shapes? (Complex edges and lobes allow leaves to get rid of absorbed heat very rapidly; smooth edges are more common in shade-loving plants because getting rid of heat is not as much of a problem.)

⟶ Why have so many leaves evolved to end in a point? (So water runs off more easily.)

⟶ Why have trees evolved to shed their leaves in the fall? (They're too thin and delicate to survive winter; snow would accumulate and break branches; water would be lost through the pores by transpiration.)

⟶ If they shed their leaves while they were still green, what would be lost? (The important minerals/nutrients that make up the chlorophyll.)

⟶ So why do leaves change color? (Trees have evolved to remove precious minerals from the leaves and store them in the wood to be used the following year. At the same time, pigments [chemicals] that were hidden by the chlorophyll become visible. These are the yellows and oranges [carotenoids]. The yellow and orange are not adaptations in themselves. The reds and purples, however, are actively produced by the leaves in late summer and are brightest when there is lots of sunshine. These pigments are called anthocyanins. Scientists are not sure what their purpose is, but they may be an adaptation. Ask the students to offer their ideas!)

Activity 10 Small Changes

• **You'll learn:** How evolution works through small changes (mutations in DNA) that accumulate over time.

• **You'll need:** Stack of paper, pencils, water, salt, clear dish soap, isopropyl alcohol, food coloring, two clear glasses.

• **Background:** A mutation is a change in DNA, the chemical that affects how every living thing looks and behaves. Mutations can be beneficial, neutral or harmful for the organism. However, mutations don't "try" to supply the organism with what it needs. They are completely random. Over time, mutations that help organisms to survive are passed on from one generation to the next.

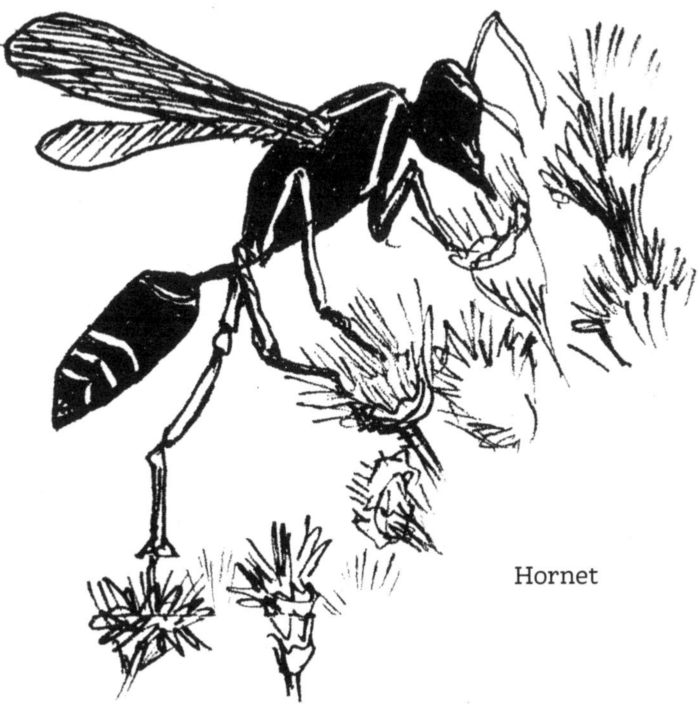

Hornet

Procedure

Telephone: This well-known childhood game can easily be played outside, maybe during a break in a hike. Start by thinking of a sentence related to the theme of evolution, such as "The frog's webbed feet allow it to move faster in the water." Whisper the sentence to the first child, who will then whisper it to the second child and so on. The last child to hear the sentence will then say it aloud to everyone. The sentence will most likely have changed as it was passed from one child to the next. The longer the chain of players, the more changes are likely.

Ask the children why they think these changes happened. Explain that it was the accumulation of small mistakes the students made in reproducing the message. The same is true of the genetic or DNA "message." Small changes called "mutations" get passed down through generations of living things. Over time, they can result in big changes. Eventually, they may even result in new species that can no longer mate with the original (ancestral) species. Emphasize, however, that evolution usually takes a huge amount of time. It usually takes thousands of years for a new species to evolve—sometimes millions! If there were no mistakes in the game, explain to the group that this is normal. In other words, DNA usually *is* copied correctly. If you want to make sure there are some mistakes, start again with a more complicated sentence, such as, "The color and spots of a fawn's coat camouflage it and help it to blend in with the forest floor and hide from predators."

The evolution of a bug: Draw a simple bug on the first page of the stack of paper. Then pass the paper on to another person and have them draw the bug as exactly as they can. They should move the original to the back of the stack. Have them pass their copy onto the next person who will try to reproduce the bug—again, as exactly as they can. Don't forget to hide the previous version behind the stack. Do this at least ten times. Compare the original to the evolved bug. Was there much of a difference? All it takes is a small variation (mutation) in each generation to create extraordinary change over time. Think of how birds evolved from dinosaurs or how whales evolved from land-dwelling mammals.

Extract and see your own DNA

1. Mix a half-quart (500 ml) of drinking water with 1 tbsp (45 g) of salt and stir until salt is dissolved.

2. Transfer 3 tbsp (14 ml) of salt water into a clear glass

3. Swirl the salt water around in your mouth for 1 minute.

4. Spit the water back into the glass. Cheek cells will be suspended in the salt water.

5. Gently stir the salt water with one drop of clear dish soap. Avoid bubbles as much as possible. (Note: Soap breaks down the cell membranes, releasing the DNA.)

6. In a separate glass, mix 7 tbsp (105 g) of isopropyl alcohol and 3 drops of food coloring.

7. Tilt the salt water cup and gently pour the alcohol–food color mixture so that it forms a layer on top (about 1 in./2 cm thick).

The black-and-white warbler is a common fall migrant

8. Wait about 2 ½ minutes. You should see small white clumps and strings forming. That's your DNA—the recipe that makes YOU!

Source: *NOVA Presents: D.I.Y. Science*

Birds

Activity 11 A Non-identification Bird Walk

• **You'll learn:** Birds, with all their interesting behaviors, are all around us.

• **You'll need:** A checklist (see Appendix page 323), a clipboard, a pencil, binoculars (optional).

• **Background:** A lot of the time, birds can be hard to see well. Learning to identify them takes time and effort, too. Unfortunately, some kids start out with lots of enthusiasm for our feathered friends but end up losing interest, especially if too much emphasis is put on identification. But fear not—it's possible to enjoy watching birds without worrying too much about identifying them. Instead, it can be fun to focus on movement, location, etc. This approach provides a good starting point for learning the art of birding.

• **Procedure:** Use the checklist to see how many items you can find. Establish a challenge based on one or more of the items, such as, How many birds can we find on this walk? How many easy-to-identify species can we find? Can we beat our record?

DARWIN: Did you know that all of the birds we see today have evolved from dinosaurs? In fact, if you had a baseball card with a picture of a bird, and then somehow got pictures of the bird's father, grandfather, great-grandfather, etc., it would take about a million cards until you were looking at a picture of the bird's dinosaur-like ancestor. The line of cards, stacked side by side, would be about a bit more than half a mile (one kilometer) long! Scientists still aren't sure how the earliest feathered dinosaurs used these feathers, but it wasn't for flight.

Activity 12 Goose Leadership

- **You'll learn:** The lessons geese can teach us about working together as a team.
- **You'll need:** Goose honker (from a hardware or hunting store), large open field.
- **Background:** Because they are primarily waterbirds, geese need to search out areas that are free of ice and where food is readily available. That's why they journey south in the fall. We are all familiar with the breathtaking sight of a flock of geese winging overhead in their characteristic V formation. What you may not know is that this "team formation" is a highly efficient way of flying, creating up to 70 percent less drag than if a single goose were to fly on its own. This is only one example of how geese work together.

(Adapted from *Lessons From The Geese* by Dr. Robert McNeish.)

More lessons from the goose

Each goose positions itself behind and a bit to the side of the goose ahead of it in the flock, so it can pick up the updraft from the swirl of air made by the beating of each wing. It also times the rhythm of its wing beats to take maximum advantage of this upwelling of air. The head goose expends the most energy as it battles against the wind to lead the way. Geese tend to share the head position; after a time, the head goose will tire and peel off, to allow another goose to lead the way.

Goose lesson 1: By working together towards a common purpose we can harness our collective energy and accomplish much more than any of us could on our own.

Goose lesson 2: It helps when we all share the task of leadership. We all have our own unique attributes and skills, and it is up to us to take on some kind of leadership role. The only question we need to ask, "How can I help?"

It is amazing how much noise a flock of geese makes. The males call out in a lower-pitched, two-noted "honk"—females make a higher-pitched honk. They all honk to encourage the geese ahead of them to keep up their speed. Scientists have determined that geese make many other vocalizations as well. Geese are constantly supporting one another by their calls.

Goose lesson 3: We all work more effectively when we support one another. A hearty "good for you" or "well done" gives each of us a bit more confidence and energy to work even harder. Don't forget about the value of encouragement.

Geese are vigilant. They are always wary, watching out for one another, especially their young. A parent will attack anything that poses a threat, even if is much larger than it is.

Goose lesson 4: We need to be mindful and aware of each other's needs. Empathy and understanding begin when we take the time to look out for one another, especially during challenging times.

• **Procedure:** Review the goose lessons provided above. Form a V in the field. Have children flap their wings and jog forward in a V formation. Make sure each child is positioned correctly back and to the side of the goose ahead. Remind the children to honk frequently to encourage one another. Stay in a V and make sure to flap at different times. Have the head goose peel off to be replaced by a new head goose every 15 seconds or so. Can you stay in formation and not suffer from V collapse?

Migrating geese

It's harder than it looks! Fly from one end of the field to another, maintaining your formation. Will you be able to keep in formation even as you round a bend? Try it and see!

Activity 13 Pishing: A Birder's Secret Weapon

• **You'll learn:** How to bring birds in close for good views and identification.

• **Background:** Fall songbird migration tends to be a quiet and somewhat secretive affair. To find birds, you'll need to watch and listen carefully. Although migrants such as warblers and vireos do not sing in the fall, they do make subtle contact calls and tend to be in mixed-species feeding flocks that often contain very vocal chickadees or titmice. Feeding in a mixed flock may provide safety from predators, since there are more eyes watching for danger. It may also make feeding more efficient, because an insect that flees from one bird may be caught by another.

• **Procedure:** A rule of thumb of fall birding is to stop, take a close look and "pish" any time you hear chickadees or titmice calling. Why? Because there are usually migrants with them. See page 46 for instructions on how to pish. This activity works best when only one or two people pish, so take turns. Not only will you attract titmice and chickadees, but migrating warblers and vireos will often approach to within 10 ft. (3 m) of you. Although some of the warblers are sporting their dull fall plumage, others look surprisingly like they did in the spring and are, therefore, easier to identify. Look for distinctive markings such as eye rings,

The blue jay's call is a common fall sound

Citizen Science Suggestions

Make a habit of submitting your bird sightings to eBird, an online checklist program that keeps track of data from thousands of birders worldwide. eBird is amassing one of the largest and fastest-growing sets of data in the world by documenting the presence or absence of species, as well as bird abundance through checklist data. Visit **ebird.org**.

Darwin: Many bird species in North America and northern Europe and Asia respond to pishing because the noise resembles the scold calls of chickadees and titmice. Given how aware chickadees are of predators, it is no wonder that other species of birds—and mammals such as squirrels and chipmunks—have evolved to pay attention to these scold calls and come in to check out the potential threat. This response has helped all these species avoid predators and is, therefore, an important adaptation shaped by evolution. A mystery to solve: some birds don't respond to pishing at all. We don't know exactly why.

Black-capped chickadee

splashes of color and stripes. After you've had a good look at the birds, refer to your field guide or app to see how many you can identify. Don't worry if you can't identify them all.

• **Suggestion:** Have a friend make a video of you pishing and the birds approaching.

Activity 14 Feeder Time is Here!

• **You'll learn:** How to attract fall migrants and resident birds to your yard.

• **You'll need:** One or more kinds of bird feeders, such as a hopper feeder, tube feeder, peanut cage or suet cage; food such as black-oil sunflower seed, millet, Nyjer seed, shelled peanuts, suet cakes; birdbath (optional).

• **Procedure:** If you want a close-up look at some of the migrants passing through in fall, September is the time to set up feeders. If possible, locate your feeders within 6–10 ft. (2–3 m) of a window. This will afford you a good view of feeder activity, and the birds won't be able to build up enough flight speed to injure themselves should they fly into the window. It is also best if the feeder is near a tree or shrub where the birds can land and find some cover.

We suggest purchasing a hopper feeder and putting it on a metal pole with a squirrel guard. The seed of choice is black-oil sunflower seed. If you have little or no backyard, try a suction-cup window feeder. A tube feeder can also be used for providing sunflower seeds; some designs are also squirrel-proof. One popular type of tube feeder, sometimes referred to as a thistle feeder, can be filled with Nyjer seed. It will attract small finches such as American goldfinches, pine siskins and common redpolls. Peanut feeders are marvelous for attracting woodpeckers and nuthatches. Suet cakes, too, can sometimes be popular with these same species. Seeds such as millet scattered on the ground will attract species like juncos, sparrows and towhees that rarely land on elevated feeders. Many of the sparrows

Common Feeder Birds by Region

All regions: black-capped/Carolina chickadee, red-breasted nuthatch, mourning dove, downy woodpecker, hairy woodpecker, northern flicker, American goldfinch, house finch, European starling, American robin, house sparrow, song sparrow, dark-eyed junco, red-winged blackbird, pine siskin, common redpoll

Marine West Coast: spotted towhee, Steller's jay, chestnut-backed chickadee, Anna's hummingbird, varied thrush, bushtit, fox sparrow, golden-crowned sparrow

Northwestern Forested Mountains: pine grosbeak, evening grosbeak, mountain chickadee, black-billed magpie

Great Plains: red-bellied woodpecker, northern cardinal, tufted titmouse, purple finch, common grackle

North American Deserts: Eurasian collared-dove, western scrub jay, black-billed magpie, white-crowned sparrow, mountain chickadee

Eastern Temperate Forests: northern cardinal, tufted titmouse, red-bellied woodpecker, Carolina wren, white-throated sparrow, white-crowned sparrow, common grackle

Northern Forests: gray jay, white-throated sparrow, white-crowned sparrow, purple finch, evening grosbeak, pine grosbeak

Note: Some species are restricted to one part of the region (e.g., house finch, gray jay) or may not occur every year (e.g., pine siskin, common redpoll). Others may only occur during migration in certain regions (e.g., white-crowned sparrow, red-winged blackbird).

Citizen Science Suggestions

Join Project FeederWatch: At regular intervals from November to April, thousands of FeederWatchers count the kinds and numbers of birds at their feeders. They then submit their observations online. Participants receive a full-color bird poster and calendar, a handbook with instructions, and the chance to contribute to a continent-wide bird research project. Go to **feederwatch.org/** for more information.

you see in the fall will be juveniles making their first migration south. Use your field guide or app to learn the differences between adult and juvenile birds.

To attract migrating warblers and other insect-eating migrants, try setting up a water drip over your birdbath. The sound of dripping water can attract birds like a magnet!

For more information, visit the "Feeding Birds" pages on the "All About Birds" website of the Cornell Lab of Ornithology at allaboutbirds.org.

Mammals

Activity 15 Dig It Up: Squirrel-watching

• **You'll learn:** How squirrels cache food items

• **Background:** Squirrels are easy to take for granted. Sometimes they seem to be everywhere. However, because we rarely take the time to observe them closely, we miss out on a number of interesting behaviors. For example, gray squirrels are scatter hoarders, animals with a distinct way of storing food for later consumption: they dig a shallow hole or "cache," deposit a single food item, then cover it with soil.

• **Procedure:** Watch for gray squirrels transporting and/or storing (caching) food such as walnuts, acorns and sunflower seeds. See if you can spot the exact location where the food is buried. Try digging up the item to see how good the squirrel was at hiding it!

Activity 16 "Oh Nuts"—A Squirrel Game

• **You'll learn:** Strategies that different squirrel species use for hiding food.

• **You'll need:** Package of dried macaroni and enough ziplock baggies for each participating squirrel. Fill each baggie with 20 macaroni noodles. Have one baggie for each squirrel (both red and gray). *Optional*—arm bands (blue for jays, red for red squirrels, gray or black for gray squirrels and yellow for red fox); see ratios below for your group (6 to 26).

• **Background:** Gray squirrels prefer to hide nuts and seeds individually, while

Squirrel Game

Character	What they'll do	# (small group)	# (large group)*
Red squirrels	Hide their food in "piles." They'll need to find their food during winter. When encountering danger, squirrels touch a tree, indicating that they have climbed to safety.	2	10
Gray squirrels	Hide their food "one by one." Like red squirrels, they'll need to find their food during winter. When encountering danger, they too touch a tree.	2	10
Jays	Can steal food. Jays are free to watch squirrels hide their food.	1	4
Red fox	Eat squirrels and jays. Foxes simply tag an animal to indicate that they have eaten it. Tagged squirrels and jays must return to the start area.	1	2
Total Number of Characters		6	26

* You can adapt these numbers to suit any size group

red squirrels hide their food in large piles. Which strategy is more effective? Red squirrels need to work hard to protect their hiding spots, since they've stored more food in fewer scattered caches. They are renowned for their feisty behavior and can often be seen chasing away gray squirrels. On the other hand, gray squirrels might spend more time looking for food, but whether they find their own seeds (most of the seeds they find are their own) or another squirrel's doesn't matter so much, as long as they can find enough food. So gray squirrels tend to be quieter and less conspicuous than their raucous red cousins. Tell the children that both species have a remarkable sense of smell to help them locate nuts and cones, even under a cover of snow.

• **Procedure:** This game works best in an open area with scattered trees where children can run without encountering hazards such as low branches. Make sure to designate clear boundaries.

• **Instructions:** Give the children roles from the table above. Select children to be gray squirrels, red squirrels, jays and foxes in the number or ratios indicated above.

Red squirrel

Citizen Science Suggestions

Take part in "Project Squirrel," a program that aims to help scientists better understand urban squirrel biology. Your task is to count squirrels in your neighborhood and report the findings online. Visit **projectsquirrel.org.**

• **Round one:** Tell the squirrels it is now fall. There is plenty of food for both species. Red squirrels prefer cones (e.g., spruce, pine), while gray squirrels prefer acorns, walnuts and various seeds. Give each squirrel one baggie filled with 20 macaroni noodles. Each noodle represents the type of food they eat. Explain that just as in real life, gray squirrels must hide each "nut" individually and the red squirrels must hide their "cones" in piles (minimum of three per pile, up to all 20 noodles). Have each child select hiding spots for their food (e.g., under leaves, in tree cavities). Foxes and jays are free to watch. They'll be joining in shortly.

• **Round two:** Call all squirrels back. Explain that some months have passed and now it is early winter. The temperature has dropped, the forest is covered under a fresh blanket of snow and, of course, both red and gray squirrels are hungry. They need food! Squirrels are now free to search for the nuts/cones they have hidden. If they find another squirrel's nuts, they can keep them. Meanwhile the jays are hungry, too. They are free to attempt to steal the nuts and cones that the squirrels have hidden (as jays will do).

The red fox, too, is hungry and would like nothing better than a taste of fresh squirrel and, as an appetizer, a jay or two. The foxes must tag a squirrel or a jay to show that they have eaten it. Remind the foxes that this is just a game and that pushing or tackling is not permitted. Tagged squirrels and jays must return to a designated home base. To indicate that squirrels can and do climb trees, any squirrel touching a tree is safe from

"**Darwin:** Fossils records show that tree squirrels like the red and the gray go back about 36 million years in North America. However, paleontologists have found fossils of squirrel-like mammals that are 208 million years old! Even in two closely related species like red and gray squirrels, evolution has resulted in two very different ways of solving the problem of getting enough food to eat."

the fox's jaws. Any jay that has flapped at least five times before the fox tags them is considered to be "flying" and is safe. If time permits, play one more round. Explain that winter is almost over and squirrels are relying on their food cache to make it until spring. Squirrels must find at least ten nuts/cones to have survived the winter.

• **Discussion:** After the game, discuss the advantages and disadvantages of hiding the nuts as a gray squirrel versus a red squirrel. Which squirrel do you think is the more aggressive and why?

Activity 17 Red Light—Green Light

• **You'll learn:** How to stalk like a fox and be attentive like a rabbit.

• **You'll need:** Two pylons or shoes for marking a starting line, a clump of keys.

• **Background:** In this game, you will learn to move with the elegance and grace of a fox as she tries to catch a very alert rabbit. Watching a red fox hunt is like watching a ballet dancer dance. A fox's front feet are slightly larger than her back feet. These she places one in front of the other, as if she were walking along a line. Her movements are fluid and graceful. Her nose is always taking short, sharp sniffs. Her ears are pointed forward like satellite dishes. If her prey looks at her, she hunkers down into the long grass and her red and gray coat helps her to melt into the landscape. She freezes until she feels it is time to stalk forward once more. When she gets close to her prey, she launches herself in the air, front feet extended and jaws open. A fox can sky pounce more than six feet (two meters) high!

• **Procedure:** Select one child to be an attentive rabbit. Practice rabbit movements such as quick head checks forward, sideways and backward; ears constantly sweeping from side to side to hear the sounds of predators; and nose twitching to catch any dangerous scents. Remember, however, that rabbits must eat, so have the rabbit bend down and simulate browsing occasionally. The rest of the group are foxes. Practice stalking like foxes (as described above).

Red fox

• How the game works: This is a version of red light/green light. Foxes line up shoulder to shoulder (with room to spare) between two pylons. The rabbit is located about 20 big steps away, facing the line of foxes. Place a set of keys in front of the rabbit. This represents her life. If any fox pounces on the keys (not the rabbit), they will have successfully captured the prey. The rabbit stays put, pretending to browse for food (e.g., clover, grass, seeds). At a given signal the foxes begin to stalk. If the rabbit's head is down, grazing for food, the foxes can move forward. However, any time the rabbit's head swings up, all foxes must hunker down and freeze. If a rabbit spots anyone moving, she points her finger at the offending fox. That fox needs to go back to the beginning between the two pylons. In real life, the rabbit would have spotted the fox with enough time to make an escape. Foxes continue stalking until one careful hunter pounces on the rabbit's keys (not the rabbit). Switch roles.

Spotted salamander

Amphibians and Reptiles

Activity 18 Hunt for Salamanders

• You'll learn: Some of the salamander species that live in your region.

• You'll need: Hands free of bug spray or sun block (might harm the animals), camera (optional).

• Background: Hunting for salamanders is great fun. You never know what you might find when you turn over the next board or rock. In order to breathe, a salamander's skin has to be moist. Therefore, salamanders live in moist, humid habitats. They often hide under objects on the forest floor to shelter from direct sunlight. One species to watch for is the red-backed salamander. Its life cycle is completed free of standing water, with no free-swimming gilled larval stage. Fully formed, one-inch (2.5 centimeter) salamanders emerge from the eggs, which hatch in the fall.

• Procedure: Salamanders are most commonly found in low-lying wooded areas or around country homes and cottages. Look under fallen logs, old boards, flat rocks and even in old piles of firewood. Carefully lift up the rock or piece of wood and peek underneath. If you find a salamander, gently place it in a container. Observe the counter shading (darker on top and lighter underneath). Notice, too, how streamlined it is—slim and flat—for fitting under things and into nooks and crannies. Red-backed salamanders can resemble earthworms, so be sure to look carefully. After you've examined the salamanders and maybe taken a picture or two, carefully put the rock, board or log back just the way you found it. Be careful not to crush the salamander.

• **Try this:** If you live near a wooded area, scatter some old boards and logs along a trail. In time, these will become "basement windows" that you can lift to discover the underworld of centipedes, sowbugs, ants, slugs and even salamanders!

Frog Hypnosis

• **You'll learn:** How to quiet a frog in the hand.

• **You'll need:** Hands free of bug spray or sun block, net (optional).

• **Background:** Frogs are normally very active. Leopard frogs, for example, have powerful hind legs that can launch them into the air to catch prey. To catch a frog on land, sweep a net over it or catch it with your hands. To catch one in the water, sweep your net upward from underneath and to the side.

• **Procedure:** This activity works best if a leader demonstrates first. Once the frog has settled down, sandwich it gently between your hands and carefully turn it on its back. Hold it in this position for at least a minute. You can also make a space between your fingers near the belly. Have someone gently rub the frog's stomach. It is said that if you do this for a minute or so your frog will become hypnotized. We've tried it and it works! Just be sure to handle the frogs gently. (See color section, figure 12.) To see videos on this activity, search "how to hypnotize a frog YouTube."

Fishes

Salmon-watching

• **You'll learn:** Some cool salmon behaviors and some of the many animals attracted by salmon.

• **You'll need:** Polarized sunglasses, broad-brimmed hat, camera.

Citizen Science Suggestions

Take part in a Herp Atlas: The purpose is to collect observational data about your state or province's native amphibians and reptiles (collectively known as herpetofauna or "herps") in order to document their distribution and changes in their populations. Participants enter data on their herp observations online. Two such projects are the Michigan Herp Atlas Project (**miherpatlas.org**) and the Ontario Reptile and Amphibian Atlas Program (**ontarionature.org/protect/species/herpetofaunal_atlas.php**).

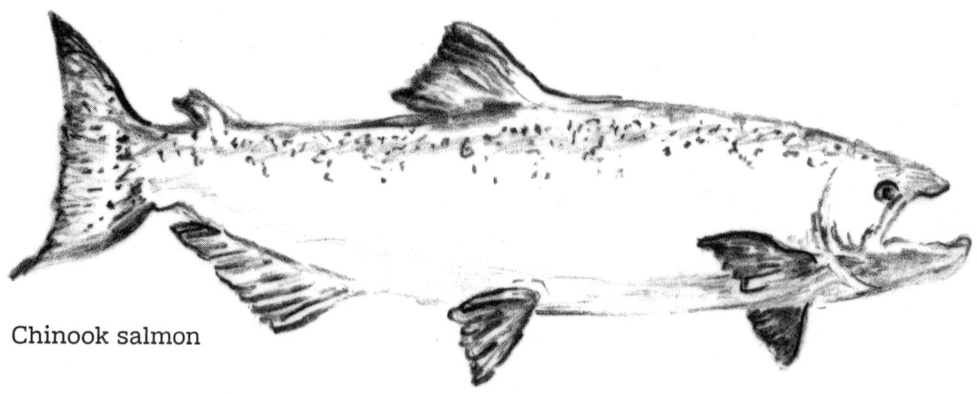

Chinook salmon

- **Background:** Salmon-watching can be an engrossing pastime, especially in the Pacific Northwest, where no fewer than five species of salmon spawn. There are also opportunities for salmon-watching at many locations on the Great Lakes. For a great classroom resource on salmon, visit salmonidsintheclassroom.ca.
- **Procedure:** Whenever you go fish watching, be sure to wear polarized sunglasses—even on cloudy days—as they cut the glare on the water's surface. Wearing a broad-brimmed hat with the sunglasses will further improve viewing. There can be great opportunities for photography, especially if you can face the fish and see their eyes. Make sure the Sun is behind you and use a polarizing filter to reduce glare on the water. Here are some guidelines.
  - Salmon-watching is best in clear streams with gravel bottoms.
  - Look for an area up above the stream, such as on top of a cutback.
  - If you visit an estuary or walk along

Darwin: When migrating, sockeye salmon typically swim up to 4,000 mi. (6,500 km) into the ocean. Years later, they navigate back to the upstream reaches of the rivers in which they were born to spawn. People have long wondered how salmon find their way to their home rivers over such huge distances. A 2013 study suggests that salmon steer themselves home by using the Earth's magnetic field. To do this, however, they have to have imprinted (i.e., learned and remembered) the magnetic field where they entered the sea as young fish. They have evolved to remember the "feeling" of home!

Citizen Science Suggestions

Think salmon: In this project in British Columbia, participate in local volunteer efforts within your own community, maybe by improving salmon habitat or by being part of a stewardship group that monitors fish, habitat and water quality. Visit **thinksalmon.com.**

Become a riverkeeper: Columbia Riverkeeper's mission is to protect and restore the water quality of the Columbia River and all life connected to it, from the headwaters to the Pacific Ocean. The strategy includes working in river communities and protecting the people, fishes and wildlife that depend on the Columbia River. Visit **columbiariverkeeper.org.**

a river in late summer or early fall, you may see salmon leaping into the air. Scientists believe the fish are trying to get used to the "taste" of their home streams' freshwater.

- Watch as the fish struggle against currents, rapids and falls. How high do they jump?
- Don't just look for adults. Watch for juvenile salmon in the backwaters and eddies; they can be identified by the dark bars or "parr marks" along their sides.
- In spawning sites, watch for white flashes underwater as the female salmon turns on her side to dig the redd (nest).
- Look for the redds themselves: areas of recently exposed, clean white gravel.
- Take a close look at any rotting salmon carcasses. Aquatic organisms on which young salmon feed depend on these for food.
- The fish aren't the only show. Watch for loons, ducks, terns, gulls and kingfishers, all of which feed on salmon fry (babies). You might also see gulls, ravens and bald eagles feeding on the carcasses, or even eagles catching live salmon. The presence of a river otter may signal that fish are near.
- Watch for predator trails along rivers and streams. Bears and wolves are the largest predators. Look for discarded morsels of salmon carcasses and examine bear droppings for salmon bones. If you find predator trails, be sure to announce your presence!

Invertebrates

Raise Monarchs

- **You'll learn:** The amazing metamorphosis of a monarch butterfly from egg or larva to adult. (See color section, figure 13.)
- **You'll need:** Monarch larvae (can be purchased from online suppliers), milkweed

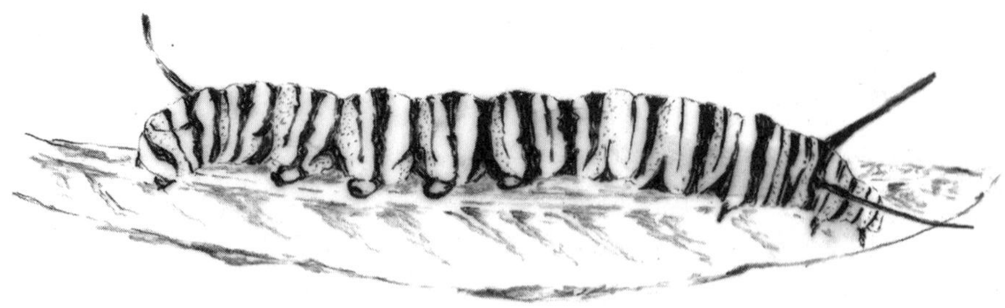

Monarch caterpillar

leaves, container. Larvae also can be purchased from online suppliers.

• **Background:** Raising monarchs is a wonderful activity for people of any age. If you are a teacher, raising monarchs in the classroom is a great way to start the school year. You and your students will witness a miracle of nature as an ungainly, worm-like creature transforms into an elegantly patterned, orange and black butterfly. Monarchs go through complete metamorphosis. After hatching from the egg, the larvae (caterpillars) pass through different stages known as *instars*. They then enter an inactive or resting stage known as a *pupa* (with butterflies, the pupa is called a *chrysalis*, the term *cocoon* refers to a case that moths and some other insects spin around the pupa). The pupa does not feed but gets its nutrition from what it ate as a larva. During pupation, adult body structures replace the larval structures. About two weeks later, the adult butterfly emerges from the pupa.

• **Procedure:** Starting in late August or early September, look for the yellow-, black- and-white-striped monarch caterpillars on milkweed plants along roadsides and in fields. Spots near wetlands and bodies of water are most productive.

Citizen Science Suggestions

Journey North: In a unique partnership, you can join students and scientists across North America to track the monarch butterfly's fall and spring migrations to and from Mexico. An app is available for this project. You can also find all kinds of information on monarchs and their migration on the Journey North website, including an interactive map showing recent sightings. Visit **learner.org/jnorth/monarch/**.

Monarch Waystation Program: Create "Monarch Waystations" (monarch habitats) in home gardens, at schools, businesses, parks, zoos, nature centers and along roadsides and on other unused plots of land. Go to **monarchwatch.org/waystations/**.

Darwin: For centuries, metamorphosis was misunderstood and even described as magic. Scientists now use the theory of evolution to explain how certain insects came to have larval and pupal stages. They believe that the larval stage is actually a worm-like, walking form of the embryo. Rather than continue to develop in the egg, natural selection "decided" that it was better to get the animal out as soon as possible and continue to develop on the move. There is an advantage to this, because it eliminates competition between the young and old, since larval insects eat very different things than adults and can, therefore, live with them in the same time and place and have a larger population. Compare this to birds where young and old live in the same places and eat the same things. When a lot of egg predators are present, many species have evolved to spend less time as an egg and more as a larva. Isn't evolution by natural selection clever? Remember, though, it was never done on purpose.

Look especially for plants with leaves that show signs of having being eaten. You will often find *frass* (larvae droppings) on these plants, too. Caterpillars are easiest to find along monarch migration routes such as the shores of the lower Great Lakes.

Put the larvae in a large jar or terrarium with a secure lid or screen on top. Make sure there is enough room for the adult to emerge and hang down unobstructed from the chrysalis. A branch will give the caterpillar a support to hang from. Feed the larvae fresh milkweed leaves every day or two. Be sure to empty the container of frass (droppings) and be careful not to handle the larvae more than absolutely necessary. When the larvae are ready to pupate, they will crawl to the top of their cage and attach themselves with a silken thread to the cage lid or some other object, such as a branch. They then form a prepupal "J" before shedding their skin for the last time. This process is fun to watch but happens quickly. The adult will emerge from the lime-green chrysalis in 10 to 14 days. When it is ready to come out, the wings will be visible through the pupa covering. Monarchs usually emerge in the morning, often between 8 and 10 AM. They can be released in the late afternoon or the following morning. A more detailed guide to raising monarchs can be found at monarchwatch.org.

Activity 22 Monarch Migration Game

• **You'll learn:** The many challenges that monarchs face migrating and on their wintering grounds.

• **You'll need:** Six pylons, 12 hula hoops (or old bicycle tires), a large playing field or gymnasium, large group.

• **Background:** In the summer, monarchs are busy seeking out milkweed plants. They lay their eggs on the underside of the leaves. After the eggs hatch, the emerging caterpillars begin consuming milkweed at an enormous rate. Milkweed sap, however, contains cardenolides (chemicals) that taste bitter to many insects and birds. Since the monarch absorbed so much milkweed sap as a caterpillar, it is poisonous to predators as an adult—in fact, the bold orange and black markings are a warning that says, "I don't taste good—don't eat me!"

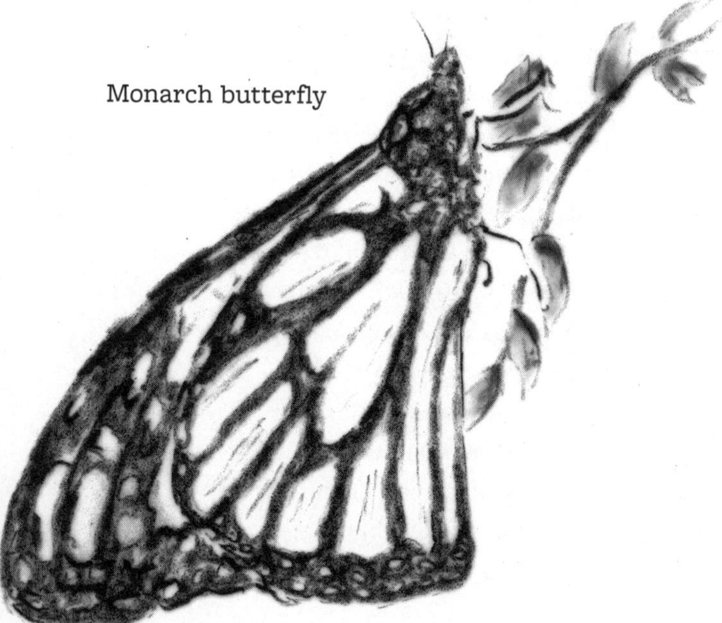
Monarch butterfly

As the days become shorter, the monarch knows instinctively that it is time to migrate south. Although being poisonous helps monarchs avoid predators, the insects still face many other challenges during migration, including storms, cars, cats, drought and deforestation on the wintering sites. During the return flight, they may struggle to find milkweed plants on which to lay eggs in many areas, due to habitat loss caused by development and modern farming techniques. For instance, the planting of Roundup-ready, genetically modified crops means that milkweed can no longer survive in corn and soya fields—something it could do in the past. These fields cover huge areas of the central United States.

• **Procedure:** Outline a large playing area with pylons, about 150 by 100 ft. (50 by 30 m). Use pylons to designate one end as the monarch's summer breeding habitat and the other end as overwintering habitat, either in Mexico or California. Scatter a dozen hula hoops between the pylons at both ends of the playing area and throughout the area in between.

Playing the game

• **Round one:** In this round you'll focus on natural hazards monarchs encounter while migrating. Have each child place one foot in a hoop in the summer breeding habitat. Two students can have one foot in each hoop. The hoops represent suitable habitat with nectar plants, cover and even puddles where the monarchs can absorb the salt and minerals they need through their long, hollow proboscises.

Yell "Go!" Monarchs begin their migration by fluttering south towards their overwintering grounds. During migration, periodically yell out "Rest!" Monarchs have three seconds to find a suitable habitat (hula hoop) to rest in. Explain that monarchs need to find resting habitats with a rich source of nectar to fuel their migration. Any monarchs that cannot find a resting spot are considered "dead" and move off to the side. Don't worry—they'll be able to rejoin the game in the next round. Alternate between the commands "Go" and "Rest" as the monarchs migrate south.

Once monarchs reach Mexico or California, they'll need to roost (rest for an extended period of time) for the winter. Here the hoops represent roosting trees. Any student who is unable to find a hoop is dead.

Explain that the trees (oyamel firs in Mexico and mostly eucalyptus trees in California) provide critical habitat, protecting monarchs from storms and sudden temperature fluctuations.

Tell the children that it is now late winter and the monarchs will be migrating north. This generation only goes a short distance before laying eggs and dying. Explain that it takes as many as three generations to return to the breeding grounds up north; in other words, the monarchs that leave the south are not the same ones that arrive on the northern breeding grounds. As before, periodically yell out "Rest!"

• **Round two:** Explain that returning monarchs lay their eggs in the spring and summer. However, only monarchs born in late summer migrate south; those born earlier die after a few weeks. All the students who perished in the last round rejoin the game. Explain that in this round, there will be a few additional limiting factors caused by humans. Begin by removing resting areas (hoops). For each area you remove, offer an explanation: for example, a new apartment complex and parking lot has taken over a field where monarchs used feed and rest or the monarchs couldn't find any milkweed plants. Leave a few areas for next round. Continue the game as before by alternating between "Go" and "Rest." After this round, how many monarchs are left?

• **Last round:** All monarchs rejoin the game. In this round, replace many of the hoops, explaining that schools, families, nature clubs and city parks have worked hard to naturalize strategic pockets of monarch habitat along the migration route. They have planted different kinds of milkweed as well as nectar plants like asters. Explain that the overwintering area in Mexico or California is now protected and patrolled.

(This is an adaptation of a game called "Migration Headache" found in *Project Wild Activity Guide.*)

Activity 23 Close-up Insect-watching

• **You'll learn:** The huge variety of insects on goldenrod, aster and other wildflowers in late summer and fall.

• **You'll need:** A viewing jar and lid, hand lens, field guide or app, camera.

• **Background:** Wildflowers such as goldenrod produce copious amounts of nectar and pollen, which attract a great number of different invertebrates. Contrary to popular belief, goldenrod does not cause allergies; ragweed pollen is the allergen to be concerned about. Unlike ragweed, goldenrod pollen is not spread through the air, because it is far too heavy. Instead, it is moved about by insects. Don't worry too much about getting stung, either. You can get very close to even a wasp or bee with your camera with almost no danger.

• **Procedure:** In a meadow or along a roadside, count how many different kinds of insects and other invertebrates you can find by visiting patches of goldenrod, aster, milkweed and other plants. Look inside the flowers and along the stems and leaves for crab spiders, grasshoppers, long-horned beetles, soldier beetles, ambush bugs, monarch and sulphur butterflies, mantids, honeybees, bumblebees, wasps, dragonflies and syrphid flies. Syrphid flies, also known as hover or flower flies, mimic bees or wasps in appearance but have only one pair of functional wings (bees and wasps have two pairs). Some syrphid flies are extremely small.

Don't worry if you can't identify all of the insects you find; just focus on the diversity. Pay special attention to the bees. You should be able to see the large, yellow pollen baskets on their hind legs. Watch, too, for insects that haven't moved for a long time, because they may still be in the clutches of a well-camouflaged predator like an ambush bug or a crab spider. Don't forget your camera, because you should be

Citizen Science Suggestions

Bee Hunt: Bee Hunt participants use digital photography to record and study the interactions between plants and pollinators. The data collected will help provide a better understanding of pollinators' importance in growing food and maintaining healthy natural ecosystems. Visit **discoverlife.org/bee/**.

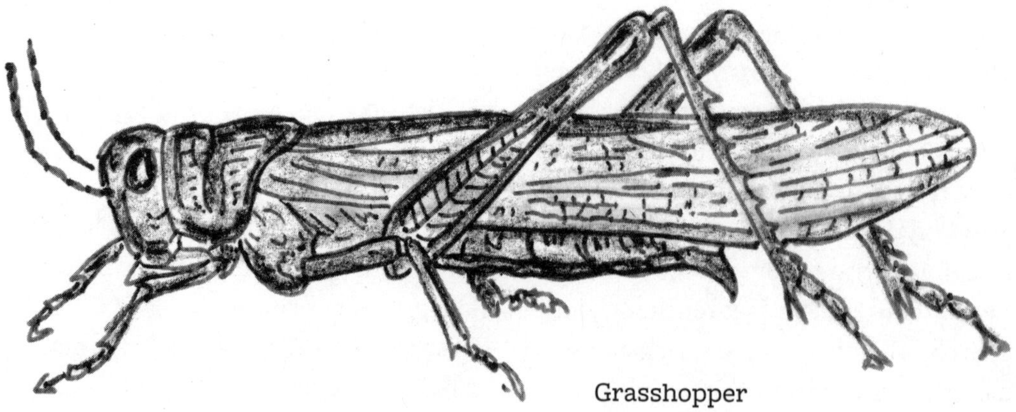
Grasshopper

Darwin: A lot of the insects you're likely to see are beetles. Of all the plant, animal and fungi species that have been named and identified, almost one quarter (350,000) are beetles! Many more kinds have yet to be named. Beetles are what got me hooked on the study of the natural world. Why are there so many kinds? One reason is that a beetle's front pair of wings have evolved into a hard, protective case. They can fold their second pair of wings away where it is protected beneath the case when not in use. This allows beetles to live and feed in places no other insect would tread, including piles of dung! Research shows that beetles also exploded into different species when they began specializing on different parts of plants (e.g., flower, root, seed, leaf). We know very little about most beetles, so there's lots left for YOU to discover.

able to get some great pictures, especially by taking advantage of the macro settings. Try capturing a few insects (avoid bees and wasps) with a viewing jar and lid. A good hand lens will allow you to see a lot of detail. See page 295 for questions to ask about the insects you've caught. Bring along a copy of a book such as Eaton and Kaufman's *Field Guide to Insects of North America* or an insect app. BugGuide.net is an excellent online resource.

Activity 24 Cheer-up Chirrup: Learn Cricket Calls

• **You'll learn:** The purpose and variety of cricket calls.

• **You'll need:** Blindfold, cricket chirrup pattern chart, pictures of a male and female cricket.

• **Background:** No late summer or early fall evening feels the same without the steady, rhythmic chorus of cricket song. Crickets sing for the same reason frogs and birds do—to attract a mate. Different species use different patterns of calls or "chirrups." Here is how they do it.

Males have two special structures on their wings—a file and a scraper. By rubbing the two together, each species of crickets creates a musical trill. Every species produces a unique sound, or stridulation. Females don't stridulate, but they do listen—using their front legs, where their eardrum, or tympanum, is located.

• **Procedure:** Any number of children can participate. You'll need one designated female cricket. The rest are males (boys and girls can be either male or female). Show the difference between male and female crickets using pictures. A female cricket has three "tails"—the middle is her oviposter used to inject eggs into the soil. Male crickets lack this structure. Tell them how a cricket attracts a mate. Demonstrate a long chirrup (a three second "prrrr" by rolling your tongue) and a short chirrup (one second) and tell them that the males will be making these sounds. Ask the males to stand in a large circle with the female in the middle. Whisper the cricket song patterns—one into the ear of each male cricket. If you have a larger group, more than one person can repeat the same pattern. Blindfold the female cricket. Whisper in the female's ear what cricket song chirrup she will be listening for as indicated in the table.

Three Long Chirrups and One Short
One Long Chirrup and One Short
Four Long Chirrups
Two Long Chirrups and One Short
Three Short Chirrups
Three Short Chirrups and One long
Five Long Chirrups
Two Long Chirrups and Two Short
Four Short Chirrups
Three Long Chirrups
One Long and One Short Chirrup
Two Long Chirrups
Three Long Chirrups and One Short

When you give the signal, have the males begin to sing out the chirrup pattern exactly as whispered. Participants can use their tongues or lips to create a simulated rolling chirrup. Just like a meadow on a warm summer's evening, there is a cacophony of cricket songs. Can the female cricket find her counterpart? She moves about the circle with her arms extended (her eardrums are there!). Remember, she lives among the stalks of flowers and plants and can't see very well, so she listens for the right species of cricket. Was the female cricket successful?

See page 297 for the unique sounds different insects make.

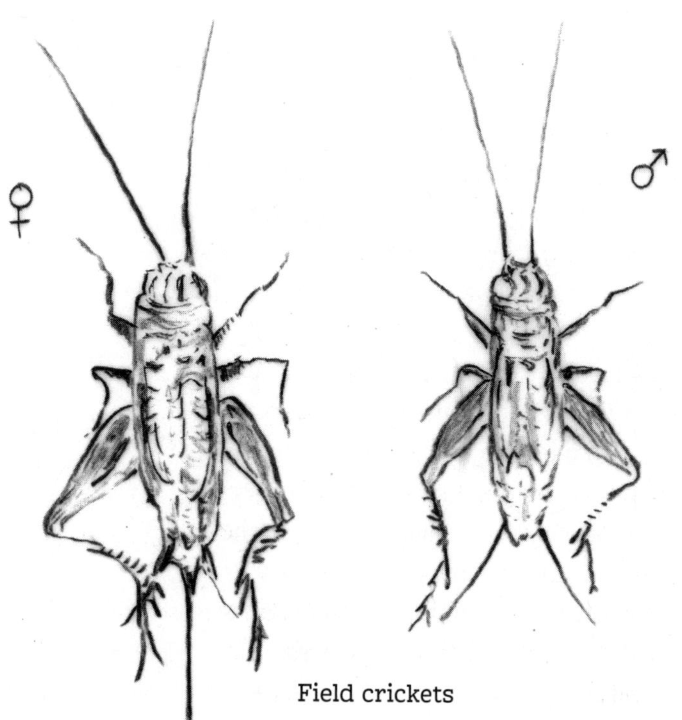

Field crickets

Activity 25 A Pet Woolly Bear

• **You'll learn:** How a woolly bear changes from a caterpillar to a moth.

• **You'll need:** Woolly bear caterpillar, container.

• **Background:** Children love caterpillars, especially the cuddly brown and black woolly bear. What could be more interesting than having a pet woolly bear and seeing it transform into a moth? According to folklore, if a woolly bear's middle brown band is wide—that is, half the body length or more—a mild winter will follow. There is no proof, however, for this.

The woolly bear overwinters as a caterpillar in the leaf litter. In the spring it rouses, eats a little grass, then starts to spin a cocoon, weaving into it hairs from its body. The finished cocoon looks like it is made of felt. By late spring, a dull yellow or orange Isabella tiger moth emerges from the cocoon.

• **Procedure:** Watch for woolly bears crossing roads and sidewalks in early fall. For fun, pick one up (it will curl up in your hand), and turn it around so that it is facing the opposite direction. See what it does when it uncurls. Almost every time, the caterpillars will swing back around and carry on in the original direction. If you want to keep a woolly bear as a pet, remember it needs to be kept outdoors on the porch or in an unheated shed. Make sure it is not exposed to direct sunlight. Put the caterpillar in a container with a layer of soil in the bottom. Provide a little grass or clover as food, replacing the plant material when it starts to wilt. Soon the caterpillar will stop feeding and become more sluggish. Remove any frass (droppings) and food plants and cover the resting caterpillar with a layer of leaves. When spring comes and the caterpillar becomes active again, give it a little fresh grass and some leaves. Watch for it to spin a cocoon. With any luck, you will have an Isabella moth in the container by late spring! Be sure to photograph the moth before you let it go.

Woolly bear caterpillar

Activity 26 Watch It Spin

• **You'll learn:** How a spider spins a web.

• **You'll need:** A large glass jar or aquarium, fine screening, a forked branch, an orb weaver spider (e.g., black and yellow garden spider), a plant mister, flies.

• **Background:** We take spiderwebs for granted. But how many of us have actually watched a spider spin a web? Spiders have special glands that hold liquid silk. The spider squeezes the silk through spinnerets, tiny holes on either side of its abdomen. By controlling the glands, it can create silk of varying thickness and stickiness. The spider sends a strand out into the breeze and feeds out the silk. When the silk attaches to something solid, the spider scampers along this strand and begins the magic of building an intricate web.

Where is my spider? Track the distribution of spiders through space and time by taking and submitting photos of any spiders you find. Visit **inaturalist.org/projects/where-is-my-spider**.

• **Procedure:** Place the forked branch in the container and the spider on the branch. Secure a screen to the top. Watch carefully as the spider spins its web. When it's done, catch some flies and let them go in the container. Watch as they get caught in the web and note how the spider reacts. It is quite a show! Spray the web with a mist of water a couple of times during the day. Return the spider to where you caught it.

Activity 27 Catch a Web

• **You'll learn:** How to preserve a spiderweb.

• **You'll need:** Black construction paper, baby powder, spray adhesive.

• **Procedure:** Locate an easy-to-access web. Apply a spray adhesive to a piece of black construction paper or cardstock. Lightly sprinkle baby powder on both sides of the web. This will make the webbing much more visible. With the black paper behind the web, slowly bring the paper towards you until it touches the web. Then, with the web on the paper, carefully cut the guylines holding the web in place. On the back of the paper, you can make a note of the date, location, type of web and the species of spider that made it.

Activity 28 Swarm Watch

• **You'll learn:** The interesting behaviors of swarming ants and their predators.

• **You'll need:** Hand lens (optional).

• **Background:** On hot, muggy afternoons, usually a few days after a heavy rain, we are provided with an intriguing glimpse into the lives of ants. This is when we see spectacular mating swarms of "flying ants." Ants only have wings during the mating phase of their life cycle. Thousands of small, winged males and much larger winged females—the potential future queens—emerge from the ground, usually pushed out by smaller wingless worker ants. The males are attracted to sex pheromones produced by the female.

The ants mate during flight. Then females bite off their wings and attempt to start their own colonies by burrowing into the soil. Males die shortly after mating but queens can live for up to 15 years.

• **Procedure:** If you come across an ant swarm, watch carefully for winged ants being pushed out of the ground (e.g., through sidewalk cracks). See if you can find both males and females. You might also be able to see shed wings lying on the ground. Watch, too, for other species feeding on the swarming ants. Can you see any birds (e.g., cedar waxwings, gulls) or even dragonflies gobbling them up? Did other people living in your region see swarming ants on the same day? It is very likely.

Citizen Science Suggestions

School of Ants: Help researchers learn about native and introduced urban ants, particularly around homes and schools, by collecting and mailing in specimens. Information at **schoolofants.org.**

Plants

Traveling Seeds: How Do They Spread?

• **You'll learn:** How plants disperse their seeds.

• **You'll need:** Ziplock bags or egg cartons, glue and paper, large wool sock.

• **Background:** Think about this. Plants can't move, so how do they spread their seeds? Well, thanks to evolution, plants have come up with a number of ingenious solutions. There are seven main ways in

Darwin: These mating flights happen on roughly the same day across huge areas of the continent. This promotes interbreeding. But how do the ants know which day to fly? It appears that they pick a day by sensing temperature, humidity and day length. However, scientists don't fully understand how this happens. Like 17-year cicadas, which all emerge on the same evening after 17 years in the ground, ants have evolved some kind of "internal clock." Once again your help is needed!

which seeds "travel" as far as possible from their parent plants in order to have room to grow:

- as a bright, tasty fruit in a bird's digestive system (e.g., cherries, grapes)
- as a sweet-smelling nut buried by a mammal (e.g., acorns, walnuts)
- as a sticky hitchhiker getting a free ride on an mammal's fur or a hiker's pants (e.g., burdock, beggar-ticks)
- as a silky parachuter (e.g., milkweed, goldenrod)
- as a spinning helicopter (e.g., maple, ash, pine) carried by the wind with the help of a special wing or blade
- as a waterproof "boat" floating on the water to a silty shoreline (e.g., water lily)
- through mechanical dispersion such as an "explosion" (e.g., jewelweed and witch hazel, which catapult their seeds in all directions using tension built up in the wall of the seed pod)

• **Procedure:** Visit different habitat types such as fields, wetland edges and woodlands and collect seeds of as many different dispersal methods as possible. Use small ziplock bags or an egg carton to keep the seed types separate. Organize the seeds by dispersal method and glue them to a piece of stiff paper or cardboard. To indicate the method of dispersal, you may want to add an icon: a picture of a squirrel or a seed-eating bird like a robin; clouds to represent the wind; a river or ocean to represent water; a picture of a Roman catapult to represent mechanical dispersal. Try these two activities.

1. Seed Race: Have a milkweed or dandelion seed race. Give each child a milkweed or dandelion seed and see how far they can make the seed go without touching

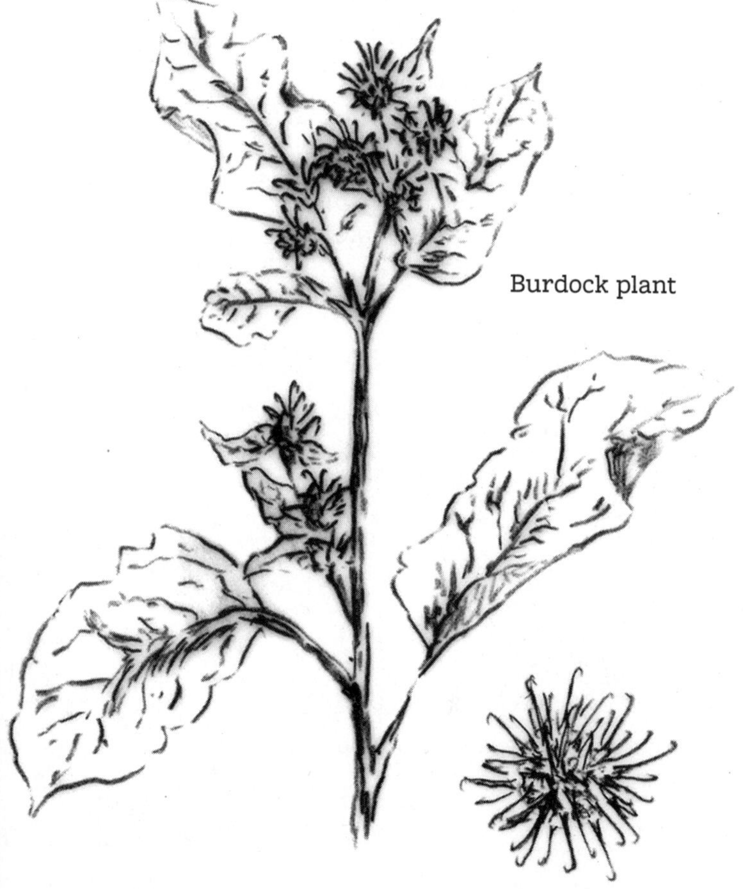

Burdock plant

Burr

Silver maple keys

it. Encourage them to blow on the seed or wave their hands about to create air currents.

2. Seed Sock Walk: Place a large wool sock over one shoe. Walk through the long grass of a field. Examine your socks. How many hitchhikers stuck on for a ride? Use a hand lens to study how the seed was able to stick to your sock. Often seeds such as burdock have a series of hooks that are remarkable at sticking to things—especially fur. In the 1950s, a Swiss engineer by the name of George de Mestral came up with the idea of Velcro after removing some very sticky burdock seeds from the coat of his dog. Why not see if your seeds will grow? Put a few in a box filled with 2 in. (5 cm) of soil. Sprinkle a little soil over them as well. Place near a window and keep moist.

My Adopted Tree

• **You'll learn:** The many changes in a tree over the course of the four seasons.

• **You'll need:** Pencils, measuring tape, camera, blackline master (page 338), nature journal (optional).

• **Procedure:** In this activity, children "adopt" a tree of their choice. They give it a name like you would a dog or cat, take various measurements and learn its key characteristics. They then take note of how the tree changes (e.g., emerging leaves, flowering, color change) through the seasons. Kids can become quite attached to their tree and even remember its "pet name" years later. The children should choose a conveniently located deciduous tree or large shrub with branches

Darwin: Believe it or not, there are plants all over the world that have evolved to trick ants into dispersing their seeds. Each seed has an *elaisome* or "food body" attached to it. These little structures are rich in fats or other nutrients that ants love. Worker ants carry them—and the seeds—back to the colony, where they remove the elaiosomes and feed these to their larvae. The ants then discard the rest of the seed, usually in an underground midden or "garbage pile," where it will germinate. This kind of seed dispersal has evolved independently in a large number of plant families, including trilliums and violets. It is an example of convergent evolution, the process whereby species that are not closely related evolve similar traits independently.

Darwin: Studies in tree evolution have shown that the first true trees, which were like ferns, appeared about 360 million years ago. Primitive conifers were the next to appear, around 250 million years ago. Hardwoods, like maples, oaks, apple trees and the tree you've adopted, only evolved about 100 million years ago. Most dinosaurs had already disappeared by then, so only a very few ever made a meal of hardwood leaves or fruit. Think about that the next time you munch on an apple!

”

they can easily reach and observe. Over the course of each season, they will complete the My Adopted Tree blackline masters in the Appendix. The children should visit the tree every week or two, and more often when changes are occurring fast. If you are a teacher, you may want to take a picture of each student (or pair of students) in front of their adopted tree in September.

Activity 31 A Fall Leaf Collection

• **You'll learn:** The variety of species, shapes, colors and textures of autumn leaves.

• **You'll need:** Newspaper, heavy books, clear contact paper, Bristol board.

• **Procedure:** Gather leaves that are still fairly fresh and pliable. Search for a variety of colors, shapes and sizes. Dry your collected leaves by placing them between sheets of newspaper. Put heavy books on top and allow a week or so until the leaves are completely dry and flat. Arrange the pressed leaves between two sheets of clear contact paper. Smooth air bubbles away with a spoon. You can then glue the leaves to a piece of Bristol board and record the species name and date collected under each leaf. You may want to group the leaves by color, by genus (e.g., all the maples together) or as simple or compound. Alternately, use the leaves to make autumn-themed greeting cards by gluing them onto folded pieces of Bristol board. (See color section, figure 8.)

• **Variation:** Stained Glass Windows—Have an adult iron your most colorful leaves between two layers of waxed papers. Tape to a window on a sunny day and marvel at how the light makes your leaf collection glow! (See color section, figure 14.)

Fall Colors by Species (Most typical colors)

Reds and purples	white ash (maroon), bald cypress, black gum, pin cherry, western crab apple, dogwoods, sugar maple, red maple, vine maple, red oak, sassafras, serviceberries, sumacs, sweet gum, tupelo, black gum, Virginia creeper
Yellows	white ash, Oregon ash, cottonwoods, tamarack (larch), bigleaf maple, sugar maple, red maple, silver maple, Norway maple, quaking aspen, bigtooth aspen, tulip tree, sassafras, sweet gum, birches, American beech, American basswood, Kentucky coffee tree, black walnut, American elm, spicebush, hickories, willows, ginkgo
Oranges	western crab apple, California black oak, sugar maple, red maple, black maple, bigtooth aspen, chokecherry, poison ivy, sumacs
Browns and coppers	American beech, white ash, red oak, white oak, eastern sycamore

Activity 32 Make a Leaf Skeleton

Here's a way to make some "friendly" Halloween skeletons. Collect a series of leaves (maple, oak and basswood work well). Leave them in a container of water for several weeks. Then take the leaves out and use a small paintbrush or a toothbrush to gently remove the soft tissue surrounding the veins. Brush from the inside towards the outside of the leaf. Rinse frequently. Soon the delicate and lacy pattern of veining in a leaf is revealed. Allow to dry for several days by placing your skeletons between several layers of newspaper. Glue your dried skeletons onto a white sheet of paper.

• **Variation:** Leaf Rubbings—Collect a variety of fall leaves. Place them under a white sheet of paper. Use the sides of crayons to rub on layers of color. Focus on the edges and the veins. Build up the colors. (See color section, figure 15.)

Leaf skeleton

Activity 33 Tree Tag

• **You'll learn:** How to identify different trees.

• **You'll need:** Location with a variety of trees.

• **Background:** When you can put names to the trees around you, it is as if you are among friends. Coniferous or cone-bearing trees keep their leaves or needles year round, while deciduous trees lose their leaves in the winter. See page 102 for why different trees have adopted these two different strategies.

• **Procedure:** Go to an area with at least four different tree species. Show the children the distinguishing characteristics (e.g., leaves, bark, shape) of the various trees. Designate a person as "it." "It" shouts out the name of a tree, e.g., "white pine!" The children need to run and touch the branch or trunk of the correct species to be "safe." Anyone tagged or who runs to the wrong tree becomes "it." As a variation—shout out "coniferous"/"deciduous" or "opposite leaves"/"alternate leaves."

• **Suggestion:** Take a picture of different trees in your area, including a close-up of the leaves. Label the pictures and post them on a wall as a reminder. You should also give each tree a memory-aid name that helps kids to remember the species, for example, "Five Finger Freddy" for the white pine, which always has clumps of five needles; "Diamond Ridge Dan" for white ash, which has diamond-shape bark; and "Toilet Paper Pete" for white birch, whose bark looks like toilet paper. Make up your own nicknames!

Activity 34 Make a Terrarium

• **You'll learn:** Characteristics of a small woodland ecosystem.

• **You'll need:** Sand or pebbles, charcoal, rotting log, woodland soil, leaves, mosses, club mosses and other small plants.

Simple bottle terrarium

• **Procedure:** You can easily recreate a mini-woodland habitat in your classroom or home by making a terrarium. It can last for weeks or even years and become the temporary home for insects, frogs and salamanders. An ordinary aquarium tank will work fine or, if you want a group of children to each have their own terrarium, you can use large jars. A screen cover may also be necessary.

- Place a layer of sand or pebbles on the bottom of the terrarium for drainage.
- Sprinkle a thin layer of charcoal pieces over the sand to keep the soil fresh.
- Take your terrarium to the woods and find a small rotting log, maybe with invertebrates underneath.
- Add soil and leaf litter from around the log to a depth of 2 in. (5 cm).
- Carefully break off a piece of the log and place it in the terrarium, scooping up some of the bugs as well.
- Dig up some mosses and small plants growing around the log and plant them in the terrarium. Press them down firmly and dampen with water (do not soak).
- If you are able to find a salamander, you could add it as well, along with a screen cover. Most salamanders will eat crickets, which can be purchased at pet stores.
- Back home or in the classroom, place the terrarium in an area where there is not too much direct sun or heat.

Fungi

Activity 35 Make Spore Prints

• **You'll learn:** That each species of mushroom has a unique spore print that is beautiful in design and color.

• **You'll need:** White paper, drinking glass, art spray fixative.

• **Background:** Mushrooms are the fruiting bodies of fungi. Unlike plants, fungi do not use the Sun's energy to make food. Instead, they absorb the nutrients they need through special roots called mycelium. When it is time to reproduce, a mushroom sprouts up. Gills from under the head of the mushroom expel thousands of tiny spores. Some of these

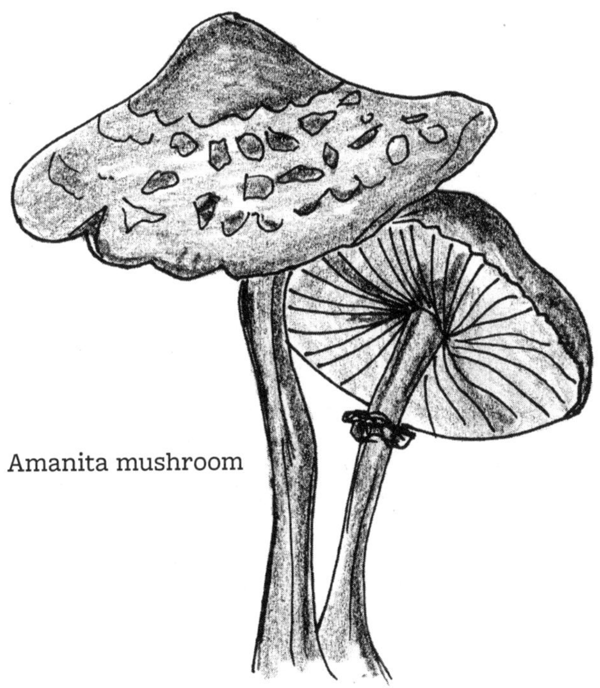

Amanita mushroom

spores will eventually drift down onto moist soil and a new generation of mushrooms will become established.

• **Procedure:** Collect several different types of mushrooms. When you are at home or in the classroom, gently remove the stalk so just the mushroom head remains. Place the mushroom heads on a piece of paper, gill side down. Experiment using dark and light paper (dark spores show up nicely on lighter paper and vice versa). Place a few drops of water on each mushroom head. Cover and leave for a few days. Remove the cover and carefully lift the mushroom straight up; avoid smudging by sliding the head from side to side. On your paper will be a beautiful and delicate spore print. Each species of mushroom leaves a print with a distinctive pattern and color, which can be used to identify the species. Spray with an art fixative (optional) to preserve. Hang up your mushroom art and enjoy! (See color section, figure 11.)

Weather

Make a Debris Survival Hut

• **You'll learn:** How to survive if you are lost in the woods in cold weather.

• **You'll need:** Area with a significant amount of deadfall and fallen leaves.

• **Background:** There is much to learn from studying animal architecture. Take a squirrel's *drey* (leaf nest), for example. This ingenious shelter uses a framework of intertwining branches and twigs to support an insulating layer of leaves, moss and shredded bark (depending on the species of squirrel). You can make a survival shelter called a debris hut based on the design elements of a drey.

• **Procedure:** Begin by making a waist-high mound of leaves at the base of a tree. Prop a branch pole about 9 ft. (3 m) long against the tree and over the mound with the other end on the ground. It should be about 3 ft. (1 m) high. Use branches to create a frame on both sides. Pile leaves, evergreen branches or whatever you can find to cover the frame on both sides. Only cut as many evergreen boughs as necessary and never do this in a conservation area or a park. Heap on as much material as you can, up to a thickness as long as your arm. Pile the same depth of material inside the hut, too. Make sure you leave a pile of dead leaves or evergreen branches in front of the entrance. After you crawl in, seal your hut by enclosing the entrance with this leafy "plug." You will have created a super insulated "sleeping bag" in the same way squirrels do when they make their winter nests. A well-constructed debris hut can help people survive even in sub-zero temperatures. It is a skill well worth practicing that one day may just save lives. (See color section, figure 10.)

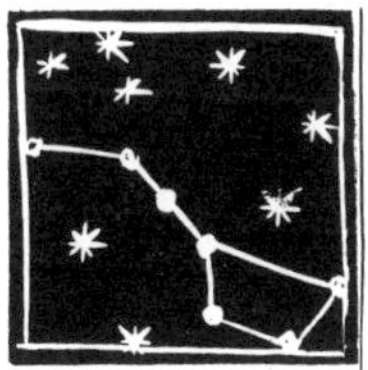

The Sky

Activity 37 Record Sunrise and Sunset Locations

• **You'll learn:** How sunrise and sunset locations change greatly over the four seasons.

• **You'll need:** Camera (optional), phenology worksheet (Appendix, page 326).

• **Background:** Review why we have seasons (see page 63).

• **Procedure:** From a window, or standing outside in your yard or near your home, try to get an unobstructed view of the eastern and/or western horizon. On or near the fall equinox, take note of exactly where the Sun rises and/or sets in relation to landmarks such as trees. Make a sketch or take a photograph of the setting or rising sun. Record on your phenology sheet. Do the same at the winter solstice, spring equinox and summer solstice, making sure to stand in exactly the same spot. You will be amazed by how much the sunrise and sunset point changes with each new season. For instance, as fall progresses, you will notice the Sun rising and setting progressively farther to the south. After the winter solstice, however, the Sun rises and sets more and more to the north.

Activity 38 Measure Your Shadow

• **You'll learn:** That shadow length depends on how much the northern hemisphere is tipped toward or away from the Sun.

• **You'll need:** Measuring tape, paper, pencil, phenology sheet (Appendix, page 326).

• **Background:** By measuring shadows from September through June, children discover that the length of their shadow changes remarkably. This is because the relative height of the Sun in the sky changes with the seasons, as a result of Earth's tilt. At the summer solstice, the noonday sun is almost directly overhead (short shadows), while at the winter

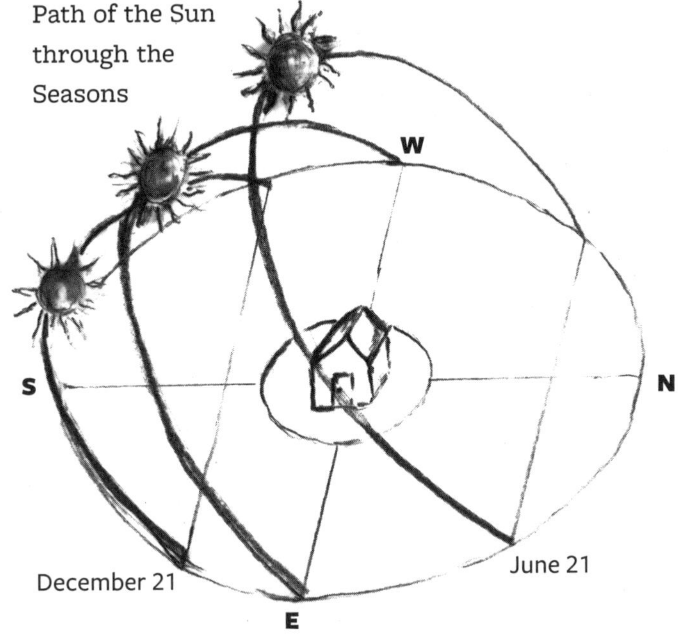

solstice, the noonday sun is much lower on the horizon (long shadows). At the fall and spring equinoxes, shadow length is intermediate between the two. This will help children to grasp the idea that shadow length depends on whether our hemisphere is tipped toward or away from the Sun. It also lays the groundwork for understanding why we have seasons (see page 63).

• **Procedure:** On a sunny day close to the fall equinox, and then again at the winter solstice, spring equinox and summer solstice, go outside at noon with a measuring tape. Stand up straight on a flat surface (e.g., lawn, asphalt) with your back to the Sun. Have a friend measure the length of your shadow. Record the length in your nature journal and/or on the seasonal phenology sheets.

Activity 39 Observe the Great Square of Pegasus and the Andromeda Galaxy

• **You'll learn:** How to find the Great Square of Pegasus and the Andromeda galaxy.

• **You'll need:** Sky chart or app (optional).

• **Background:** The Great Square, part of the Pegasus constellation, is an easy-to-see "asterism." It is can be used much like the Big Dipper to help you find other sky treasures—in this case the Andromeda galaxy. At 2.3 million light years away, Andromeda is the most distant object the human eye can see without the aid of binoculars (although it is easier with them!). It is closer to our own Milky Way than any other galaxy. At 220,000 light years across, Andromeda is also more than twice as big as our Milky Way.

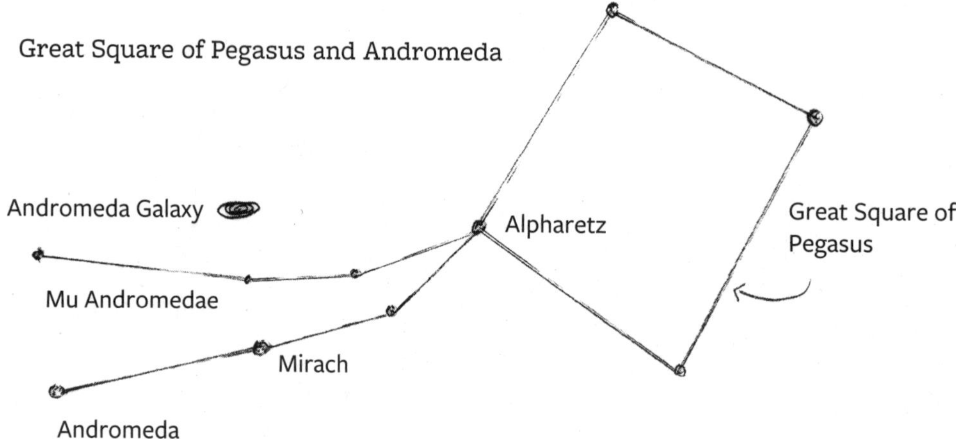

Not surprisingly, Andromeda probably contains twice as many stars—close to 1,000 billion!

• Procedure: If you can, observe the sky from a rural area, away from the bright lights of the city. Start by locating the Great Square in the southeastern sky. Extending from the star Alpheratz on the left side of the Square, you will see the two "arms" of the Andromeda constellation. From Alpheratz, locate the two stars Mirach and Mu Andromedae in the illustration. An imaginary line drawn upwards from Mirach through Mu Andromeda points directly to the Andromeda galaxy. It appears as a faint oval of fuzzy light. Not everyone can see Andromeda with the unaided eye, so binoculars may be necessary.

Disillusion Yourself

• You'll learn: That it is an illusion that the Moon appears largest near the horizon.

• Background: An optical illusion makes the full Moon look larger when it's near the horizon. How this illusion works is still being debated.

• Procedure: When the Harvest Moon is close to the horizon just after sunset, hold a dime at arm's length with one eye closed. Note how much of the Moon the dime covers. Later in the evening when the Moon is higher in the sky and appears smaller, repeat. You will see that the dime covers exactly the same amount of the Moon. You can also trick your mind out of the Moon illusion by bending over at

SAGAN: To get an idea of how far Andromeda is from Earth, let's turn the tables. Imagine that at this very minute, you are on a planet orbiting a star in the Andromeda galaxy. Imagine, too, that you have an incredibly powerful telescope and can see Earth. You would see no cities, no Great Pyramids and no Great Wall of China. With luck, all you might see would be a small band of early humans out hunting on the African plains. You would be seeing Earth as it was 2.3 million years ago. Why? Because it would take that long for light from our solar system to travel to Andromeda. Wow!

Neil deGrasse Tyson: Yes, the Harvest Moon might appear gentle and calming, but its origins were anything but! What you are looking at is actually an ancient chunk of our Earth. Scientists now believe that when Earth formed 4.5 billion years ago, other smaller planetary bodies were also taking shape. One of these crashed into the Earth and blew out rocky debris. Some of the debris went into orbit around the Earth and eventually clumped together to form the Moon. Moon rocks have a similar composition to Earth rocks, whereas meteorites and rocks from other planets do not. Now, isn't that cooler than the Moon being made of cheese?

the waist and watching the rising Harvest Moon upside down between your legs. For most people, the illusion of bigness disappears!

Activity 41 A Month of Moon-watching

• **You'll learn:** The different phases of the Moon.

• **You'll need:** Nature journal, pencil, camera (optional).

• **Background:** The long, comfortable evenings of early fall are ideal for moon watching. Fall is also the season of the Harvest Moon, which adds extra interest and can serve as a good starting point for observing the other phases. Like the Sun, the Moon appears to rise in the east and set in the west. It follows roughly the same path as the Sun through the sky and is visible during the day as much as at night. But unlike the Sun, the Moon rises each day an average of 50 minutes later than the day before. We see the Moon because it reflects the light of the Sun. It takes the Moon 29½ days to go through the full cycle of eight distinct phases.

1. Full Moon: The beautiful full Moon rises at sunset and sets at sunrise. It often appears like a huge orange ball as it climbs above the eastern horizon in the evening. When it is full, the Moon is on the side of the Earth farthest from the Sun, so the Sun lights up its entire visible side.

2. Waning gibbous: The waning gibbous Moon rises after sunset and starts to take on the shape of a football or a C. The Moon is "crumbling" away.

3. Third (last) quarter: This "half Moon" phase rises in the middle of the night and sets at midday.

4. Waning crescent: What is left of the crumbling Moon rises and sets just before

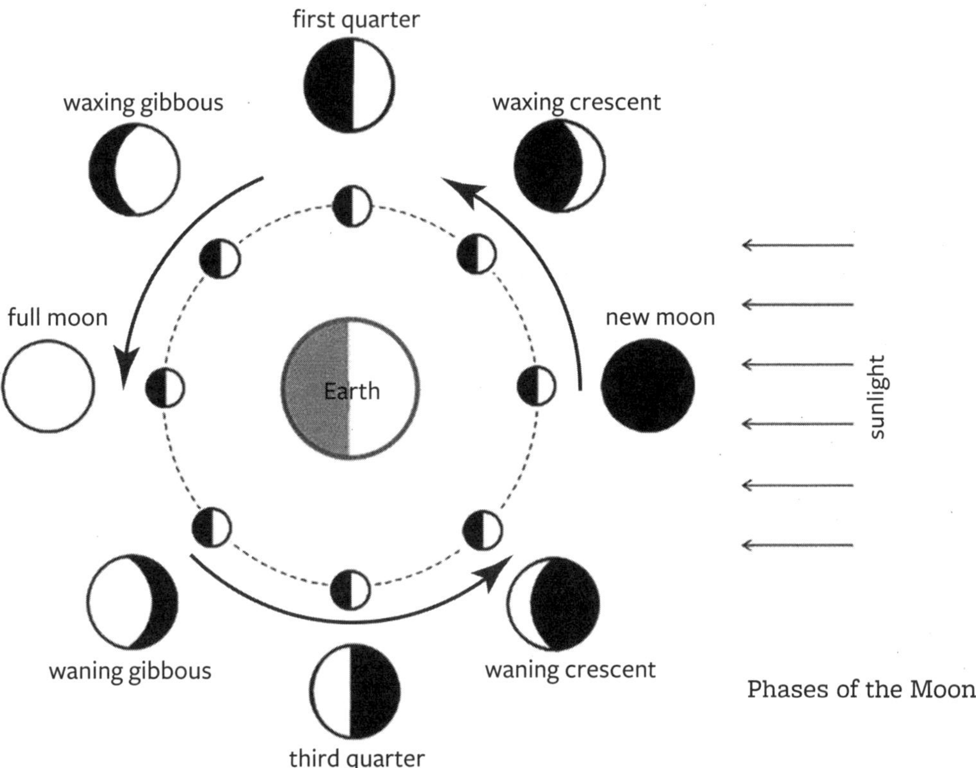

Phases of the Moon

the Sun and stays in the sky most of the day. It is exquisitely beautiful at dawn.

5. New Moon: The new Moon rises and sets with the Sun and stays close to it during the day. The Moon is between the Earth and the Sun, so the Sun shines only on the far side of the Moon, making it invisible.

6. Waxing crescent: The Moon now rises and sets shortly after the Sun and is quite striking in the evening twilight, low in the west. Earthshine (sunlight reflected off the Earth onto the Moon and back again to our eyes) *dimly* illuminates the Moon's surface to the left of the crescent. Looking like the rounded part of a D, the waxing crescent is "Developing" towards the full Moon.

7. First quarter: Like the last quarter phase, this is the familiar "half Moon." It is called a quarter Moon, however, because it has completed one quarter of its cycle. A first quarter Moon rises around noon and sets around midnight. This is the best phase for looking at the Moon's surface through binoculars.

8. Waxing gibbous: The word gibbous means "like a hump." The somewhat football-shaped waxing gibbous Moon rises late in the day and shines most of the night. Within a few days it looks very similar to the full Moon.

• **Procedure:** Try to observe the Moon each day that the sky is clear. Each time you see the Moon in one of the eight phases, draw it in your nature journal and write down the date and time. If you wish, take a picture of the Moon in each phase, print it and glue it in your journal.

Activity 42 Make Your Own Phases

• **You'll learn:** Why we see the different phases of the Moon.
• **You'll need:** A strong flashlight or projector, Styrofoam ball or orange, a pencil.
• **Procedure:** In a dark room, place the light source on a shelf or stepladder at about eye level. Stick the pencil into the orange or ball. Stand facing the light, holding the ball out in front of you at arm's length and a little higher than your head. You are looking at the new Moon, since only the back of the ball is illuminated. Turn slowly to the left, keeping the ball in front of you. Soon you will see a little crescent form (waxing crescent). Keeping turning until you see the entire right side of the ball illuminated. This is the first quarter. Rotating a little farther, you will see the football-like waxing gibbous phase. When your back is to the light, the full Moon appears. As you carry on, you will be looking at the waning gibbous, the last quarter and the waning crescent. A full rotation brings you back to the invisible new Moon. (See color section, figure 9.)

Honoring the Season

Activity 43 Celebrate the Fall Equinox

In late September, organize an "Equinox Experience." Since day and night are of equal duration, black (night) and white (day) can be the theme of a party. Just use your imagination! You might, for example, want to serve sandwiches with one slice of pumpernickel and one slice of white bread, make a cake that is half chocolate and half vanilla, dress half in white and half in black and maybe even decorate with black and white balloons. For a table centerpiece, use dark objects (e.g., bark) and bright objects (e.g., goldenrod blossoms) along with black and white candles. Have a countdown in the last minute leading up to the equinox. (Adapted from *The Kids' Nature Almanac* by Alison Smith.)

Activity 44 Celebrate Halloween

Elementary school teachers will tell you that children get more excited about Halloween than just about any other event of the year, including Christmas. There are many ways to inject an element of nature into the celebrations, both in the home or classroom and outside. Here are a few ideas:

- Wear "naturized" costumes: Attach natural objects like pine needles, twigs with leaves or bunches of grass to costumes—or even dress up as a tree or animal.
- Organize a Halloween bike parade: Decorating your bike for a Halloween parade could be fun for the whole neighborhood. A scary plant or animal theme allows for lots of creativity!
- Research plants and animals associated with Halloween: What do bats do in the fall? What owl species live in your area? How do spiders get through the winter? What plants are associated with Halloween? Can any of them be found locally?
- Take part in an owl walk: Many nature centers such as Audubon sponsor evening "owl prowls" in late October.
- Discuss fear of nature: Why are so many people afraid of bats, snakes and spiders? Is there an evolutionary reason? If we are afraid of something, does that mean we should persecute it (e.g., kill snakes)? How can fear be positively channeled into fascination, curiosity and exploration? What should we *really* be afraid of in the natural world? (See page 5 in Introduction.)

Activity 45 Celebrate the Harvest and/or Thanksgiving

- Guess the seeds: Put the seeds from a pumpkin or two into a jar. Have each child guess how many seeds there are. Empty the jar and count the seeds. The closest guess wins. This is also a fun way to teach about estimation.
- Piling leaves: You will need plenty of leaves on your lawn to play this game. Divide the children into two teams and then place two hula hoops—or similar

Boreal owl

round objects—on the ground. Give each team a rake and tell them they have five minutes to build the highest pile of leaves possible. When five minutes is up, the team with the tallest pile wins. Don't forget to jump into your piles when you are done.

- Treasure in a leaf pile: Make several piles of leaves and then bury some small treasures in each—things like wrapped candy, coins, peanuts in the shell and stickers. Give the children a bag each and send them on a treasure hunt! This game can also be a competition, where the child who finds the most items wins. It is fun for children of all ages.
- Harvest centerpiece: Hollow out a pumpkin and place a small jar of water inside. Go for a hike and gather natural items (e.g., fall grasses, wildflowers gone to seed, twigs with berries, twigs with brightly colored leaves, cattails) and put them in the pumpkin. You can also decorate the outside by sticking in cloves, maybe by spelling out a word such as "thanks." For an added touch, hang pictures of all the members of your family from the twigs or flowers.

Quotes on fall for contemplation

For man, autumn is a time of harvest, of gathering together. For nature, it is a time of sowing, of scattering abroad.

—**Edwin Way Teale**

Everyone must take time to sit and watch the leaves turn.

—**Elizabeth Lawrence**

Autumn is a second spring when every leaf is a flower.

—**Albert Camus**

Winter

the great exhale

As winter winds blast across brown or white fields and the temperature dips, the land seems to breathe out—cleansing itself of the remnants of last summer's growth. We hear the chattering of dried leaves, feel the ground becoming firm beneath our feet and sense a new sharpness in the air. This is the time of the great exhale, a moment of rest and release. And despite the cold and the starkness of the season, we place hope in the promise of a new cycle of regeneration and rebirth that is yet to come.

Some Key Events in Nature in Winter

Overview

The "early winter "period runs from about the start of December to mid-January. "Late winter" covers the period from approximately mid-January through February. Timing will vary depending on latitude, elevation and the vagaries of the weather. Climate change, too, is accelerating some events and delaying others. The sequence of events, however, is always the same. The references point to an activity based on a given event.

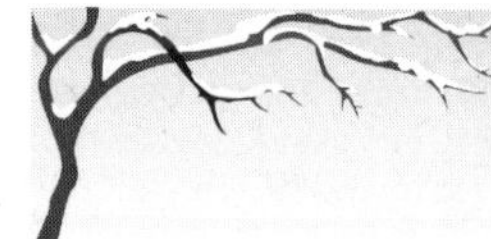

Continent-wide Overview

Birds

General

- Feeders attract a wide selection of birds over the winter, especially when a variety of different foods are provided. (See Activity 14, page 108.)
- Every year from December 14 to January 5, the Christmas Bird Count (CBC) takes place across North America. This is followed in mid-February by the Great Backyard Bird Count (GBBC). These are important citizen science events that collect data on how bird populations are changing. (See Activity 10, page 163 and Activity 11, page 164.)
- The number of many winter birds varies greatly from one year to the next, depending on whether "winter irruptives" show up. These species include many of the finches (e.g., redpolls, pine siskins) and owls such as the snowy and great gray.
- Some resident species forage in mixed flocks, which often include chickadees, nuthatches, woodpeckers, creepers and kinglets.
- Many species of waterfowl can be found wintering on open bodies of water.
- Snow buntings, horned larks and Lapland longspurs can often be found in farm fields.

Early winter

- Rarities that have wandered out of their normal range sometimes show up at feeders.
- Small numbers of waterfowl, loons and grebes linger on lakes and rivers until freeze-up.

Late winter

- Bird song begins once again as pair bonds are established or renewed. Among the first species to sing are cardinals and chickadees. (See Activity 12, page 165.)

- Ducks such as common goldeneye show courtship behavior, bobbing their heads and whistling loudly. Ravens begin their aerial mating displays and great horned owls start nesting.
- Early migrants such as American crows, Canada geese and red-winged blackbirds begin to return.

Mammals

- Early snowfalls reveal the nocturnal world of mammal activity. Coyotes, deer, squirrels, mice and voles are just a few of the many species that leave their tracks—and other signs such as tunnels, scat and chew marks—for us to decipher. (See Activity 13, page 167 and Activity 14, page 169.)
- Holes in standing dead trees (snags) often provide valuable shelter for birds and mammals in winter. (See Activity 17, page 171.)
- Some mammals are true hibernators and enter a death-like state (e.g., groundhogs). Others, such as bears, enter a state of deep sleep. Raccoons and skunks sleep much of the time but will venture out of their refuge during mild spells. For mammals like foxes, coyotes and deer, however, winter means business as usual as they search for food. (See Activity 16, page 171.)
- Moose and deer lose their antlers.
- In January, black bears give birth, usually to two cubs.
- By late winter, skunks begin to emerge from dens to find a mate. Their telltale scent is one of first datable events of the new year.
- Mid-January through February is also mating time for beavers, foxes, wolves, coyotes, squirrels, raccoons and minks.

Amphibians and Reptiles

- Some salamanders remain active all winter long. These include mudpuppies, an entirely aquatic salamander, and eastern newts. (See Activity 20, page 174.)
- In northern latitudes and at high elevations, some frog species (e.g., wood frog, chorus frogs) spend the winter frozen in the leaf litter of the forest floor. (See Activity 21, page 175.)

Fishes

- Fish such as bass are relatively dormant during the winter, while others, like pike, walleye, perch and trout, are active and continue to feed.
- Fishing through the ice, anglers pursue a variety of species in winter, including walleye, perch, pike and trout. (See Activity 22, page 176.)

Invertebrates

- The galls of the goldenrod gall fly are a common sight in many areas. (See Activity 23, page 176.)
- Most insects are now in diapause, a stage of halted development in which they overwinter as eggs, larvae, pupae (cocoons), nymphs or even adults. With a little searching, it is possible to find them in all these stages. (See Activity 24, page 178.)
- Snow fleas can be fairly common on woodland snow on mild, sunny days. Watch for what looks like jumping specks of spilled pepper!
- Many species of pollinating insects are in serious decline. Now is a great time to sit down and draw up plans for a pollinator garden to give these insects a helping hand. (See Activity 25, page 179.)

Plants

- Conifers attract our attention now that deciduous trees have lost their leaves. Their needles and the different shapes of the trees are useful in identification. (See Activity 26, page 181.)
- The unique buds, leaf scars and twigs of deciduous trees stand out clearly and are a great tool for identification. (See Activity 29, page 184.)
- Fields and roadsides are scattered with the remains of last summer's wildflowers, most of which still contain seeds.
- Evergreen wildflowers, ferns, mosses and club mosses catch the eye in snow-free areas.

Fungi

- Bracket fungi (e.g., turkey tail, tinder polypore) are conspicuous on tree trunks. Look, too, for puffballs (e.g., pear-shaped puffball) and jelly fungi (e.g., witch's butter).
- On mild winter days when moisture is sufficient, lichens are able to carry out photosynthesis and actually grow. (See Activity 30, page 185.)

Weather

- Snow covers much of the continent and directly shapes the composition of our plant and animal life. It is the cause of many fascinating adaptations but is also fascinating in itself. (See Activities 31–33, pages 187–190.)

- Daylight returns slowly and is most noticeable in the afternoon as the Sun continues to set farther and farther north. Longer days are quite apparent by late January.
- By February, days are as long as in October. More than an hour of sunlight has been gained since December 20.

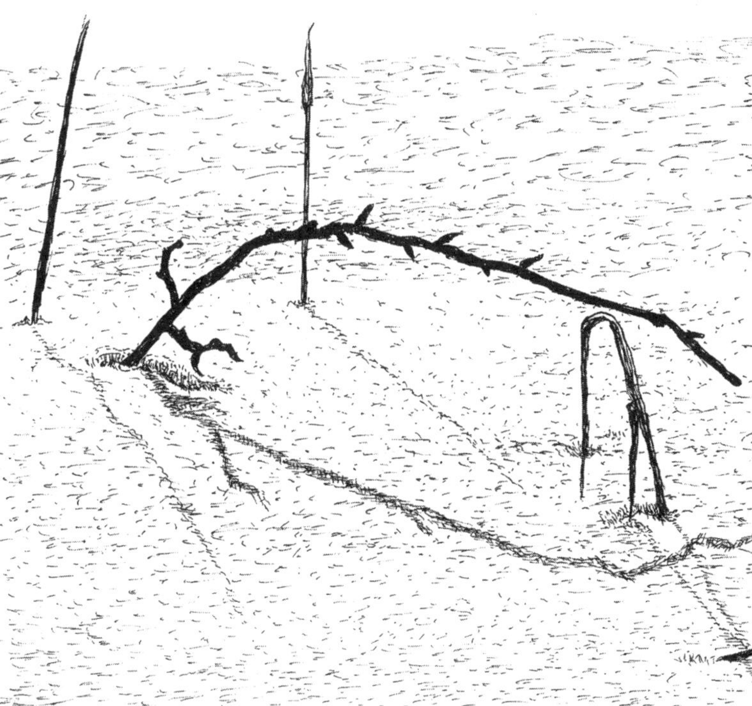

Winter scene—note snow melt at base of stems

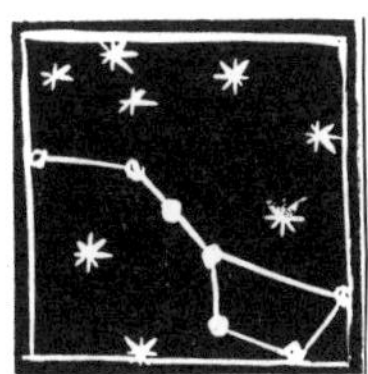

The Sky

- The winter solstice marks the shortest day of the year as the Sun traces its lowest and shortest arc through the sky. Even at noon, it remains far lower in the sky than at any other time of year. (See Activity 34, page 190.)
- The winter constellations shine brightly and are easy to pick out. In the southeast, look for the Winter Six: Canis Major, Canis Minor, Gemini, Auriga, Taurus and, of course, Orion. The most prominent stars in these same constellations form an asterism known as the Winter Hexagon. (See Activity 37, page 191.)
- The Big Dipper (in Ursa Major) is standing upright low in the northeast. The Little Dipper (in Ursa Minor) and the North Star (Polaris) are to its left. Cassiopeia is high in the northwest.
- The early winter full Moon rides higher in the sky than at any other season and passes nearly overhead at midnight.
- Because the waxing crescent moon is fairly high above the horizon at sunset in late winter and early spring, this time of year provides the best showing of "earth-shine"—the faint lighting of the dark portion of the Moon during the waxing crescent moon phase.
- The early morning hours of December 13 and 14 are peak viewing for the Geminids meteor shower. The Quadrantid meteor shower takes place January 3 and 4.
- Winter is a good time to see "sun dogs," short rainbow arcs that form on either side of the Sun and create a halo of light.

Winter Nature Highlights by Region

1. Marine West Coast

- Bodies of freshwater and saltwater host thousands of waterfowl. In winter many of these birds form pair bonds and have interesting mating displays (e.g., bufflehead). Other common species include American wigeon, northern shoveler, red-breasted merganser, surf scoter, Barrow's and common goldeneye, brant, snow geese (estuaries), western grebe, horned grebe, common loon and red-throated loon.
- Large numbers of snow geese and, in some areas, trumpeter swans feed in corn fields.
- Anna's hummingbirds take advantage of non-native plantings and feeders to overwinter in much of the region.
- Thousands of dunlin and black-bellied plover remain to winter along the coast.
- Raptors, including peregrines, bald eagles, northern harriers and red-tailed hawks, are most abundant at this time of year.
- You can see migrating gray whales along the Oregon coast in December. Some remain near the coast throughout the year. Bundle up and grab binoculars!
- Song sparrows, pacific wrens and red-winged blackbirds may begin singing in late winter.
- The Pacific treefrog (*Pseudacris regilla*) symphony begins in February. When Hollywood moviemakers wanted frog calls to convey the feeling of nighttime outdoors, they recorded treefrogs, so now their *ribbit* call is known to all.
- One of the first native shrubs to flower is Indian plum. Its creamy-white flowers provide a glimpse of spring at a time of short days, clouds and rain.
- In some areas, Oregon grape blooms as early as December in bright yellow clusters of flowers. Other early bloomers include red alder and western skunk cabbage.
- Mushrooms that can be found in winter include morels, cauliflower mushrooms (*Sparassis herbstii*) and hedgehog mushrooms (*Hydnum umbilicatum*).
- Weather is rainy and cold, even though temperatures rarely drop below freezing on the coastal lowlands.
- Howling winter gales make for great storm-watching. Tofino and Ucluelet on western Vancouver Island are popular destinations.

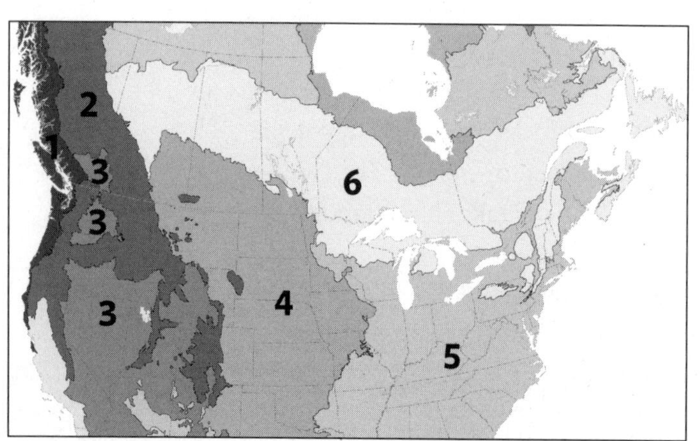

Ecological Zones of North America

2. Northwestern Forested Mountains

- A few species that can be seen in many areas in winter include mountain chickadee, Clark's nutcracker, Steller's jay, black-billed magpie, common raven, Townsend's solitaire and pine grosbeak.
- Winter is an excellent time to see mammals. For instance, if you visit Yellowstone National Park in winter, you should be able to see mule deer, pronghorns, bighorn sheep, elk, American bison, coyotes and gray wolves.

3. North American Deserts

- Bald eagles, northern harriers and rough-legged hawks overwinter in the region. Watch, too, for short-eared owls.
- In January and February, bald eagle numbers at Klamath Basin in Oregon and California peak at over 500 birds. There are also abundant wintering waterfowl.
- Lake Lowell (Deer Flat National Wildlife Refuge in Oregon) is the winter home to as many as 150,000 ducks and geese and to the many raptors attracted by the large flocks of waterfowl.
- Elk often wander down to the grain fields to browse in the evenings and head back up to the safety of the forest at first light.
- Oregon spotted frogs, a species of special concern, start breeding in February or March at lower elevations.

4. Great Plains

- Rough-legged hawks and golden eagles can be common in some locales. Small numbers of bald eagles will also winter in the area.
- Snowy owls are often seen.
- Other hardy birds like ring-necked pheasants, sharp-tailed grouse, gray partridge, great horned owls and snow buntings are active.
- Eastern red cedars, the only native evergreen on much of the Great Plains, become a vital source of shelter for many birds and mammals during severe winter weather.

Ring-billed gull in non-breeding plumage

5. Eastern Temperate Forests

- In late November and December, the Niagara River is one of the best places in the world to see a wide variety of gulls, including rarities like little gulls.
- In the Upper Mississippi River Valley, hundreds of wintering bald eagles congregate near open water and snatch fish with their talons. In the northeast, eagles spend the winter along the coasts of Maine, around Delaware Bay and on large, unfrozen lakes throughout the area.
- Amherst and Wolfe islands, west of Kingston on Lake Ontario, attract large

Red-shouldered hawks

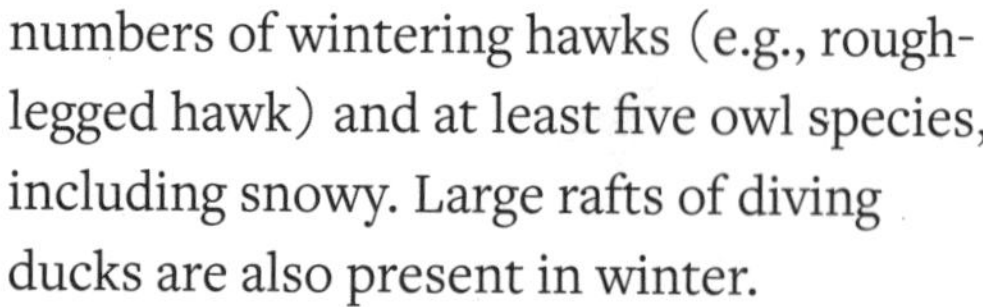

numbers of wintering hawks (e.g., rough-legged hawk) and at least five owl species, including snowy. Large rafts of diving ducks are also present in winter.

- Kemptville Creek at Oxford Mills, Ontario, is one of the best places to see mudpuppies in large numbers throughout the winter months. Organized mudpuppy-viewing outings take place.
- By late February, eastern skunk cabbage may begin poking through the snow. Evening rains may bring about a chorus of wood frogs and spring peepers in southern parts of the region as they prepare to lay eggs in vernal ponds.

6. Northern Forests

- Some years, when conifers produce a lot of cones, large flocks of crossbills will show up and glean seeds from the cones. They are also fond of the salt and grit put down on roads in winter.
- Both great gray and northern hawk owls sometimes show up along the southern edge of the region (e.g., central Ontario) when rodent numbers crash in the north.
- Northern flying squirrels will sometimes soar down from trees to visit bird feeders at night. Floodlights outside don't seem to bother them, and they can be very tame and approachable.
- White-tailed deer travel to wintering areas, where they "yard up." These spots are often large stands of lowland conifers such as cedars or hemlocks, which provide food and shelter from the wind and snow.

Stopping by Woods on a Snowy Evening

Whose woods these are I think I know.
His house is in the village though;
He will not see me stopping here
To watch his woods fill up with snow.

My little horse must think it queer
To stop without a farmhouse near
Between the woods and frozen lake
The darkest evening of the year.

He gives his harness bells a shake
To ask if there is some mistake.
The only other sound's the sweep
Of easy wind and downy flake.

The woods are lovely, dark and deep,
But I have promises to keep,
And miles to go before I sleep,
And miles to go before I sleep.

— Robert Frost

Silhouettes of different conifers

Collection Challenge

Winter items for the collection box and/or nature table (see also page 54 in "Connecting with Nature"):

- Various galls (see page 176 for more about galls)
- Seed heads from winter wildflowers such as Queen Anne's lace. Put them in a vase or jar with a piece of white paper underneath. Observe the seeds that fall onto the paper.
- Different kinds of lichen taken from tree bark, rocks, tree branches, etc.
- Needles and cones from different conifers
- Leaves that cling to twigs all winter (e.g., beech, ironwood, oak)
- Plants such as amaryllis or paper whites
- Twigs of spring-blooming trees and shrubs in a jar of water to force into bloom. Try willows, dogwoods, forsythia, red maple, spicebush, etc.
- Smells of winter: conifer needles and poplar buds to rub and smell
- Laptop: websites showing common feeder birds

Evolution display: artificial selection

1. Bring in the six different vegetables derived from *Brassica oleracea*, also known as wild cabbage. Pictures are available online. This was done over hundreds of years by selecting seeds of plants with certain characteristics. Kale was created by selecting seeds from wild cabbage plants with large, crinkled leaves; kohlrabi, by selecting seeds from kale plants with short, fleshy and fat stems; cabbage, by selecting seeds from kale plants with tight clusters of large leaves; broccoli and cauliflower, by selecting cabbages with tight clusters of flowering heads; and Brussels sprouts, by selecting cabbages with tightly packed leafy buds on the stem. Be sure to eat all these delicious foods afterwards, maybe in a salad or with a "Darwin Dip"!

2. Ask the children to bring in pictures of purebred dogs—maybe their own pets—to show all of the dog breeds obtained by selective breeding (artificial selection). Ask the kids what they think the breeders were selecting for in order to create each breed.

Art in the Park

Ideas for what to sketch and photograph in winter:

- Early snowfalls when there are still some colorful fall leaves clinging to trees
- A leafless tree silhouetted against white snow or an interesting sky
- Long winter shadows in a forest or grove of trees. Black-and-white photography can be very appealing for shots like these in winter.
- Hoar frost on old fences, grass and trees.

- Lingering leaves on trees such as American beech and hophornbeam
- Vines such as wild grape that still bear fruit
- Close-ups of the bark—often covered with lichen—of different species of trees
- Interesting ice formations and vegetation frozen in the ice around the edges of running water, ponds and lakes
- Tree shadows on the snow at the full Moon
- Morning fog, mist and frost, such as mist over a half-frozen river

What's Wrong with the Scenario?

Can you find the six mistakes?

It was a beautiful early winter's day and a great time to just be outside. The Sun, high in the northern sky, shone brightly and made the snow sparkle. Although it was quite cold, birds were singing loudly. Some were even carrying nesting material. I watched as big flocks of chickadees all ate together at the feeder, obviously enjoying sunflower seeds. At one point, a gray squirrel provided entertainment too, as it tried time and time again to get at the seed. It was beautiful in its white winter coat. Before going inside, I gathered a few maple and oak twigs to make a craft. Looking at the bare twigs, I couldn't stop thinking about how nice it will be when the buds finally appear in the spring!

Turn to the Appendix, page 342, to see how you did!

The Story of Night Cap, the Chickadee

It is early January and the temperature has dipped to a chilly −5°F (−15°C). To fuel her small body, Night Cap must always look for food. She searches for seeds and berries, or for insects and eggs hidden in the folds of bark. Night Cap's head and eyes are continually moving, glancing up, behind and to either side. She flits to a gypsy moth egg mass pasted to the side of a thick branch and feasts on the protein-rich snack. But out of the corner of her eye, Night Cap spots a whirl of feathers, streaking towards her. A sharp-shinned hawk, with short, rounded wings and narrow tail, is closing in fast! Uttering a sharp *zeek* alarm call, Night Cap launches herself into the air, twirling, darting and zigzagging, using whatever evasive action she can. By flying in and out of thick cedar bows, she manages to shake off the hawk.

Night Cap hides herself deep within the cover of evergreen boughs. Eventually, when she is sure it is safe, she lets out several short, soft *tseet*, *tseet* calls to contact the rest of the chickadees in her flock. Soon they gather round using the familiar *chickadee*, *chickadee* call to stay together. During the winter, Night Cap flies in a flock of 6 to 12 chickadees. Sometimes she is joined by nuthatches and kinglets. There is safety in numbers with all those eyes to watch for danger!

Night comes quickly to the winter forest. The flock finds a grove of birch trees, some of which are dead. Each bird excavates an overnight roosting site by pecking through the bark of a few of the rotten trees. This affords some good protection from the north winds and plummeting temperatures. Night Cap puffs her feathers out, trapping dead air and she falls fast asleep. She shivers often to warm her small body. Her feet don't get cold because there isn't much blood circulating there. At night, Night Cap's body temperature can drop more than 14°F (8°C) to save valuable energy. While it wasn't easy, Night Cap survives another night in the heart of winter.

What you can do

- As you watch chickadees, notice how only one bird ever feeds at a time. A flock usually forms around a dominant pair and contains six or more birds, depending on how much food is available. Some are juveniles, some are paired adults and some are single adults. Each member of the dominant pair dominates all other male or female birds. They also get to eat first. To pick out the dominant pair, watch for chickadees that approach the feeder directly, scaring off other birds that are feeding. Less dominant individuals wait until the "top dogs" have eaten their fill. You will sometimes see them approach and then veer off at the last second without perching on the feeder, intimidated by another chickadee.
- Are you always seeing the same dozen or so chickadees at your feeder? Banding has shown that there are far more different chickadees coming than you might think.
- Watch for a chickadee puffing out its plumage on a cold winter's morning. This is a way to stay warm—it traps extra air around down feathers, which prevents heat loss.

Black-capped chickadee

Hand feed chickadees

There is something magical about feeling the clutch of tiny feet and the brush of feathers as a delicate, winged being takes a seed straight from your outstretched hand. Frank Glew calls this "That Chickadee Feeling" (in his lovely children's book of the same name). You can train chickadees and nuthatches to eat out of your hands. All it takes is a bit of patience and determination. Here's how:

- Fill a bird feeder or a container with black-oil sunflower seeds. This is the food of choice for chickadees and other small birds.
- Keep your feeder stocked so the birds get used to visiting you on a regular basis.
- Stand about ten feet (three meters) away from the feeder and watch the birds feed for ten minutes or so. Every day, move in just a bit closer. In time, the birds won't mind if you stand right next to the feeder. Be as still as you possible can. If you like, make soft *pishing* noises.
- Next, take away your feeder and fill a bowl or cup with sunflower seeds. Hold this out with your hands, right next to the place where you had your feeder. The birds are used to this spot and will return. The trick is not to move! Even the slightest gesture will scare a chickadee. Instead, transform yourself into a bird feeder—your arm outstretched and your hands, eyes, head and body perfectly still.
- After a few days, try using your open hand instead of a bowl. It won't be long before you experience "That Chickadee Feeling," a feeling you won't easily forget! (See color section, figure 26.)

At Your Magic Spot

Sonogram: You'll need a pencil and paper. To start with, get comfortable. Now close your eyes and really listen. Use focused hearing (see Activity 2, page 270). Do you notice how, at this time of year, the sound has a different quality? Sound doesn't travel as well through cold air, and snow (if there is any) tends to muffle sound waves. What do you hear? A chickadee's contact notes, a squirrel's chatter, the rustling of dried leaves or needles? Can you draw these sounds on paper? Here is one way:

The left side of the page represents how loud the sound is: higher up the page means louder, lower down, softer. The bottom of the page represents how long the sound lasts. Does your sound curve upward? Does it rapidly increase and decrease, or slowly build? See if you can make at least three different sonograms. The next time you visit your spot, can you still hear some of the same sounds? If so, how have they changed?

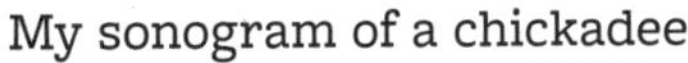

My sonogram of a chickadee

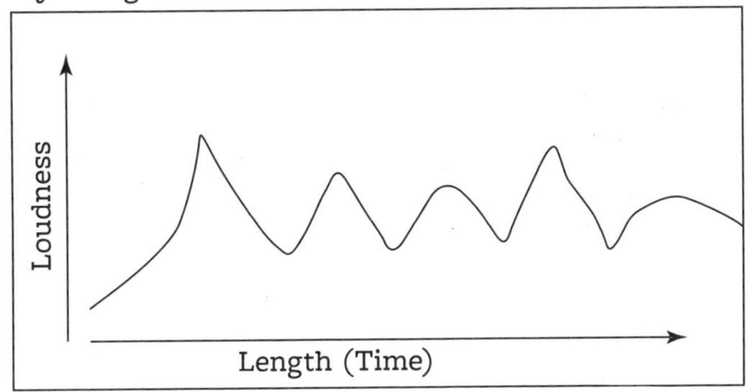

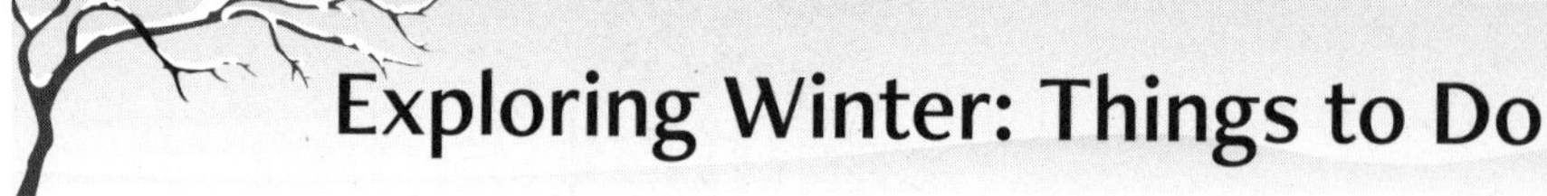

Exploring Winter: Things to Do

Winter looks like...

- The beauty of tree shadows on the snow at night when the Moon is full
- The exquisite design of a snowflake
- The winter sky in late afternoon and at sunset as the stars come out
- The subdued but varied colors of the winter woods
- The special quality of the light, the sky, the landscape or even your backyard. How do winter colors and light compare to those of summer and fall?

Activity 1 Tree Faces

The human brain is very good at seeing "faces," even when they are not really there. Now that the leaves are off most of the trees, hidden faces in the bark are easier to spot. Look for eyes, a nose and a mouth. The face you see may only have one or two of these features but still look strangely human. Try to see, too, how the tree is feeling. Be sure to show the face to others. Are they able to see it? Do they agree with how the tree is feeling? Old willow trees are a good choice for this activity. Extension: Look for faces in the leaf scars. (See color section, figure 29.)

Winter sounds like...

- The silence of the winter woods, especially when snow is gently falling
- The wind blowing in the branches of trees. Pines make a distinct whooshing sound, while oaks and beech chatter from last year's leaves that still cling tenaciously to their branches.
- The groaning, cracking and booming of lake ice as it grows and expands in cold weather
- The crunch of snow underfoot and how the sound changes, depending on the temperature
- The gentle contact calls of a flock of chickadees

Two Ears are Better Than One

This game shows the importance of two ears. Mark an X on the ground with a stick. Walk in a straight line and mark points every 5 ft. (1.5 m) from the X, labeling each one (5 ft./1.5 m, 10 ft./3 m, 15 ft./4.5 m, etc.) with a small piece of paper. Now place a blindfolded subject on the X. Stand on one of the points away from the subject and say his or her name. The subject must now tell you which line you are standing on. Try it when the subject uses one and both ears. Make it harder with shorter distances from the X. Are two ears better than one in judging distance? For most people, it will be easier to judge distance using two ears. Like owls, we use the loudness of sounds and the time it takes for them to reach each ear to determine where sounds come from. Without this, owls would not be able to hunt at night.

Winter tastes like...

- The sweet pulp of rose hips, which can be eaten raw
- Watercress from a winter stream; it too is tasty raw
- A small piece of wintergreen leaf from the forest floor
- Root vegetables like carrots and turnips
- A snowflake landing on your tongue

Forest Tea

As you walk, harvest a handful of needles from trees such as cedar, pine, spruce and Douglas fir. Choose the freshest looking. When you get home—or over an outdoor fire—toss about 1 oz. (30 g) of needles into 2 pt. (0.5 L) of boiling water. Try combinations of different needles, such as white pine and eastern white cedar. Let steep for at least ten minutes. The resulting tea will be bitter but refreshing, and your tongue will dance with a pungent but evocative taste of the forest! As always, make sure you positively identify the species *before* you make tea—and don't drink too much! (See color section, figure 28.)

Winter smells like...

- The smoke from a fireplace or wood stove
- Leaf mold of the snowless forest floor on a damp early winter day
- A Douglas or balsam fir Christmas tree and the delicious aroma of holiday food
- The resinous odor of conifers, especially on mild, sunny days, when you rub their leaves
- The spray of a skunk on a damp, late winter evening

Learn the Winter Woods by Smell

Go out for a walk in the woods, allowing each child to have a pair of scissors or, for older children, a small jackknife. Stop at various trees of interest and allow the children to snip off some foliage (cedar, pine, fir, hemlock, etc.), a large bud (balsam or black poplar) or a twig (yellow birch, tamarack, sassafras). Gather some resin from a pine and maybe a fir. Place each item in a separate small ziplock bag. Be sure to smell each sample as you take it. Crushing the foliage with the sides of the bag works well and keeps the oils off your fingers. You may need to cut the twig along its length or whittle it with the knife to release the smell. Tell the children the name of each species and, as a group, try to describe the smells. Write the name of the plant and a description of the smell on a piece of paper. Practice smelling for a few minutes while looking at the list. Then, working in pairs, try to identify each odor while wearing a blindfold. Poplar buds smell like the air on a spring day. Sassafras twigs have a particularly pleasant citrus scent. Larch twigs have a particularly pleasant smell. Who has the most accurate nose?

Winter feels like...

- The bite of cold wind and snow on your face
- The smoothness of an icicle
- The sheer pleasure of walking through fluffy snow
- The excitement of running and sliding on an icy surface
- The warmth of a wood fire

Meet a Tree

In this game, children work in pairs. One child is blindfolded and led through a forested area by the other to a given tree, perhaps 30 ft. (10 m) away. The blindfolded player explores the tree with his or her arms and hands and tries to get an idea of the diameter, the texture of the bark, whether it has any branches, lichens, holes or large roots, etc. The blindfolded child is then guided back to the starting point, taking a circuitous route. The blindfold is removed and the child has to find his or her tree.
(From *Sharing Nature with Children* by Joseph Cornell.)

White pine cone

Phenology

Winter Phenology: Track Seasonal Change

• **You'll learn:** How the local climate changes through the seasons and how plants and animals take their cues from these changes.

• **You'll need:** Winter Phenology Chart. (See the Appendix, page 329.)

• **Procedure:** As in the fall (see page 99), complete the Phenology Chart. After completing the chart, discuss how typical the season was compared to the long-term average. What really stands out?

Evolution

Meet the Beast Within You

• **You'll learn:** Some remnant body parts and behaviors that link you to your distant past.

• **You'll need:** Mirrors, plastic claws, ice or snow, tails made from twisted cloth, safety pins, string, items to smell, dog or dog photos.

• **Background:** Vestiges are body parts or behaviors our ancestors needed in the past, but that we no longer use today (or very little). Our bodies carry dozens of reminders of how we used to be five, seven or ten million years ago. However, humans are very different now: we no longer walk on all fours, we don't wear a thick coat of fur and we don't have a talent for climbing trees. Over time, we have evolved into the smooth-skinned, small-nailed, big-brained creatures we are today.

• **Procedure:** Follow the suggestions outlined in the chart on the following page.

Winter Adaptations Scavenger Hunt

• **You'll learn:** That almost every characteristic of an organism is an adaptation that helps it to survive.

• **You'll need:** Scavenger hunt sheets, (see Appendix, page 317), pencil, clipboard.

• **Background:** Especially in winter, all living things need strategies to deal with the cold, dryness, and lack of food. Through millions of years of natural selection, they have evolved traits (adaptations) to help them survive this difficult season. Some of these are behavioral (e.g., insect-eating birds like swallows migrate south where food will be available), others physical (e.g., birds fluff up their feathers to trap pockets of insulating air).

• **Procedure:** Visit an area with various habitat types, preferably including field, forest and wetland. Ask the children to try to find as many plant and animal adaptations to winter as possible from the following list. Encourage them to add

Our animal body part	Why we have this feature	What to do
Coccyx: The coccyx is located at the very bottom of your backbone and is the remnant of a lost tail.	Our early ancestors had a tail. Monkeys, who are fairly close relatives to humans, still do. None of the apes (a group that includes humans) has a tail, however. Humans still have a tail-like structure during part of the time they are an embryo. It is later absorbed and disappears (usually) before birth. Tails in the great apes may have disappeared because they were no longer needed for walking upright.	Have each child make a colorful animal tail. Ask them to tape this on the seat of their pants, just below the waist. Practice moving your tail in different ways to communicate different meanings. How do animals use their tails?
Canine teeth: Our early ancestors had much bigger canine teeth.	Canines were used for defending against attacks and for shredding tough meat and vegetation. Deep roots meant they would stay put when tearing into tough flesh. Today, they are not as noticeable in some people as in others.	Use a mirror to examine your own teeth. Have children feel for their canines—a set of pointy teeth located two teeth to the left and two teeth to the right of your two middle front teeth (top and bottom.) What do you notice? Are they longer and sharper? What animals do you know that still have long canines? Have everyone look at a dog's canines. How do you think they help a dog (wolf) survive? How would canines have served our early ancestors?
Smiles: When you make a big smile, the muscles in your face pull back, your skin wrinkles and all your teeth are revealed.	Smiles were an early human's way of scaring an enemy into running away, thereby avoiding a fight. They were no less than snarls. Today, smiling has the opposite meaning. A smile's meaning is not the same everywhere, however; in some Asian societies, people smile when they are embarrassed, angry, sad or confused.	Ask the children to make as wide a smile as possible, showing all their teeth. Discuss what "smiles" used to mean for early ancestors. How has the meaning of a smile changed? How might this have come about? Practice with a partner—was that a grin or a grimace?
Rhinarium: In humans, a rhinarium is a little depression or low area above your top lip and below your nose. Sometimes there is a ridge on each side.	Millions of years ago our rhinariums were not unlike those of a dog—a moist area of flesh that helped us to smell. Even today, if you wet your rhinarium, your sense of smell improves.	Ask children to run their finger along their rhinarium. Show the group the dog's rhinarium (bare, dark flesh around the nostrils). Ask them what the purpose of the rhinarium in ancient humans might have been. Explain that moistness improves the sense of smell. Have the children moisten their upper lip (see page 98). Try smelling different leaves, flowers, buds, etc. to see if you notice a difference.

Our animal body part	**Why we have this feature**	**What to do**
Ear wiggling: Early humans could move their ears to help in hearing, just like deer and some dogs do today.	The gene that controls your ear muscles has mutated in most humans and no longer works. Today, only about 10–20 percent of the population can still wiggle their ears.	Ask the children to wiggle their ears. Can anyone in the group do so? Ask them what animals can still do this and how it might be a useful adaptation. Ask them if it's a useful adaptation for modern humans.
Fingernails: Fingernails evolved from claws.	Over thousands of years our fingernails have been gradually disappearing in length, thickness and sharpness, due to gene mutations. At one time, they were important for defending us against our enemies.	Have the children hold up their hands and examine their fingers. Ask them what they think their fingernails evolved from and what purpose they served. Let the children put on some play claws and try doing some nimble activities like tying shoelaces or zipping a jacket. Ask them why they think claws evolved into fingernails?
Goose bumps: These bumps are the body's way to erect the thick hairs we once had.	Goose bumps are formed from tiny muscles called arrector pili. Raised hair insulates the body by trapping air, so we feel warmer. Raised hair also makes us look larger and more ferocious. You often see this when two dogs meet face to face for the first time: the hair on their back stands up immediately.	Have the children stick their arm in some cold water or snow until their skin looks like a "plucked goose." Ask them if they have ever felt the hair rise on their back of their neck or seen a dog's hair rise. What emotions are tied to this? Ask the children why our hairy coats may have disappeared.
Anger: A powerful emotion that overcomes us if we feel we have been wronged.	Long ago anger served a very important purpose. If our ancient ancestors had never became angry, they would have ended up losing everything to other people: their food, their spouse, etc. Now, thanks to civilization, education and our larger brains, we are better able to control our emotions and consider the implications of our actions.	Practice making the angriest face possible. Show one another your angry face. Who looks the angriest? Ask the children why getting angry would have evolved and been an advantage to early humans in some situations. How do modern humans control their anger?

other probable adaptations they see that are not on the list. The adaptation story for some items is explained. Then have the children provide their own ideas about what special adaptation(s) are associated with each item. Discuss the adaptations they found on their own.

Birds

Winter Bird Checklist Challenge

• **You'll learn:** The names and behaviors of the birds visiting your feeder and in your community.

• **You'll need:** Bird feeder, binoculars, bird guide or app.

• **Procedure:** Make a winter bird checklist using a large piece of Bristol board or a computer spreadsheet with the headings as they appear in the chart below.

In order to know what birds to put on your checklist, go to Project FeederWatch at feederwatch.org and click on Explore. Choose "Top 25 Birds" and then the year of your choice (probably the most recent). Click on your state or province from the dropdown menu. Look at the birds from several previous years as well. You may see that some species were quite common one year and lacking altogether in other years. These birds tend to be finches such as redpolls, grosbeaks, pine siskins and crossbills. They, too, should be added to your checklist, even though they may not appear every year. Depending on where you live in the state or province will also make a difference; feeder birds in lowland areas, for instance, can be quite different from those in mountains. How many species on the checklist can you attract to your yard and identify over the winter?

In addition to feeder birds, you might also want to include 25 other species you can see in your region in winter. Find this

Winter Bird Checklist

Bird species	Where seen?	Date	Time	Weather conditions	Food it was eating
Black-capped chickadee	at feeder	Feb 1, 2016	10 am	Clear, cold, –10°C	Black-oil sunflower seeds
Common goldeneye	on river	Feb. 5, 2016	2 pm	sunny, mild, 0°C	

Common redpolls, pine siskin and American goldfinch

information by going to eBird.org, clicking on Explore a Region, typing in the name of your county, clicking on Bar Charts and looking to see what species (in addition to the feeder birds) have thick green marks for December, January and February. How many of these 50 birds can you see between December 1 and the last day of February?

Activity 10 A Christmas Bird Count for Kids

• **You'll learn:** How to identify and count winter birds, while having a lot of fun.

• **You'll need:** Binoculars, bird guide or app.

• **Background:** Every year since 1900, "Christmas Bird Counts" (CBCs) have taken place across North America. They are rigorous dawn-to-dusk "citizen science" events designed mainly for adults and birding clubs. To get more young people involved, Tom Rusert and Darren Peterie of Sonoma Birding created CBC4Kids in 2007 in California. This stand-alone half-day event incorporates many of the features of the adult version, such as counting the numbers of different species of birds seen, but it is far less rigorous and is designed more like a game for kids aged 8 to 16. The objective is to contribute to citizen science while having fun and potentially creating a "hometown team" of birders and conservationists for the future. It is a wonderfully simple, healthy, holiday celebration for families, schools, youth groups, nature clubs or other environmental organizations.

• **Procedure:**

→ Start simple... it only takes two or three teams to get started! Target a date between the second weekend in December and early January.

→ Participants are divided into teams (named by the kids after a favorite bird!), each with an experienced adult as leader.

→ The teams pass through "Binocular Boot Camp" to hone binocular skills and birding basics.

- With their list of the most likely species to be seen, the teams have 90 minutes to cover a designated route and record the kinds and numbers of birds.
- The teams return for lunch and a much-anticipated result tabulation and celebration.
- Two kids from each team present some of the morning's highlights to the assembled crowd.
- The compiler tallies the overall results on a computer and enters them into the eBird database.
- Local clubs and businesses will often agree to sponsor a CBC4Kids event, by providing funding for food, field guides and maybe even a few pairs of binoculars.

Barn owl

Detailed step-by-step information can be found in the free "CBC4KIDS Playbook," which can be downloaded from the Sonoma Birding website (sonomabirding.com). In the U.S., you can contact Sonoma Birding for additional support documents and event coaching; in Canada, contact Bird Studies Canada at education@birdscanada.org.

Activity 11 The Great Backyard Bird Count (GBBC)

• **You'll learn:** Same as above.

• **You'll need:** Binoculars, bird guide or app.

• **Background:** Like the Christmas Bird Count, results (checklists) submitted during the GBBC help researchers at the Cornell Lab of Ornithology and the National Audubon Society learn more about how birds are faring and how to protect them and the environment we share. In 2014, more than 140,000 participants submitted their bird observations online. The GBBC is held over four days in mid February.

• **Procedure:** Simply count and identify the birds you see in your yard (or any other location) for at least 15 minutes. Count in as many places and on as many of the four days as you like. Go online and submit a separate checklist for each new day, for each new location, or for the same location if you counted at a different time of day. Estimate the number of individuals of each species you saw. You can count from any location, anywhere in the world! To make the event more kid-friendly, invite other children and their families to join you. You could even organize a "feeder party" with snacks and games. For more information, go to: gbbc.birdcount.org/.

 Prepare for Spring!

• **You'll learn:** The most common bird songs that herald spring.
• **You'll need:** Bird ID Skills: How to Learn Songs and Calls web page at All About Birds, allaboutbirds.org.
• **Background:** To the practiced ear, a chorus of bird song is like a symphony in which you recognize each of the individual instruments. Knowing at least the common songs adds a great deal to one's enjoyment of nature. The purpose of bird song is to attract mates and to "advertise" ownership of a nesting territory. Instead of singing, woodpeckers hammer on trees with their beaks to produce a "song," while ruffed grouse "drum" by using their wings to compress air and make a thumping sound. In North America, mostly males sing.

Birds also emit calls, which are much simpler than songs—often just one note long. Birds use calls to communicate with other birds such as family members. One common use of a call is to alert other birds about the presence of predators.
• **Procedure:** The easiest way to begin learning songs is to listen to recordings. Listen in the car, at home—anywhere and anytime. Start by listening to the most common species in your region, especially those species that are residents or return earliest in the spring. Memorizing bird song as pure sound is difficult. To make the task more manageable, convert each song to a mnemonic, a memory aid. For example, the red-breasted nuthatch sounds like a child's toy horn, while the American bittern's call is reminiscent of the sound of an old pump. Come up with your own gimmicks for remembering

"**Darwin:** Birds have evolved some pretty cool adaptations to the cold. Feathers are the first line of defense. Small muscles have evolved to control each feather, which they can both raise and lower. Using these muscles to "fluff up" their feathers, birds create tiny air spaces that drastically reduce heat loss—just like a down ski jacket! We are still not sure how low the temperatures can get before many species of birds can no longer stay warm."

a song. If a bird sounds like a squeaky clothesline, write this mnemonic down in your field guide. In addition to the mnemonic, pay attention to a quality of the song that really stands out. Is it the rhythm, pitch, tone or repetition?

Here are mnemonics for the songs of some common species. Others can be found online.

- Black-capped chickadee: *swee-tie* or *hi-cuty*—a clear, two-note whistle. The last note drops in pitch and is often double-pulsed. The chickadee's call is the well-known *chick-a-dee-dee-dee.*
- Northern cardinal: *cheer-cheer-whit-whit-whit-whit* or *birdy-birdy-birdy-birdy*—a loud, rich and persistent song, usually sung from a high perch.
- American robin: *cheerily-cheery-cheerily-cheer*—a series of short, sweet, musical whistles, rising and falling.
- European starling: *wheeee-err*—a long, down-slurred "wolf whistle," accompanied by an unmusical series of chips, squawks and squeaky notes. Starlings often sing from telephone wires.
- House finch: think of this bird as "the mad warbler" because of its loud, bubbly, quick-paced, warbled song. Harsh *churr* notes are often included.
- Mourning dove: *there's nothing to do*—very slow and "mourning," it could be mistaken for the hoot of an owl.
- Red-winged blackbird: *kon-ka-reeeee*—a harsh, gurgling song ending in a trill.
- Song sparrow: *maids-maids-maids-put-on-your-tea-kettle-ettle-ettle*—a variable, complex series of notes that includes one long trill in the middle.

Some simple games

- Play a recording to the children and have them guess what species is singing. Award points.
- Challenge the kids to make up their own mnemonics for common birds, instead of just using the traditional ones. The others could guess the species.
- Have one child imitate a bird's song by a means other than a word mnemonic—maybe by whistling or using some object—while the others try to guess the species.

Red-winged blackbird

Darwin: Bird song can evolve quite quickly. As vegetation has reclaimed former farmland in California, Oregon and Washington over the last 35 years, male white-crowned sparrows have lowered their pitch and slowed down their singing so that their love songs would carry better through heavier foliage. This is the first time that anyone has shown that bird songs can shift with rapid changes in habitat. Some birds also adapt their songs to noisy conditions such as cities by singing louder or longer.

Mammals

Activity 13 Make Tracks... What's Your Story?

• **You'll learn:** How to read the fascinating story of tracks.

• **You'll need:** Animal Tracking Table (on the following page); groups of three or more.

• **Background:** Winter is a wonderful time to study animal tracks. These are more than just marks crisscrossing the landscape; they tell a fascinating tale. Like words written on the ground, tracks record stories. With a few hints, a keen eye and bit of patience you too can learn to read the stories written in the soft mounds of snow or mud by the feet of local mammals and birds.

• **Procedure:** Practice reading tracks with this simple activity. Find an area with fresh snow. Ask your group to stand in a straight line with their backs to you. Make sure there is undisturbed snow behind them. As a way to distract your group and to disguise the noise you make, have them sing a song in unison. Now, right behind your group's backs, make a tracking pattern. Here are some suggestions:

- Jump with two feet
- Walk on all fours
- Lie in the snow
- Walk normally then run
- Hop on one foot
- Turn around and walk backwards

When you have a clear track, have your group pivot in the same spot and study the story you've just made. Don't forget to remind them that their feet are just like big erasers, able to wipe out your freshly made tracks. Can they tell you what happened? Here are some questions your group can try to answer when they encounter a track. Use your tracking story as a guide.

Animal Tracking Table

Pattern of Tracks	Example in snow	Who else walks this way?	Notes
Big Foot Little Foot	Raccoon: Hind—4″ (10 cm) Front—2½″ (6.4 cm) 5 toes each foot.	Porcupine	These animals tend to be stout-bodied. The larger hind foot lands close to or beside the front foot.
Hopping	Grey Squirrel: Hind—2½″ Front—1½″ 5 toes hind foot, 4 toes front foot	Rabbit Snowshoe Hare	Note how the back feet land ahead of the front feet. For squirrel racks, the front feet are usually beside each other (and a bit turned out). For rabbits, the front feet often land one in front of the other.
Bounding	Mink: Each foot 2½″ 5 toes on each foot	Weasel Martin Fisher	A 2 × 2 diagonal bound. If you are lucky enough to find river otter tracks, there will be a series of bounds along with a noticeable slide.
In a Line	Fox: Each foot 2½″ 4 toes on each foot	Fox Coyote Deer Wolf House Cat Dog	Tracks are generally in a straight line. This is an efficient mode of travel and saves energy (one foot falls right into the next). Some, like deer, are a bit offset. On the other hand, foxes travel with one foot right in front of the other. Because dogs aren't in a rush and are well fed and they don't need to save energy, their tracks tend to be a bit more erratic.

1. Which way was I going? Look for scuff marks: small but discernable marks that often appear at the rear of tracks. These can help you establish the direction of travel.
2. How far apart are my tracks? Most animals have a "harmonic gate"—their normal walking speed. When they run, their stride (the distance between their tracks) increases.
3. What was I doing? During the day, a white-tailed deer will often rest on the side of a hill. Sometimes you can spot the area where it has lain down (called a bed).
4. What pattern do my tracks have? This is often a clue to what animal has left the tracks. For example, rabbits hop with their two back legs beside each other and their front feet landing behind their back feet, one in front of the other. Raccoons often walk with their bigger rear foot beside their smaller front foot. Weasels, minks and other members of the mustelid family bound. Deer, fox and coyotes walk in fairly straight lines.

Something to think about

Now, after putting all the clues together, can you read the story of this track? Ask your group if they can tell you, just by looking at your tracks, exactly what you were doing. This activity is an excellent way to begin the art of tracking. Think about ways in which it might help you read other animal tracks.

Next step—take your group tracking!

When you encounter tracks, hunker down and look closely at their patterns. Here are some questions you can ask your group:

- Can you figure out which way the animal was going?
- Was it walking or running?
- Follow the tracks for a while. Do they disappear at a tree? Do they go into a bush or under the snow?
- Can you find any evidence that the animal was eating something (browsing)? Can you find any scat or urine?
- Did it meet any other animals? What do you think happened here?
- Who do you think made these tracks? Don't be too quick to decide. Try putting all the clues together—habitat, pattern of tracks, number of toes, what it was doing.

Use the Animal Tracking Table on the previous page to guess what animal might be passing by.

Make a Tracking Stick

• **You'll learn:** How to follow tracks when there is no snow.
• **You'll need:** A ¾-in. (2-cm) dowel about 2 ft. (60 cm) long; two hair elastics.
• **Procedure:** Place a hair elastic on each end of the dowel. If you find tracks in the soft mud, slide the hair bands up and down on the tracking stick to measure the animal's stride (the distance between the heel of one paw print and the heel of the next print). Once the tracks leave the mud, flip the tracking stick over to work out were the next paw print *should* be. Look for subtle disturbances (bent grass, scuff mark, scratches, etc.). Follow the trail as far as you can.

Activity 15 Animal Signs in Winter: Scat

• **You'll learn:** How to identify animals by their scat.

• **You'll need:** Scat scarf (available at Acorn Naturalists) or pictures/drawings of scat, sticks to probe scat.

• **Background:** Kids are fascinated and repelled by animal pooh in equal measure. Animal "scat" (as scientists like to call it) helps us identify what animals share our green spaces, as it is one obvious sign they have been passing by.

• **Procedure:** If you find some scat, examine its shape, color and consistency. Some questions you might ask are:

- Does it have hair in it? (If so, it probably comes from a carnivore like a coyote or fox.)
- Is it long and tubular with blunt ends? (It may be from a raccoon.)
- Is it a pellet? (Round pellets indicate cottontail rabbit or hare; longer pellets may indicate deer; curved pellets may be from a porcupine or grouse.)
- Is it twisted, with pointed ends? (It may be from a weasel or mink.)
- Is it woody in consistency? (Might be from a beaver.)
- Did you find it in the middle of a trail? (Some animals, like coyotes, use scat to mark their territory).

Try this scat rap on for size. Start by alternating between slapping your thighs and clapping your hands, in rhythm. Have kids repeat each line of the rap as you slap and clap.

Scat Rap

It starts with an "S," ends with a "T."
It comes out of you, and it comes out of me.
I know what you're thinking, but don't call it that,
Be scientific, and call it SCAT.

If you wanna find out what animals eat,
Take a good look at what they excrete.
Stuck in the scat are all kinds of clues,
Parts of the food that their bodies can't use.

Down by the creek on a hollow log,
Scat full of berries and bones of frogs.
Fresh last night he was out with the Moon,
Hunting crawdads, it was Mr. Raccoon.

You park your car by a wood or field,
Gonna find scat on your window shield.
Full of seeds, purple and white,
You just got bombed by a bird in flight.

If you wanna know what's in the woods or around,
Take a good long look at the scat on the ground.
It tells us what they eat and tells us who they are,
And that's what we know about scat so far.

White-tailed deer scat

Activity 16 Browse or Chew Marks

• **You'll learn:** What animals are in the area by the way they feed.

• **Procedure:** Watch for signs that animals have been feeding on plants. Evidence includes cut or seemingly broken branches. Naturalists refer to these as "browse marks." Different animals leave different chew signs. Here are some chew signs to watch out for:

- Deer have a hard palate instead of teeth on their upper jaw. So when a deer forages, it tends to leave behind a torn, ragged-looking browse mark.
- Rabbits have sharp teeth on their upper and lower jaws. When they chew, it looks almost as if someone cut a twig with a knife—often at about a 45-degree angle.
- Red squirrels love to chew on cones (pine, spruce, hemlock, fir). You can find piles of loose scales and the center core of cones near logs and trees.

Activity 17 Hole Patrol

• **You'll learn:** That holes in trees provide valuable shelter for animals.

• **You'll need:** Hole cards, forest with dead trees and natural cavities.

• **Background:** It may be hard to believe, but a dead tree can often provide more valuable shelter for animals than a live tree. Standing trees that are dead are referred to as *snags*. Perhaps due to a lightning strike, disease, old age, drought or too much shade, these standing "hotels" provide critical shelter for birds, mammals, insects, reptiles and amphibians, which use them as nurseries, roosting sites, for food storage, etc. Sometimes the size of the cavity in a snag can give us a clue about what critter might occupy it.

• **Procedure:** Photocopy the Hole Patrol Cards provided on the following page and distribute these to the group.

Go for a walk in a forest with some older trees, where there are likely to be snags. Use the Hole Patrol Cards to help you guess which species may live in your neighborhood. Compare the size of your hole with your card. Look for additional clues such as feathers, scat, pellets, chewed cones, tracks and scratch marks.

Suspended Animation—Mammal Hibernation

• **You'll learn:** How much the breathing and heart rates of "true hibernators" slow down.

• **You'll need:** Watch or smartphone.

• **Background:** One way to survive the cold winter is to hit the "pause (paws) button." In other words—fall into a deep, deep sleep until spring, when the weather warms up and more food becomes available. The mammals that can do this—including groundhogs and jumping mice—are called true hibernators. They enter into a near death-like state. Others, such as bears, enter a state of deep sleep called torpor. Some, like raccoons and skunks, sleep much of the time but will venture out of their refuge during mild spells.

Hole Patrol Cards

1½ in. or 3 cm
chickadee, flying squirrel, downy woodpecker, brown creeper, house wren, little brown bat, nuthatch

3 to 4 in. or 7 to 12 cm or more
gray and red squirrels, American kestrel, wood duck, screech owl, bufflehead

1.6 to 2 in. or 4 to 4.5 cm
tree swallow, hairy woodpecker, great crested fly catcher, white-breasted nuthatch, saw whet owl, northern flicker, red-headed woodpecker

Darwin: Evolution has done some amazing things when it comes to groundhog hibernation. The animal's heart rate slows from between 80 and 100 beats per minute to around four or five beats. A groundhog will breathe in and out only once every six minutes! Its body receives the small amount of nutrition it requires from the fat layer the animal built up in the summer and fall. A groundhog's body temperature drops from 98°F (36.7°C) to only 38°F (3.3°C), which is almost as low as the air temperature of the burrow itself. Hibernation can last anywhere from two to five months, depending on the region.

For mammals like foxes, coyotes and deer, however, winter means business as usual as they search for food.

• **Procedure:** Sit down for a while. Now count your resting heart rate. How many beats per minute? Count your breathing. How many breaths in and out per minute? Now compare this to a hibernating groundhog. Who do you think uses more energy—you or the sleeping groundhog?

Activity 19 Stay Warm

• **You'll learn:** How well you can create a shelter to keep your imaginary "critter" warm.

• **You'll need:** Film canisters or yogurt containers with tight-fitting lids, warm water, thermometers.

• **Background:** Even in the coldest of winters, animals can survive. Many use whatever material is at hand to protect them from the cold. A deer will find a hillside and a hollow away from the prevailing winds. A snowshoe hare might scoop out a hollow under the overhanging branches of an evergreen, a vole could weave grasses together to create a cozy nest and a fox may curl its warm brush (tail) around itself.

• **Procedure:**

- Have children go outside and make a shelter for their "critter." Use whatever insulating materials that may be at hand, e.g., dried grass, leaves, moss and/or snow. Think about design considerations:
- What natural materials will best insulate it?
- Make sure your critter will be insulated all the way around: above, beside and below.

- Think about how much insulation you'll need. It might be helpful to consider how a squirrel's drey, a bird's nest and a beaver's lodge is made.
- Fill canisters with warm water. Measure the temperature and record.
- Carefully close the lid.
- Place your critter in the shelter you've made for one hour.
- Remove and measure the temperature. How did you do?

• **Modification:** Use liquid Jell-O instead of warm water. Here the idea is to stop your critter from turning into solid Jell-O. You can eat the results!

• **Try this:** Can snow act like an insulator? Use mounded snow and place your canister inside for one hour—compare this to a canister left in the open air for the same length of time. Which canister was warmer? Why?

Deer mouse and tunnel in snow

Amphibians and Reptiles

Activity 20 Go Winter Salamandering

• **You'll learn:** Some behaviors of salamanders in winter.

• **You'll need:** Field guide or app.

• **Background:** A winter-active salamander is the eastern newt. There are two distinct stages in a newt's life. As a juvenile, these salamanders are bright orange and live entirely on land. In this stage, they are known as "red efts." As adults, however, they become olive-green with black-rimmed red spots, and are mostly aquatic.

• **Procedure:** Well-vegetated ponds, marshes and ditches with pristine water are the preferred habitat of adult-phase eastern newts. Large numbers can sometimes be seen swimming or resting in ice-free water or even viewed through a layer of ice. Why newts congregate like this in winter (sometimes 100 or more!) is not known, so keep your eyes open when visiting ponds in winter. Maybe your observations will shed new light on the mystery of newt convocations!

Darwin: Eastern newts have toxins in their skin as a defense against predation. In the red eft stage, they are brightly colored, and as adults they have showy red spots. In this way, evolution has also ensured that predators are forewarned of the poisonous nature of these tiny creatures, because it doesn't help the salamander very much if it ends up being spit out of a predator's mouth as a sodden mass! Its colors say, 'Back off. I'm dangerous!' Brightly colored monarch butterflies, poison dart frogs and coral snakes have evolved the same early-warning system. How cool is that!

Activity 21 Frozen, but Alive!

• **You'll learn:** How glucose protects hibernating frogs.

• **You'll need:** Basin, thermometer, two small glasses, ice cubes, water, salt, sugar packet, marker.

• **Background:** Glucose, like the antifreeze in your car's engine, lowers the freezing point of water. In this activity, think of the sugar as a form of glucose. The lowering of the freezing point of the liquid in a cell protects it from freezing and ripping open (remember, liquid expands when it freezes). In species that overwinter frozen in the leaf litter—"frogsicles"—the frog's liver converts glycogen to glucose, which prevents ice crystals from forming in the cells and killing the frog. Any water outside of the cells does freeze, but does no damage.

• **Procedure:** Fill a basin with about .5 pt. (250 ml) of ice and water and wait until the mixture reaches 32°F (0°C). Use a thermometer to check. Add ¼ c. (60 g) of salt, which will lower the temperature of the water even further. Add 2 tsp. (10 ml) of cold tap water to two small glasses labeled A and B. Add sugar to B. Place both glasses into the basin containing the salted ice water. Wait about ten minutes and compare the two glasses. The water in glass A should have frozen, while the water–sugar mixture in glass B should have remained liquid. Why do you think that was? What does this tell us about how frogs (and nearly all insects) survive the winter?

Fishes

Take the Kids Ice Fishing

• **You'll learn:** How to catch fish through the ice.

• **You'll need:** A sled or toboggan to transport your fishing gear, an ice auger, a skimmer, an ice chisel, a bait bucket (should you choose to use live minnows), a small folding chair or bucket to sit on, needle-nose pliers to remove hooks, a jigging rod and/or tip-up, hooks (no. 10 or 12 for panfish), lures, light monofilament line, leaders, hot chocolate and snacks, a cell phone, small stove, a portable shelter if you have one.

• **Procedure:** Just because it's winter doesn't mean you can't go out and have some fishing fun. Some of our best-tasting fish are biting, including bluegills, yellow perch, northern pike, walleye, and rainbow trout. Furthermore, there's something special about being out on a frozen lake on a calm, clear winter day. Just be sure to bundle up, since it's hard to have any fun if you're cold. This means wearing a knitted or fleece hat that covers your ears, a scarf or neck gaiter, mittens, layers of warm clothes, thick wool socks and insulated winter boots.

The main concern when going ice fishing, of course, is making sure that the ice is safe. This means waiting until that it is at least 4 in. (10 cm) thick. The following mnemonic can come in handy: "Thick and blue, tried and true. Thin and crispy, way too risky." Once you've found a promising location on the lake, drill a hole 1 ft. (30 cm) wide completely through the ice with an auger. Let the kids help with the drilling. You may also want to widen the hole with an ice chisel. When the hole is ready, get out your special lures, jigging sticks (short fishing rods) or tip-ups (a special "pole" for ice fishing), portable seat or bucket and a skimmer to clear the hole of ice and slush. Once everything is set up and your line is in the water, keep a close eye on the line or watch the flag on the tip-up to see if you've caught a fish. For something truly memorable, enjoy a fish lunch right out on the ice. All you need is a small stove, a frying pan and maybe some butter. Fresh fish and hot chocolate on a crisp winter's day makes for an unforgettable experience. (See color section, figure 27.)

Invertebrates

You've Got a Lot of Gall!

• **You'll learn:** To understand how some insects overwinter as larvae in plant galls.

• **You'll need:** Scissors or pruning shears, small knife.

- **Background:** Imagine sitting in the snow with no coat or jacket, no boots or shoes, no hat or mittens. You would be freezing within minutes! Insects face this same dilemma. They have to find strategies to help them survive the crushing cold of winter. Different kinds of insects have evolved to overwinter in different stages of their life cycle: crickets as eggs, woolly bear caterpillars and gall flies as larvae, swallowtail butterflies as pupae, dragonflies as nymphs and honeybees as adults.

The goldenrod gall fly (*Eurosta solidaginis*) is found throughout much of North America and only lays eggs on goldenrod. Only ¼ in. (5 mm) in size, the adult fly emerges from the gall in late spring. As with most insects, its adult life is brief—only about two weeks. This just gives these flies enough time to find a mate and for the females to deposit their eggs on the tip of newly emerging goldenrod stems. They lay more than one egg in each stem, but only one larva tends to survive for each gall. The larva eats its way into the plant stem and creates a chamber. The plant responds to the chewing of the larva and its saliva by growing a round deformation around the chamber. The larva spends the winter in this cozy shelter. In the spring, it chews out a tunnel as an escape route, almost to the outer surface of the gall. It then moves back towards the center and pupates in a cocoon-like puparium. The adult emerges from the puparium, wanders down the tunnel and, by inflating a spiny, balloon-like structure on its head, pushes its way out of the gall. And so begins another life cycle!

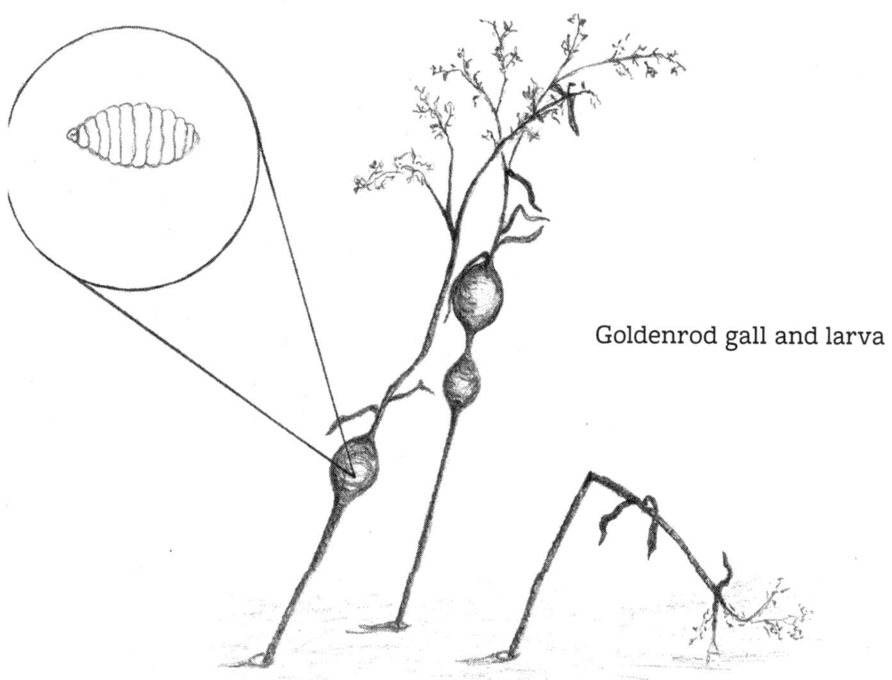

Goldenrod gall and larva

• **Procedure:** Visit a field or roadside with goldenrods and look for galls. If you find one with a ragged hole in the side, this means it has been robbed! A chickadee or downy woodpecker has pecked open the gall and eaten the grub inside. When you find healthy galls, allow each child to use pruning shears to remove these (along with an inch or so of stem) from the plant. Carefully push the blade of a knife into the gall along the stem axis (parallel to the stem), inserting it no more than ¼ in. (1 cm). Twist the knife blade sharply until the gall splits open. Look for the small white grub (fly larva) inside. You may need to try more than one gall before you find a healthy grub. Depending on the age of the children, you may allow everyone to do this individually. Explain once again that the grub will pupate inside the ball in the spring and exit as an adult fly. You can also try putting the grub into a freezer for a couple of hours. When it's frozen, remove it and watch it warm up and start squirming again. Now, how amazing is that!

Allow each child to take a gall home to witness the rest of the life cycle. Place the gall upright in a glass jar and put this in an unheated spot like a balcony or garage. Starting in early May, check the jar for signs of life. With luck, you should eventually find an adult goldenrod gall fly in the jar.

Winter Insect Scavenger Hunt

• **You'll learn:** The signs of insects, even in mid-winter.

• **You'll need:** Insect sign checklist (next page), pencil, hand lens.

• **Procedure:** A winter outing can be made all the more enjoyable by keeping an

Darwin: You might wonder why the fly larva doesn't freeze to death in the winter. Well, it's because many kinds of insects have evolved freeze tolerance. In the fall, the larva starts to produce large amounts of glycerol, which acts as an antifreeze and stops the insect's body cells from freezing. If the cells froze, they would split open and the insect would die. In the spring, glycerol levels drop again. Amazingly, freeze tolerance has evolved separately in at least six groups of insects, including beetles, butterflies and flies. It has also evolved in some frogs, turtles, plants, fungi and bacteria.

1. Sketching in a nature journal (see p. 49)

2. Nature photography with a smartphone (see p. 51)

3. School birding club (see p. 32)

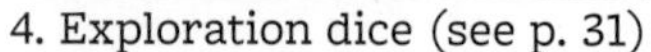
4. Exploration dice (see p. 31)

5. Basement windows activity (see p. 31)

6. Humans are the universe becoming aware of itself (see p. 78)

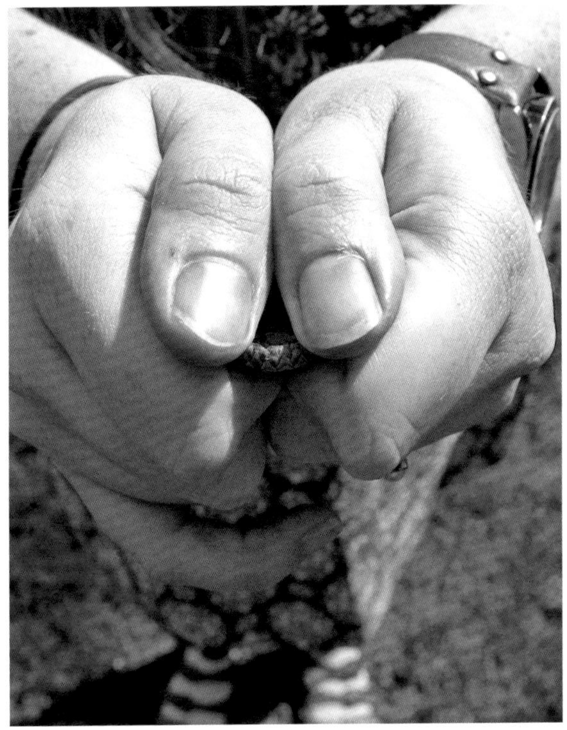

7. Acorn whistle (see p. 97)

8. Pressed fall leaves (see p. 130)

9. Understanding the phases of the moon (see p. 140)

10. Debris survival hut (see p. 134)

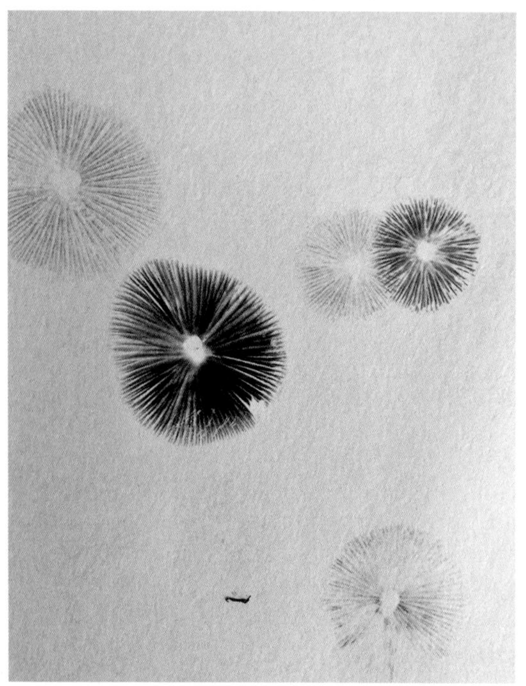

11. Mushroom spore prints (see p. 133)

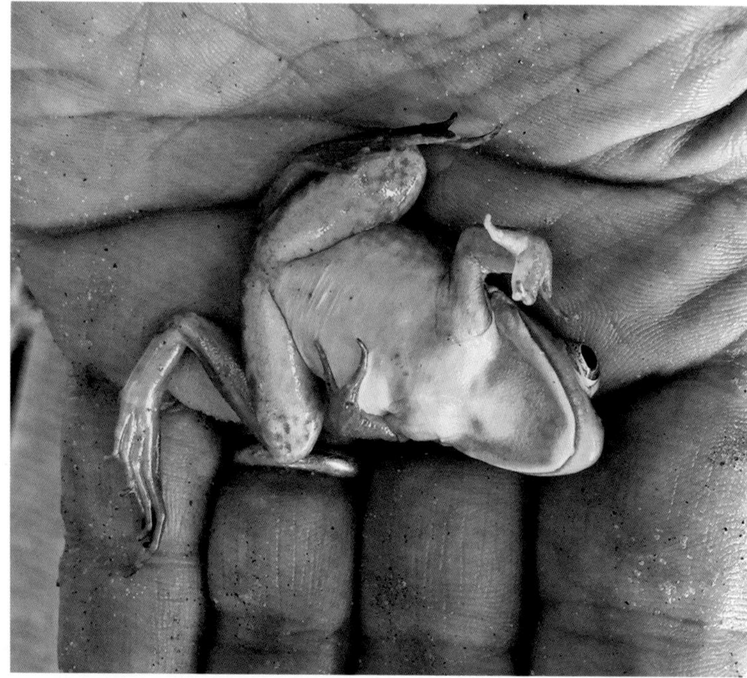

12. Hynotized frog (see p. 115)

13. Watching monarch emerge from chrysalis (see p. 117)

14. Stained glass window (see p. 130)

15. Leaf rubbings (see p. 131)

16. Barefoot walk (see p. 99)

17. Monarch on mexican sunflower (see p. 179)

18. Lichens come in many shapes and colors (see p. 185)

19. Snow snake (see p. 194)

20. Ice lantern (see p. 193)

21. Flowerpot sundial (see p. 190)

22. Paper snowflakes (see p. 190)

23. Quinzhee (see p. 187)

24. (L to R) Honeysuckle, ash, maple, lilac, viburnum, elderberry, dogwood (see p. 184)

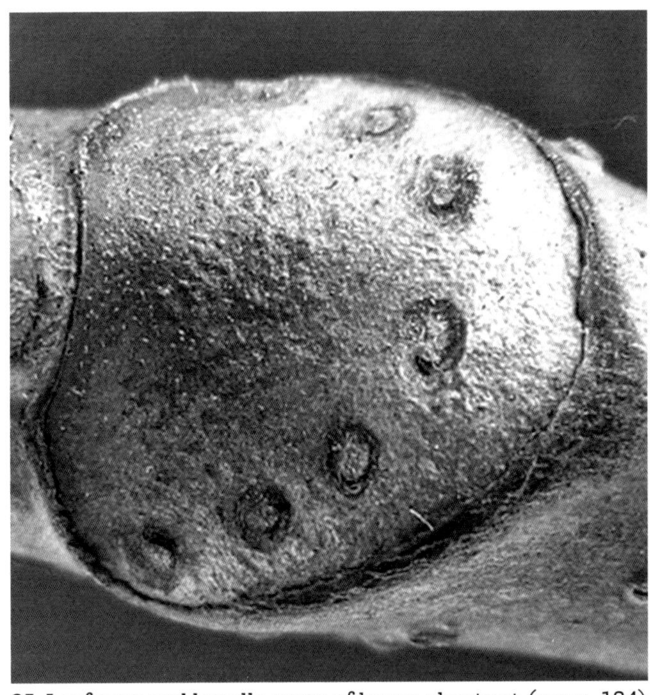

25. Leaf scar and bundle scars of horse-chestnut (see p. 184)

26. Hand-feeding chickadees (see p. 154)

27. Ice fishing (see p. 176)

28. Forest tea (see p. 157)

29. Tree face (see p. 156)

30. Celebrating Earth Day (see p. 252)

31. Cloud in a jar (see p. 249)

32. Artist's Conk (*Ganoderma applanatum*) (see p. 246)

33. Hammered plant pattern (see p. 245)

34. Gyotaku fish print (see p. 236)

35. Snake slither (see p. 233)

36. Smell cocktail (see p. 217)

37. Micro trail (see p. 213)

38. Spreading bark chips in naturalized area of schoolyard (see p. 252)

39. Pistil & multiple stamens in flower (see p. 241)

40. Decorating Easter eggs (see p. 252)

41. Tide pool on the coast of Oregon (see p. 287)

42. Worm fiddling (see p. 290)

43. Identifying pond invertebrates (see p. 294)

44. Twig Weaving (see p. 299)

45. Playing the Great Green Gobbler (see p. 285)

46. Focused hearing (see p. 270)

47. Pirate eye (see p. 269)

48. Fossil hunting can be an engrossing pastime (see p. 274)

eye open for evidence of previous insect activity or even seeing insects themselves in all stages of their life cycle. Here are a few things to look for. Be sure to record all other signs of insects that you discover as well. Take some time, too, to look at galls, insect eggs and any live insects with a hand lens. Oak apple galls are especially interesting to cut open and look at.

- □ Goldenrod galls containing larval fly (ball on stem of goldenrod plants).
- □ Oak apple gall containing larval wasp (apple-like, on oak trees).
- □ Pine cone willow gall containing larval midge (pine cone-like, on willows).
- □ Tunnels made by bark beetle larvae in logs or tree trunks.
- □ Ragged fall webworm nests on numerous broad-leaved tree species.
- □ Empty tent caterpillar nests on cherry trees.
- □ Tent caterpillar eggs (inside of shiny, brown rings encircling twigs of cherries).
- □ European mantis eggs in foamy, tan-colored cases on twigs and stems.
- □ Cocoons (pupae) such as the 2-inch- (5-cm-) long, brown, silken cocoon of the *Cecropia* moth.
- □ Insect nymphs and larvae on or under rocks and branches in streams.
- □ Hibernating adult insects such as butterflies and queen wasps nestled under loose bark.
- □ Active, adult snow fleas, spiders, wingless scorpion flies, wingless winter crane flies and winter stoneflies on snow.

Plan a Pollinator Garden

• **You'll learn:** That with a bit of planning, you can attract a variety of pollinators to your yard.

• **You'll need:** Paper, pencil.

• **Background:** Pollinators are animals that transfer pollen, allowing flowers to be pollinated. We can thank pollinators for the grapefruit we have for breakfast, the carrots in our snacks and many of the wildflowers that carpet our forests and fields. Bees are our most important pollinators, but flies, moths, butterflies, beetles, hummingbirds and certain bats pollinate as well. When we think of bees, most of us think of the honeybee, a species introduced from Europe. Although incredibly valuable, many native bees, such as mason bees, sweat bees, squash bees and bumblebees, are actually more effective and efficient pollinators. Most of these bees are solitary, which means each female makes her own nest, deposits some food, lays her eggs and provides little further care. Bumblebees, however, do form a small colony, which starts anew each spring with just the queen. Like any bee, solitary bees and bumblebees are unlikely to sting unless directly threatened. As with honeybees and monarch butterflies, our native North American solitary bees and bumblebees are under threat for many reasons including habitat loss, pesticides and disease. By creating a pollinator-friendly garden, you will be helping our native pollinators.

• **Procedure:** Winter is a good time to sit down with a paper and pencil and plan how you can help bees and other pollinators on your property. The two key features of good bee habitat are a wide range of bee-friendly flowers and lots of good nesting sites. As for monarchs, milkweed plants are a must. Many of the species listed below (e.g., Mexican sunflower, fireweed) will also attract hummingbirds. Here are some guidelines to follow:

⊸ Use (or plan for) a garden in a sunny location.

⊸ Choose mostly native plants, because many exotics produce very little nectar and pollen. If you do plant exotics, try to find heirloom varieties.

⊸ Be sure to include plants that will provide pollen and nectar from early spring through fall.

1. Spring: Wild strawberry, wild geranium, wild apple (*Malus pumila*), blueberry, chokecherry, serviceberry, staghorn sumac, dogwood, willow, lilac (*Syringa meyeri 'Palibin'*)

2. Summer: Bergamot, buttonbush, purple coneflower, Culver's root, meadowsweet, New Jersey tea, milkweed, hyssop, Joe-Pye weed, common sunflower (*Helianthus annus*), pumpkin/squash, lamb's ear, comfrey, Russian sage, nodding onion, prairie clover, native roses, fireweed

3. Late summer and fall: Aster, goldenrod, blue vervain, cup plant, false sunflower (*Heliopsis helianthoides*), Mexican sunflower (*Tithonia rotundifolia*), butterfly bush (Buddleia), Verbena (*Verbena bonairiensis*)

⊸ Plant clusters of three to five of each flower species.

⊸ Provide a shallow dish of water, with partly submerged stones as perches, and

Monarch butterfly

a muddy patch where bees can collect mud for nesting.

- In addition to the garden, allow a corner of your yard to go wild with grasses, weeds, etc.
- Consider planting a patch of soil-improving plants, such as clovers, alfalfa and buckwheat, which provide a veritable feast of nectar and pollen.
- To attract night-flying moths, some good choices are evening primrose and yucca (e.g., *Yucca glauca* if you live in the central U.S.).
- Establish and protect suitable nesting sites for bees. If you have a large property, reserve some south-facing slopes and field margins for this purpose (keep grass cut short). Some species will also nest in sandy areas, including abandoned sandboxes. If you grow raspberries, don't destroy the old stems, but keep them in vertical bundles in the garden for at least a year. Yellow-faced and leafcutter bees will use them for nesting.
- You can also make artificial nests for stem-dwelling bees, including mason and leaf-cutters, by bundling together the hollow stems of Phragmites (also called common reed). Cut 20 stems to a variety of different lengths of about 6–8 in. (15–20 cm), bundle them together with string and place them in a plastic pail or similar container lying on its side. This provides protection from the elements. Attach the pail to a branch or post, so that the stems face east or southeast. Xerces.org provides information on building a variety of native bee nesting structures. You can also purchase commercially made bee nesting tubes from websites such as crownbees.com—their BeeEndeavour Kit is excellent. (See color section, figure 17.)

Plants

Activity 26 We're "Needling" You

• **You'll learn:** How to identify conifers by their needles and their silhouettes.

• **Background:** Knowing the common conifers adds to our enjoyment of the holiday season and of nature in general. Although the needles are your main clue, many species also have a distinctive silhouette that allows identification at a distance.

• **Procedure:** On the following page you will find a list of the needle characteristics of the main conifer families as well as some helpful memory aids or mnemonics to remember them. To practice these mnemonics, try to identify the evergreens in your holiday decorations, in your yard, in your neighborhood, during a winter nature walk, or even those you see from the car. You might also want to make a display of the different types of conifer needles (and cones, if you wish) in your area.

On the next page is a chart on needle characteristics and mnemonics. Remember: The mnemonics begin with the same letter or sound as the type of conifer.

Get the Point: Needle Characteristics and Mnemonics

Spruce needles **spiral** along the branch and are sharp like **spikes**, so they are painful to the touch. Because they are rounded, they roll or **spin** between your thumb and finger.
Fir needles are **flat** and very **flexible**. They don't roll!
Pine needles are usually very long like **pins**. White pine, a common species in the east, has the same number of needles as the number of letters in the word *white*, namely five.
Cedars have **scale**-like, flattened leaves, just like fish that live in the sea! (*"sea"dar*).
Hemlock needles are very small, green on top and appear white underneath. To connect the needles to the word hemlock, think of the prefix **hemi**, which means half. Hemlock needles are half white and half green.
Juniper: two types of leaves (often on the same tree), small scale-like leaves, similar to those of a cedar, as well as longer (¼-in./6-mm) dark blue–green needle-like leaves. Think of a **pair** of different leaves and *juni"pair."*
Larches or tamaracks are **leafless** in winter. The rest of the year, they have tufts of up to 20 very soft, **limp** needles.

Shapes of some common conifers

Identification by shape

- White spruce: symmetrical, conical, wide, not pointed at top.
- Balsam fir: narrow, symmetrical, tapered, pointed at the top. Resembles a church spire.
- Douglas fir: pyramidal; unique cones with a protruding, tongue-like, three-pointed bract.
- Eastern white cedar: dense, cone-shaped branches often go right to the ground.
- Western hemlock: irregular, horizontal branches; top often bent, drooping branchlets giving a graceful appearance.
- White pine: often asymmetrical; branches at right angles to trunk, sometimes look like large wings.

My Adopted Tree

• **Procedure:** As explained in the Fall chapter (see page 129), complete the winter section of "My Adopted Tree" on page 339.

Darwin: Trees have evolved some pretty incredible adaptations to survive winter cold. Remember, a tree is about half water—and water freezes! If you are going to survive winter, you can't allow your living cells to freeze. How does a tree do this? 1. As winter approaches, a lot of the water moves out of the cells and into spaces between cells. The cells, therefore, shrink and occupy less space. 2. In the fall, trees convert starch (made in photosynthesis) into sugar, which acts like a natural antifreeze. Cell fluids become concentrated with these sugars, which lowers the freezing point inside the cell. Sugar-free water between cells is allowed to freeze. The sugary fluid in the cell becomes so thick that it appears almost glass-like; however, no damaging ice crystals form. To do all of this, trees need a lot of genes, which are like sets of instructions. As it turns out, they have many more genes than even humans; the black cottonwood poplar (*Populus trichocarpa*) has more than 45,000 genes, about twice as many as we do. Remember, too, that trees are our distant cousins. In fact, we still share many of the same genes. For example, about 50 percent of human genes can also be found in banana trees! This is an amazing example of the common heritage we share with all other forms of life.

Activity 28 Hey, Bud!

• **You'll learn:** To identify the deciduous trees by their buds, leaf scars and twigs.

• **You'll need:** Hand lens, twigs from a variety of deciduous trees.

• **Background:** Like meeting old friends while you are out strolling around town, walking through the woods—even in winter—is more enjoyable if you can recognize at least some of the trees and shrubs you see. Buds, twigs and even leaf scars can help us. Let's begin with buds. They are located on twigs, which are the part of the branch that grew the previous summer. At the point where a twig begins, you will see two to five rows of narrow grooves that appear jammed together. Twigs have a different color, texture and patterning from the older branches. Contrary to popular belief, buds don't suddenly appear in the spring but have actually been present on the twig since the late summer. Hidden inside are the beginnings of next spring's leaves, stems and, sometimes, flowers. Thick, overlapping scales protect the buds from the cold, snow and ice. (See color section, figure 25.)

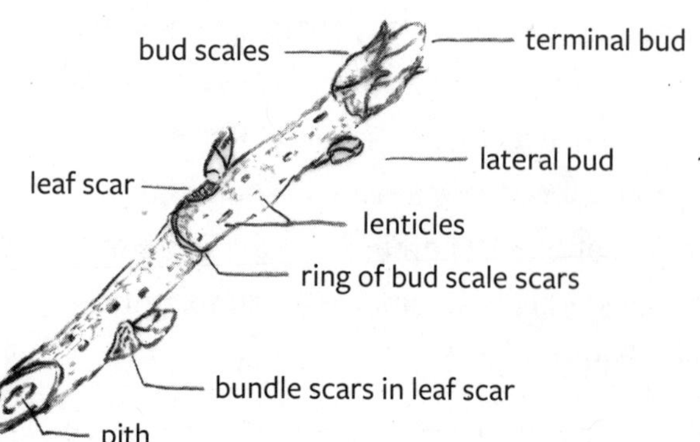

Twigs usually have buds growing from the side (lateral buds) and a bud or buds growing at the end (terminal bud), where most of the new growth will come from. Each bud also has a leaf scar right below it. This is where last summer's leaf was attached. Leaf scars are visible to the naked eye but are best appreciated by using a hand lens. If you look carefully inside the scar, you will see tiny markings known as bundle scars where veins passed from the stem of the leaf into the twig. These veins carried water into the leaf and food—made through photosynthesis—back out into the twig and to the rest of the tree. The bundle scars often make the leaf scar look like a little face. Because buds almost always form in the angle between the stem and the stalk of the leaf, both leaves and buds have the same arrangement on the twig. This arrangement is usually alternate (staggered) or opposite. Most species are alternate. Honeysuckle, ash, maple, lilac, viburnum, elderberry and dogwood are the principal tree and shrub genera with opposite leaves and buds; just about all the others are alternate. The following mnemonic—which unintentionally sounds like a rallying call for animal rights—may be helpful in remembering these seven genera: HAM LIVED! (each genus except lilac corresponds to one letter in the mnemonic; Lilac corresponds to LI). Start by learning the opposite buds, especially maple, ash and dogwood, and then move on to some of the common and distinctive alternate species like poplar, elm and willow.

• Procedure:

1. See what's inside a bud? Try opening some buds to see what's inside. Lilac and horse chestnut buds work especially well. Using your fingers and/or pins, try peeling back the scales and unfolding the contents. Count the tiny leaves inside. A hand lens will come in handy. Can you already see the shape of the leaves? Children are often amazed to see so many tiny leaves hidden inside such a small object. Horse chestnut buds may have flowers in them. For small children, try cutting open some Brussel sprouts, which are actually large, immature leaf buds containing tightly overlapping leaves.

2. Make a twig collection: Collect the twigs of the most common trees and shrubs of your area. Attach these to a piece of cardboard with a glue gun, grouping them by opposite and alternate. Make sure you include twigs with both side and terminal buds. Cutting the twigs at an angle will expose the pith (the inside of the twig), which can also help in identification. Label each species.

3. Twinkle (a combination of a twig and a wrinkle): Find a big deciduous tree (one that loses its leaves in the winter). Get comfortable and sit with your back against its trunk. Look up. Your tree has a shape and a character that is completely unique. That's partially because of the kind of tree it is and partially because of the particular soil, and the amount of water and sunlight that have nurtured it. It is perfectly suited to be in this spot at right this time. There will never be another tree exactly like this one, just like there will never be another person just like you! Observe the intricate patterning of branches and twigs of your tree. Now study the wrinkles on the palm of your hands. Notice how they branch just like the twigs of a tree. Can you find a branching pattern in the tree that exactly matches these wrinkles? Somewhere on that tree is a close match! (See color section, figure 24.)

Fungi

Activity 29 Like Lichens!

• You'll learn: To identify and appreciate the diversity of lichens.

• You'll need: Hand lens, natural area with lots of lichens.

• Background: Of all the conspicuous organisms, lichens are probably the most overlooked. However, with fewer plants and mushrooms around to compete for your eye's attention, winter can be a good time to get to know this interesting division of the fungi kingdom. Lichens are actually "dual organisms" consisting of an alga and a fungus living together as a single unit for mutual benefit. The fungus—the visible portion of the lichen—provides the alga with protection and a "house" to live in. It also supplies the alga with mineral nutrients and water, both of which the fungus absorbs from the surrounding surface and directly from the air. The alga, in turn, makes food for the fungus by using sunlight to photosynthesize glucose.

Lichens survive the cold of winter by drying out to the point of becoming brittle. If temperatures climb above freezing, however, and they can get enough moisture, they can photosynthesize and grow even in winter. Lichens come in four growth forms: leaf lichens (e.g., rock tripe), cup lichens (e.g., British soldiers), shrub lichens (e.g., reindeer moss) and hair lichens (e.g., old man's beard). They grow on everything from bark and rock to even bricks. Ruby-throated hummingbirds use parmelia lichens to build their nests. Lichens can also tell us about air quality, because many species die when the air gets polluted.

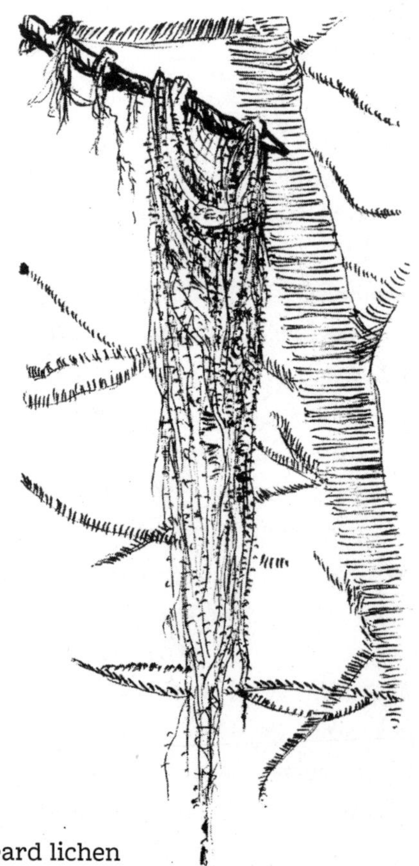
Old man's beard lichen

• **Procedure:** Tell the children what a lichen is, then look at some pictures of lichens online and tell them where they are found. Head outside to an area rich in lichens and challenge them to find as many different kinds and colors of these organisms as they can. Younger children can simply focus on the lichen's color: bright green, gray-green, blue-green, yellow-green, orange, red, pink, black, etc. Older children may want to draw, photograph or even collect a small sample of each kind of lichen they find. As a general rule, the more lichen you see (in color and quantity), the cleaner the air. Make sure the children take time to carefully examine the lichens with a hand lens. Older children may also be interested in identifying some of the species they find. An excellent resource is Lichenland Lite, at ocid.nacse.org/lichenland/LichenLite/processor.php.

Three common lichens to look at through a hand lens:

- British soldiers (Cladonia family) is often found on decaying logs. Through the lens you will see a beautiful color contrast between the frosted green branches and the little red tips. The tips are fruiting structures that produce spores for reproduction.
- Waxpaper or cracked lichen (Parmelia family) grows on tree trunks and rocks. It is whitish gray to grayish green. Through

Darwin: In 2011, researchers from Duke University compared two lichens that were absolutely identical in all outward appearances. One was from North America and the other from Australia. When they looked at the genes, however, they realized that they were not closely related and actually separate species. In their evolution, the lichens had developed exactly the same adaptations to survive in very different regions of the world. They are an example of "convergent evolution," in which two species evolve separately but end up looking very similar, like the Tasmanian wolf (a marsupial) and the American wolf. Don't let anyone tell you that lichens are boring!

the lens you can see a net-like pattern of white cracks.

⟶ Old man's beard (Usnea spp.) lichens hang from tree branches and look like upside-down trees themselves, with a central cord from which other cords branch. With the hand lens, look for powdery structures called *soredia* that produce spores. (See color section, figure 18.)

Weather

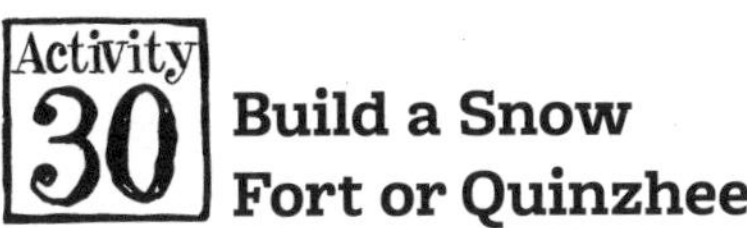

Activity 30 Build a Snow Fort or Quinzhee

- **You'll learn:** How to build a survival snow fort.
- **You'll need:** Snow that is at least 6 in. (15 cm) thick.
- **Background:** While it feels cold to the touch, snow is actually a wonderful insulator. Animals such as voles and mice live under the snow in the *subnivean* environment, away from the severe chills of winter winds and plunging temperatures at night. If the temperature is a frigid −40°F (−40°C) above the snow, it can be 65 degrees warmer, 25°F (−4°C), right at ground level. Voles and mice take advantage of this blanket of insulation by creating a network of tunnels underneath the snow.
- **Procedure:** To discover how well snow insulates, try making a winter survival shelter called a *quinzhee*.

When the snow is at least 6 in. (15 cm) deep, use shovels to mound up snow as high as you can—a big pile about 6 ft. (2 m) high and 12 ft. (4 m) across is ideal. Make sure your pile slopes gently. Smooth the sides into a symmetrical dome shape. Here is an important tip: *You must leave the mound for a minimum of three hours!* This will give the snow crystals time to coalesce (bind). If you can, leave it overnight. After the pile has settled, find a series of sticks 6 in. (30 cm) long and push them into the pile so that one end is at the surface and the other end is deep inside. There should be a stick every 3 ft. (1 m) or so over the entire surface of the quinzhee. Next, begin hollowing out the mound. Make sure you have snow pants and an insulated jacket with a hood; this can be cold and wet work! Use your shovel and start scooping snow out. Have your children haul the snow away from the entrance. Keep digging until you come across the butt end of one of the sticks. The sticks serve as a guide so that you know the walls are of an even and consistent thickness. When the quinzhee is sufficiently hollowed out, use a larger stick or your fist (5 in./12 cm in diameter) to poke three or four holes through to the outside (one overhead, the rest along the sides). These holes will provide ventilation, helping to bring fresh air inside. If you are up for an adventure, insulate the bottom of the quinzhee with a tarp and sleeping pads, then add warm blankets and a sleeping bag. If you are well dressed and there is enough insulation above and below you, you and your children can spend a cozy and unforgettable night in a snow fort of your own creation. (See color section, figure 23.)

Activity 31 How to Catch a Snowflake!

• **You'll learn:** To catch and examine individual snowflakes.

• **You'll need:** Laminated black Bristol board (snowflake catcher), hand lens.

• **Background:** A snowflake will form on the tiniest particle of dust. As the snowflake tumbles through the air, it forms a complex and beautiful snow crystal. When first formed, a snowflake is likely to be a hexagonal prism. As it grows larger, arms of crystals form at the corners and begin to take on ever more complex and stunning shapes. A fully formed snowflake crystal is nothing short of magic!

• **Procedure:** Laminate enough black Bristol board so that each child has a piece. On a calm day when it is snowing, go outside and catch some snowflakes as they fall. Many of the most interesting shapes form when the temperature is close to freezing. Make sure your Bristol board (snowflake catcher) has time to cool before starting. Can you find stellar crystals, hexagonal plates, needles or columns?

Read the story opposite to children. Do any of your snowflakes match those in the pictures?

The Story of a Snowflake

It all began 1,000 years ago. A volcanic eruption in the Philippines sent a cloud of dust and ash skyward 8 mi. (12 km) above lofty mountains. For many years one particle of ash tumbled around the sky buffeted by winds, mixing with the upper and lower atmosphere. On one December night, this small particle ended up in a part of the atmosphere that was supercooled and stable, about –4 degrees Fahrenheit (–20°C). Moisture in the air gradually increased as winds blew warm ocean air upward over the mountains. A lone particle of ash bumped against molecules of water and a snow seed was born—a microscopic crystal so small even the world's most powerful microscope would have trouble seeing it. One by one other molecules were pulled towards the growing crystal, fusing and becoming larger. Within two hours, the snow crystal had grown a thousandfold into a perfect hexagon. The snow crystal, now a snowflake, had become so heavy it began to fall. Slowly at first, and then gathering momentum, it danced towards the Earth. Every layer of air it fell through had slightly different levels of moisture and temperature. And each layer sculpted the flake into a more complex and beautiful shape. I was walking with my two children in the first snowfall of the season, tongues outstretched to catch the tumbling crystals from above. One delicately made snowflake fell upon my daughter's warm tongue, and she smiled as it melted into the tiniest droplet of water, so soft it was almost never there.

Some common snowflake shapes

Activity 32 Make Your Own Anatomically Correct Snowflake

• **You'll learn:** How to make an anatomically correct snowflake with six sides.

• **You'll need:** Sharp scissors, paper.

• **Procedure:**

1. Cut out a circle of paper. (You can trace around a small plate).

2. Fold this in half.

3. Fold this in thirds. Careful, this is a tricky step for some people! You should have three equal sections.

4. Fold this in half and begin cutting. Use the folded part as your spine. The more snowflakes you make, the more delicate and beautiful your designs become. You need to be brave in your cutting. As long as one part of your spine stays together, you'll have a whole snowflake. If you like, iron the flake between two layers of wax paper. Create a snowflake mobile or hang your creation on a Christmas tree! (See color section, figure 22.)

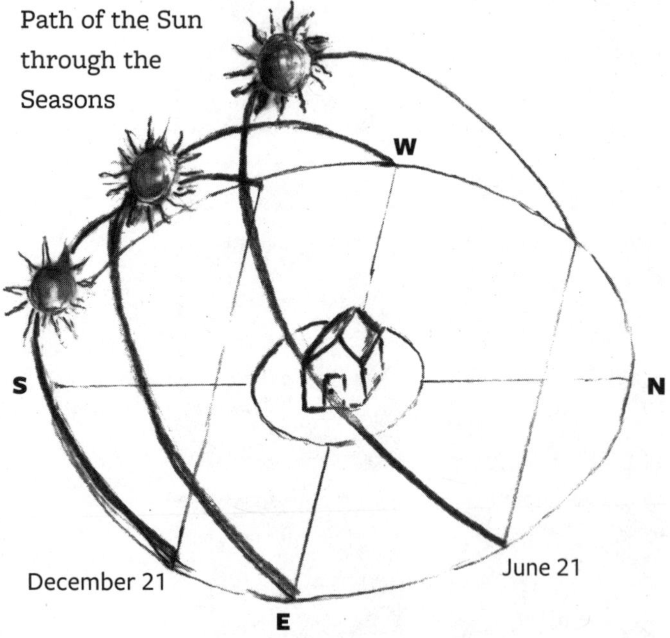

Path of the Sun through the Seasons

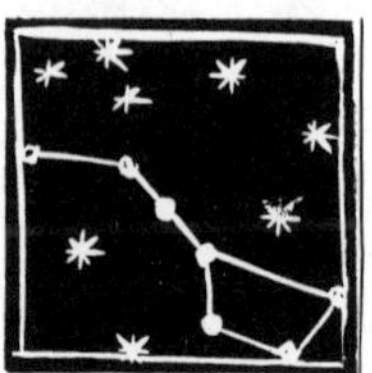

The Sky

Activity 33 Record Sunrise and Sunset Locations

• **You'll learn:** To record sunrise and sunset locations on or near the winter solstice.

• **Procedure:** As in the fall (see page 135), take note of exactly where the Sun rises and sets in relation to landmarks on the eastern and western horizons.

Activity 34 Measure Your Shadow

• **Procedure:** As you did in the fall (page 135), go outside at noon and measure the length of your shadow.

Activity 35 A Flowerpot Sundial

• **You'll learn:** How to make a sundial.

• **You'll need:** Clay flowerpot (bigger the better), black permanent marker, modeling clay, a stick or dowel twice the length of the flowerpot.

• **Background:** A sundial is a simple clock that shows the time by the shadow of an object (the gnomon) cast by the Sun onto

SAGAN: Over 5,000 years ago in Ireland, ancient peoples built a circular, stone burial mound called Newgrange. Its purpose was to be a marker of the winter solstice. Newgrange was constructed in such a way that on the morning of the solstice, a shaft of sunlight would pass through a window and passageway, beam across a chamber and shine upon a stone wall for about 17 minutes. Newgrange may have been initially designed so that the Sun would illuminate the ashes of the dead, buried deep in the tomb. This may have been done to offer the departed a chance for "rebirth," by bathing them in the light of the reborn sun. For these people to have built such a complicated celestial clock, the solstice obviously had to have had a huge significance in their lives.

a plate. The hours of the day are marked on the plate. This activity works well with young children.

• **Procedure:** Starting in the morning if possible, choose an area near your house that receives lots of sunshine. Place a flower pot upside down on the ground (or other flat surface). Push the stick through the hole and, if possible, into the ground or packed snow. Place some modeling clay around the stick to hold it vertical. Trace a straight black line over the stick's shadow and write down the time next to the line. You may wish to do this exactly on the hour (e.g., 9 AM, 10 AM, etc). Repeat each hour, maybe by setting a timer to remind you. You will now have a way to tell the time on sunny days. Just remember to keep the sundial in exactly the same place after you have made it. (See color section, figure 21.)

Activity 36 Gems of the Winter Sky

• **You'll learn:** To recognize the Winter Six constellations and the Winter Hexagon.

• **You'll need:** Sky chart or app.

• **Procedure:** Like the Big Dipper, Orion is useful in locating other stars and constellations. The belt acts as a pointer in two directions. To the right, it points to Aldebaran in Taurus, the Bull, and then on towards the Pleiades. To the left, the belt points to Sirius in Canis Major, the brightest of all the stars. A line extended from Rigel through Betelgeuse points to Gemini, the Twins (Pollux and Castor). Orion, along with Canis Major, Canis Minor, Gemini, Auriga and Taurus, make up a group of constellations known as the Winter Six. The most prominent stars in these same constellations form an asterism called the Winter Hexagon. You can see it by imagining a line joining Rigel, Sirius, Procyon, Pollux/Castor, Capella, Aldebaran and back to Rigel.

Activity 37 Tin Can Constellations

• **You'll learn:** How to make your own mini-planetarium.

• **You'll need:** Empty tin cans, water (optional), hammer and nails, glue, scissors, printouts of constellation patterns (from Google Images).

• **Procedure:**

- If you wish, fill the can with water and let freeze. If there is ice in the can, the bottom will not bend as easily when you hammer nails into it and you will make more accurate patterns.
- Cut out and glue the constellation pattern of your choice to the bottom of the can. Let dry.
- Punch holes in the can where the stars are.
- If you used ice, let the ice melt and pour out the water.
- Shine a bright flashlight through the can toward the ceiling or wall in a dark room.

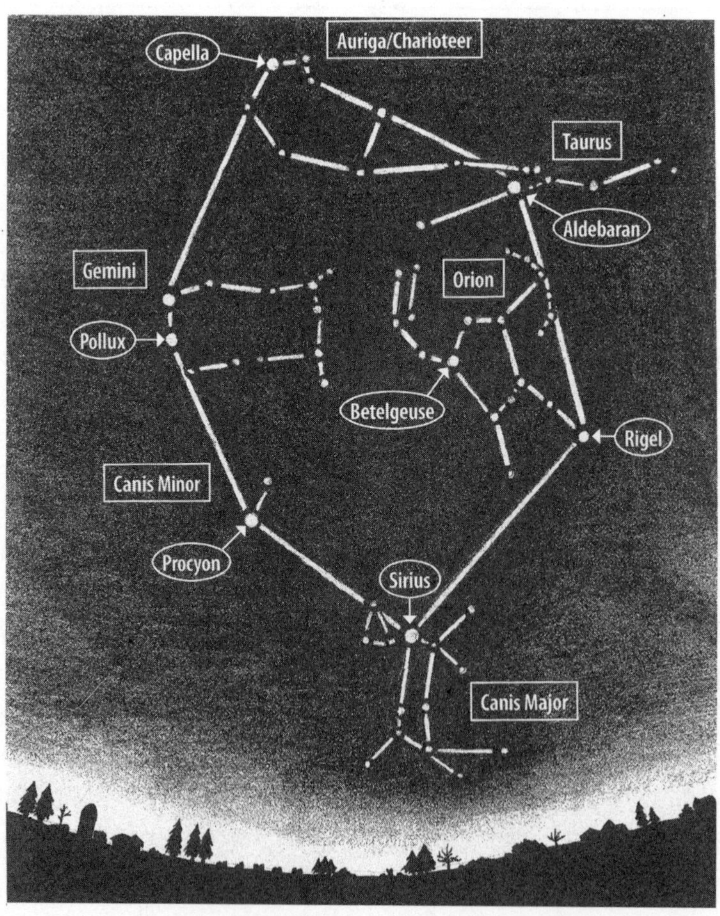

Stars and constellations of the winter sky

> **Neil deGrasse Tyson:** Even though Betelgeuse lies some 430 light years from Earth, it is one of the brightest stars in our sky. This is because Betelgeuse is a supergiant star. Its amazing brilliance means that it's due to explode. In fact Betelgeuse is now near the end of its lifetime. Some day soon, it will run out of fuel, collapse under its own weight, then rebound in a spectacular supernova explosion. The kind of explosion that creates new elements like oxygen, carbon and iron—the stuff we are made of! When this happens, Betelgeuse will brighten enormously for a few weeks or months. It may be as bright as the full Moon and visible in broad daylight! As to when this will happen, no one really knows.

Honoring the Season

Activity 38 Celebrating the Winter Solstice and Christmas

The winter solstice represents the assurance that the days will once again grow longer and spring indeed will come. Ancient cultures all over the northern hemisphere noticed and celebrated this event. Now more and more people are once again celebrating the spiritual and symbolic dimensions of the solstice, often as a part of Christmas and other holiday season festivities.

Make a solstice corsage: Head out for a solstice nature walk, taking along a small length of thread. As you walk along, watch for any small natural objects that catch your attention (e.g., small section of a conifer twig, bark with lichen). Bind the objects together with the thread. You may wish to make a loop so that you can attach it to a button on your coat. You could also wear it in your hair or around your neck, attached to a piece of string. When you leave, you will be able to take your memories of that special nature walk with you.

Make ice lanterns: You'll need balloons (any size), colored dye (optional), a large bowl, water and tea light candles. If you want to use dye, add a few drops inside the balloon. Attach the balloon to a water faucet and fill to desired size. Tie off the balloon. Put the balloon in a bowl and place it either outside or in a freezer for six hours or until the outside is frozen but there is still water inside. Carefully cut and peel away the balloon. Working over a sink or outdoors, drain the water away by making a hole in the weakest part of the base with a kitchen knife. The hole will have to be large enough to slip over the tea light candle. Refreeze the globe until completely solid. Make a hole at the top, either with a drill or a flame. Place your candle outdoors and cover with the ice lantern! (See color section, figure 20.)

Make frozen mandalas: Take sprigs of your favourite winter plants (e.g., dogwood, holly, conifer needles). Use a flat and shallow container (e.g., empty tuna can, Tupperware). Fill with fresh water. Place your sprig(s) inside. Place a twig in the upper middle and allow this to freeze overnight. The next day, gently ease your decoration from the container. Remove the twig. Place a ribbon or twine in the hole and create a loop. This will make a handy hanger. Hang on a tree outside. Watch as the winter side light filters through the beautiful textures of ice and plant material.

Cut your own tree: Head to a local Christmas tree farm and cut down your own tree. A real tree is the most environmentally friendly choice. Go for a nature walk the same day and collect natural ornaments with which to decorate the tree. A few ideas include cones, colorful twigs, birch bark, berries and shells. When Christmas is over, use your tree as a backyard shelter for birds, possibly placing it near your feeder.

Decorate an outside tree (preferably near a window) for the animals and birds: Conifers work well. String pieces of apple, dried fruit, peanuts in the shell and popcorn over the boughs. You can also hang out pieces of suet and pine cones covered in peanut butter and rolled in bird seed. It won't be long before wildlife discover your creation.

Common mullein

Decorate the table with a winter wildflower bouquet: The gray, brittle remains of last summer's field and roadside flowers have a beauty and grace all their own, especially if you take time to look at them closely. When you are out for a walk, why not snip off a few and make your own winter floral arrangement? Some of the most attractive are the dry stalks and seed pods of milkweed, Queen Anne's lace (wild carrot), evening primrose, mullein, burdock and the numerous types of grass. For a splash of color try adding some of the fruit that often still lingers on shrubs and vines in winter (e.g., sumac, mountain ash, highbush cranberry).

Activity 39 Arctic Winter Games

During the long winter when the Sun hung low or disappeared altogether, the First Nations and the Inuit traditionally played games in order to hone hunting skills, develop balance and test their strength. These games also helped to pass the time during blizzards and severe cold. This was often known as the storytelling time.

Now every two years, athletes gather from far and wide across the world's northern circumpolar regions for an exciting week of sporting competition. This unique event is an occasion for people living around the Arctic Circle to compete in many different sports and to share cultures from around the world.

Here are some traditional Inuit games:

- **The Toe Jump:** This game, which sounds easy, can be surprisingly difficult. Simply grab your toes and jump as far as you can. But you can't let go of your toes! The winner is the one who jumps the furthest, but I can tell you it probably won't be more than a few inches!
- **The Knee Jump:** Kneel down with your shins flat to the ground and the back of your toes extended behind you (not curled underneath). The idea is to jump as far as you can and land on your feet. Jumps of more than 6 ft. (2 m) have been recorded!
- **Toe Tag:** Two participants face each other, hands behind their back. Each attempts to touch the other person's toes with their own before their rival touches theirs. Lots of leaping and prancing is required for this one!
- **Kicking Games:** The essential element for these games is the object that is kicked, called the seal. It can be made out of a piece of fur, a stuffed sock or rolled-up paper—anything that can be suspended from a rope. Make the seal about 6 in. (15 cm) long and 3 in. (7 cm) wide. Then tie it to a some string about 12 ft. (4 m) long and throw it over a low-lying limb of a tree, so you can adjust its height.
- **The One-foot High Kick:** This is perhaps the most popular of all the kicking games. The contestants approach the seal at a trot and jump as high as possible, leaping from both feet. They then attempt to kick the seal. Contestants must land balanced and in control *on the foot that they kicked with*. Kicks of more than 8 ft. (3 m) have been recorded!
- **The Alaskan High Kick:** The contestant positions themselves underneath the seal. One hand must hold the opposite foot and the body weight should be placed on the other arm. With the free foot the contestant tries to kick the seal without releasing the held foot. The behind cannot touch the ground during this kick.

A First Nations game

Snow Snake: This traditional game was played by the Oneida, Haudenosaunee (Iroquois), Anishinaabe and other indigenous peoples of North America. Contestants tossed a carved stick (snow snake) as far as they could along a grooved track. If the conditions were right, tosses of more than .5 mi. (1 km) were not unheard of. Snow snakes were carved from various types of hardwood. Some were carved flat with an upturned front, while others were completely round with a metal tip to create extra weight. In many areas, the game is still played today.

How to make a simple snow snake:

- Purchase a ¾ in. (1.5 cm) diameter hardwood dowel. Smooth the doweling with sandpaper (suggested sequence: 80 grit, 100 grit, 200 grit) and clean off with a cloth.

- Use paints, burner, markers to create a snow snake design.
- Soak in linseed oil or varnish with an exterior varnish. Allow 24 hours to air dry.
- Coat the snake liberally with paraffin wax. Apply at least three to four coats.
- Allow the snake to cool before using (it will work better if it is the same temperature as the air).
- Experiment with different lengths: a long snow snake (6 ft./2 m long), a short snake (3 ft./1 m) and a snow dart (a ⅜-in.- or 5-mm-diameter dowel 10 in./ 5 cm long).

How to make a simple snow snake track:

- Mound snow into a long track (about 50 yd./m long and 18 in./50 cm) wide). Taper the track downward so it begins at waist height and slowly descends toward the ground.
- Run a log about 8–10 in. (20–25 cm) in diameter over the track several times.
- If you can, spray water along the track to create an ice surface.

How to play

- Launch your snow snake. The farthest toss earns two points, the second farthest one point.
- When all participants have tossed their snakes, the round is over.
- Switch throwers and continue playing until one participant reaches ten points. (See color section, figure 19.)

Mossy rose gall, goldenrod gall and pine cone willow gall

Quotes on winter for contemplation

Winter, a lingering season, is a time to gather golden moments, embark upon a sentimental journey, and enjoy every idle hour.

— John Boswell

No winter lasts forever; no spring skips its turn.

—Hal Borland

In the depths of winter I finally learned that within me there lay an invincible summer.

—Albert Camus

To see a hillside white with dogwood bloom is to know a particular ecstasy of beauty, but to walk the gray winter woods and find the buds which will resurrect that beauty in another May is to partake of continuity.

—Hal Borland

Spring
the greening season

Spring usually begins as a tug-of-war with winter. Just when we think warmer weather is here to stay, we are hit with another blast of cold and snow. However, the change of season is always apparent if you take the time to look and listen: the Sun is higher in the sky, daylight is with us until early evening and bird song has returned. Soon, wetlands come alive with a chorus of frog song, new plant life slowly appears and even the smell of the air changes. Before we know it, the explosive growth of buds, flowers, shoots and leaves totally transforms the landscape and provides a feast for countless insects. Then, just like clockwork, the much-anticipated birds of spring arrive to devour this smorgasbord of protein and food for their young. A surge of life is all around us.

Some Key Events in Nature in Spring

Overview

The "early spring" period runs from about the start of March through mid-April. "Late spring" covers the period from approximately mid-April through May. Timing of events will vary depending on latitude, elevation and the vagaries of the weather. Climate change, too, is accelerating some events and delaying others. The sequence of events, however, is always the same. The page references point to an activity based on this event.

Continent-wide Overview

Birds

General

⊸ From early March through early June, birds are returning from their wintering grounds. However, millions die from window collisions and cat predation during migration each year. Make sure your windows are bird-safe (i.e., visible to birds). Go to allaboutbirds.org for ideas. It is equally important to always keep your cat indoors.

⊸ Spring is a season of ardent song and courtship displays as birds make claims to nesting territories and try to attract mates. Listen, too, for the hooting of owls, the drumming of ruffed grouse, the winnowing of Wilson's snipes and the hammering of woodpeckers. (See pages 276–277.)

⊸ Starting in April and continuing through early summer, it is nesting time for most species. Baby birds are inevitably

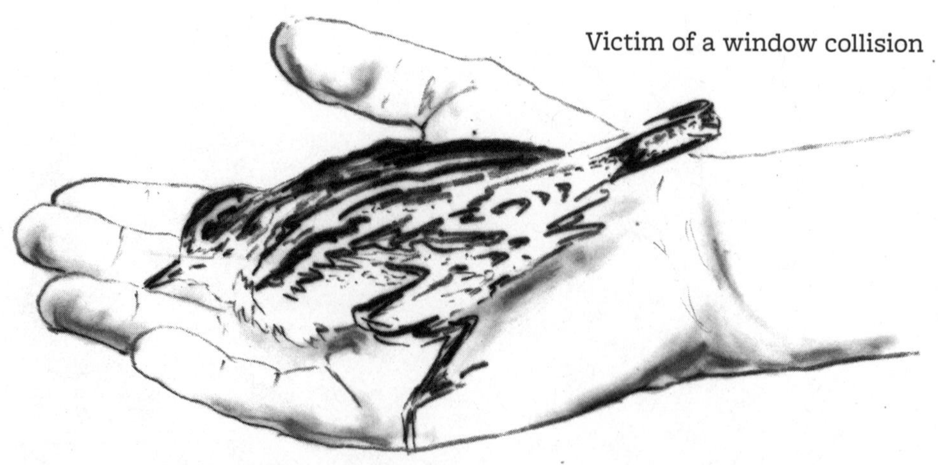

Victim of a window collision

found and believed to have been abandoned. Rarely is this the case. They are best left alone or relocated close by where they are out of danger from predators—especially cats—and where their parents will find them. (See Activity 13, page 223.)

- Don't be surprised if a half-crazed bird, maybe a robin or bluebird, starts aggressively pecking at one of your windows in an attempt to drive the "invader"—its reflected image—out of its nesting territory.
- Feeders can be very busy, both with resident species and northbound migrants such as a variety of sparrows.

Singing hooded warbler. Note tulip tree in background

Early spring

- The first migratory songbirds return with red-winged blackbirds, American robins and song sparrows leading the way in many areas.
- Ducks and geese move north in large numbers and often gather in huge flocks on ice-free sections of lakes and rivers and in meltwater ponds in fields. Watch, too, for loons and grebes.
- Early nesters include Canada geese, common ravens, ospreys, American robins, European starlings and house sparrows.
- The early-morning chorus of robins, sparrows and doves, along with the drumming of woodpeckers, can be overwhelming!

Late spring

- Birding is at its best in late April through mid-May as most of the long-distance migrants from the tropics return. These include hummingbirds, warblers, vireos, orioles, tanagers, flycatchers, thrushes and many species of sandpipers and plovers.
- Migratory hummingbirds like the ruby-throated and the rufous are back by early May and make a beeline to feeders. Their natural food in spring includes tree sap oozing from sapsucker drillings.
- Tropical migrants like thrushes and warblers begin nesting.
- Bird song is so rich and diverse that it is often difficult to distinguish all the voices.

Mammals

Early spring

- Wolves, coyotes and foxes may bear young by the end of March, followed shortly by raccoons, skunks and many kinds of squirrels and weasels. This baby boom requires a high degree of hunting and foraging skill on the part of the parents. (See Activity 14, page 225 and Activity 15, page 227.)
- Chipmunks and ground squirrels emerge from their dens, often while there is still snow on the ground.
- Male muskrats range widely looking for mates.
- Other mammals mating in early spring include skunks, ground squirrels, rabbits, hares, chipmunks, red squirrels and flying squirrels.
- The white winter coats of weasels and snowshoe hares change back to brown.

Late spring

- The mammalian baby boom continues in May with the arrival of baby beavers, deer, moose and many of the species that mated in early spring.
- Moose-watching can be excellent, especially in places where the animals are attracted to salty roadside puddles.
- Antler growth on deer and moose accelerates dramatically because of the increased daylight.
- Young foxes make their first appearance in the open and are entertaining to watch.

Amphibians and Reptiles

Early spring

- Depending on latitude and the vagaries of the weather, the first frogs and toads begin calling. Sometimes, the chorus can be deafening. Most frog and toad calls are distinctive and easy to learn. (See Activity 16, page 228.)

Spotted skunk

- When the first frogs start calling, salamanders breed in woodland ponds and can be seen crossing roads on wet, mild nights. It is also possible to observe the frogs as they call. (See Activity 17, page 230.)
- Soon after they start calling, frogs lay masses of gelatin-like eggs, while toads lay their eggs in what looks like a tube of jelly. It is fascinating to watch the eggs hatch and the tadpoles develop into adults. (See Activity 18, page 232.)
- Snakes emerge from their dens and often bask in sunny spots. Garter snakes begin mating in what looks like a "knot" of snakes, entwining themselves around each other. (See Activity 19, page 233.)
- Turtles come out of hibernation and can be seen basking in the sun on logs and rocks.

Spring peeper—not much bigger than a bumblebee!

Late spring

- More frog and toad species add their voices to the amphibian chorus.
- In northern latitudes, baby painted turtles emerge from their ground nests where they overwintered, frozen almost solid.

Fishes

Early spring

- Spring is an excellent time of year for fish-watching, as many species are spawning near shore. (See Activity 20, page 235.)
- Northern pike move towards sun-warmed shallows in search of food and spawn sites.
- Shad, smelt and rainbow trout, too, move upstream to spawn. Rainbow trout can be a spectacular sight as they jump at fish ladders.
- Other early spawners include walleye, yellow perch and suckers.

Late spring

- Many non-game species such as minnows, sticklebacks and darters are laying their eggs.
- Members of the sunfish family such as bass and pumpkinseeds begin spawning in the basin-like nests that the males make in shallow water.

Invertebrates

Early spring

- Honeybees become active and search out nectar and pollen from early-blooming trees, shrubs and flowers. They communicate the location of food sources to other bees in the hive. (See Activity 22, page 237 and Activity 23, page 239.)
- Butterflies that overwintered as adults begin to appear on mild days and are often seen feeding on tree sap oozing from stumps or broken branches. These include tortoiseshell butterflies like the mourning cloak. (See Activity 24, page 240.)
- The first mating swarms of midges can be seen over trees, often along lakes and rivers.
- Woolly bear caterpillars, having overwintered as larvae, become active once again.
- If the weather is warm, spring azure and elfin butterflies may appear.

Late spring

- Insect numbers explode and provide protein to millions of birds and their nestlings.
- Mayflies emerge from lakes and streams and form large mating swarms. These transparent-winged insects have long, forked tails. Their adult life lasts only two days.
- The first dragonflies and damselflies change from forbidding aquatic nymphs to gracious adult flying machines. Common green darners are often the first species seen.
- Large pregnant queen bumblebees search out suitable underground chambers in which to nest and start new colonies.
- Biting flies emerge en masse with black flies appearing first, followed soon after by mosquitoes.
- Tent caterpillars hatch out and start feeding heavily on the new foliage of cherry trees. The tents are a common sight along roadsides.

Mourning cloak butterfly basking in spring sun

- Swallowtail butterflies emerge and are often seen at puddles on dirt roads.
- Spittlebug (froghopper) nymphs secrete frothy white masses of spittle on the stems of plants in weedy areas.
- The first monarch butterflies arrive in northern latitudes in late May or early June; these are often the "grandchildren" of the monarchs that flew south to Mexico and California the previous fall.
- The first fireflies emerge and light up meadows in a dreamy flickering.
- Spectacular giant silk moths like the Polyphemus take wing as June approaches.

Pussy willow catkins

Plants

Early spring

- The sap of the sugar maple is running, and people collect it to make maple syrup.
- The furry catkins of pussy willows and aspens poke through bud scales and become a time-honored sign of spring.
- By late March, skunk cabbage is already in bloom. Its unpleasant smell attracts early flies and bees.
- The first wildflowers appear, including coltsfoot with its dandelion-like flowers.
- In woodlands, wild leek pokes through patches of late March snow. Dandelion blossoms will soon turn lawns and roadsides into a riot of yellow.
- Fiddleheads of ostrich and cinnamon ferns appear.
- A pastel wash of swelling tree buds and the flowers of wind-pollinated trees spreads over the landscape, giving distant trees a soft, hazy appearance. (See Activity 26, page 241.)
- As flowers burst into bloom, we often forget that the brightly colored petals are not designed to please humans but to attract insects, birds and even bats to pollinate the plants. (See Activity 30, page 243.)

Late spring

- By mid-April, carpets of wildflowers such as trilliums brighten still-leafless woodlands. (See Activity 31, page 245.)
- By late April, trees are quickly leafing out. Among the first are weeping willow and quaking aspen.

- White flowers abound, including dogwoods, serviceberries, chokecherries and hawthorns.
- Pinks and reds, too, are a signature color. Watch for rhododendrons in many areas.
- Many plants release their seeds to the wind, including aspens, willows and dandelions.

Fungi

- Edible morel mushrooms fruit. The cap has a series of pits and ridges.
- Watch for fairy rings, which are a circle or arc of mushrooms. The edible fairy ring mushroom (*Marasmius oreades*) sometimes grows in this form.
- A common and widespread bracket fungus to watch for in deciduous and mixed woods is the artist's conk. (See Activity 32, page 246.)

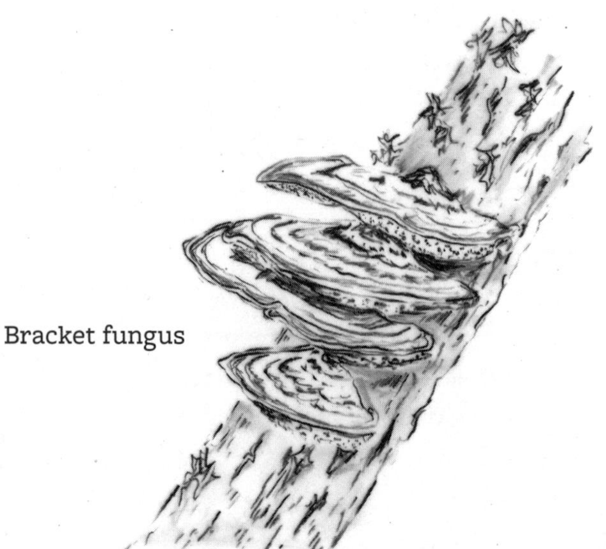

Bracket fungus

Weather

- We go from about 11 hours of daylight in early March to over 15 in late May!
- In much of North America, early spring is a time without rules; just about any kind of winter or spring weather can be expected.
- By late spring, there are usually periods of summer-like weather, which bring about an explosive greening of the landscape.
- Warm weather means spending more time outside, gazing at the sky and appreciating the wonder and beauty of clouds. (See Activity 33, page 247.)
- Vernal ponds—small, temporary bodies of spring meltwater and rain—create crucially important breeding habitat for amphibians.

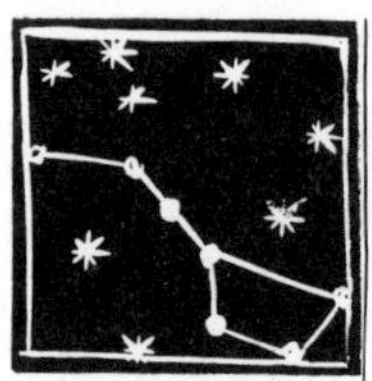

The Sky

Early spring

- No other season offers as many bright stars and constellations as spring. There are no fewer than 11 first-magnitude stars visible.
- On or about March 18, day and night are almost exactly equal in duration.
- The spring equinox falls on or about March 20. Both the Moon and Sun rise due east and set due west that day. (See Activity 35, page 249.)

- In the evening, watch the northeastern horizon for Arcturus, the brightest star of summer and the harbinger of spring.
- The signature constellation of spring is Leo, the lion. Although somewhat dim, it really does look like a crouching lion. (See Activity 37, page 250.)
- The Big Dipper is standing upright, high in the north sky.

Late spring

- Two meteor showers take place: the Lyrids in the northern sky from April 20–22 and the Eta Aquarids in the southeast around May 5.

Spring Nature Highlights by Region

1. Marine West Coast

- From April through mid-May, there is an influx of hundreds of thousands of shorebirds, particularly western sandpipers and dunlin. They are migrating towards their Arctic breeding grounds. Some key stopovers include San Francisco Bay, Grays Harbor (Washington) and the Fraser River Delta/Boundary Bay (British Columbia).
- Spring is a time for courting, nest building and brood rearing among seabirds on offshore rocks and islands.
- Large numbers of bald eagles nest in the Lower Mainland of British Columbia and in Washington state.
- Spring provides excellent whale-watching opportunities as more than 20,000 gray whales migrate north up the coast. Mothers and calves stay close together. They are easily seen during whale-watching excursions and may be spotted from shore. It is possible to see whales at almost any time of year along the Pacific coast.

Gray whale

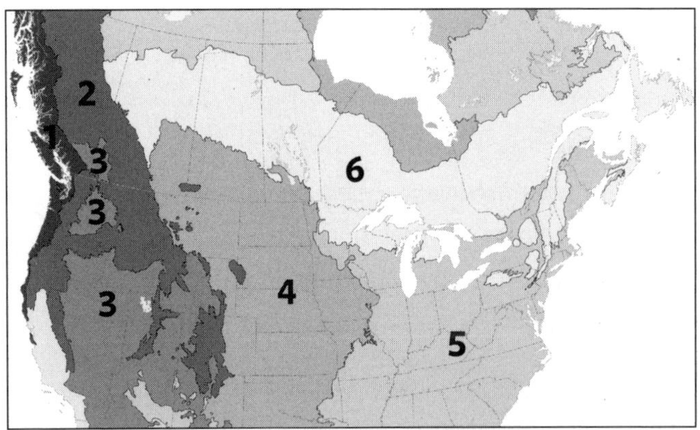

Ecological Zones of North America

- In early spring, Pacific treefrogs, red-legged frogs and rough-skinned newts begin the overland trek to lay eggs in ponds.
- Each spring, peaking in March, Pacific herring return to spawn in protected inlets in the Strait of Georgia and elsewhere on the coast of British Columbia. The event draws thousands of marine birds and mammals to feed on the nutritious bounty.
- Early-flowering plants like salmonberry and Indian plum provide nectar for returning rufous hummingbirds.
- In early spring, western trilliums and calypso orchids bloom in woodlands. Iconic arbutus trees (madrone) blossom in drier, coastal regions in April or May.
- A huge display of wildflowers (e.g., California goldfields, California buttercups, Douglas iris) explodes around San Francisco Bay.

2. Northwestern Forested Mountains

- In early spring, male elk and deer shed their antlers. Bighorn sheep graze along roadsides.
- In late spring, baby bighorn sheep are born and are often seen at lower elevations.
- As a result of climate change, the wildflower-blooming season now lasts from late April to late September, longer than ever before.
- In late spring, in the drier montane zone below 6,000 ft. (1,800 m), pasqueflower, geranium, mariposa lily and miner's candle bloom. Pipsissewa, lupine and blue columbine follow in higher elevations.
- The most spectacular wildflower show occurs above 11,000 ft. (3,400 m) in the alpine zone, where bistorts, alpine forget-me-nots, yellow-blossomed avens, marsh marigolds and snow buttercups create a veritable alpine flower garden.

3. North American Deserts

- Sage grouse begin displaying on their dancing grounds (leks) in late March. The chest drumming and elaborate strut of the male is a renowned spectacle of the high desert.
- The staccato call of the greater sandhill crane announces the beginning of spring in many areas.
- The Oregon spotted frog, a species of special concern, starts breeding in February or March at lower elevations.
- Some native wildflowers blooming are yellow Oregon sunshine, dwarf purple monkeyflower, sulfur buckwheat, Indian paintbrush and mariposa lily.

4. Great Plains

- In April and May, sharp-tailed grouse are performing their mating dance.

- Endangered whooping cranes migrate through the region, using area wetlands and grain fields for feeding.
- A number of shorebirds are nesting, including marbled godwit and long-billed curlew.
- Sandhill cranes stop to rest on their way north and are very vocal.
- In late spring, western grebes begin their mating ritual by "dancing" in synchronized pairs across the water.
- American white pelicans arrive as the cold weather retreats in April. They begin nesting in May.
- Tiger salamanders, which often live in rodent burrows during much of the year, migrate to shallow ponds to breed in the spring.
- Lavender-blue pasqueflowers are blooming on hillsides, sometimes even in the remnants of snow.

Barred tiger salamander

5. Eastern Temperate Forests

- In early March, when the weather delivers a pattern of sunny, thawing days and freezing nights, sweet sap starts "rising"—traveling throughout the tree—in sugar maples.
- A highlight of spring evenings is the courtship "sky dance" of the American woodcock. As the bird circles high overhead, its outer wing feathers make a distinctive twittering sound.
- As the shadbush flowers (serviceberry), millions of bluish-green and silver American shad leave the Atlantic Ocean and migrate up eastern rivers such as the Connecticut to spawn.
- Red and silver maples shine in pastel reds as flowers begin to emerge. The brownish flowers of elms and the tiny golden-yellow flowers of spicebush appear as well.
- In April, the forest floor is transformed from an expanse of monotonous brown to a patchwork of white, yellow, green and shades of red as wildflowers announce spring's arrival. In order of bloom, some of the most anticipated are hepatica, trailing arbutus, bloodroot, trout lily, marsh marigolds and white trillium. Soon after, the abundant flowers of redbuds, tulip

American woodcock

trees and flowering dogwoods dazzle the eye with purple-reds, oranges and whites.

- Early May means birding at its best. The highlight for most people is the arrival of more than 30 species of warblers whose brilliant colors, melodious voices and constant movement are a sheer delight.
- Migrating rose-breasted grosbeaks, and sometimes even indigo buntings, drop in at sunflower feeders.

6. Northern Forests

- April is usually the month of greatest snowmelt and ice-out.
- In early spring, sugar maples are tapped. Honeybees, mourning cloak butterflies, noctuid moths and even red squirrels come for the sweet, dripping sap.
- Merlins are among the more noticeable early nesters. Not only are they very noisy, but they often scatter songbird carcasses below their nests, which are often in conifers.
- American woodcock perform their famous "sky dance" flight in damp meadows at dusk. Sharp-tailed grouse also put on a remarkable spring courtship display, which can be seen on Manitoulin Island in 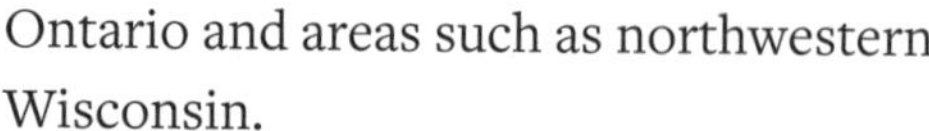Ontario and areas such as northwestern Wisconsin.
- In early April, northern gannets return to Quebec's Bonaventure Island to nest. Atlantic puffins and many other seabirds can also be seen on the island.
- In some areas, like Ontario's Algonquin Provincial Park, moose can be seen along the side of the highway in late spring. They are attracted by puddles of salty snowmelt from winter road maintenance.
- Ruby-throated hummingbirds return in early May and are especially common along the southern edge of the Canadian Shield in Ontario.
- It is estimated that at least three billion land birds, water birds and shorebirds breed in the northern forests each year, including almost 30 species of warblers.
- The frog chorus usually begins in early April, with wood frogs leading the way. By May, nearly all of the region's frog and toad species can be heard calling at some time in the month.
- May is also the month when black flies are at their worst. The larvae require cold, clear, running water to develop—a common habitat in the northern forests.
- Usually starting in late April or early May, deciduous and mixed forests display a profusion of spring ephemeral wildflowers. By late May, orchids begin to bloom, including abundant yellow lady's slippers lining roadsides of Ontario's Bruce Peninsula.

Painted trillium

Through all the frozen winter
My nose has grown most lonely
For lovely, lovely, colored smells
That come in springtime only.
The purple smell of lilacs,
The yellow smell that blows
Across the air of meadows
Where bright forsythia grows.
The tall pink smell of peach trees,
The low white smell of clover,
And everywhere the great green smell
Of grass the whole world over.

— Kathryn Worth

Marsh wren building a nest

Collection Challenge

Spring items for the collection box and/or nature table (see also page 54 in "Connecting with Nature"):

- Aquarium with frog or toad tadpoles
- Flowers from different trees as they come into bloom (e.g., alder, elm, maple)
- Old bird nests
- Fragments of eggshells or entire eggs (when found abandoned)
- Plants that you are starting from seed for transfer to the garden
- Common roadside wildflowers in a vase
- Smells of spring: vase with balsam poplar or black cottonwood twigs (with leaves and/or buds), cherry blossoms, lilac blossoms
- Terrarium: tent caterpillars with cherry leaves to eat. Keep for a day or two.
- Laptop: websites with amphibian calls and bird songs
- Evolution display: timelines showing evolution of various species (e.g., horse, humans, birds)

Art in the Park

Ideas for what to sketch and photograph in spring:

- The same tree at regular intervals to show progression of leaf-out. Begin when the tree is still entirely leafless and continue until all the leaves have emerged and fully opened.
- A landscape scene over a period of weeks (or days, when change is happening fast) as it changes from leafless to fully cloaked in leaves
- Returning waterfowl, especially the brilliantly plumaged males
- A frog or toad calling, with its vocal sac fully extended
- Bees on early blooms such as crocuses
- Thawing ice on lakes
- Returning warblers and other songbirds perched in leafless trees
- Activities of nesting birds
- Day-to-day images of an individual bud opening up and leaves and/or flowers emerging
- Spring wildflowers in a deciduous forest

What's Wrong with the Scenario?

How many mistakes can you find?

It is a lovely spring evening. Swallows are flying above me carrying grass to line the nests they've made in the branches of a nearby pine tree. Soon the babies will be born and they'll be swooping in with their parents to feast on seeds at my backyard feeder. Asters and goldenrods are blooming in the meadow and, as it grows darker, you can make out the Big Dipper high in the southern sky. In the distance, I hear the whistle of an American bullfrog coming from the marsh. All of a sudden, there is a crash behind me, and I turn just in time to see a majestic buck white-tailed deer with a full rack of antlers. How I love the spring!

Turn to the Appendix, page 342, to see how you did!

The Story of Night Cap, the Chickadee

It is early April. The sun, higher and warmer now, is slanting through the tree branches and everywhere snow is soft and melting. Suddenly, from the top of an old pine tree, Night Cap hears a melodious whistling—a two-noted song, which to human ears sounds much like *sweetie*. Then she hears another burst of the *sweetie* song, this time coming from a grove of cedar trees. Then another. These are male chickadees singing for a mate! They are in the middle of a "song battle." Night Cap knows the males are saying something like, "Hey honey, I'm over here... but boy oh boy... if you're another boy, back right off—this is my part of the forest." Her head is never still as she listens to all the male songs. She seems intrigued. Finally, she flies to one of the males whose voice is a little deeper and a little louder, which suggests he's a larger, healthier male. His name is White Cheek.

In time, Night Cap and White Cheek mate. Together, they find a birch tree that has died and is beginning to rot. Night Cap and White Cheek excavate several nesting sites. They make at least three holes about 3 in. (8 cm) in diameter and 10 ft. (3 m) off the ground. Soon, Night Cap selects one of the holes and lines it with moss, feathers, shredded bark and even animal hair. She lays six tiny white and brown speckled eggs, only about a half-inch (12 mm) in size. White Cheek faithfully feeds his mate a steady diet of caterpillars, insect eggs and spiders. Night Cap uses the warmth from her body and special brood patch to keep her eggs warm. She keeps still and quiet, incubating her eggs. Then late one afternoon she hears a series of strange *queedle* sounds. A crested bird with shimmering blue feathers is peering into her nest. A jay—known to eat baby birds and eggs! Night Cap lets out a startled hissing noise. There is a flurry of white and gray feathers as White Cheek rockets in from a nearby tree. Surprised by a series of acrobatic tumbles, twists and pecks from White Cheek, the harried jay flies off.

After 14 days, six baby chickadees hatch out—hairless, eyes bulging but closed—as fragile as any new beginning.

What you can do

- Listen for song battles between male chickadees.
- Can you imitate the black-capped chickadee's springtime song (*sweet-ee*)? Listen to allaboutbirds.org/guide/Black-capped_Chickadee/sounds. If you can,

Chickadee feeding from maple sap bucket

pitch your song just a bit lower. A female chickadee is attracted to chickadees that sound big and healthy, and a lower tone signifies a larger, stronger bird. Does a chickadee respond to your imitation?

Make a chickadee nesting box

Construct a nesting box as outlined at nestwatch.org/learn/all-about-birdhouses/. Place the box in an area that receives sunlight about half the day. Chickadees do well in habitats such as woodlots, fields, backyards with mature trees, and the edges of forests or meadows. Your box needs to be at least 5 ft. (2 m) above the ground.

Install your box before the breeding season begins. In the south, mount your nesting box by February. In northern regions, put it up by mid- to late March. It may take a while for chickadees to discover your box, so don't be discouraged!

At Your Magic Spot

Albert Einstein once said, "Imagination is more important than knowledge. For knowledge is limited to all we now know and understand, while imagination embraces the entire world, and all there ever will be to know and understand."

Imagination is a wonderful ability all of us have—especially at our Magic Spot. So, using the power of your imagination, shrink yourself down to the size of an ant. What would your Magic Spot look like if you were only a fraction of an inch (less than a centimeter) tall? What points of interest might capture your attention? Perhaps a funny-colored mushroom? Maybe a chewed leaf or a groove along that fallen log? Using Popsicle sticks (or small branches) and string, create a micro-trail about 30 ft. (10 m) long. Press the sticks into the soil next to every point of interest. Find at least eight points of interest a few steps from each other. Connect them all with the string, wrapping it around each stick to make a long string trail. When you are finished, sit down and watch your trail quietly for ten minutes or so. Did anything of note happen? Then take a trip along the trail, keeping your head close to the ground. Don't forget to use a hand lens. Take someone special to your micro-trail and give them a guided tour of your discoveries! (See color section, figure 37.)

One step further:
Make a backyard nature trail

Walk around your yard or nearby green space and look for interesting features. These might include notable trees and plants, a wet area, a large rock, an animal burrow or maybe even invertebrates under a log. If your property has little of interest, consider adding features that will attract wildlife. You might plant shrubs, make a brush pile, bring in a big log or create a small wet area using a plastic liner or a wading pool sunk into the ground.

Make a narrow, windy path that passes by these interesting features. Identify the path with markers such as wood chips, small pieces of ribbon, dead branches laid down along the edge or maybe by cutting an extra-low swath with the lawn mower. Consider adding a bench, chair or log as an observation point at one or more locations. Label species and features of interest along the path by using plain aluminum write-on tree tags, which can be attached to branches or small posts. They are inexpensive and available online. In addition to the name, add an interesting fact about the species or feature and maybe a number.

Place tags at different levels so visitors will look around as they walk. You may even want to make a little interpretive guide that provides more information on features of interest. Numbers can be painted on wooden stakes to tell visitors where to stop and read about a given feature. Add new tags as you find or add new species or other details. Become an expert on the species and special features of your trail. Lead friends and family on nature trail walks, too!

Exploring Spring: Things to Do

Spring looks like...

- The pastel greens, browns and reds as tree buds swell and leaves and flowers slowly emerge
- The amazing variety of shades of green of the fresh new vegetation
- The return of vibrant color to the landscape, especially the white carpets of trilliums, the yellow surf of dandelions and the mauve splashes of lilac
- The vivid colors of birds such as male mallards and American goldfinches in their breeding plumage
- Bright stars like Arcturus rising over the eastern horizon

Group Observation

It is an incontrovertible fact of physics: no two people can occupy the same space at the same time. This means that no matter what you are looking at—a tree, a bird or a boulder—you have a unique perspective. You see the object from a vantage point that no one else can. Your eyes are the only ones looking at that object from that precise angle, at that time and at that place. When out for a walk, choose a natural object of interest (a stump, a hole, a vista). Have each participant, in turn, look at that one object and describe exactly what they see. By sharing our insights and our perspectives, we gain a more holistic view of the object. We also learn to value other points of view—literally.

The Beauty of Emerging Leaves

If you can't wait for spring's greenery to arrive, snip off a few twigs (e.g., willow), with pruning shears. Put them in water and place near a window. With any luck, the buds will open up and leaves and/or flowers will emerge. Be sure to sketch some of the twigs and emerging leaves in your nature journal.

Spring sounds like...

- The tinkling of lake ice as it melts and breaks up
- The morning songbird chorus, with new voices appearing as the season advances
- The drumming of ruffed grouse and the hammering of woodpeckers

- The chorus of frog and toad song emanating from wetlands
- The pitter-patter of spring rains

Activity 3 Sound Maps

Choose a site and time of day with a variety of natural sounds. Edge habitats near a marsh can be excellent. Give each child an index card with an X in the center. Tell them the card is a map and the X is where they'll be sitting. Each time they hear a sound, they should mark its location (direction and distance) and represent it with a simple symbol (e.g., a few parallel lines for wind, a musical note for bird song, a number after the note for each different bird). Show them how to cup their hands in front of and behind their ears to hear sounds from all directions (see Focused Hearing, page 270). Make sure each child finds a listening place well-separated from other children. Listen for 5–10 minutes, depending on the variety of sounds and the age of participants. Encourage kids to share their maps with a partner, identifying both natural and human-related sounds. Bring the group together and discuss the following:

- How many different sounds did you hear?
- Which sounds did you particularly like?
- What sounds were new to you?
- Who/what may have made them?
- Which were natural and which were caused by humans?
- Do some of these sounds have a purpose? If so, what might this be?

Sound map

Spring tastes like...

- The mildly sweet sap of sugar maples, which doesn't need to be boiled down to taste wonderful (although not as sweet, the sap of Manitoba maples, big-leaf maples and white birches is also tasty)
- The return of salads and early veggies like asparagus and new potatoes to the dinner table
- The delights of the edible wild such as wild leeks, dandelion leaves, sheep sorrel, fiddleheads and morel mushrooms
- The bright green tips of new growth on Douglas fir (see recipe below)
- The purity of a raindrop

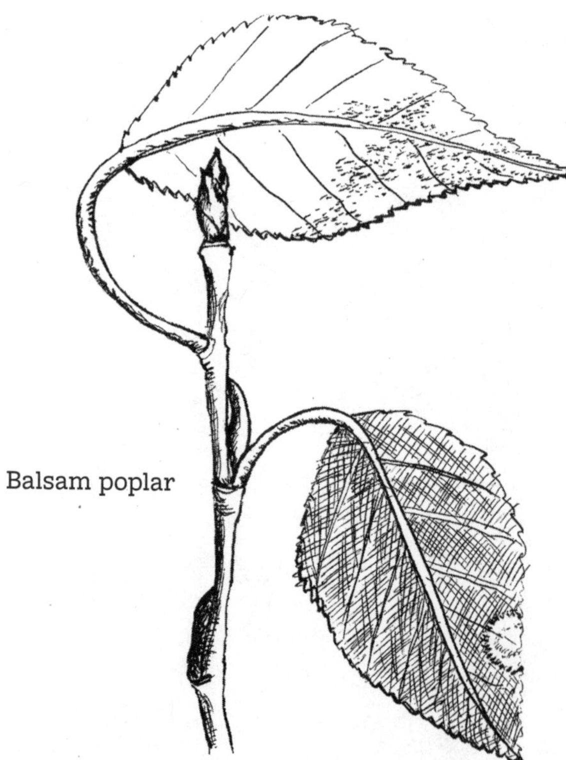

Balsam poplar

Activity 4 Douglas Fir or Spruce Sorbet

Try the following edible wild treat, which uses the bright lime-green tips of new growth on Douglas fir or spruce trees.

Combine 3 c. (700 ml) of water and 1 c. (237 ml) of organic cane sugar in a saucepan. Heat to a boil. Add 4 c. (1 L) of fresh or frozen tips and, if you wish, 3 c. (700 ml) of redwood sorrel (*Oxalis oregona*) leaves. Completely submerge in water. Remove from heat, cover and let steep for 30 minutes. Pour the liquid through a strainer and then into ice cube trays. When fully frozen, mix the cubes in a blender and serve as a sorbet. Garnish with a few extra tips.

Spring smells like...

- The sweet aroma of evaporating maple sap from a sugar shack
- The earthy smell of soil, leaf mold, rotting twigs and earthworms
- The rich fragrance of black cottonwood and balsam poplar resin emanating from sun-warmed buds as they open
- The scent of flowering shrubs and trees like cherries and lilacs
- The smell of freshly mown grass

Smell Cocktail

You'll need a few paper cups and a small twig as a swivel stick. As you hike, encourage the kids to selectively harvest tiny "bits" of the forest (e.g., a pinch of soil, a part of a leaf, a petal of a wildflower, a bud, a flake of bark). Place each item in your cup. Add your swivel stick. This is your smell cocktail! Give each creation a name, perhaps "Petaltopia" or "Forest Fragrance." Take time to smell each other's creations. Can you identify the fragrances? (See color section, figure 36.)

Spring feels like...

- The tenderness of a freshly opened leaf or the new growth on a conifer
- The softness of a pussy willow catkin
- The sliminess of a wriggling earthworm or slug
- The squelch of mud under your feet
- The warmth of the sun on your face

Let Your Fingers Do the Identifying

Can your fingers guess what mysterious natural object is in a box or bag, just by feeling? To make a Touch Box, use a medium-sized cardboard box with a hand hole cut in the side. For a Touch Bag, use an old pillowcase. Place five to ten familiar objects into the box or bag. These might include a leathery leaf such as an oak, a soft leaf like a maple, different kinds of seeds like maple keys and acorns, the cones of different conifers, a feather, a milkweed pod, a small bracket fungus, the seed head of a grass, a fern, a mussel shell, egg fragments, etc. Taking turns, have each child write down a) how many objects are in the bag, b) what each item is and c) a word or two describing the texture of each object. For fun, try the activity again wearing a pair of dishwashing or latex gloves. How was this different? Why?

Phenology

Activity 7 Spring Phenology: Track Seasonal Change

- **You'll learn:** How the local climate changes through the seasons and how plants and animals take their cues from these changes.
- **You'll need:** Spring Phenology Chart. (See Appendix, page 332.)
- **Procedure:** As in the fall (see Activity 8, page 99) and winter, complete the Phenology Chart. After, discuss how typical the season was in comparison to the long-term average. What really stands out?

Evolution

Reproduction Adaptations Scavenger Hunt

• You'll learn: That plants and animals have adaptations that allow them to reproduce.

• You'll need: Copy of the scavenger hunt sheet (see Appendix, page 319), pencil, clipboard.

• Background: For many plants and animals, spring is a time of mating and reproduction. Over millions of years, special adaptations have evolved to make this process possible. These include adaptations for attracting a mate and others for keeping away competitors for mates or breeding sites. In the case of plants, a common adaptation is having your genes (pollen) spread by the wind or an animal pollinator.

Egg showing speckled markings for camouflage

• Procedure: Visit an area with various habitat types, including field, forest and wetland, if possible. Ask the children to try to find as many plant and animal adaptations from the sheet. Encourage them to add other probable adaptations that they see. The purpose of some of the adaptations from the sheet are explained; however, some purposes are left blank. After completing the activity, have the children provide their own ideas as to what purpose these adaptations might serve. Have them do the same with the adaptations that they found on their own.

Camouflaged Eggs

• You'll learn: That eggs of birds that nest in the open, especially on the ground, are highly camouflaged.

• You'll need: Hard-boiled eggs, different colored markers or tempera paint, paint-brushes.

• Background: Explain that many birds such as killdeer and grouse nest on the ground. As a result, their eggs are exquisitely camouflaged, not just in color but in pattern, too. They will also choose the substrate (e.g., dark sand instead of light sand) that offers the best match to the egg color and pattern. In other words, birds and their eggs have evolved to maximize camouflage. Species that nest in cavities often lay all-white eggs, because camouflage is not a concern.

• Procedure: Show the children pictures of real eggs from ground-nesting birds.

Think about the most effective colors and patterns. Visit the area where the eggs will be hidden. Ask the children to think about how to best camouflage their eggs. Each child then takes two to three eggs and uses paint or markers to camouflage them as well as they can. Have them hide their eggs in a designated area or areas. Hide a few unpainted white eggs as well for comparison. Excluding their own eggs, how many can they then find within a given amount of time? Which eggs were the best camouflaged? How easy was it to find the white eggs?

Activity 10 Toilet Paper Timeline

- **You'll learn:** To visualize the massive time scale of life on Earth.
- **You'll need:** Roll of toilet paper of 450 sheets (tear off 50 from a roll of 500), sticky notes, large open area or hall.
- **Background:** It is hard to believe but the Earth is over five billion years old. However, from a child's perspective, there isn't much difference between numbers like 1,000, one million or one billion; these are difficult concepts to grasp, even for adults. This activity helps children to imagine just how recent human existence is in the incredibly long history of life on Earth.
- **Procedure:** Find a large open space. If you are outside, choose a calm day. Unroll the entire roll of toilet paper. The beginning of the roll represents the ancient past 4.5 billion years ago. Each square of

Toilet paper roll

toilet paper represents about ten million years. Write down each stage on a sticky note. Place each of the sticky notes at the squares indicated along the roll of toilet paper. Take a walk along the timeline.

Note: BYA = billion years ago; MYA = million years ago

- 4.5 BYA: The Earth is formed, along with the other planets (first square)
- 3.7 BYA: Earth's crust solidifies (square 80)
- 3.5 BYA: first life appears in oceans (square 100)
- 3.25 BYA: photosynthesis begins in oceans (square 125)
- 2.4 BYA: oceans contain significant amounts of oxygen (square 260)
- 1.9 BYA: first cells with nuclei appear in oceans (square 260)
- 650 MYA: first multicellular organisms appear (square 385)
- 500 MYA: first land plants with inner vessels (square 400)
- 250 MYA: mass extinction of 99 percent of all life (square 425)
- 245 MYA: Age of Dinosaurs begins (square 425)

- 200 MYA: the first mammals appear (square 430)
- 150 MYA: supercontinent breaking up; continents drifting apart (square 435)
- 65 MYA: Age of Dinosaurs ends, with mass extinction of 70 percent of all living things (square 444)
- 3.5 MYA: first proto-humans appear, in what is now Africa (last square, 3.6 cm from the end)
- 100,000 years ago: first *Homo sapiens*, our species, appears (last square, 1 mm from end)
- 10,000 years ago: recorded human history begins (last square, 0.1 mm from end)

Questions to ponder

- What did you learn about how long life has existed?

Chimpanzee

- How long, relative to the Earth's history, have humans inhabited the Earth?
- How might this timeline guide us in treating the Earth?

Alternative: Imagining your ancestors

As an alternative, consider creating an ancestor timeline, based on "Imagining Your Ancestors" on page 75. To do so, find a grassy, open area at least 200 ft. (60 m) long. It should be parallel to a long, straight road or at the beginning of a trail, depending on how far along the "bookshelf" you want to walk. Using stakes, make a line of string at least 33 ft. (10 m) long. This represents the start of the bookshelf. Use the Monkman family pictures in the Appendix or pictures from another family, going back as far as there are photos available. Place the photos on top of a stack of photo-size paper about 5 in. (13 cm) thick. Any kind of paper or light cardboard will do. Place a picture of a long-haired, bearded human at 4 in. (10 cm) down the pile, maybe with a sticky note attached so it's easy to find. Turn the pile on its side and place it on the ground at the start of the string line. Use Popsicle sticks to keep the pile upright. At about 40 in. (1 m) down the string, place a picture of a human with a thicker skull, especially under the eyebrows. Put some blank cards or photo-sized paper before and after this picture to represent the idea that we have to imagine an unbroken chain of ancestor photos. Do the same with the

Homo erectus picture at 33 ft. (10 m; about 13 steps from start). If you have enough string (not necessary), extend it to 200 ft. (60 m; about 80 steps from start) and place a picture of the common ancestor with chimpanzees (a chimp-like photo). If you wish, you can keep going, maybe along a road or trail, and place a lemur photo at 2,100 ft. (650 m; about 840 big steps) from the start. After that, refer to landmarks (e.g., a building, park) or towns and/or cities the kids would know that are located at 2.5 mi. (4 km; shrew photo); 9 mi. (15 km; big lizard photo); an additional 1,000 ft. (300 m; amphibian photo); another half-mile (0.8 km; ancient fish photo); and 1,000 mi. (1,500 km) from the start (first life on Earth; blue-green algae photo). You may wish to read aloud and discuss "Imagining Your Ancestors" (see page 75) as you walk—or even bike or drive—along the imaginary bookshelf with the group, stopping to pull out photos as you go.

Birds

Bird Song Ensemble

- **You'll learn:** That different species of birds have distinctive songs they use to stake out their territories and attract mates.
- **You'll need:** Song cards (see Appendix, page 313), song recordings at allaboutbirds.org, large group.
- **Background:** There is nothing quite like hearing the chorus of bird song on a warm spring day. In this activity, you'll take children through a day in the life of a forest, meadow and wetland. They will hear the pulse and rhythm of bird song during an entire spring day and night. Since birds sing at different times of the day, this activity helps children experience the rising and falling crescendo of sound as it occurs in nature. Birds, usually only the male, sing for two principal reasons: to attract a mate and to establish and defend a nesting territory. A rough translation of a bird song into English might be something like,

Gray catbird singing from gooseberry bush

"Hey, if you're a girl bird of my kind, I'm right here! But, if you are a boy bird, you better back off…this is my piece of the woods!" Learning bird calls and songs can be tricky. It is helpful to have some kind of memory aid or mnemonic. See Winter for some suggested bird song mnemonics. (See Activity 12, page 165.)

• **Procedure:** Hand out one of the bird song cards (see Appendix, page 313) to each child. Have the children listen to recordings and practice their mnemonic a few times. Have them study the times of day when their birds sing. Tell them that when they hear the time indicated on their card, they should begin to sing energetically and continue the song until they hear the stopping time. Using your storytelling skills and as much drama as you can muster, read aloud the unfolding of the day. Each time given is a prompt for children to look at the time on their card. Here is the story:

Imagine you want to experience bird song through an entire spring day. So one morning you get up very early and head out to a secret spot. This is where a forest, a meadow and a wetland all come together. You were told that an amazing variety of birds can be found there.

It is now 4 o'clock in the morning. You have a thermos of tea, a thick sweater and loads of patience. You rest your back against the trunk of a tree and wait for the world to wake up.

At 5 o'clock, the first fingers of light spread across the land and you marvel at the golden side light. The bird chorus begins to build.

At 6 o'clock, the mist is visible as it hovers over the still waters and the nodding heads of flowers. The air is filled with a cacophony of sound!

You open your thermos and enjoy a hot cup of tea and a sandwich at 7 o'clock. You savor the rising and falling tones of the symphony of birds!

At 8 o'clock, you get up to stretch and walk around a little. At 9 AM, you notice things are a bit quieter and the heat is building. You take off your sweater.

10 AM and all is well, but all is surprisingly quiet. At 11 AM, most self-respecting birds are taking a siesta. At noon, you notice the Sun is almost overhead.

At 1 PM, it's getting uncomfortably hot. The sun is warming your cheeks, so you take cover under a canopy of leaves. At 2 PM, the air feels humid, hot and heavy. At 3 PM, however, you hear some familiar friends. The shadows begin to stretch.

It is now 5 PM and you can feel the air beginning to cool. There is a lovely bronze side light that warms the edges of everything you see. At 6 PM there is something in the quality of light that is astounding.

At 7 PM the Sun is noticeably lower in the sky. By 8 PM, it is nudging the horizon. The clouds are dipped in pink, blue and gold. At 9 PM, the Sun has slipped below the horizon. It is now that lovely, darkening time between night and day—a blue and inky black that no artist can quite capture. At 10 PM you hear the hoot of a great horned owl saying *who is awake? me too!* and you decide it is time to leave. And so on stiff legs, you stumble home, refreshed and amazed at how the natural world comes alive with the chorus of bird song!

Activity 12 Listen for Your Mate

• **You'll learn:** How birds attract a mate through song.

• **You'll need:** Three photocopies of each bird song card from "Song Ensemble" activity (see Appendix, page 313), blindfolds.

• **Background:** This game is best played a little later in spring after the tropical songbirds have returned. Select a large open area, free of obstacles.

• **Procedure:** See the Bird Song Ensemble game (page 221) to find out why birds sing and call. Listen to real recordings of each of the songs used in the game. An iPod or smartphone with a bird app such as Sibley's and a small, portable speaker work well for this. Have children form pairs. Give each pair a blindfold and two copies of the same bird card. Participants should not discuss with other groups what species they are. Allow a few minutes for everyone to practice their song. Decide who will be the male and who will be the female in each pair. The females each take a blindfold and spread out randomly about 20–30 ft. (6–10 m) away. Ask them to tie on their blindfolds. Then ask the males to spread out a little. When the leader yells, "Sing your hearts out!" all of the males begin singing their species-specific song loud enough so the females can hear. The females try to find their mates. Afterwards, have everyone switch roles and/or species cards.

What challenges were there in finding a mate? What would happen to a songbird that wasn't able to find a mate? How would bird song travel in different habitat types? What might the effects be of noise pollution? Try replaying recordings of the real songs to see if the participants can now identify them more easily. Encourage everyone to get up before sunrise one spring morning and listen to the real bird chorus!

Activity 13 Can You Make a Robin's Nest?

• **You'll learn:** That making a nest is not easy!

• **You'll need:** A bucket of warm soapy water, nice gooey mud (mix soil and water), lots of dried plant fibers (e.g., dried grass) and, of course, patience!

• **Background:** A bird egg is a beautiful thing. Within this fragile, round container is the promise of new, feathered life. Bird eggs come in a surprising variety of shapes, sizes and colors. However, no matter what they look like, there is one indisputable fact: eggs roll! And a rolling egg is not a safe egg. Keeping their eggs both warm and safe from danger is the challenge every mother bird faces. That is why she makes a nest. Sometimes a bird nest is an elaborate affair like the woven, hanging nest of an oriole, and sometimes it is as simple as a hollow scrape in the ground like that of a killdeer. At first blush, making a bird's nest doesn't seem that remarkable. But if you think about it, birds have a handicap. They have no hands! In the case of robins, the nest is built by the female over the course of about six days.

She often locates it on a ledge or a forked tree branch and constructs it mostly from dead grass, twigs and mud. A robin nest can contain 350 individual pieces of vegetation! The bird drops grass on top of a layer of mud and molds it into shape by sitting, squirming, pushing with the wrist of her wings and stamping with her feet. Then she turns several degrees and goes through the same process again. By the time she is finished, she may have made several complete rotations.

• **Procedure:** Begin by making a mud and plant fiber pancake. Mix fibers together with globs of mud. Mix, knead and mix again. You should have a pancake about 6 in. (18 cm) across and ½ in. (1 cm) thick.

- Make four long fiber and mud cigars, about 4 in. (10 cm) long and ¾ in. (2 cm) thick. Roll, mix and roll again.
- Using mud, stick these mud cigars to the perimeter of the pancake. Knead them all together using plenty of mud.
- Sculpt the sides. Add more mud as required.
- Line with soft grasses and tufts of downy seeds. Let dry.
- Place your nest on something sturdy and admire your creation. You never know—maybe a robin will adopt it as its very own!

• **Suggestion:** You can also try to find out what human-made materials birds like for their nests. In early spring, cut 6-in. (15-cm) and 9-in. (22-cm) pieces of four different colors of yarn, string and cloth (narrow strips). Gray, brown, red and yellow work well. Put some on the ground close to a window and place the rest between the scales of pine cones—just loose enough so birds can easily pull the pieces out. Maybe add some hair from a hairbrush. Using string, suspend the cones outside the window. Keep track of what materials and colors the birds prefer. Why?

Blue-headed vireo on nest

Citizen Science Suggestions

NestWatch is a continent-wide monitoring program designed to track status and trends in the reproductive biology of birds. This includes when nesting occurs, how many eggs are laid, how many eggs hatch and how many hatchlings survive. The data is used to study the current condition of breeding bird populations and how they may be changing over time. The NestWatch website also has information on bird boxes. Visit **nestwatch.org** or **birdscanada.org**.

Mammals

Activity 14 Predator Stalk

• **You'll learn:** The art of stalking your prey.

• **You'll need:** Open field, blindfolds, large open space, large group.

• **Background:** After breeding, foxes seek out a den site, such as an old groundhog burrow, a hollow log, under a thick bush or an excavated hole along a hillside. The pups are born any time from early March until the end of May. During the spring, the vixen needs to find enough food for herself and her growing pups. Knowing how to hunt effectively is, therefore, an

"**DARWIN:** There is tremendous variety in the nests of birds. Huge differences can be found in nest location, shape, materials and more. However, we know very little about the forces in the environment that shaped the evolution of this incredible variety. For instance, it may be that domed-shaped nests (e.g., the inverted bowl the ovenbird makes from weaved grasses and leaves, with a concealed side entrance) arose because of increased competition for nesting sites forcing some species to nest on the ground. The risk from predators is greater on the ground so nests need to be better hidden. Birds don't just choose any colored material to build their nests, either. Zebra finches, for example, avoid colors that clash with their surroundings."

important survival skill. Foxes are direct register walkers. They carefully place one foot in front of the other, making virtually no noise because of the soft and hairy pads beneath their feet. A fox's rear paw is slightly smaller than the front paw, and they place it in the exact same spot as the front paw when they walk.

• **Procedure:** Practice walking like a fox. Be smooth, be careful, but mostly, be quiet! Select two volunteers and seat them about 15 ft. (5 m) apart. Make sure their eyes are closed or that they are blindfolded. Have the rest the group line up about 30 ft. (10 m) away. Acting just like foxes, can this group—one at a time—sneak between the spotters? Every time a volunteer hears a noise, they point to exactly where it is coming from. If they are pointing directly at a fox, that fox needs to hunker down and stay put. Can the foxes successfully stalk between the listeners without being heard? It is harder than you might think!

Variation: Tug-o-mouse

• **You'll need:** Several "Tug-o-mice," blindfolds, large open area, judge.

• **Procedure:** To make a Tug-o-mouse, take a 6 × 6-in. (15 × 15-cm) scrap of fur or cloth. Roll it up tightly and tie one end of a 20-ft. (6-m) rope around the middle. Form groups of three, made up of one meadow vole (also known as a field mouse), one fox and one judge. Spread out along the playing area. The meadow vole is blindfolded, because voles live in fields and their vision is obstructed by long grass. They can't always see approaching danger. Extend

Red fox

Darwin: Like wolves, foxes are closely related to dogs. In a famous Russian experiment with silver foxes from fur farms (where foxes are still quite aggressive), researchers wanted to try to recreate the evolution of wolves into dogs. Starting in 1959, they took 130 foxes and began breeding them. In each generation of fox kits, the researchers selected only the tamest ones to breed for the next generation. In just 20 generations, more than one third of the foxes were as tame as golden retrievers. Unlike wild foxes, the domesticated foxes also had floppier ears and patterns on their fur, and wagged their tails!

the Tug-o-mouse all the way out. Have the meadow vole hold one end. The fox needs to be at least 30 steps away from the end of the Tug-o-mouse; the judge can estimate the proper distance. When the judge says "Go," the fox begins to stalk. Every time the vole hears a dangerous sound, she pulls on the Tug-o-mouse, hauling it in (a bit at a time). This represents a vole moving along a meadow trail. The fox tries to pounce on the fur bit at the end. Continue until the vole is caught or safely hauled in. Any disputes are resolved by the judge! Switch roles.

Activity 15 Scent Trails

- **You'll learn:** How animals follow scent trails.
- **You'll need:** Lemon, almond, wrapped mint, maple or orange extract, blindfolds.
- **Background:** Imagine this. Your eyes are closed and you hunker down. You fill your lungs full of fresh spring air and you pick up a scent. It is the familiar odor of your friend Rick, and you can tell that he passed right by your front door, headed for downtown. You use your nose and you follow his scent right to a convenience store just in time to share his bag of chips.

If only that were true! Unfortunately, our human nose isn't sensitive enough to follow scent trails. However, many animals *can* follow scent trails. Canids—members of the dog family, including foxes, coyotes, wolves and dogs—have an incredible sense of smell, many thousands of times better than a human. A larger portion of their brain is given over to scent perception. They can distinguish between many different types of smell. We might say, "hmmm, mac and cheese." They might say, "Hmmm, noodles and cheese and butter and salt and milk and bread crumbs and metal pot and Aunt Marge must have just made this." Animals take short and deep sniffs to isolate and follow a scent.

• **Procedure:** In this game, you'll be given a "helping nose" so that you can follow a scent trail to something delicious! Work in partners. One person is blindfolded while the other lays down a scent trail with extract. You only need a drop or two every foot or so for about 30 ft. (10 m). Try to lay down a curving, sweeping trail to make things more challenging. At the end of the scent trail, place a wrapped mint. Guide the blindfolded partner to the beginning of your trail and let them use their nose to follow the trail. If you are lucky, just like a hunting fox following the trail of a rabbit, there might be something tasty at the end of your journey!

Amphibians and Reptiles

Activity 16 The Frog and Toad Orchestra

• **You'll learn:** The songs of your local frogs and toads.

• **You'll need:** Frog song descriptions, six or more participants.

• **Background:** One of the wonders of spring is to listen to the melodious strains of an amphibian orchestra, courtesy of your local frogs and toads. Frogs sing for the same reason birds do: the males are trying to attract a mate, and many species are also fighting for territory. To appreciate this natural concert, walk to a nearby marsh, swamp or bog in early spring, just as the Sun is starting to set. Remember to use focused hearing (page 270). Depending on where you live, listen for the high, piercing peep of a spring peeper, or maybe the trilling bursts of sound from the chorus frog. By late spring, you might also hear the low *jug-o-rum* of the bullfrog. Some species call earlier during spring, some later. During the day, you might even hear the bird-like trill of a species such as the gray treefrog. To learn to identify the frog songs in your province or state, go to frogwatch.ca (Canada) or aza.org/frogwatch/ (U.S.).

• **Procedure:** Explain to the children that you are the conductor and they are the various frog and toad species found in your region. Use the table (opposite) as a guide. Have the children imitate each of the sounds as best they can. Listen to the real sounds of frogs by going to the websites mentioned above.

Leopard frog

Spring Sounds

Species	Region	What they sound like	When they sing
Spring peeper	Eastern Temperate Forests, Northern Forests	High *peep-peep* sound	Early spring
American bullfrog	Eastern Temperate Forests, Northern Forests, Great Plains, Northwestern Forested Mountains, North American Deserts, Marine West Coast	Deep, resonant *rr-uum* or *jug-o-rum*	Late spring–early summer
Wood frog	Eastern Temperate Forests, Northern Forests	Sounds like a quaking duck	Early spring
Green frog	Eastern Temperate Forests, Northern Forests	*Gulp, gulp* deep from the throat	Late spring–early summer
Leopard frog	Eastern Temperate Forests, Northern Forests, Great Plains, Northwestern Forested Mountains	A throaty *ahhhhhhhhhh....*	Early spring
Chorus frog	Eastern Temperate Forests, Northern Forests, Great Plains, Northwestern Forested Mountains	Short bursts of trills made with your lips or tongue	Mid- to late spring
Eastern cricket frog	Eastern Temperate Forests	Use your tongue to make *click-click-click* sounds, reminiscent of pebbles clicked together; cricket-like	Late spring–early summer
Gray treefrog	Eastern Temperate Forests, Northern Forests	Slow musical bird like trill lasting 2 to 3 seconds. Use your lips or tongue	Late spring–early summer
Fowler's toad	Eastern Temperate Forests	Nasal, sheep-like *waaaaa*	Late spring–early summer
American toad	Eastern Temperate Forests, Northern Forests	A sustained trill from lips or throat, lasting up to 30 seconds	Early to late spring
Western toad	Great Plains, Northwestern Forested Mountains, Marine West Coast	Soft, quickly repeated *peep-peep*	Late winter–early spring
Great Basin spadefoot toad	North American Deserts	Short, harsh, nasal-sounding snores at 1-second intervals	Late spring–early summer
Great Plains toad	Great Plains	Rapidly repeated, harsh, machine gun-like trill; 20–30 seconds in length	Late spring–midsummer
Plains spadefoot toad	Great Plains	Short, harsh, *ouak-ouak* barks at 1 second intervals	Late spring–early summer
Pacific treefrog	Marine West Coast	*Rib-it, rib-it, rib-it*	Late winter–late spring
Red-legged frog	Marine West Coast	Weak series of 5–7 notes lasting 1–3 seconds: *uh-uh-uh-uh-uh*	Late winter–early summer
Sierran treefrog	Marine West Coast, Northwestern Forested Mountains, North American Deserts	*Rib-it* or *krek-ek*, with the last syllable rising in inflection	Nov–July (depending on location)

Citizen Science Suggestions

You can learn to be a citizen scientist by counting the frog and toad species you hear. Reporting this data to either **Frogwatch Canada** or **Frogwatch USA** will give scientists a better idea of the impacts of climate change and the general health of wetlands in your area.

As a conductor, you need to give clear signals to your orchestra. When you point to a frog species, it begins to sing. When you cross your hands and swipe them outwards (like a referee), they stop singing. When you raise both hands simultaneously upwards, the individual sound becomes louder. When you lower your hands, the sound becomes quieter.

Begin with the wood frog (or the earliest to sing in your region), and add additional frog and toad songs until all the species are singing in joyous chorus. Come to a dramatic crescendo and then fade out. You will have conducted a rendition of a wetland symphony, courtesy of your local frogs and toads!

Activity 17 Amphibian-watching

- **You'll learn:** To observe frogs, toads and salamanders as they prepare to breed.
- **You'll need:** Rubber boots, flashlights, camera, sound recorder (optional), amphibian guide or app.
- **Background:** The frogs of early spring usually begin calling when nighttime air temperatures have warmed to at least 45°F (8°C). Calls are usually loudest at dusk and during the first few hours of darkness. The best weather conditions

Wood frog

for hearing a full chorus are mild, damp, windless nights that follow a period of rain. Evenings when a light rain is falling can also be excellent. These are also the conditions when many salamanders move to breeding sites.

- **Procedure:** Grab a pair of rubber boots, a strong flashlight and a camera (your smartphone will do) and try to arrive at the wetland before it gets dark. Take a few minutes to make a sound recording or video of the wetland and chorus. Try to identify the various species calling. If necessary, use an app like "Audubon Reptiles and Amphibians" or a website such as Amphibiaweb.org. Then slowly walk in the direction of the calls. When you first approach, some of the frogs and toads will probably stop calling. All you need to do is pick a promising spot and wait. Eventually the calling will start again. Softly rubbing two stones together or whistling an imitation of a call will sometimes jump-start the chorus. Try to pinpoint the calls of one individual and shine your flashlight in its direction. Scan the water, the floating plant debris and the lower stems of the vegetation. Remember that many species such as chorus frogs are only the size of bumblebees and drably colored. They are often easiest to find by looking for the

Citizen Science Suggestions

Snapshots in Time is a long-term citizen science project aimed at mobilizing people to monitor the timing of spotted salamander and wood frog breeding throughout their respective ranges. The project aims to investigate possible effects of climate change on the timing of reproduction. Go to **oriannesociety.org.**

Darwin: In 2016, a species of salamander-like cavefish was discovered in Thailand. Known as *Cryptotora thamicola*, it is able to climb steep rocks and waterfalls in a way comparable to a four-footed amphibian, reptile or mammal—known together as tetrapods. The fish does this by planting and moving its two front fins and two back fins as if they were feet. *Cryptotora*'s skeleton has adaptations that have never been seen before in fish. For example, it has as pelvis built for walking. So, here's more proof that tetrapods evolved from fish! ”

shiny throat sacs moving in and out with every call. Some species such as wood frogs might be floating on the water itself; their vocal sacs are on the sides of their bodies. If you are close enough, take some pictures, either with a flash or by having another person shine the flashlight on the frog. You can always try to slowly move in closer for a better look as well.

There is also a good chance that salamanders will be on the move. They are most easily seen by driving slowly along back roads that pass through low, swampy woodlands or where there are flooded ditches adjacent to the woods. By watching carefully, you may be able to see some salamanders on the road. If you do, park your car, get out and walk. Take time to photograph these beautiful animals. Shine the flashlight on a few roadside pools as well—if you are lucky, you may see salamanders mating in a sort of underwater dance.

Activity 18 Nature's Amazing Magic Act: Raising Toads

• **You'll learn:** All or part of a toad's life cycle.

• **You'll need:** Toad eggs, pail (1-gal./ 4 L) with lid, pond water, terrarium, fine screening, food for tadpoles and adult toads, hand lens, small viewing bottle.

• **Background:** Raising toads allows you to see one of nature's most amazing magic tricks: the complete metamorphosis of an amphibian from egg to adult. Some key milestones to look at are: the tiny gills of young tadpoles, the small bumps that appear on both sides of the tadpole near the base of the tail, the appearance of the hind legs and then the front legs, the gradual disappearance of the tail, and the change in shape of the mouth as it gradually widens.

• **Note:** It is much more difficult to raise frogs to the adult stage (which takes a year or more in many species). If you cannot find toad eggs, use frog eggs instead, but return the tadpoles to their pond of origin when the legs appear. Frog eggs look like a floating mass of jelly-covered eggs.

• **Procedure:** In spring, when the toads are calling, look for long strings of jelly-covered toad eggs in the vegetation of small ponds and flooded ditches. Reach into the water and take or break off a string of a dozen or so eggs. If you have too many tadpoles, the larger ones will

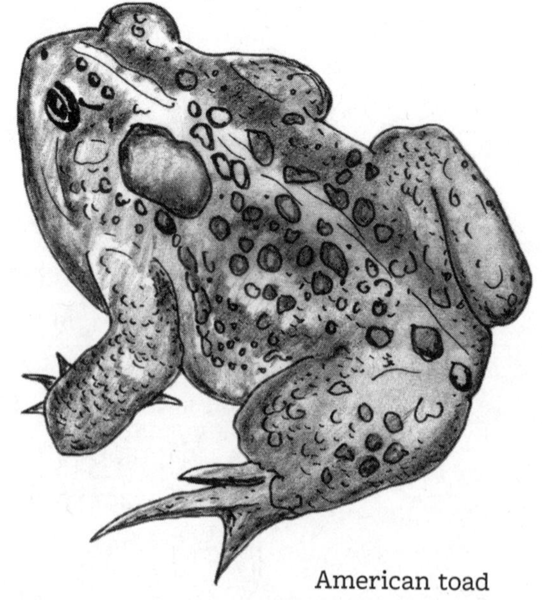

American toad

eat the smaller ones. Put the eggs in a pail with about 6 in. (15 cm) of pond water. At home or in the classroom, place the pail in a bright area but not in direct sunlight. Keep a hand lens and a small plastic viewing bottle beside the pail so the children can look at the eggs and tadpoles as they develop.

The eggs should hatch in 3–12 days. Notice the external gills on the tadpoles. They will become internal after a few days. Tadpoles eat tiny algae in pond water, so change half the water twice a week, using water from the same pond (never use tap water). You can also feed the tadpoles with bits of boiled lettuce or hard-boiled egg. Remove any old food before adding more. When the tadpoles start to develop legs (hind legs first), add some pieces of bark so they can climb out of the water. After about two months when their tails disappear, you will need to move the tiny toads to a terrarium. (See Activity 34, page 132 for directions on making a terrarium.)

Make sure there are pieces of loose bark, twigs and stones in the terrarium for the toads to hide under; plants are not necessary. Place a shallow bowl of pond water flush with the soil at one end of the terrarium. Add a few small stones to the bowl and continue to put in fresh pond water twice a week. Place four to five toads in the terrarium and return the rest to the pond. Tape a screen to the top of the terrarium to keep the toads from escaping. Try feeding your toads the smallest insects available at the pet store, such as tiny crickets or mealworms. You can also try giving them the smallest earthworms you can find. After a week or so—sooner if they won't eat—return the toads to the edge of the pond where they came from.

Be sure to take lots of pictures (e.g., the pond, the eggs in the water, eggs at home, newborn tadpoles) of each stage of development. Make notes and sketches in your nature journal, too, and don't forget to make regular use of your hand lens. Who knows? You might even be able to use your notes and photos as a project for an upcoming science fair at school.

Snake Slither

• **You'll learn:** How snakes move without using legs.

• **You'll need:** Open area, six or more participants, a scarf or long ribbon.

• **Background:** Although they are not loved by all, snakes are an important part of many ecosystems. They control rodent and insect populations and are in turn eaten by many other species. Scientists have recently discovered that venom from a number of poisonous snakes can be used to treat various illnesses such as heart disease, cancer and Parkinson's disease.

As the temperature rises in spring, snakes are on the move. First, they need to bask in the sun to warm up their bodies; you'll find them lying on rocks, paths and even along roadways, soaking up the sunshine. Then they slither off in

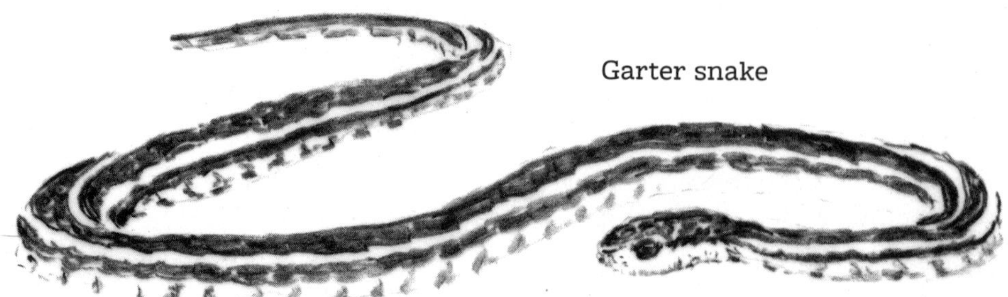

Garter snake

search of food. Snakes don't have legs, so they have to use something else in order to move. They accomplish this by contracting a series of muscles and using the scales on their belly as "tire treads" to help them wind their way forward. Twisting their bodies back and forth, they move about in a process known as lateral undulation.

• **Procedure:** Like a conga line dance, have children hold onto the person in front of them (not too tightly). Your snake will need a head (the front person) and a tail (the back person). Loosely tuck a scarf or a ribbon on the back of the tail so that it can easily be removed.

While everyone is hanging on, can the head grab the scarf from the tail, without the snake falling apart? The tail tries to avoid being caught. What is interesting about this game is that the movements the group spontaneously creates are very similar to those of a real snake. (See color section, figure 35.)

Darwin: Snakes evolved from lizards and, like lizards, the earliest snakes still had legs. Their main food source at that time was small mammals, so snakes that could easily enter the holes where the mammals lived were most successful. Over time, natural selection favored those individuals that had a wave-like form of locomotion in which they alternately flexed their bodies to the left and right. For these animals, legs only got in the way. Therefore, legs slowly disappeared. Paleontologists have found snake fossils where stubby, hind legs were still present but probably no longer functional. Boas and pythons still have tiny remnant legs, complete with bones. ”

Fishes

Watch Fish Spawn

• You'll learn: Some behaviors of spawning fish.

• You'll need: Polarized sunglasses, strong flashlight, canoe (optional).

• Background: Watching fish can be almost as much fun as catching them. From shore, from a canoe or, even better, from under the water with a mask and snorkel, fish-watching is an absorbing pastime. Don't limit your viewing to game species, however. North America boasts a wide diversity of fascinating non-game fishes that are often found in nearby streams and ponds. Just remember that a pair of polarized sunglasses will help to eliminate the glare from the water's surface.

• Procedure:

1. Northern pike spawn in the early spring shortly after the ice goes out and the water temperature is between 40°F–50°F (5°C–11°C). Look for them in weedy, shallow bays and flooded marshy areas, where they scatter and then desert their eggs. Pike will sometimes spawn in water so shallow that the fish's upper half sticks out into the air. Watch for what looks like a sleek, miniature submarine cruising along the edge of a cattail bed or between grassy hummocks.

2. Walleye also spawn in spring, when water temperatures reach about 40°F (5°C). Some populations spawn in fast-flowing shallow water over gravelly and rocky bottoms, which often makes for excellent fish-watching conditions.

Bluegills over nest

Although some fish can be seen during the day, large numbers are usually observed only at night, when the actual egg-laying takes place. You will, therefore, need a strong-beamed flashlight. The walleye's eyes glow when a light is shone upon them. Suckers are often seen in the same spawning locations as walleye.

3. Many of the fish in the minnow family spawn in clear streams in late spring, when water temperatures reach about 60°F (16°C). A good example is the creek chub, a popular, coppery-colored bait minnow. The female deposits her eggs in a mound-like nest of stones constructed by the male. Spawning males develop large, sharp tubercles on the head. Watch for the male guarding the eggs from predators.

4. Bluegills breed later in the spring, when the water warms to at least 66°F (19°C). They often spawn near docks in colonies sometimes numbering up to 50 nests. The male sweeps away gravel and other debris from the bottom with his caudal fin. At the same time, he holds his side fins out and pushes water forward to remain stationary. You may see him swim out, "greet" an approaching female and try to drive her into his nest. There is an elaborate courtship between the pair in which the two fish swim in a circular path, side by side, with their bellies touching. After the eggs are fertilized, the male remains at the nest to vigorously defend the eggs and fry.

5. In late spring or early summer, at about the same time bluegills spawn, watch for largemouth bass spawning in amongst the lily pads and in the shaded waters under overhanging trees, old docks and boathouses. The male constructs the nest at a depth of about 3 ft. (1 m). He uses his caudal fin to "sweep" a shallow depression free of loose silt and debris. The male and female then engage in pre-spawning rituals that involve rubbing and nipping each other. Like the bluegill, the male bass remains to jealously guard the eggs and later to protect the young fry, which swim in a school close to the nest.

Activity 21 Make Fish Prints: A Traditional Japanese Art Form

• **You'll learn:** The patterns and scale structures of different kinds of fish.

• **You'll need:** A whole fish, a newspaper, acrylic paint, paintbrushes or rollers, paper towels, paper (e.g., tissue paper, construction paper, rice paper, paper plates), fabric (e.g., T-shirt).

• **Background:** Gyotaku, or fish printing using rice paper and ink, originated more than 100 years ago in Japan as a way for anglers to record the size of their catch.

• **Procedure:** Cover the work area with newspaper. Wash off any mucus on the fish and pat dry with paper towels. Place the fish on the newspaper. Slather paint all over the exposed side of the fish using rollers or brushes. Make sure you cover one entire side of the fish. Place a sheet of paper or fabric (e.g., T-shirt) over the fish and press it down firmly, trying hard not to move it. Smooth down.

Carefully remove the paper or fabric and allow to dry. You can use the fish again for another print. Just carefully wash off all of the paint under a tap. (See color section, figure 34.)

Invertebrates

Activity 22 Bee-ware: Know Your Bees

Honey bee

• You'll learn: Bee dances, trivia and lots more.

• Background: Honey on toast. Delicious! But did you know that it takes 60,000 flights to bring back enough nectar for honeybees to make one teaspoon (5 milliliters of honey? Honeybees also pollinate close to one third of all the world's crops. A typical colony of honeybees has between 50,000 and 60,000 bees. Almost all are female worker bees, plus a few hundred drones (males) and one queen. Worker bees look after the young, protect the hive and search out food sources.

Bees are adapted for collecting pollen and nectar. They have special pollen baskets on their rear legs, a pollen brush and comb, and loads of hair (even on their eyes). Because pollen is sticky and worker bees are hairy, pollen attaches itself easily to them. Bees carry nectar back to the hive in a special honey stomach filled with enzymes. Once there, the bees regur gitate the nectar, which is then "chewed" by other worker bees and fanned by the wings of yet other bees (to evaporate any extra water). Eventually the sugary nectar transforms into honey, which is sealed in honeycombs. Bees use the honey as a stored food source for the winter months.

• Why honeybees dance: While it might be entertaining, we wouldn't think of telling our friends the location of a good restaurant by breaking out in an interpretive dance. Here's the thing: honeybees do. They use a special "dance language" that not only communicates how far away nectar-rich flowers are, but in which direction. The dance is easy to learn and fun to do. Here is how it works.

• Round dance: If the flowers are less than 300 ft. (100 m) away, the scout bee performs a "round dance." She begins to dance in a tight circle, making sure to attract the attention of the colony. First she moves in one direction; then she switches back the other way, always dancing the outline of a circle. Worker bees touch her with their antennae to pick up the scent of the flowers. Then off they go. They know the flowers are somewhere nearby the hive.

• **Waggle dance:** If the flowers are more than about 300 ft. (100 m) away, the scout bee does a "waggle dance." This dance is in the shape of a figure-8. The bee peels off to the right in a tight circle. Then, as she comes back to the center, she begins to waggle her abdomen and move towards the starting point in a straight line. This straight line part of the dance is known as the "run." The longer the run, the further away the flowers are. She then peels off to the left in a tight circle and begins the run again. Now here is something remarkable. The angle of the run in relation to the Sun tells the bees which direction to fly. Remember the combs in a hive are vertical. In this way the waggle dance tells the bees how far away and in what direction the flowers are.

• **Procedure:** Try out some honeybee trivia—BEElieve it or not! (from: beeman .ca/id26.html). How many answers did you get right?

Trivia question	Answer
How fast do honeybee wings beat?	11,400 times per minute (that's why we hear their buzzing)
How many flowers must honeybees visit to make a single pound (450 g) of honey?	About two million
How far does a hive of bees fly to bring you 1 lb (450 g) of honey?	Over 55,000 mi. (89,000 km)
How much honey does the average worker honeybee make in her entire lifetime?	1⁄12 tsp. (0.4 ml)
How fast can a honeybee fly?	About 15 mph (25 km/h)
How much honey would it take to fuel a bee's flight around the world?	About 2 tbsp (30 ml)
How long have bees been producing honey from flowering plants?	10–20 million yrs.
How many flowers does a honeybee visit during one collection trip?	50–100

The Bee Dance Drama Activity

• **You'll learn:** How bees communicate flower location through "dance."

• **You'll need:** Four plastic flowers of different colors (or real ones in a pot), a large field, honey-flavored candies, eight or more participants.

• **Procedure:** As leader, hide the four flowers in both different directions and distances from one single point in the field. Two of the flowers should be less than 300 ft. (100 m) away. Leave some candies at each flower. Have everyone form a large circle facing inward. This represents the outline of the hive. Create an open gap that is several feet (1 m) wide. This represents the entrance to the hive. Explain that everyone in the hive is a worker bee—all females and all performing different duties. If there are enough participants, place two or three bees near the hive to fan their wings, to bring fresh air into the colony. Explain that scout bees have gone out to find a source of nectar. You, as leader, are one of these scout bees and are going to tell the colony the direction and distance to the flowers. However, you are going to use a special dance to communicate this—just like real honeybees. (See Activity 22.)

Hold your index fingers up on your head to indicate antennae. Do the round dance first, for the flowers you've hidden close by (see explanation above). Have

Darwin: It is believed that the ancient ancestors of bees were wasps. In 2006, a 100-million-year-old bee fossil was found preserved in amber. Although clearly a bee, it shared some features of a carnivorous wasp. Like today's wasps, ancient wasps ate other insects. One hundred million years ago, flowering plants were starting to evolve and spread wide and far. They began depending more and more on insects to spread their pollen. One way in which bees could have evolved is that wasp larvae were fed prey insects that were covered in pollen from having visited flowers. A genetic mutation may have given some wasps a taste for protein-rich pollen, and this group may have eventually evolved into bees. It's interesting, too, that only female bees sting. That's because the stinger evolved from the ovipositor (an organ for laying eggs), which only females have. Remember, evolution can only work with or change body parts that already exist.

students "buzz off" to find the nearby flowers. If they do, they can take a honey candy or some other appropriate sweet treat. Next, do a waggle dance for each of the flowers hidden farther away. Waggle your behind. Remember the angle of the waggle is the direction of the flowers. The longer the waggle run, the farther it is to the flowers. Can the children read your waggle dance and find the hidden flowers? If there is time, have each child hide the flowers and dance the round and waggle dances.

Magic Butterfly Goop

- **You'll learn:** How to attract butterflies and moths.
- **You'll need:** 1 c. (237 ml) of white sugar, 1 can of beer, 4–5 over-ripe bananas, water, half-gallon (2-l) jar with lid.
- **Background:** We know spring is well and truly here when we spy the gentle flutter of a butterfly (or as one poetic person rephrased it, a "flutterby") sailing from flower to flower. Butterfly visits, however, can be few and far between. You can increase your chances of seeing butterflies by creating your very own magical potion. This recipe can attract such beauties as mourning cloaks, viceroys, swallowtail butterflies and, at night, even moths. It even works on a balcony. If you examine the ingredients you might think—hey, that's a bit strange! It turns out that some butterflies love fermented fruit, tree sap, mud and even mammal dung.

With a bit of patience, you'll be amazed by who visits your potent butterfly bait. Have a camera ready so you can take some pictures. Be aware that the bait may also attract wasps.
- **Procedure:** Mix sugar, bananas and a little water in a blender. Pour mixture and beer into jar. Top off with more water to make a half gallon (2 L). Place lid on jar loosely (contents will ferment). Pour the mixture into a shallow dish outside or paint on trees, rocks, etc. You can even soak a

> **Darwin:** When insects split from their crustacean cousins (e.g., crabs) and evolved to live on land, they needed a way to detect smells in the air. Over millions of years, they evolved smell-gathering organs (sensilla) on their antennae. Now we know that scent molecules arrive at the sensilla and enter through pores. Nerve cells in the sensilla then convert the scent into an electric impulse, which travels to the animal's brain. The insect has "smelled" the odor and will set out in search of the food.

sponge in the goop and hang it from a tree branch. Check your bait sites (at night, too) to see what winged splendors are enjoying your magic potion!

Plants

Activity 25 My Adopted Tree

• **Procedure:** As explained in the Fall chapter (see Activity 30, page 129), complete the spring section of "My Adopted Tree" on page 340.

Activity 26 The Wonder of Pollination

• **You'll learn:** The parts of a flower and how pollination works.

• **You'll need:** Hand lens, large flowers in full bloom with easy-to-see parts (e.g., tulip, lily, daffodil, gladiolus), toothpicks, clear plastic spray, cardboard (mosquito netting, duct tape are optional).

• **Background:** That beautiful flower you see? To our eyes, a flower might seem delicate and colorful, and may even inspire poetry. However, never forget that flowers evolved for one thing and one thing only: to produce seeds (e.g., berries, acorns) through pollination. This is one of the most amazing stories in nature and a triumph of evolution. It happens when pollen grains are spread from the male part of a flower (stamen) to the female part of the same or another flower (pistil). The two flowers must be the same species. When the pollen lands on the stigma (the sticky top of the pistil), it produces a tiny tube which travels down the style and pierces the ovary wall. Male cells from the pollen grain then travel down the tube and fuse or "mix" with eggs in the ovary. When this happens, we say that the plant has been fertilized. The fertilized eggs grow into seeds and the ovary wall becomes the encasing fruit around the seeds. So the next time you eat an apple, remember that you are eating an apple flower's ovary! A milkweed pod, too, is simply a ripened ovary containing seeds. Some plants have two kinds of flowers—some male, some female—that are separate from each other, either on the same plant or on different plants. Male flowers have stamens with pollen and female flowers have pistils with ovaries. Other plants have "perfect" flowers, with both male parts and female parts in the same flowers.

Flowers have evolved in countless ways to achieve pollination and fertilization. These include an amazing array of colors, markings, shapes, fragrances and even different flavors of nectar. Some plants (mostly trees like maples, aspens and conifers) rely on the wind to move their pollen. This kind of pollen is light and dusty. The flowers often hang loosely like caterpillars in order to be swayed by the wind, which helps to release the pollen. They often have no petals and no fragrance. These flowers usually appear before the tree's leaves come out. Sometimes you can see clouds of pollen in the air or on the surface of the water. Other plants rely on animals such as insects, birds and bats to spread their pollen. Animals visit flowers in search of food, such as nectar and pollen itself, shelter, nest-building materials and sometimes even mates. Some animals, such as many bees species, intentionally collect pollen as food, while others, such as many butterflies and birds, feed on nectar. Markings in the flower guide the animal to the nectaries where the nectar is located. They move pollen by accident, because it sticks to their bodies as they feed. This kind of pollen is not only sticky but too heavy to be moved very far by the wind. When the animals fly to another plant, the pollen on their bodies accidentally falls onto or brushes up against the sticky top of the pistil.

• **Procedure:** First, try to see and identify the parts of a flower as shown in the diagram. Be sure to smell the flower and to admire the beauty of each part. Remember to use the hand lens at each stage of the dissection. Carefully pull off the green sepals, which protect the flower in the bud stage. Take a close look at the color of the petals and any markings on them. Then remove the petals and look for the stamens with their club-like heads (anthers). Gently touch an anther to see if any pollen rubs off. Pull off the stamens and look closely at the pistil, which is thicker and often taller than the stamens. Identify all three parts. Touch the stigma. Is it sticky? Remove the pistil(s) and break open the ovary to see the ovules inside. Each ovule contains an egg which, when fertilized, will develop into a seed. Sketch and label each flower part in your nature journal. You can reconstruct the flower if you wish, gluing the pistil, several stamens

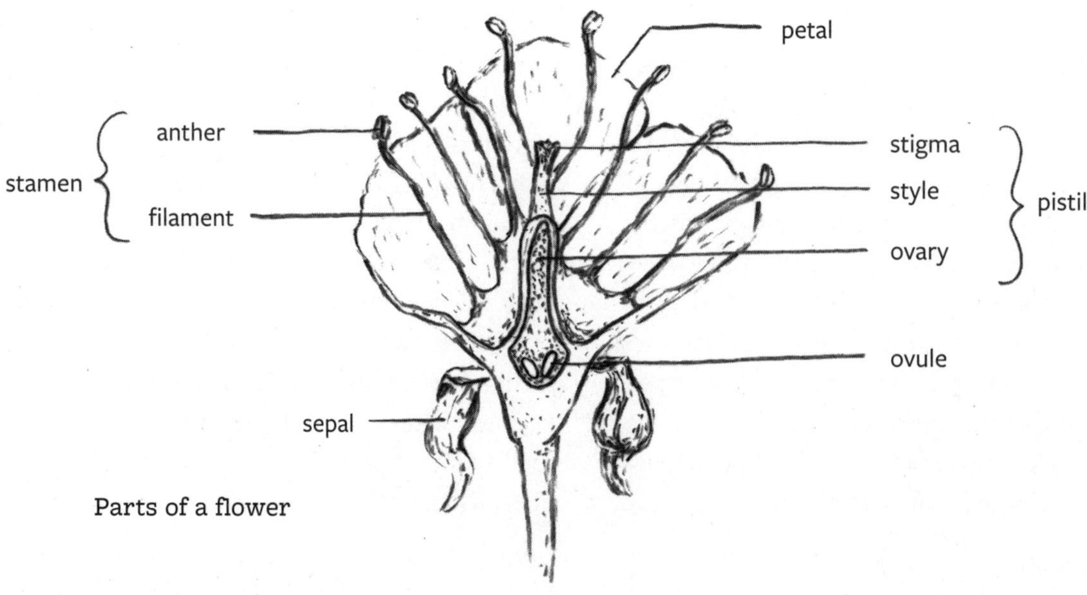

Parts of a flower

and a couple of the petals and sepals to a piece of cardboard. Label all of the parts. Apply a clear, plastic spray to preserve the flower parts.

• **Suggestion:** Whenever you are admiring flowers in a garden or on a hike, take a moment to try to see the various structures. The shape, color and location of these parts have evolved in different ways in different kinds of flowers because of the wide variety of pollinator-flower relationships. This is especially true in orchids. (See color section, figure 39.)

Activity 27 Pollen Transfer

Using either a small paintbrush or the tip of a finger, have children carefully touch the anthers to see if some dust-like, yellow pollen grains rub off. Then, flying like butterflies if they wish, have them move to another plant of the same species and rub the grains onto the stigma at the tip of the pistil. If there is no pollen to be found, give each child a little flour to rub onto the stigmas to see if it will stick.

Bee-watching

Spend some time observing bees visiting flowers such as those of an apple tree. Try to see the pollen grains on their "furry" bodies. An adult might want to carefully catch a bee in a viewing jar. You should be able to see a little ball of pollen on each of its back legs. These are pollen grains that the bee has brushed off into "baskets," which are made up of stiff hairs on its legs. A magnifying glass or hand lens will allow you to see more detail. The bee will carry the pollen back to the hive where it is fed to young bees.

Proving Pollination is Real

Have you ever wondered if pollination is "real"? Well, here's a way to find out. In the early spring, before the buds open, find a fruit tree. Get a piece of mosquito netting and use it to loosely encase the end of a twig—almost like you were putting on a loose sock—that has lots of big buds. Make sure there's plenty of room for the leaves and flowers that will soon come out. Use duct tape or string to secure the netting to the twig so it won't fall off and insects won't get inside. The netting should stop any insects from pollinating the flowers. When the petals have all fallen from the flowers, remove the netting. Check to see if any of the flowers within formed fruit. If they did, there must have been a hole somewhere!

"Busy Bee" Pollination Game

• **You'll learn:** How bees pollinate flowers.

• **You'll need:** For the bee: black and yellow clothing, a woolly hat with two antennae made from straws; for each flower: three or four large blue or purple cardboard petals, three socks for stamens, a woolly hat for a stigma, six ping pong balls with Velcro attached for pollen, one plastic bottle with juice representing a nectary, one can of floral room freshener spray, large space, 17 or more participants.

• **Background:** This game illustrates how pollen is transferred from the stamen of one flower to the pistil of another. See Activity 26 for an explanation of how pollination takes place.

• **Procedure:** The game requires at least two flowers, each consisting of a group of children representing the different flower parts. For each flower, you need three or four children holding the petals; two or three as stamens, wearing a sock on a hand and two or three ping pong balls stuck to the sock; one as a pistil, wearing a woolly hat and standing a little higher than the stamens (on a block or log, if necessary); one person with the juice bottle; and one person with the room freshener. Explain the role of each flower part: the petals and perfume (three squirts maximum) try to attract the bee as it buzzes around; the bottle of nectar is offered to the bee as food; stamens transfer one ping pong pollen grain onto the bee's back; the pistil transfers pollen from the back of the bee to its woolly hat (stigma). One person volunteers to be the bee. The pollen-free bee buzzes around until it is attracted to one of the flowers. It brushes up against the stigma (no pollen yet to transfer), drinks some nectar and brushes up against the stamen socks (the stamens each transfer one ball to the bee's hat). The bee then moves on to another flower, brushing up first against the pistil as it drinks (who takes a pollen grain and puts it on the hat); the bee then brushes up against the stamens (pollen transfer), drinking a little all the while. The bee then leaves to visit other flowers, including a second visit to the first flower. At the end

Bumblebee in columbine

Citizen Science Suggestions

Project BudBurst: Help scientists understand changing climates in your area by making regular observations of your plants. You will be paying special attention to the timing of leafing, flowering, and fruiting of plants. Visit **budburst.org**.

Darwin: For millions of years, flowering plants have been evolving to attract their pollinators, which in turn have been adapting to changes in the plants. Each species evolves to its own benefit. For example, some plants like skunk cabbage are "warm blooded"— they generate heat. This warmth, along with the plant's putrid smell, attracts early-spring insects, which are looking for food and a spot to warm up. In exchange, the insects end up pollinating the plant. In the case of bees, they are attracted to blue and yellow flowers and to flowers with lines leading to the nectar. Therefore, bee-pollinated plants have evolved to have these traits. If pollination is to work, however, the bees have to transfer pollen effectively. This is why they have evolved traits like hairiness, to accidentally pick up and transfer pollen. We call this coevolution.

of the game pollen will have been distributed onto the stigmas of the various flowers. Switch roles if you play again. (Adapted from "Games for the Outdoor Classroom," *Farming & Countryside Education.*)

Activity 31 Hammered Flower and Plant Activity

• **You'll learn:** Flowers and leaves can act as natural dyes.

• **You'll need:** Plastic or paper bags for harvesting, scissors, boards (or any hard surface like a picnic table that can be dented), hammers, paper towel, watercolor paper and/or white cloth (e.g., a handkerchief, a T-shirt), acrylic preservative (optional).

• **Background:** After the grays, whites and browns of winter, our eyes are hungry for the vibrant colors of spring. From pale violets, butter yellows and glorious pinks to the many intense shades of green, spring is a feast for the eye! You can capture some of this beauty by hammering colored flowers and plants to release their natural dyes onto either paper or fabric. Please note: You'll need adult supervision for this activity. Also, be sure you can identify any noxious plants that might be in your area such as poison oak, poison ivy or giant hogweed.

• **Procedure:** Go for a walk and harvest various flowers and leaves that you know are safe to touch. You are looking for plants and flowers that aren't too juicy or too dry. Take just a few leaves or flower

Darwin: Richard Feynman, a famous American physicist, had an artist friend who said that a scientist can't appreciate the beauty of a flower the way an artist can. His artist friend felt that by studying a flower scientifically and 'taking it all apart,' the flower loses its beauty. Feynman disagreed. He said that, as a scientist, he sees more beauty and wonder in a flower—not less—than even an artist sees. Scientists can imagine the cells, the complicated actions going on inside them and the fact that the colors evolved to attract insects to pollinate the flower. Scientific knowledge only adds to the excitement, mystery and awe we feel before a flower.

heads from any one place. Place these in your collection bag. Don't ever harvest anything that isn't in abundance. Next, place your watercolor paper (or cloth) on top of the hard surface. Artfully arrange a variety of flower heads and plants on the paper. Cover this with two or three layers of paper towel. Now, methodically and carefully, hammer on top of the paper towel, trying to make sure you hit each part of the plant hidden below. Don't hit too hard! And careful for your fingers too! You may need to experiment with a variety of flowers and plants.

When you are done hammering, peel away the paper towel and the plant. You should have a lovely imprint of your plant on the watercolor paper or cloth. Admire your creation and savor the beauty of the natural world! You may wish to spray it with acrylic preservative to protect it. (See color section, figure 33.)

Fungi

Activity 32 An Artist's Canvas in the Forest

- **You'll learn:** How to make a beautiful piece of art with a shelf fungus.
- **You'll need:** Artist's conk fungus, knitting needle or dull pencil.
- **Background:** Artist's conk (*Ganoderma applanatum*) is a shelf fungus that grows throughout North America where dead or dying hardwoods are present. It projects straight out from tree trunks or fallen logs and is woody throughout. The upper surface is shades of brown and/or gray, with a white tip in younger specimens. The underside (the surface from which spores are released) is a perfect white color.

Darwin: Fungi are an amazingly old and diverse kingdom of life, yet we know very little about them. In fact, names have been given to only about 5 to 10 percent of the more than one million species thought to exist. This is a great area for curious young scientists to get involved. You'll soon learn that the vast majority of fungi are not mushrooms, which will lead you to start to wonder about all the rest. A good starting point for learning more is Jens Peterson's book *The Kingdom of Fungi*. It is full of amazing pictures of the incredible diversity of these organisms. You'll find yourself wishing for a really good hand lens because teeny-weeny fungi are really beautiful—and cool!

When it is touched or etched, the underside "bruises" and turns dark brown very quickly. This makes it easy to draw on.

• **Procedure:** When you find an artist's conk, be sure that the underside is soft and can be etched before picking it. Depending on where you live, etching may not be possible until later in the spring. Remove the conk, take it home, and do your etching as soon as possible. Use a knitting needle or the tip of a dull pencil. You can make detailed drawings or even print short poems or nature quotes, depending on the size of the conk. Kids will love doing this. You may, however, wish to have them do a practice drawing first on a piece of paper of the same size as the conk before working on the real thing. Artist's conk etchings will last for years and make a wonderful addition to your nature table or even the mantle in your living room! (See color section, figure 32.)

Weather

Activity 33 Cloud-watching

• **You'll learn:** The different kinds of clouds and the types of weather they are associated with.

• **You'll need:** Cloud reference chart from a book or online (e.g., National Weather Service), nature journal, camera or sketching materials.

• **Background:** Clouds come in many shapes and sizes and each has its own characteristics. Starting with just four basic cloud types (cumulus, stratus, cirrus and nimbus) nature composes an endless symphony of interesting variations. By taking time to really LOOK at them, you will appreciate an amazing spectacle of form, color, thickness and light and shadow. Sunset and sunrise provide some of the most beautiful cloud spectacles. Clouds are also like giant billboards in the sky, telling us what weather conditions are on the way. Some of the easier clouds to identify and relate to weather are the following:

- Cirrus: High-altitude, wispy clouds, which indicate fair weather
- Cirrocumulus: Clouds that look like ripples of water on the surface of a lake and are a sign of good weather
- Cumulus: Large, white, fluffy clouds, which indicate fair weather when they are widely separated. If they are large with numerous heads, they can bring intense showers.
- Nimbostratus: Low blankets of cloud, which indicate rain or snow
- Stratocumulus: A lumpy mass of clouds covering the entire sky, which may produce light rain
- Cumulonimbus: Low clouds with a characteristic flat, anvil-like top. They often bring strong winds, thunder, lightning and even hail.
- Stratus: A low, fog-like layer of clouds, which may produce drizzle

When your personally made forecast comes true, you end up feeling more connected to nature, since your information came from the sky and not from a screen or radio. Like nature observation in general, cloud-watching is an antidote to boredom. You will never be bored when you get in the habit of looking at the sky.

• **Procedure:**

1. Record cloud types and predict the weather: Go to srh.noaa.gov/srh/jetstream/clouds/cloudwise/types.html to see 10 basic cloud types. Over several weeks, watch the sky and try to take a photograph or make a sketch of each of the ten types. In your nature journal, write down the date, the cloud type and your weather predic-

Cumulus clouds before a rainstorm

tion. The following day, write down what kind of weather actually occurred. Were you correct? If you took photos, glue them in your journal. No special techniques are required to take good cloud pictures. However, if you want dramatic shots, try taking a picture when the Sun is at its brightest and is directly appearing or disappearing from behind the clouds. If you shoot clouds during sunset, you will be able to capture a variety of unique colors.

2. Display cotton cloud types: In this activity, you will make cotton ball representations of the types of clouds you see. For instance, on a sunny day, you will often see puffy cumulus clouds. On a large piece of blue cardboard—leave enough room for all ten cloud types—stretch the cotton balls into the shapes of clouds you just saw and glue them to the cardboard. Write down the date, time and cloud type. You can also write down how the weather changed (or stayed the same) over the following hours or day. Use watercolor paint to make the cotton balls gray for rain clouds.

Activity 34 Make a Cloud in a Jar

• **You'll learn:** How a cloud forms.

• **You'll need:** A glass jar and lid, boiled water, a can of hairspray, ice.

• **Background:** When moist air cools, the water vapor in it will condense on any nuclei in the air, such as dust or smoke particles, forming a cloud. In this experiment, all three ingredients are present.

• **Procedure:** Pour about 1 in. (2 cm) of boiled water into the jar. Screw the lid on and shake the jar a little so that the water heats up the sides. Remove the lid, turn it upside down and use it to hold a couple of ice cubes. Set the lid with the ice cubes on top of the jar for a few seconds. Remove it and quickly spray some hairspray into the jar. Place the lid and ice back on top of the jar. Watch carefully as a cloud forms inside the jar and swirls around. You can then take the lid off and watch as the cloud escapes. (See color section, figure 31.) (Adapted from kidspot.com.au/things-to-do/activities/how-to-make-a-cloud-in-a-jar)

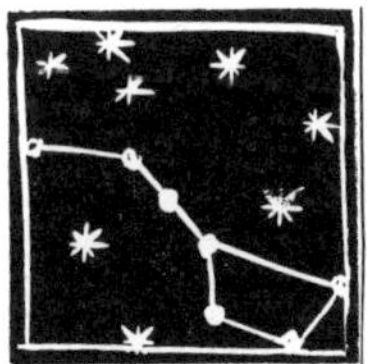

The Sky

Activity 35 Record Sunrise and Sunset Locations

• **You'll learn:** To record sunrise and sunset locations on or near the spring equinox.

• **Procedure:** As in the fall (see Activity 37, page 135) and winter, take note of exactly where the Sun rises and sets in relation to landmarks on the eastern and western horizons.

Measure Your Shadow

• **Procedure:** As you did in September (see Activity 38, page 135) and December, go outside at noon and measure the length of your shadow.

Sagan: Our Earth, like the other planets, formed as chunks of rock and debris in the early solar system collided and then clumped together because of the pull of gravity. This increased the gravitational pull of the early Earth. Eventually, Earth was big enough to start rotating like a straight-up spinning top. However, it probably attracted a huge piece of space debris that knocked the early Earth off-kilter and into the tilted position it's in today. Just think. We enjoy seasons because our Earth was smacked by a huge space rock!

Path of the Sun through the Seasons

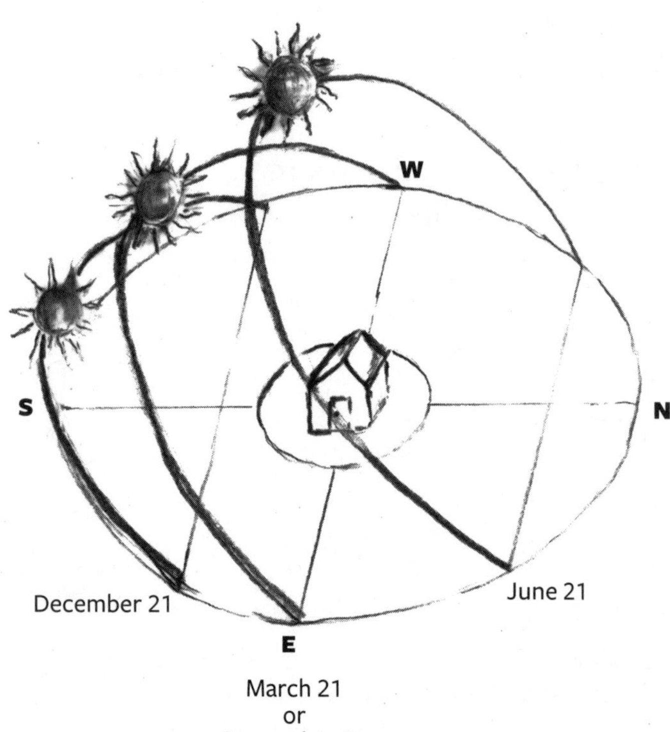

Activity 37 Observe Leo the Lion and Other Spring Constellations

• **You'll learn:** To identify spring constellations.

• **You'll need:** Sky chart or app.

• **Background:** Ancient peoples throughout the world recognized this constellation as a large animal. The Greeks and Romans saw it as a lion, the Chinese perceived a horse and the Incas are believed to have seen it as a cougar.

• **Procedure:** Leo is found high in the southern sky from early April to late June. The easiest way to locate this large but rather dim constellation is to find its brightest star, Regulus. First, face north to locate the Big Dipper and the two stars that form the end of the Dipper's bowl closest to the handle. Extend an imaginary line southward from these two stars to the next bright star you encounter—

a magnificent white star high in the sky. This is Regulus, and it marks one of the Lion's forepaws. Now, face south, so the Lion appears right side up, and to see the remaining parts of the beast. His proudly arched neck and head are formed by an asterism known as the Sickle, located a little north of Regulus. Working back towards the east, look for the stars that outline his hindquarters, tail and rear legs. If you look to the west, you should be able to see the Twins, Castor and Pollux, of the constellation Gemini. These stars represent the Twins' heads. Try to imagine them prancing along, arm in arm. Just to the south of Pollux you should see a large, bright star, Procyon, accompanied by a smaller star. Together they form the constellation Canis Minor, the Little Dog. Yes, it's nearly impossible to make a dog out of two stars, but use your imagination! Try to imagine him as a friendly puppy, tagging along faithfully behind the Twins as the Lion approaches.

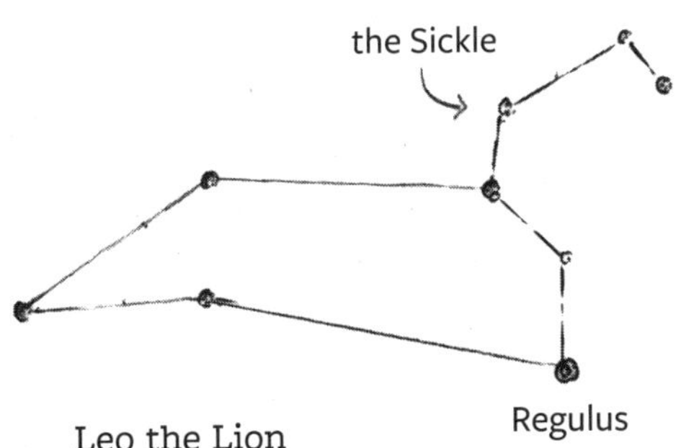

Honoring the Season

Activity 38 Spring Equinox (March 21)

The spring equinox, also known as Ostara (Eostre), occurs on or close to March 21. It marks the beginning of spring and in many traditions is the start of the New Year. Buds swell in the strengthening Sun's light, animals breed and the quiet of winter is replaced by the exuberance of spring. It is a time of new beginnings.

- Hold an Equinox Experience (see Activity 43, page 140 in Fall), and adapt it to spring
- Decorate your home or classroom with early blossoms or bouquets of bought flowers
- Understand why the Easter bunny lays eggs. This comes from an ancient Saxon tale about their lunar (or spring/summer) goddess, Eostre. In one version of the tale, Eostre found an injured bird and changed it into a hare to save its life. However, the transformation was incomplete. To thank Eostre for saving her, the hare laid eggs and decorated them as gifts. Parts of the myth were absorbed into the modern Easter celebration.
- Plant seeds inside to be transplanted outside after the last risk of frost. Mexican sunflower (tithonia) is a good choice. It is a great plant for attracting both hummingbirds and butterflies.

- Decorate eggs. Boil a single onion skin with a few eggs to get a soft orange. Adding more onion skins produces rust, a half-teaspoon (2.5 g) of turmeric gives a sunny yellow and beet juice and vinegar make pink. You can also decorate with markers. (See color section, figure 40.)
- Fly kites. Go to a hilltop and run like a spring hare! Laugh out loud and enjoy the wind! Try to feel this season of new beginnings that you have been craving.
- Hold an egg-balancing contest. Try balancing a hard-boiled egg on your finger. Run a relay race with spoons and a hard-boiled egg. Or try egg tossing. Set up two lines facing each other. Start close up and toss to the person across from you. After each catch, take a step back. See which pair can toss the farthest without breaking an egg!
- Create a spring nature table. If you aren't doing this already, cover a table with green and yellow cloth and then decorate with signs of spring: catkins, pieces of birds' eggs, flowers, etc.

Activity 39 Earth Day (April 22)

Earth Day, which takes place on April 22, has always been closely linked to education. First held in 1970, it was framed as a "national teach-in on the environment." It brought together people to fight for a single cause: protecting the environment. Schools often prefer to celebrate the event over an entire week, "Earth Week." It is important to do more than just a simple litter clean-up or other token measure. Use this book to plan outings that actually engage children with the natural world in a meaningful, personal way and help them to become more knowledgeable and appreciative of nearby nature. Although most of these suggestions apply to school settings, many can be modified to be done at home or with friends and neighbors.

- **Schoolyard or backyard naturalization project:** Starting in the fall, develop a plan to transform a corner of the schoolyard or your own backyard into a natural habitat with native trees, flowers and pathways. (See color section, figure 38.)
- **Earth Day assembly:** Your assembly might include a guest speaker, classroom displays, classroom sketches/plays/songs about nature, everyone dressing up as an animal or plant and bringing in an environmental storyteller. (See color section, figure 30.)
- **Yard sale fundraiser:** Kids can sell their old toys, video games and books. The money raised could then be donated to a conservation organization.
- **Art and photography exhibit:** Display photographs, sketches and other art pieces on the theme of students' personal experiences in the natural world.
- **Birdhouses and feeders:** Using a plan for birds that are common in your school area, find volunteers to pre-cut the parts of a birdhouse. Children can then nail the boxes together with the assistance of several adults. Some of the houses can be erected around the schoolyard, while others can be taken home. You could also sell some boxes to raise money.
- **A pledge board:** Provide a pad of sticky

notes for students to record their nature pledges for the year: "I will play outside at least one hour a day" or "I will set up and maintain a bird feeder for the next year," to name a couple.

- **Local plants and animals:** Hold an event such as an assembly or science fair on the theme of local plants and animals. Prepare information posters, have a PowerPoint slide show, watch videos from YouTube and maybe even have classrooms prepare field guides to everything from neighborhood birds to fungi. Have kids share some experiences they've had with these species.
- **YouTube Earth Day film festival:** Show YouTube videos on the theme of Earth Day and how people are helping the environment. Inspire kids to feel like they can make a difference for our planet. Among the best are "Get 'em Outside!" (5:35), "The Earth Day Network's Education Department" (2:10), "Natural Growth: Connecting Urban Youth with Nature" (4:07), "Change the World in 5 Minutes: Everyday at School" (4:33) and Jane Goodall's "Roots & Shoots" (4:29).

Quotes on spring for contemplation

If we had no winter, the spring would not be so pleasant.

—Anne Bradstreet

If I had my life to live over, I would start barefoot earlier in the spring and stay that way later in the fall.

—Nadine Stair

In June as many as a dozen species may burst their buds on a single day. No man can heed all of these anniversaries; no man can ignore all of them.

—Aldo Leopold

Every spring is the only spring—a perpetual astonishment.

—Ellis Peters

The world's favorite season is the spring. All things seem possible in May.

—Edwin Way Teale

Dandelion and seeds

Summer

the crescendo

The preparations of spring bear fruit in summer. Eggs become fledged birds, flowers become ripe berries and tadpoles transform into small frogs and toads. Summer is a treat for all of our senses. Roadside flowers provide a parade of ever-changing color. The warm air is full of the smell of blossoms and, in late summer, insects replace birds as the source of most song. Our palates, too, are well served with all manner of cultivated and wild berries. But despite weather that is often hot and sultry, signs of fall arrive early. By mid-summer, shorebirds are already heading south and a few splashes of color change are apparent in the leaves. As Henry David Thoreau observed, "How early in the year it begins to be late."

Some Key Events in Nature in Summer

Overview

The "early summer" period runs from about the start of June until mid-July. "Late summer" covers the period from approximately mid-July through August. Timing of events will vary depending on latitude, elevation and the vagaries of the weather. Climate change, too, is accelerating some events and delaying others. The sequence of events, however, is always the same. The references point to an activity based on this event.

Continent-wide Overview

Birds

Early summer

- With migration completed, June is the month of peak nesting activity. Fledgling birds such as ducklings and goslings are a common sight.
- Hummingbirds are a constant source of wonder and delight and they visit our gardens and feeders all summer long. (See Activity 9, page 275.)
- Bird song is at its strongest and most diverse. The different drumming patterns of woodpeckers are noticeable too, if you really pay attention. (See Activity 10, page 276.)

Late summer

- Many birds are replacing their feathers through a process called molting. (See Activity 11, page 278.)
- Many species flock up and roost in large, clamorous flocks. Swallows start congregating on wires.
- Shorebirds stream southward in large numbers, to the delight of birders. (See Activity 12, page 279.)
- With a few exceptions, bird song soon ceases.
- Songbird migration is in full swing by late August, particularly for warblers. Migrant songbirds can be attracted to backyard birdbaths, especially if there is water dripping into the basin to catch their attention.

Mammals

- Many mammals are active at dawn and dusk and can often be seen then. Some are also active at night. (See Activity 13, page 281 and Activity 14, page 282.)

Early summer

- This is a time of baby mammals such as deer, bear, raccoons, skunks and red foxes. They are often seen along roadsides and even in suburban backyards. Sadly, a great deal of roadkill occurs.
- Observing bats can be a fascinating activity, especially on warm June evenings.

Late summer

- Food becomes plentiful as countless berries ripen. Among the most important for mammals are blueberries.
- Some bat species begin to congregate at mating and hibernation sites.
- Wolves and coyotes are often very vocal.

Amphibians and Reptiles

- Reptiles are a common sight all summer and most often seen basking in the sun. (See Activity 15, page 283.)

Early summer

- Early June nights resound with the calls of numerous species of frogs and toads. These include the mighty voice of the bullfrog, a voracious feeder. (See Activity 16, page 285.)
- Turtles are often seen crossing roads and laying their eggs along roadsides and in other locations with loose soil.
- A variety of young frogs complete their development and emerge from natal ponds.

Late summer

- Garter snakes give birth in July and August. The young are born live and may number as many as 50 in a brood.
- By late July or early August, the frog chorus comes to a close.
- A number of species of baby turtles are born.
- Frogs are often abundant in fields adjacent to wetlands.

Fishes

- Bass, carp and bluegills continue to spawn in early summer and make for interesting fish-watching. (See Activity 17, page 286 and Activity 18, page 286.)
- In mid- to late summer, many fish move to deeper, cooler waters.

Invertebrates

- Summer is a great time to visit tide pools and explore beach habitats. Look for "seaweeds" like kelp, small fish like sculpins and all manner of invertebrates from anemones to sea stars. (See Activity 19, page 287 and Activity 20, page 288.)
- All summer long, earthworms are often found on lawns at night, especially during or after a soaking rain. (See Activity 21, page 290.)

Painted lady butterfly

Early summer

- Butterflies abound, as do damselflies and dragonflies. This is a great time for both butterfly- and odonate-watching, as explained on pages 35–39. (See Activity 22, page 290.)
- Watch also for giant silk moths (e.g., Prometheus).
- Fields alive with fireflies provide entertainment by night. (See Activity 23, page 292.)
- Aquatic insects are active and plentiful, making this a great time of year for pond studies. (See Activity 24, page 293 and Activity 25, page 294.)
- Biting insects such as deerflies, horse flies, mosquitoes and stable flies are abundant in many areas.
- Hawk-moths, like the hummingbird clearwing, nectar at garden flowers all summer long.
- By early July, cicadas start to fill the void left by the decrease in daytime bird song.

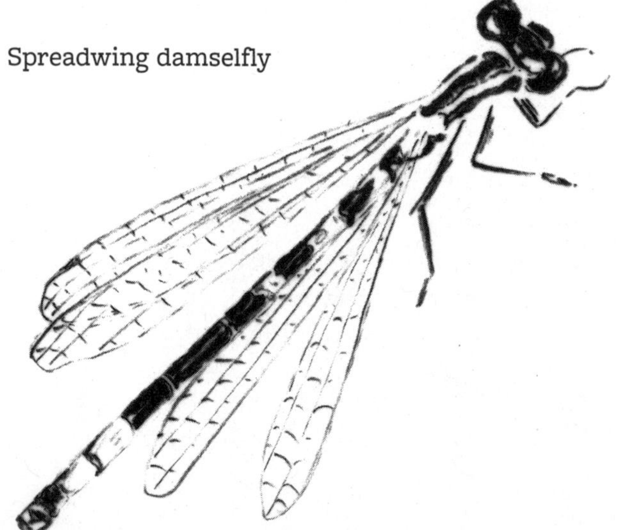
Spreadwing damselfly

Late summer

- The insect world explodes wide open, with many species reaching peak numbers. (See Activity 26, page 295.)
- The calls of insects such as ground crickets, tree crickets, grasshoppers, bush katydids and cicadas dominate the soundscape. (See Activity 27, page 296 and Activity 28, page 298.)
- Sulphur butterflies and, sometimes, monarchs are quite noticeable.
- Watch for small, usually red or yellow dragonflies called meadowhawks, which belong to the Sympetrum genus.
- Fall webworm feeding nests are very noticeable in many areas.
- Yellowjacket wasps become increasingly present and annoying, especially at a picnic!
- Carolina grasshoppers are conspicuous with their crackling flight and yellow-bordered wings.
- Underwing moths (Catocala group) become more common. They are just some of the many moths that can be attracted by lights or bait. (See Basic Skills, pages 36–38.)

Plants

Early summer

- With the longest days of the year, plant growth proceeds at amazing rates.
- Dozens of species of orchids bloom in late spring and early summer.
- The annual roadside flower parade kicks off, with mustards, buttercups and daisies leading the way.
- The yellow pollen of pines and other conifers dusts the land and water. Conifers, like other trees, have evolved chemical defense systems. (See Activity 32, page 299.)
- Wetlands deliver a full spectrum of color as a variety of shrubs and herbaceous plants bloom.
- A wide variety of grasses is also in flower.
- The wildflowers of coniferous and mixed woodlands bloom. Many are white.
- A profusion of ferns adorns fields, wetlands and forests.
- The flowers of common milkweeds fill the air with their rich, sweet scent.

Late summer

- The roadside flower display continues with white sweet clover, Queen Anne's lace, black-eyed Susan and tansy among the many blossoms.
- A profusion of ripe wild fruits can be found on various shrubs and small trees, much to the delight of birds and mammals.
- Jewelweed, purple loosestrife and Joe-Pye weed brighten wetlands.
- The first fall colors start to appear on species such as poison ivy and chokecherry.
- Ragweed is in flower, setting off the beginning of another hay fever season. Goldenrods, which are approaching peak bloom by now and turning fields yellow, are not to blame for allergies.
- Lady's tresses orchids bloom in late summer, as do various gentians.

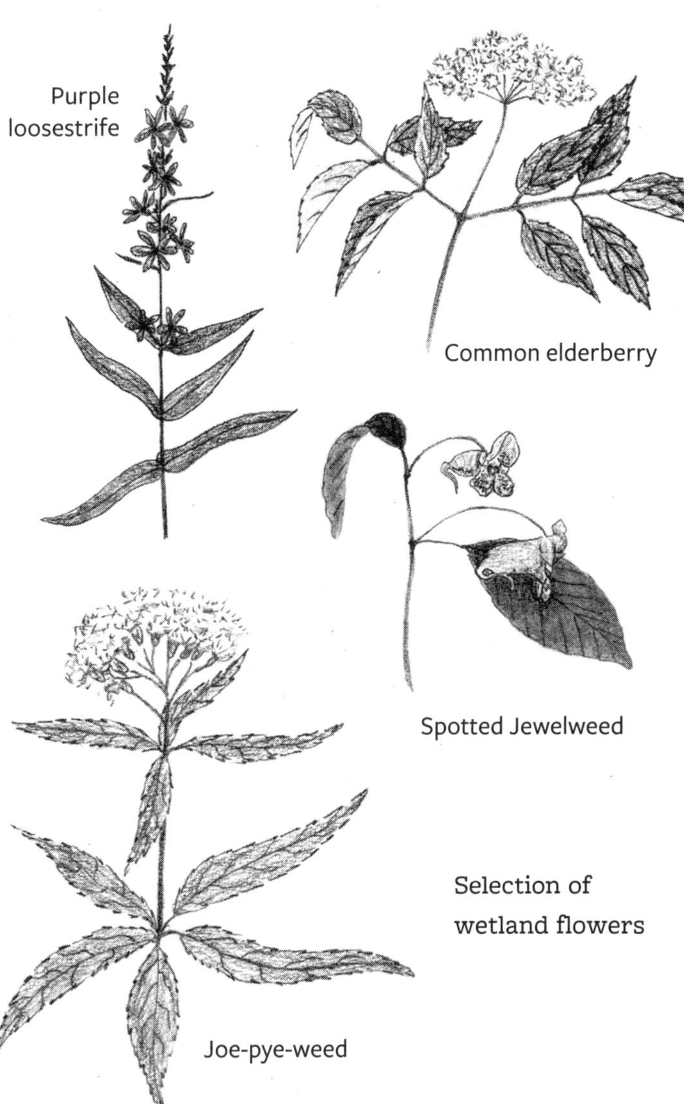

Selection of wetland flowers

Fungi

- Mushrooms are often at their most diverse and abundant in late summer, especially during wet years. (See Activity 33, page 300.)

Agaricus mushroom

Weather

General

- With more than 15 hours of sunlight (depending on latitude), early summer days convey a sense of unending time.
- Summer often brings severe thunderstorms. (See Activity 34, page 301.)
- Nights are warm and a wonderful time to explore the natural world after dark. (See Activity 35, page 302.)
- By late summer and early fall, heavy morning mists, especially in valleys and over lakes, complement the beauty of sunrise.

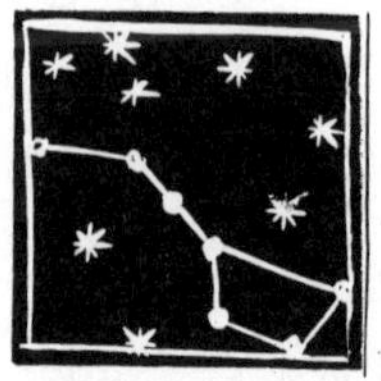

The Sky

General

- Summer officially begins on or about June 21 with the summer solstice. The Sun rises and sets farther north than at any other time of the year. (See Activity 36, page 305.)
- The summer stars have arrived. The three stars of the Summer Triangle, namely Vega, Deneb and Altair, can be seen low in the eastern sky after dark. The most easily recognizable constellation associated with them is Cygnus, the Swan. (See Activity 38, page 306.)
- Look high overhead for Arcturus, the star that heralded the arrival of spring. It is now the brightest star in the sky.
- In early summer, the Milky Way is at its most spectacular. Generally warm and pleasant weather makes for comfortable stargazing. (See Basic Skills, pages 42–44.)
- The Big Dipper holds sway over the northwestern sky.
- On or about August 12, the year's best meteor shower, the Perseids, reaches its peak. (See Activity 39, page 308.)

Summer Nature Highlights by Region

1. Marine West Coast

- In early summer, seabird colonies are teeming with loud, awkward, quickly growing chicks. Visit Canon Beach, Oregon, for tufted puffins and other nesting seabirds
- A small population of gray whales—200 or so—feed off the coasts of northern California, Oregon, Washington, British Columbia and southeast Alaska from May to October, rather than migrate to the Arctic.
- Orcas of the salmon-eating "southern resident population" may be seen in the Salish Sea (Georgia Strait, Puget Sound, Juan de Fuca Strait) of British Columbia and Washington from June through September. Orcas belonging to the transient, seal-eating population occur throughout the year.

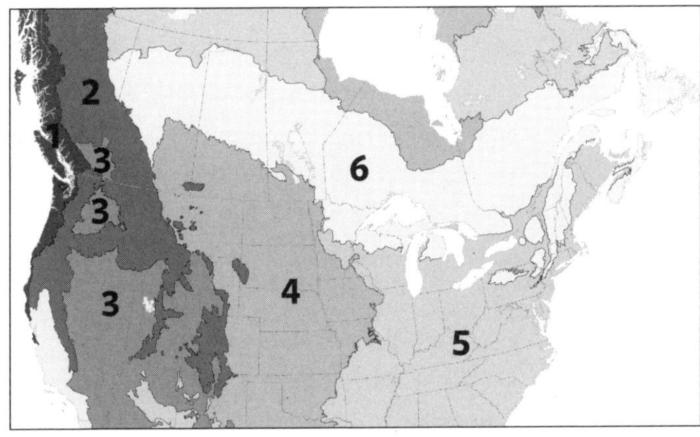

Ecological Zones of North America

- Take a whale-watching/seabird tour to see gray whales, humpback whales and orcas and other marine mammals like sea lions, seals and dolphins. With any luck, you will also be able to observe seabirds such as tufted puffins, marbled murrelets and rhinoceros auklets, as well as shorebirds like black oystercatchers.

Orca whale

- Harbor seals are pupping on secluded beaches or reefs.
- By July, shorebirds from the Arctic start arriving as they make their way south. Fall migration is more drawn out than spring migration.
- In late summer, flocks of barn and violet-green swallows congregate on wires, preparing for migration.
- Native wildflowers in bloom include California poppy, Oregon sunshine and red columbine.

Harbor seal

2. Northwestern Forested Mountains

- In early summer, a host of interesting waterfowl and waterbird species such as harlequin ducks and western grebes are nesting and raising young. Watch for western grebes doing their dramatic courtship display on mountain lakes.
- American dippers flit among the rocks in creeks.
- Bald eagles are nesting and can be easily observed around the nest.
- Northern harriers, red-tailed hawks and American kestrels are commonly seen hunting over fields.
- The subalpine and alpine wildflower display includes sulphur flower, scarlet gilia, orange agoseris, California corn lily and various penstemons.
- In late summer, large numbers of southbound shorebirds come to feed on exposed mudflats in many areas.

3. North American Deserts

- In early summer, a wide variety of duck broods can be seen, including ruddy ducks and cinnamon teal.
- In late June and July, watch for young shorebirds such as American avocets and black-necked stilts. You may also see baby western grebes riding atop a parent's back.
- Southbound shorebirds start arriving in July and can be seen feeding on exposed mudflats.
- Large numbers of American white pelicans are common on many lakes.
- Wildflowers in bloom include peppergrass, monkeyflowers, pale stickweed and cutleaf daisy.

4. Great Plains

- A host of interesting species—some very rare—are nesting and raising young in and around prairie potholes (flooded depressions in the ground). These are fascinating habitats to visit in summer, and many are close to major roads. Look for spectacular ducks such as cinnamon teal and canvasback; grassland birds such as bobolink and Sprague's pipit; waterbirds like American white pelicans, western grebe and eared grebe; and shorebirds such as American avocet and Wilson's phalarope.

- The songs of grasshopper sparrows, western meadowlarks, upland sandpipers and dickcissels fill the air. Later in the summer, the insect chorus takes center stage.
- On telephone poles, watch for birds of prey such as Swainson's hawks.
- Migrating shorebirds begin arriving in mid-July with peak migration in August. These include large numbers of long-billed dowitchers.
- In pockets of native and restored prairie, the Great Plains is one of the best places to see a variety of wildflower blooms in summer. Some species that can be seen throughout the region include blue and purple scurf peas; mostly purple wallflowers; yellow and orange blanket-flowers; blue and purple spiderworts; yellow evening primroses; pink, orange and red milkweeds; and yellow and purple coneflowers.
- Other interesting prairie plants that flower in summer include various sage-brushes, plains prickly pear, buckbrush, chokecherry, Saskatoon berry, wild prairie rose, wild barley, blue grama grass and alkali grass.

5. Eastern Temperate Forests

- In one of the northeast's most spectacular annual events, mountain laurel blooms in June with large, showy, white and pink blossoms. About three weeks later, closely related rhododendrons also bloom.
- In the downtown core of many towns and cities, pairs of chimney swifts can be seen and heard in courtship flight.
- Late June sees peak activity of the firefly, an insect curiously absent from the western United States. Seeing a roadside or meadow alive with thousands of blinking lights on an early summer night is one of the most unforgettable experiences of nature.
- The loudest, most famous player in the summer insect chorus of the eastern United States is the common true katydid. Individual males make their loud, harsh calls from dusk into the night, forming huge choruses that drown out nearly all other sounds.

Eared and western grebes

- A succession of delicious fruits ripen throughout the summer: blueberries, huckleberries, raspberries, blackberries and dewberries, to name a few.
- In August, the vast expanses of the mudflats of the Bay of Fundy attract huge numbers of southbound shorebirds, including hundreds of thousands of semipalmated sandpipers. Among the best places to see this spectacle are Mary's Point, New Brunswick, and Wolfville, Nova Scotia.

6. Northern Forests

- The last migrants pass through in the first week of June and include Arctic-bound shorebirds such as dunlin and whimbrels.
- A huge variety of songbirds are nesting, including almost 30 species of warblers.
- Throughout most of June and July, summer evenings echo with the calls of thrushes such as hermit, Swainson's and the veery.
- Five-lined skinks, Ontario's only lizard, mate in early June and are active and visible. Look for them on open, south-facing Canadian Shield rock outcrops with deep cracks, and scattered rocks.
- In early summer, the gray treefrog chorus of melodious, bird-like trills reaches its peak.
- More than 20 species of orchids bloom in early summer, including the showy lady's slipper. This is also the best time to explore the intriguing plants of bog habitats such as bog laurel, bog rosemary, Labrador tea and pitcher plant. A variety of wildflowers are also blooming in woodlands where conifers dominate. These include fringed polygala, Canada mayflower, bunchberry and bluebead lily.
- In June, the male cones of pines, fir and spruce release their pollen and powder both land and water with a yellow "dust."
- In late summer, fireweed blossoms turn fields, forest edges and burned-over woodlands a riot of pink.

Black-and-white, black-throated green and American redstart warblers

Midsummer Night Itch

Mosquito is out,
it's the end of the day;
she's humming and hunting
her evening away.
Who knows why such hunger
arrives on such wings
at sundown? I guess
it's the nature of things.

—N. M. Boedecker

Purple-flowering raspberry

Collection Challenge

Summer items for the collection box and/or nature table (see also page 54 in "Connecting with Nature"):

- Green leaves of different sizes, shapes, edges, texture, shades of green—labeled
- Summer mushrooms (e.g., boletes)
- Abandoned eggs such as a robin's
- Egg fragments from turtle nests that have been dug up by predators
- Shed snake skins
- A vase of invasive exotic plants to learn (e.g., dog-strangling vine)
- Dragonfly exuviae (cast skin) and a variety of dead insects
- Laptop: insect calls
- Smells of summer: vase with wild bergamot, milkweed flowers, basswood flowers, etc.
- Evolution display: Biodiversity—poster of tree of life, specimens and/or pictures of groups of plants or animals with high biodiversity (e.g., orchids, beetles, moths)

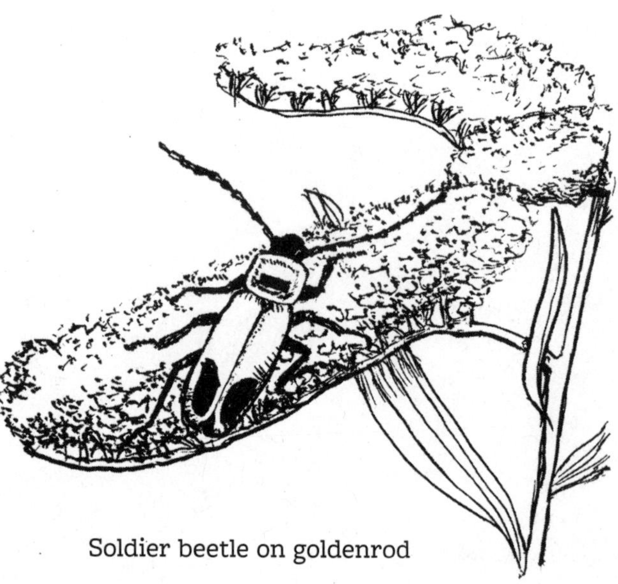

Soldier beetle on goldenrod

Art in the Park

Ideas for what to sketch and photograph in summer:

- In early summer, orchids and other flowers of mixed forests
- Wild berries on the vine or twig: strawberries, raspberries, Juneberries (serviceberries)
- Scenic shots of fog and mist as well as close-ups of dew on plants and cobwebs
- Use the video function on your camera to record the insect chorus in a meadow or grassy wetland
- While on a walk along the beach or on a forest path, collect an assortment of natural objects and put them in your pockets. When you get home or somewhere to sit down, place them on a surface in an interesting arrangement and either sketch or photograph them.
- A collection of flowers, all of the same color or shape.
- Collect moths at night, leave them in the fridge overnight and sketch and/or photograph them before they warm up enough to fly away. (See Basic Skills, page 36.)

- Time exposure of flowing water in a forest stream
- Bales of hay in a field at dawn or dusk
- Lie on your back in a field and photograph tall wildflowers from below, against sky

What's Wrong with the Scenario?

Can you find the six mistakes?

In the summer meadow, monarch butterfly caterpillars munched heartily on the leaves of the goldenrods, while dragonflies drank nectar from the plant's numerous tiny yellow flowers. The goldenrod looked beautiful, but its pollen made me sneeze and my eyes water. On the edge of the road, the young crows that were born in April were now finding food all on their own. They looked just like their parents but, being much younger, were only half the size. Just about the only sounds I heard this summer day were the musical, cheery whistles of cicadas, high above in the trees. Now that August was here, sunset was earlier than in June. We stayed up until it got dark enough to see summer's most beautiful constellation, Leo the Lion.

Turn to the Appendix, page 342, to see how you did!

The Story of Night Cap, the Chickadee

For the first few days, Night Cap stays with her newly hatched chicks, while White Cheek flies out into the forest to search for food. Four tiny bills tilt to the sky as White Cheek crams them full of insects, seeds and caterpillars. The youngsters grow quickly and are soon covered with feathers. Both White Cheek and Night Cap remove any fecal sacs (waste) to keep the nest clean. As the baby birds' appetites increase, Night Cap also joins in on the never-ending task

Cicada

of feeding—sometimes as often as 14 times per hour! Do you eat that much? I hope not!

After 17 days, Night Cap makes a few encouraging peeps and four little heads poke out of their nesting cavity to see a brand new world!

Night Cap continues to encourage her young to try out their wings. You should see their first flight! It looks as though they are a little tipsy as they lunge and careen through the forest air. But soon they gain confidence and experience. They learn to be nimble, flitting from branch to branch, always staying close to Night Cap and White Cheek.

But something else is watching, too. A flash of red and a blur of fur and a red squirrel charges from a nearby branch. She is hoping for a small morsel of baby chickadee. Red squirrels occasionally snack on eggs and baby birds. Luckily, both Night Cap and White Cheek are vigilant. They both give alarm calls and swoop straight towards the squirrel. With flashing wings and quick dips and turns right in front of the squirrel's face, they manage to drive her away, as she gives out her loud chattering *tchheeeer* call. Red squirrels need to eat, too. But today baby chickadee will not be on the menu.

For five weeks Black Cap and White Cheek stay with their young, feeding them and teaching them how to be chickadees. They don't tell them, they show them: How you hang upside down to eat from an insect egg mass, how you always move your head about to be on the lookout for danger and how you fluff out your feathers at night to stay warm.

Soon there are six beautiful gray, black-and-white-winged wonders—two adults and four children—zigging and zagging through the forest. Maybe you've seen them?

And so begins a whole new story. If you take the time to observe, I'm sure you'll discover your very own animal story. See if you can write your discoveries down in your journal!

Black-capped chickadee

What you can do

- Can you find a family group of chickadees? The juvenile black-capped chickadees will have a smaller beak, a shorter tail and, usually, ragged-looking feathers.
- Can you hear the sounds of the juvenile chickadees? They are constantly making soft, high-pitched begging calls. When they see an adult, the begging becomes more intense, and they flutter their wings.
- Can you spot parent chickadees feeding their young?

At Your Magic Spot

Pirate Eye!: Arrgghh! Here is a pirate activity that gets you to think about the colors you see!

While sitting quietly in your magic spot, shut one eye and cover it with your hand. Leave your hand there for at least three minutes. Observe your spot through your one open eye. Notice anything? You've lost depth perception. Predators like hawks, owls and humans need to see in three dimensions in order to catch their prey. Each eye provides a unique angle.

After three minutes, switch between your eyes, opening one eye, then the other. Do this repeatedly. What do you notice? The shades of colors have completely changed between your eyes! That is because one pupil (the black spot in the middle of your eyes) dilated—got bigger—when you closed it. When you open your eyes again, the world looks brighter through this eye. The other eye, with a smaller pupil, creates darker shades. So which color is real? Do you think all humans see exactly in the same shades? We humans can distinguish between two to three million shades of color. Many insects like bees can see beyond the visible spectrum and detect ultraviolet light. To bees, flowers have totally different-looking patterns and colors. For example, the ultraviolet light often reveals stripes on the petals which guide hungry bees to the nectar. (See color section, figure 47.)

Exploring Summer: Things to Do

Summer looks like...

- Fireflies lighting up a damp meadow
- A family of geese swimming gracefully across a pond
- Moths buzzing around the porch light and landing on the screen door
- The ever-changing species and colors of roadside flowers
- Deep blue skies and big, puffy white clouds

Camouflage Trail

For every step we take in the wild, we miss observing dozens of insects, birds and even mammals. Nature is the master of camouflage. But with a bit of practice you can get better at seeing what is normally hidden from view. Here is a game to help you become a better "all-around watcher" (see Splatter Vision, page 26).

Mark the beginning and the end of a trail through a meadow or forest. Obtain a dozen or more plastic insects (try to purchase as many native species as you can) from a dollar store (we use ours over and over again). Hide them along the trail, thinking about camouflage as a guide. For example, place a grasshopper on a leaf, a cricket against the dark soil, a spider on a stem. Remember where you hide them. Ask the children to count how many they can spot along the trail. Who has the sharpest eye? Turn around and collect all the insects.

> The real voyage of discovery consists not in seeking new landscapes but in having new eyes.
>
> —MARCEL PROUST

Summer sounds like...

- The electric buzz of the cicada in the midday heat
- The huge chorus of cricket and katydid song in the evening
- The quiet dawns of late summer as bird song disappears
- The booming and shaking of thunder on a hot afternoon
- The buzz of biting flies circling around your head

Focused Hearing

Take your two hands, squeeze your fingers together and then cup your hands behind your ears. If you can, push your ears out. This simple gesture enhances your hearing up to tenfold. Try this: listen to a natural sound in the distance without your hands. Then slip your hands behind your ears as described. You'll hear a noticeable difference! Your ears have become "deer ears"—large parabolic dishes that capture sound waves. With your "deer ears" on, listen to the wind through the trees, the gurgling of water along a stream, the squelch of mud underfoot. Your hands have focused sound right into your ear. This is a perfect way to begin learning the sounds of summer insects, many of which are quite faint. (See color section, figure 46.)

Summer tastes like...

- Wild strawberries, blackberries, huckleberries and serviceberries (Saskatoons)
- The new, light-green growth on the tips of conifer branches
- The petals of elderberry flowers. Shake a branch over a paper bag to collect them, then use the petals to infuse cream and syrups with a floral, honey-like sweetness.
- Fresh tomatoes and sweet corn
- The sweetness of a blade of grass

Activity 3 Nature's Supermarket

Those who harvest the edible wild refer to cattails as "nature's supermarket"—there are parts of the plant you can harvest during every season. In summer, go to an area where cattails are growing, away from buildings and roads. Pull one up and you'll notice a white lower portion. Peel away the outer layers until you come to the tender center. If you eat this raw, it will taste very similar to cucumber; if you fry it up, the flavor is reminiscent of corn. Cattail stalks are an amazing source of vitamins A, B and C as well as potassium and phosphorus. When cattails are in flower, you will notice distinctive yellow pollen on their stalks. You can use this as a thickener for soups and stews. All you need to do is bend the cattail head and shake the pollen into a paper bag. In late summer, keep your eye out for green flower spikes. These can be eaten raw and are quite tasty! Because cattails are known for absorbing pollutants, be careful where you harvest.

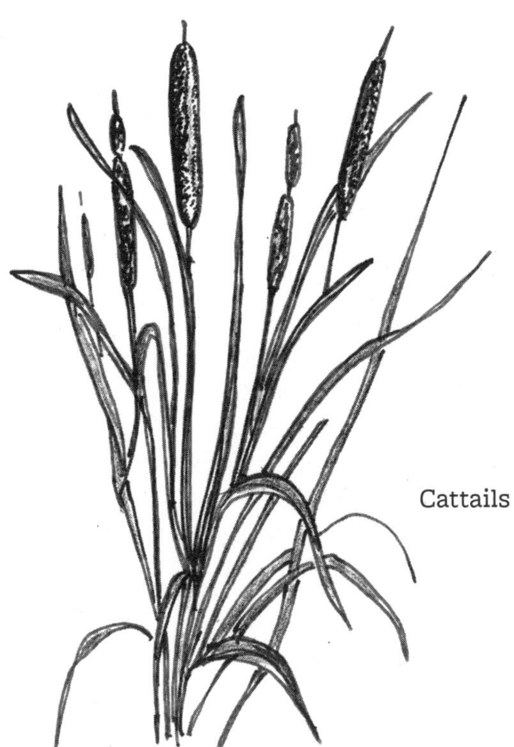

Cattails

Summer smells like...

- The perfume of countless flowers, from milkweed and black locust to little-leaved linden trees and wild bergamot
- A meadow of sagebrush
- Freshly cut hay curing in the sun
- Petrichor—the strong scent in the air when rain falls after a dry spell
- The strong citrus scent of unripe green walnut husks

Activity 4 Make Your Own Perfume

Place 1 c. (237 ml) of water in a bowl. Add 1 c. (225 g) of fresh chopped flower blossoms, leaves and/or buds to the water. Let the mixture sit overnight. (Flowers with strong smells: common milkweed, lavender, orange blossoms, linden; buds with strong smells: balsam/black poplar; leaves with strong smells: wintergreen, bergamot, spice bush, etc.) Strain the water through a coffee filter into a clean spray bottle. Spritz over yourself and your friends and enjoy the sweet scent!

Summer feels like...

- The heat of the sun on your skin and sweat on your brow
- The refreshing sensation of jumping into a lake
- The itch of insect bites
- Walking barefoot on a beach, a lawn or even through mud
- The soft, wet skin of a frog held in your hand

Activity 5 Mudilicious: The Magic of Mud Therapy

Ever wonder why kids delight in playing in the mud? More than one exasperated parent has hosed down their child, murmuring "Why, why, why oh why?" There is a good reason why kids like mud and seem to know this instinctively. Mud makes us happier.

It turns out that soil contains a bacterium called *Mycobacterium vaccae* which boosts the level of seratonin in our brains. Seratonin is a chemical that helps us feel positive, relaxed and happy.

Mud Pie: Take an aluminum pie plate and fill it with gooey mud. Decorate the top with flowers, twigs, leaves and stones. Make imprints by pressing something with texture into the soft mud and carefully removing it. Try using shells and leaves.

Mud Pit: Take an old wading pool and fill it with a mixture of soil and water until you have a fine goop. Watch the kids wallow. Have a hose handy and give them a good wash before allowing them back in the house! You can also use a wheelbarrow for a more controlled mud experience.

Phenology

Activity 6 Summer Phenology: Track Seasonal Change

- **You'll learn:** How the local climate changes through the season and how plants and animals take their cues from these changes.
- **You'll need:** Summer Phenology Chart (see Appendix, page 335.)
- **Procedure:** After completing the chart, discuss how typical the season was in comparison to the long-term average. What really stands out?

Evolution

Activity 7 Making a Good Impression

- **You'll learn:** How fossils are formed and how to make your very own fossil.
- **You'll need:** Paper cups, 4.5-lb. (2-kg) box of plaster of Paris or modeling or pottery clay (do not use Play-Doh or

Darwin: Next time you think you've seen a monarch, be careful that you are not actually looking at its look-alike cousin, the viceroy. These two butterfly species have evolved almost exactly the same striking wing color and pattern. However, they are only distantly related. The reason they look so similar is because of mimicry, which is the ability of a species to imitate something other than what it really is. Why would mimicry have evolved? In the case of the viceroy, mimicry tricks predators into thinking that it is an inedible species. Predators quickly learn that monarchs are distasteful and eating them causes vomiting. They, therefore, learn to avoid them. Viceroys find protection by closely resembling their distant cousins. However, there is also some newer research showing that the viceroy itself may actually be poisonous and that both the viceroy and monarch mimic each other. Now, isn't evolution amazing!

Plasticine because they aren't able to hold an imprint), objects to make your fossils with (shells, leaves, bones, seeds). You'll also need water, a mixing bowl and a large spoon.

• **Background:** Fossils provide us with a direct link to the ancient past and show a panorama of evolutionary change over billions of years. They clearly show that life is incredibly old and has changed massively over time. It is amazing that we can touch something that was once alive thousands, even millions of years ago.

Fossils are the remains or impressions of ancient creatures preserved in rock (often the bones or shells). Different layers of rock contain different fossils. The further down the stack of layers you go, the older the rocks and, consequently, the older the fossils. Fossils often form after a creature's body settles on sediment (the sea floor or earth). As years pass, the body is covered by more and more sediment. As pressure increases, harder parts slowly transform into rock. What remains is both a mold—the original impression of the creature—and a cast, the minerals that have replaced the body. In this activity you'll be making both the mold (modeling clay) and the cast (plaster of Paris).

• **Procedure:**

1. Flatten the modeling clay into the bottom of the paper cup. Select an object

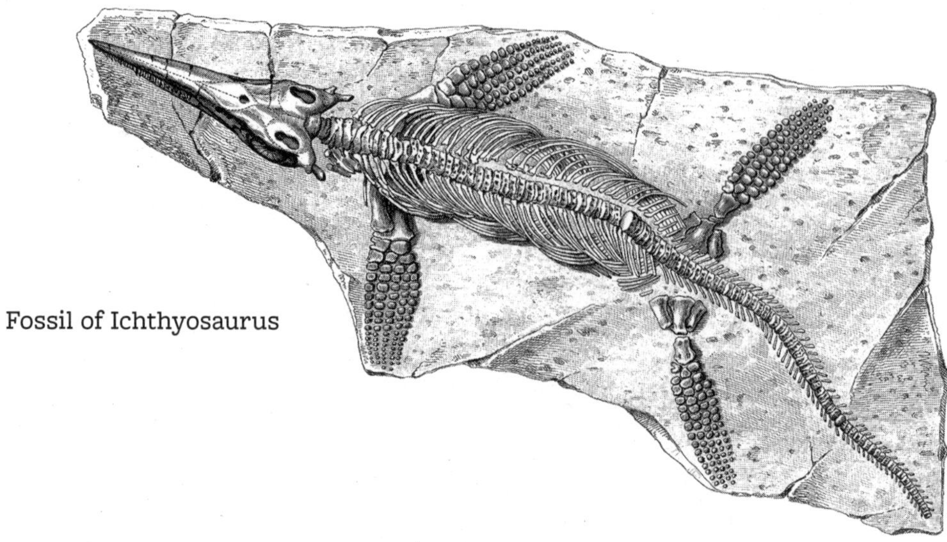
Fossil of Ichthyosaurus

that will make a good impression. Press firmly down and remove the object. Make sure you have a well-defined impression.

2. Mix up the plaster of Paris. Add water to the powder and stir continuously. Keep stirring until you have the consistency of thick pancake batter. You'll need to work quickly because the plaster begins to set almost immediately. Make sure all cups are within easy reach. Pour the mixture into each cup until you have a layer over the clay that is at least 1 in. (2.5 cm) thick. Allow a minimum of one hour to dry.

3. Test the plaster to see that it has well and truly set. It should be hard as rock. If so, tear away the paper cup. You'll have both a mold and a fossil cast. Set up a fossil table. You can even use the fossils you've made to create prints by dipping them in paint and pressing these onto a sheet of paper.

• **Suggestion:** Go fossil hunting! Contact local rock hounds for good fossil locations near you. Go to fossils-facts-and-finds .com for more information. (See color section, figure 48.)

Bat and Moth Game

• **You'll learn:** How one species can affect the evolution of another.

• **You'll need:** Large playing area, blindfolds, 12 or more participants.

• **Background:** Evolution isn't just a response to environmental conditions. Sometimes species evolve in response to each other. A good example of this is coevolution. Coevolution occurs when two species are closely associated. When one species develops an evolutionary advantage, it often triggers a change in the other. This change, in turn, may initiate another evolutionary change in the first species, and so on. For example, bats evolved to use echolocation (pulses of sound) to detect and catch their prey. Moths, in turn, have evolved to detect the echolocation calls of hunting bats. When moths detect bats, some species begin evasive flight maneuvers; they dip, weave, dive and even barrel roll. Some moths reply with their own ultrasonic clicks to confuse the bat's echolocation.

• **What to do:** Have everyone make a large circle, so that when your arms are extended, you form a continuous barrier with no gaps. This forms the wall of a cave and the habitat of the little brown bat, a species common throughout North America. Select one bat and one moth. Blindfold each. To show that the bat is using echolocation, have the bat say in a loud clear voice, *Bat!* To show that the sonar produced by the bat is bouncing off the moth, have the moth clearly say *Moth!* each time the bat utters *Bat!* Like in the game Marco Polo, the bat is trying to find and catch (tag) the moth. As you play, point out the following:

- What is the difference between slow bursts of sound and much quicker bursts of sound? Bats send out at least 20 sonar clicks per second, with a top speed of 200 per second. The more clicks, the more information. Have the bat use a slower, then a faster rate of clicks. What happened?
- Now have the moth use clicks whenever it likes and not just in response to the bat's call. This mimics the sonar that some moth species are able to use to confuse the bat. Did it work?

If you can, obtain a bat detector. This device changes the sonar clicks, normally beyond the range of human hearing, to sound that we can hear. The frequency of the sound will also be a clue as to what bat species is hunting. (Adapted from *Project Wild*)

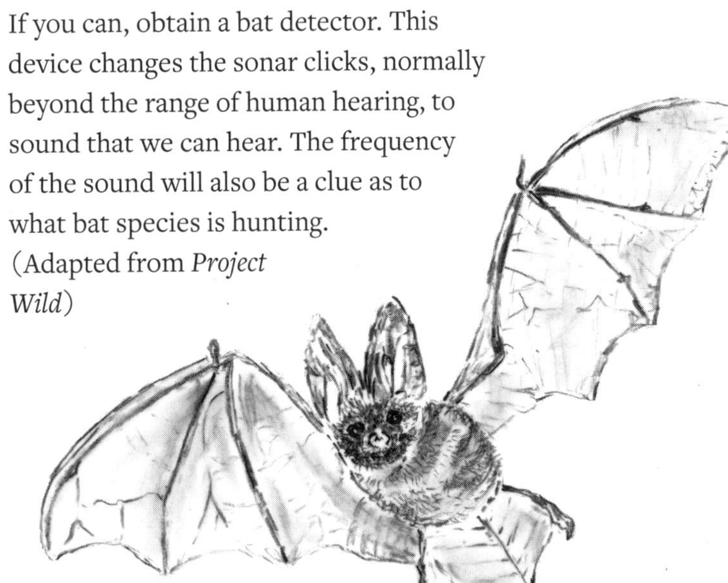

Townsend's big-eared bat

Birds

Activity 9 Hummingbird Challenge

• **You'll learn:** Some amazing hummingbird abilities and behaviors.

• **You'll need:** Hummingbird feeder

• **Background:** A hummingbird can flap its wings more than 700 times in 10 seconds. This rapid movement, assisted by special chest muscles that can contract and release at incredible speeds, enables a hummingbird to fly forward, hover and even fly backward. Hummingbirds are also famous for their aggressiveness. They are quick to drive off other hummingbirds (and sometimes other bird species) that enter their nesting territory or feeding area. Some aggressive behaviors include fast-paced chirping, the flaring of throat and tail feathers, puffing themselves up to look bigger, diving at or chasing away an intruder, and sometimes even fighting, using the bill and claws as weapons. Watch, too, for male courtship behavior in spring or early summer as it flies up and down in a large U-shaped pattern.

• **Procedure:** You probably think you are stronger than a hummingbird. Well, let's put your strength to the test. Extend your arms straight out. Now flap. You need to reach up past the top of your head and all the way down to below your hips. That is one just flap; if you are a hummingbird, your flap is more like a figure-8. So how many times can you flap in 10 seconds? 15–20 times? Try it and see! How did you measure up? Remember, just because something is small doesn't mean it isn't strong or fast.

• **Set up a hummingbird feeder:** There are many commercial hummingbird feeders available. Just make sure it's red. Feed the birds a mixture of one part sugar to four parts water. Bring to a boil and let stand to cool. Change the nectar once a week or more often if becomes cloudy. Clean your feeder at least once a month with a mixture of one part vinegar to four parts water.

- What species of hummingbird are visiting the feeder?
- What aggressive behaviors are you seeing?
- Watch for the male's courtship flight.
- In late summer, watch for young hummingbirds at the feeder. Can you spot them?

Activity 10 Woodpecker Drumming Game

• **You'll learn:** That different woodpecker species use different drumming patterns to attract a mate.

• **You'll need:** One hardwood dowel (¾ in./2 cm wide by 24 in./60 cm long) per child, a treed area.

• **Background:** Imagine slamming your head repeatedly into solid wood without getting a headache. That's got to hurt! Luckily, woodpeckers have specially reinforced skulls and extra neck muscles

Ruby-throated hummingbird

Drum Patterns

Species	Pattern
Hairy woodpecker	As quick and as fast as you can for about 3 to 5 seconds—rapid, even beats—pause for 7 seconds—resume. A real hairy can drum 25 times per second!
Pileated woodpecker	Slow, resonate, rolling taps that last for 5 seconds or so and then begin again. Like knocking on a door.
Sapsuckers	Slower, Morse code-like taps, like tap tap, tapity tap, tap, tap tapity tap. Some slow.
Red-headed woodpecker	Very fast rolling drum tap lasting only for a second or two. Resumes after a pause. Like a military drum roll.
Black-backed woodpecker	Slower drumming that accelerates towards the end, lasting several seconds. Starts like knocking on a door, then accelerates to sound like a drum roll. Fairly soft.

to help them excavate even the hardest of woods. See Darwin (next page) for other amazing woodpecker adaptations. While many birds attract a mate through song, woodpeckers use drumming to do so. Both males and females drum. They select a hollow tree (or even metal signs, downspouts, etc.) that resonates well, and then hammer repeatedly with their beaks to produce a rhythmic drumming pattern.

• **Procedure:** Demonstrate the drumming patterns described above. Let the kids practice the patterns. Tell them that they will either be performing one of these patterns or listening for it. Whisper a pattern to each child, along with the name of the woodpecker that makes it. Make sure that each pattern is whispered to two children (i.e., a male and female of the same species). However, don't let them know who their partner is. Give one of each species a dowel. At a given signal

Yellow-bellied sapsucker

Darwin: Woodpeckers are one of the best examples of how evolution has shaped an animal to live the way it does: strong bills for drilling and drumming on trees; long sticky tongues with bristles for grabbing and pulling out insects deep within a hole; adaptations to prevent brain damage from repeated blows; a membrane that closes a millisecond before contact with the wood to protect the eye from debris; special feathers covering the nostrils; the best toe arrangement for walking vertically up a tree trunk; short, strong legs; and tails with extremely stiff feathers for optimum support.

(whistle), have each of the "drummers" find a tree and start drumming their pattern. Encourage them to try two or three trees to see which sounds loudest. Hollow ones work the best. Explain that no words should be spoken; drumming only, please! After a minute or so, tell the remaining children to find their mate by listening for their pattern. When everyone thinks they have found their mates (remember, no talking), bring all the children together and ask the drummers to divulge what species they were.

Activity 11 A Close Look at Feathers

• **You'll learn:** Some amazing characteristics of feathers.

• **You'll need:** Body or flight feather, hand lens.

• **Background:** Like a reptile's scales and your fingernails, feathers are made of keratin. They are not only necessary for flight but also critically important in body temperature control, camouflage and breeding display. Most feathers consist of a stiff central shaft (rachis) with a series of parallel barbs that branch away from the shaft on each side. All of the barbs taken together form two flat vanes, one on each side of the shaft. Many tiny barbules branch off the barbs and, thanks to a system of tiny hooks called barbicels, hold the barbs together. This interlocking system allows a feather vane to perform as one surface as air flows over it. Bird feathers require daily maintenance to keep them clean, free of parasites and aligned in the best position in relation to other feathers for more efficient flight. This is called preening. While preening, birds also spread an oily substance on each feather from the preen gland, located at the base of the tail. This oil waterproofs the feathers and keeps them flexible.

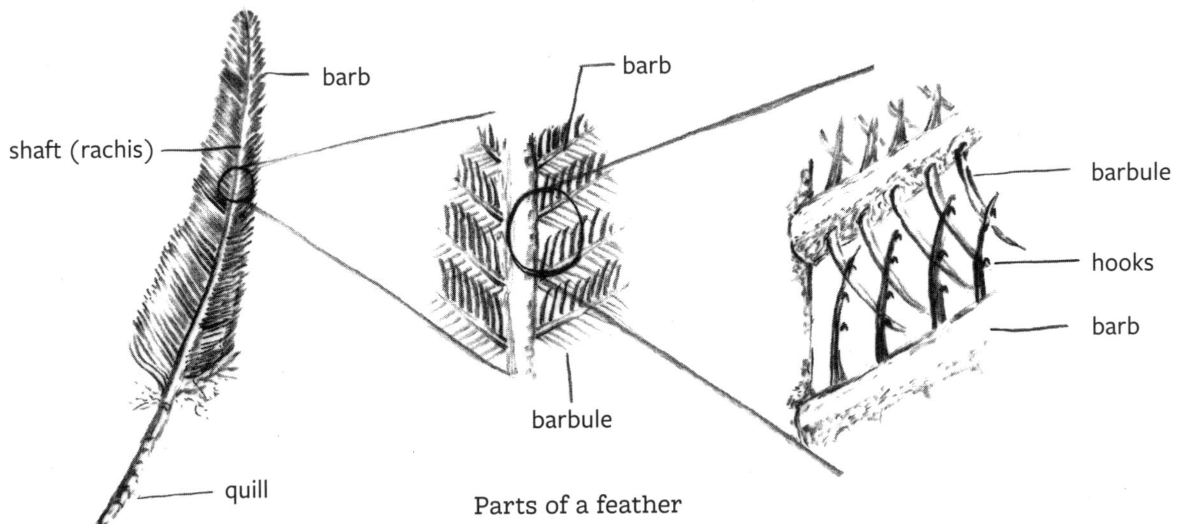

Parts of a feather

• **Procedure:** With your hand lens, examine the base of the shaft. You will find that it is hollow with a small opening at the end where the blood vessels enter the growing feather. Next, hold the feather up to the sky or a bright light and look carefully at a section of the vane. Look for the barbs extending out to the side from the shaft and for the many barbules on each barb. The barbules interlock with each other, thanks to tiny hooklets. This gives the feather its stiffness, makes it waterproof and allows the feather to trap air for warmth. If your hand lens is strong enough, you should be able to see these hooklets. If not, you may need to look through a microscope.

Activity 12 Go Shorebird-watching

• **You'll learn:** To identify shorebirds and observe some interesting behaviors.
• **You'll need:** Binoculars, bird guide or app, hat, sunscreen, spotting scope (optional).
• **Procedure:** Bird-watching can be excellent in late July and August, when shorebirds are migrating in large numbers. They turn up anywhere there are beaches or mudflats. Check the "Hotspots" in eBird (ebird.org) for good shorebird locations near you. Common species that can be expected across the continent include lesser and greater yellowlegs, semipalmated plover, and least sandpiper. Many more species can be seen regionally. Shorebirds are especially interesting because they allow the observer to get quite close and to take long, leisurely looks. This makes them a great group of birds for kids to look at and, with help, identify. Identification is not always easy, however, and sometimes you just have to appreciate the bird's beauty and forget putting a name to it. There is also a special aesthetic in shorebirds' tightly knit flocks that twist and turn on a dime, their restlessness, and the vast distances they travel. These are birds that represent the ends of the Earth.

Shorebirds

Darwin: Have you ever stopped to wonder why some birds such as waterfowl and shorebirds move about in flocks? Well, scientists have. Birds seem to gain information about good feeding sources by following other birds. Another advantage to flocking is that it may reduce the amount of time each individual bird has to spend watching out for predators, so it has more time for feeding and preening. In a flock, there will always be some individuals with their heads up looking around. Scientists have even shown that on islands with few predators, birds tend to form flocks less often. Some birds that evolved on islands with few predators also became flightless. If something is not necessary (i.e., escaping enemies through flight), evolution gets rid of it!

When you are watching a juvenile sanderling on an August day, you can't help but feel moved by a 2-oz. (50-g) bundle of feathers that was born mere weeks before on Canada's Baffin Island and will fly all the way to southern Argentina, without the aid of adult birds to show the way.

Mammals

Activity 13 Critter Cam

• **You'll learn:** Some of the animals that are secretly visiting your property, both at night and during the day.

• **You'll need:** A trail (game) camera, preferably at least an 8-megapixel with infrared detection (IR); SD card of 8GB plus.

• **Background:** Depending on the species, being active at night is an adaptation for avoiding daytime predators (e.g., mice avoiding hawks) or avoiding conflict over the same food resource (e.g., owls hunt mice at night; hawks hunt them during the day). However, before trail cameras, nocturnal animal activity was hardly ever seen. Trail cameras are not only weatherproof but also designed for extended, unmanned use. They have both motion and heat detector switches that snap photos or take video of animals when they walk past. They are able to reveal the mysterious world of nighttime—and daytime—animal activity. With infrared detection, the animal will never know it is being photographed, so the behavior you see is natural. In winter, we suggest using lithium-ion batteries, which work to 40 degrees below zero.

• **Procedure:** Start by setting a camera up in your own backyard. Place it 2–10 ft. (1–3 m) from a focal point, usually food. Dog food, both wet and dry, works well. Feed them, and they will come! You may wish to stop putting out food after a few nights, however, to avoid future problems with what your neighbors might consider to be "nuisance animals." If you own or have access to rural property, set the camera up in an area where there are already animal signs such as tracks and scat. The transition zones between two or more habitat types (called an *ecotone*)

Raccoon

can be productive, as are locations near water, gaps in fences and fence lines themselves. Beaver wetlands are also excellent locations. You may wish to install a small salt lick, which will attract a wide variety of mammals from moose and deer to beaver and raccoons. You will love the candid moments you capture with your camera and the special feeling of seeing the private lives of many of our elusive birds and mammals. You will be astonished at the variety of wild creatures that are active at night. When you have your images, you might want to post them to a social media site like Pinterest or YouTube. You should also print off some of your best color and IR photos; you will be the hit of the schoolyard or the party! More importantly, you will engender respect and concern for wildlife, especially if you tell a story with each picture.

Things to See from a Car

Mammal-watching from a Car

• **You'll learn:** To find and identify mammals by driving through promising habitat.

• **You'll need:** Binoculars, vehicle.

• **Background:** One of the best ways to see mammals is from a car. During a daytime drive, you can usually spot squirrels on lawns and in parks. Depending on where you live, woodchucks are often seen in grassy areas close to roads and ground squirrels and even deer can be a common sight in roadside fields. Mammal-watching can be especially good at night. Most of us have seen this. While driving after dark, we spy a pair of eyes gleaming out at us from the darkness of the woods, looking for all the world like two floating alien orbs. What on earth (or not of this earth) causes eyes to shine like this? Many nocturnal animals have a mirror-like layer in the retina that reflects light, the *tapetum lucidum* ("bright carpet"). This gives visual pigments a second chance to absorb light and improves vision in low light. When a flashlight or a car's headlights shine light on the tapetum, it is mirrored back to our eyes in a variety of interesting colors.

• **Procedure:** To maximize your chances of seeing the more elusive mammals (e.g., coyotes, foxes, bears, raccoons and weasels), go out at dawn, at dusk or at night. Drive slowly along backroads that wind through different habitat types such as wetlands, fields and woods. Remember to watch for animals crossing the road well ahead of the car. If there is a municipal dump in your area where the garbage is not containerized, you may also wish to make a brief stop there to look for bears. Or stop the vehicle and sit quietly in an area where two habitat types come together, such as a field and a woodlot. Use the binoculars to scan distant field edges. When driving at night, watch for

Darwin: Have you ever wondered why humans have color vision while many other mammals don't? We used to think that this ability evolved because it made finding fruit in the forest much easier. Now, some scientists think that it probably had more to do with being able to detect emotions or the health of other people. We have all noticed how skin color changes when people blush or get extremely angry. When people are sick, their skin often becomes pale. It's easy to understand how sensing emotions or health in others would be important for survival.

the luminous eye reflections of mammals along the roadside, where some species scavenge for roadkill. Try to identify the animal by noting the color of its eye shine. The color varies from species to species and with the angle at which the eyes are seen. Here is a quick field guide to eye shine color.

Eye color	Species
Red	Coyote, fox, opossum, rodents, bears, weasels, birds
Green	Cats, dogs
Bright yellow	Raccoon
Amber	Skunk
Yellow-green to white	Deer
Bright White	Fox
Orange	Opossum, flying squirrel

Amphibians and Reptiles

Activity 15 Reptile-watching

- **You'll learn:** How to find different kinds of reptiles.
- **You'll need:** Camera, field guide or app, binoculars.
- **Background:** In order to find reptiles, you should first learn as much as you can about the species you are interested in: its geographic range and preferred habitat, whether it is nocturnal or diurnal and any particular habits it may have. As for snakes, even if you don't particularly like them, seeing and identifying the various species can be fun and may help you get over your phobia. Explain to the children the importance of not persecuting snakes. In many areas, they are in drastic decline.

• **Procedure:** Spending a summer day observing and photographing reptiles can be a lot of fun. At the start of the walk, have the children lie on a rock in the sun to appreciate what cold-blooded reptiles are feeling. Be sure to visit a variety of habitat types but especially areas close to water. Turtles love to bask on emergent logs, rocks and beaver lodges in ponds, shallow lakes and marshy areas. If a turtle ducks under the water, remember that it will soon resurface and eventually climb out of the water to continue basking. Many kinds of snakes, too, are found near water. Water snakes sun themselves on rocks and sometimes climb up onto vegetation. Garter snakes often turn up in fields near wetlands, where they hunt for frogs. They are easy to catch and cannot harm you. Make sure everyone who wants to gets to hold or at least touch the snake. Snakes such as the northern redbelly are often found around the foundations of abandoned buildings. Try turning over rocks, boards or pieces of sheet metal to see if there are any snakes hiding underneath. Other places you might find snakes include woodpiles (both on the pile and in between the logs), rock piles in fields, roads that cross wetlands or forests (often early or late in the day) and sheds. Some snakes like to stretch out on the horizontal beam where the wall meets the roof to absorb the heat.

Lizards, too, like areas where they can bask in the sun such as rock outcrops, sand dunes, boards, logs, building foundations, walls and bridges. They, too, often hide under rocks and boards. Lizards are most active when the Sun shines directly on their habitat. Keep an eye open for the shed skins of snakes and lizards as well. They are a great addition to the nature table.

Western painted turtle

Activity 16 The Great Green Gobbler

• **You'll learn:** How bullfrogs hunt for their food.

• **You'll need:** Open field, hula hoops.

• **Background:** They may look like they are slow and bumbling, but bullfrogs are incredible hunters. They've been known to catch birds, spiders, mice, bats, dragonflies and even their own kind. A bullfrog is a still hunter, which means it waits for prey to show up. When it detects prey moving near its territory, it rotates its body so that its mouth is oriented towards the prey. If necessary, it may make a few approach leaps. A bullfrog's back legs are very powerful, like tightly wound springs. Once the frog is close enough, it extends its back legs and launches itself into the air, eyes closed and mouth wide open. Timing is everything. If the aim is true, a bullfrog will unfurl its massive mucus-covered tongue and fling it outward—often covering up its prey like a blanket. It then retracts its tongue as its jaws clamp down. If the prey is large enough, the bullfrog uses its forearms to stuff any remaining bits into its massive mouth.

• **Materials:** Half of the group will be bullfrogs and the other half dragonflies. Have the bullfrogs set up their territory using hula hoops. Make sure frogs are at least three big steps away from each other. Bullfrogs crouch in their hula hoops, back legs folded and bent, front legs in between back legs. Here they wait patiently for dinner. Dragonflies are busy catching their

Darwin: Believe it or not, in 2014, researchers from Rutgers University found a new species of frog right in the middle of one of the most highly populated parts of the U.S.! The Atlantic coast leopard frog, *Rana kauffeldi*, lives in wetlands from Connecticut to North Carolina. By examining the genes and mating calls of leopard frogs from various parts of the Northeast, the scientists were able to prove that this frog is, in fact, a new species. Citizen scientists provided crucial information about where the frogs are living and what they look and sound like, such as their distinct *chuck* call. This shows how important it is to get out and study the plants and animals in your own backyard, because you never know what new information you might discover—maybe even a brand new species!

”

American bullfrog

own prey in and among the bullfrogs. They dart forward; they hover, zigging and zagging—flying backward, zooming forward. The quicker dragonflies are, the less likely they'll be caught. On a given signal, the dragonflies flit among the frogs, trying to catch insects. Meanwhile bullfrogs try their best to catch a dragonfly. It is all about timing the leap. Can they tag a dragonfly with one of their hands extended, representing the unfurled tongue of a bullfrog? It is more challenging than you might think. Try it! (See color section, figure 45.)

Fishes

Make a Fish Viewer

- **You'll learn:** To see and appreciate the underwater world with a homemade viewer.
- **You'll need:** Large coffee can or an 18-in. (45-cm) section of 4-in. (10-cm) or greater PVC pipe; heavy clear plastic wrap or Plexiglas (cut about same size as pipe); elastic band; duct tape or GOOP plumbing adhesive.
- **Procedure:** Although inexpensive commercial fish viewers are available, it's easy to make your own. For a simple viewer, use a large coffee can. Remove both ends and stretch clear plastic wrap over one. Secure with several elastic bands or duct tape. For a more solid and longer lasting viewer, use a section of 4-in. (10-cm) or greater PVC pipe. Glue a piece of Plexiglas to one end with GOOP or similar adhesive. Then place the plastic wrap or Plexiglas end under the surface of the water and look through the other end. Move quietly along. You'll be amazed at how clear the underwater world becomes with your homemade fish viewer! Try taking pictures or even video.

Catching Fish for Close-up Looks

- **You'll learn:** Different behaviors of fish.
- **You'll need:** Glass jar or aquarium, fishing gear and/or net.
- **Procedure:** Catching fish for identification and close observation is not only fun but can become an absorbing hobby. A barbless hook and worm work well for catching species such as sunfishes, perch and small bass. Just file the barb off a regular hook. If the barbless hook is not working, try a small barbed hook. When you catch a fish of the right size, drop it into a wide-mouthed gallon jar or aquarium full of water out of direct sunlight.

You can also catch fish with a net. Walk into a shallow stream or pond. When you see a fish, make a downward swoop with the net, cover the fish and drag the net shoreward along the bottom. You may need to reach into the water with your hands and direct the fish up into the netting, so it remains trapped there when you take the net out of the water. You should be able to find various species of minnows, shiners, dace, darters, sculpins, sticklebacks, etc. Transfer your catch into the jar or aquarium.

You can then study the actions of your fish and take pictures of them at leisure. Watch how they breathe, how they move their fins, the shape of their bodies, the different colors, etc. Identify each species you have caught and start a list in your nature journal of the fish you have found in your region. Make sure there are columns for the species' name, date, location and a brief description. You may also want to add a sketch or a photograph. Keep the fish for a day or two and then let them go where you found them. At some point you may wish to set up a permanent aquarium in your house with several of your favorite native fish.

• **Visit a fish hatchery:** A trip to a state or provincial fish hatchery can help a child learn a great deal by observing fish in all stages of development. Most hatcheries have regular visiting hours. If there is none located near your home, you may be able to visit one during a vacation trip. Fish hatcheries are located in many areas of Canada and the United States.

Invertebrates

Activity 19 Explore a Tide Pool

• **You'll learn:** The wide diversity of life in a tide pool.

• **You'll need:** A pocket guide or app to seashore life, water sandals or other shoes with gripping soles that you can get wet, shorts or swimwear, hat, sunscreen, bucket, camera, hand lens.

• **Background:** Tide pools are seawater-filled depressions along the seashore that form twice a day as water is caught when the tide goes out. They range from small, shallow puddles high up on the shore to rocky holes nearer to the sea. They are much like natural aquariums and can be teeming with animals and plants. Tide pools, and the intertidal zone in general, are home to many marine algae (seaweeds), invertebrates and vertebrates. Some algal species are found on the Pacific coast (P), and others on the Atlantic coast (A). They include green algae like sea lettuce (A,P) and hollow green weed (A,P); brown algae like sea potato (A,P), rockweed (P), sea palm (P), giant kelp (P) and oar kelp (A); and red algae like nori (P) and dulse (A). The latter two are popular edible species. Most of the animals in tide pools are invertebrates such as sponges, sea anemones, molluscs (e.g., chitons; gastropods like limpets, abalone, snails and nudibranchs; bivalves like mussels; cephalopods like octopuses; echinoderms like brittle stars, basket stars, sea stars, sea urchins and sea cucumbers), arthropods (e.g., crustaceans like barnacles and crabs); and annelids like sandcastle worms. You may also be able to find some vertebrates like small fishes adapted to the tide pool environment. Some of these are bony fish like sculpins, opaleyes and clingfish.

• **Procedure:** Plan to visit the seashore during the hour before and after low tide and dress appropriately (see You'll need). If you have small children with you, remember that walking over the rocks can be difficult for them. Be aware, too, of slippery seaweed and try not to step on any marine life. When you arrive at a tide pool, explore from the edge. See how many different seaweeds and animals you can find and identify. Keep your field guide handy. You may also want to take pictures of some of the species. Don't try to remove or pick up any animal that appears stuck and resists you, such as limpets, mussels, barnacles, starfish and sea anemones. If you wish, just touch them. Seaweed, crabs, snails and sea cucumbers can be picked up. Unless you are in an area with very few visitors, you should resist the temptation to lift rocks to see what is underneath. On many seashores, thousands of people visit the tide pools each year.

As you move along the shore, don't forget to look under seaweed. As you lift up the plant, watch for crabs, a variety of snails and maybe even a starfish. Fill your bucket with seawater to hold a few of the snails and crabs for closer examination. Use your hand lens. Be sure to let them go within a few minutes. To really do a tide pool visit justice, try to take part in an interpretive program such as a guided visit with a park naturalist. In many areas, you can also hire local guides to explain tide pool ecosystems to your family. If possible, combine your tide pool exploring with a visit to a marine aquarium. (See color section, figure 41.)

Starfish (Seastar)

Activity 20 Walk the Swash and Wrack Zones

• **You'll learn:** The wide diversity of life on ocean beaches.

• **You'll need:** Same as above activity, small shovel, plus binoculars and bird guide (optional).

• **Background:** The area along the beach where waves roll up and down is called the swash zone. The top few inches of sand are home to abundant burrowing animals such as mud worms, digging amphipods (tiny, shrimp-like crustaceans with no carapace) and certain species of clams (e.g., coquina clams) and crabs (e.g., mole crabs). Because they are small and can dig very fast, seeing them is challenging but fun. Shorebirds like sandpipers and plovers feed on many of these creatures. Further up on the beach is the wrack line, located just above the high tide line. It is a ribbon of seaweed, garbage and other flotsam—collectively known as wrack. The decaying organic matter provides food for creatures such as shrimp-like amphipods; because they literally jump out of the wrack, these are also called beach hoppers or beach fleas. Some can be up to an inch (2.5 cm) long. As adults, many of us beachcomb, not only for the little treasures but also because it offers us a walking meditation in nature.

• **Procedure:** The best time to go beach-combing is two to three hours before low tide or an hour or so after. It can be especially interesting to go after a big storm, when all kinds of things can get washed up on the beach. Walk the swash zone, stopping to catch the odd burrowing animal. You may need to dig down with your shovel. Look out for shorebirds—you should be able to get quite close to them. Next, head up to the wrack line and poke around in the seaweed for amphipods. It's fun to watch them jump in the air; try to catch a few for a closer look. The wrack line is also a place to look for shells (e.g., clams, oysters, mussels, jingles, scallops and cockles), the molted carapaces of crabs, egg cases, bones and driftwood. You might also find exquisite smooth pebbles and maybe even fossils. Don't take too many shells home with you, especially if the beach receives a lot of visitors.

How to present your beach treasures

A pizza box makes a nice display tray.

1. Fill the box with crumpled newspaper and tape it shut.

2. Glue colored felt to the top and sides.

3. Arrange your objects on the box and hold them in place with pins placed around the edge of each object.

4. Make label cards and pin or glue them to the felt.

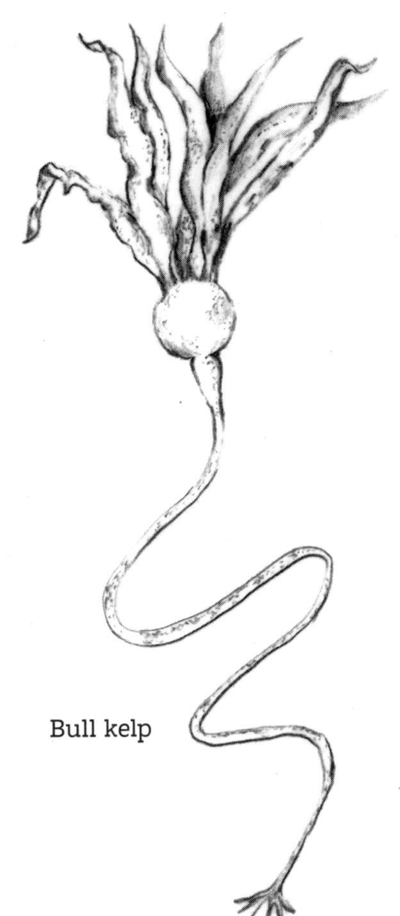

Bull kelp

Activity 21 Fiddle for Worms

- **You'll learn:** How to conjure up worms from the soil.
- **You'll need:** Two hardwood dowels (see below), saw.
- **Background:** Also called worm charming or worm grunting, fiddling for worms is the art of coaxing worms up to the surface with the help of homemade worm fiddlesticks. There are competitions throughout the United States and in Canada to find the best worm charmer. Maybe it is you? Want to find out? See Darwin below for more information on why worm fiddling works.
- **Procedure:** You'll need two ¾-in. (2-cm) hardwood dowels—one 4 ft. (120 cm) long and the other 2 ft. (60 cm). Use a saw to cut notches in the longer piece every few inches or so. Find a moist, wooded location. Place one end of the longer dowel with ridges into the ground. Hold the dowel firmly in the upright position. With the other stick, rub up and down vigorously just like a fiddle player playing a jig. You should hear a distinctive rasping noise. Keep at it for at least 5 to 10 minutes. The vibrations attract worms to the surface. Try it! (See color section, figure 42.)

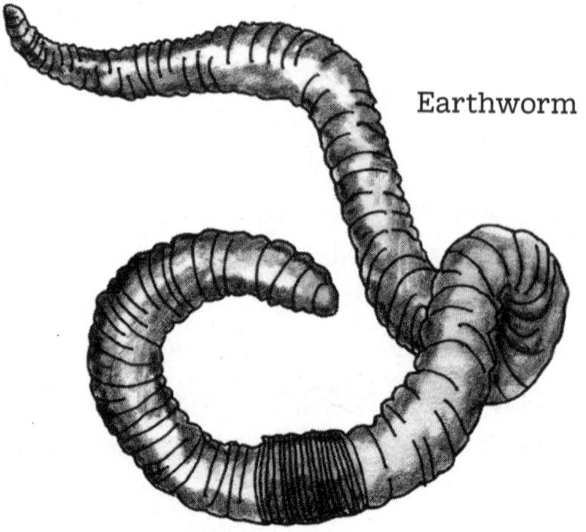

Earthworm

Activity 22 Dragonfly Dragster Drama

- **You'll learn:** How to move like a dragonfly.
- **You'll need:** Ten participants or more.
- **Background:** Don't like mosquitoes? Dragonflies do. One dragonfly can eat more than 100 in an evening, depending on the species. Mosquitoes are one of the

Darwin: Why would worms behave in such a strange way? Well, it has to do with moles, one of the worm's worst enemies. Moles are quite noisy when they dig tunnels through the earth. Worms have, therefore, evolved to flee to the surface whenever there is a strong vibration, because it usually means there is a mole around! Worm grunting vibrations overlap with those that moles make.

most acrobatic of all the flying insects—they can fly straight up and down, hover and even fly backwards, so dragonflies need to be fast and nimble fliers to catch their prey on the wing. To do that, they need remarkable vision. Most of a dragonfly's moveable head consists of two compound eyes, each containing more than 30,000 lenses. They can see from almost every angle except directly behind them. Watch "Investigating the Secrets of Dragonfly Flight" on Youtube.

• **What to do:** You'll be making a large, flying dragonfly using everyone as a body part. Head: two participants side by side, each with one arm crooked (left side—left arm; right side—right arm) to signify compound eyes. Thorax: four participants. This is the part where the four wings of a dragonfly are joined to the middle part of the body. Left side participants extend their left arms out, right side participants stick their right arms out to simulate wings. Abdomen: the remaining four participants line up behind the thorax. They lift their shoulders up and down at the same time to mimic a dragonfly as it breathes through spiracles, tiny holes in its abdomen.

How to flap like a dragonfly

To fly up, both right and left wings flap. The wings are horizontal to the ground.

- To fly forward, both right and left wings flap. The wings are pitched forward with thumbs angled downward.
- To fly backward, right and left wings flap. The wings are pitched backward with thumbs angled upward.
- To bank right, left wings are lifted upward, and right wings are tilted downward while flapping.
- To bank left, right wings are lifted upward, and left wings are tilted downward while flapping.
- To hover, both right and left wings flap in a figure-8 pattern, alternatively tilting forward and backward.

Dragonfly commands

The key to this dramatic activity is that participants need to stay together as one unit, one dragonfly. Have a designated person shout out the following commands:

- Fly forward
- Fly backward
- Fly straight up
- Bank right, Bank left
- Hover

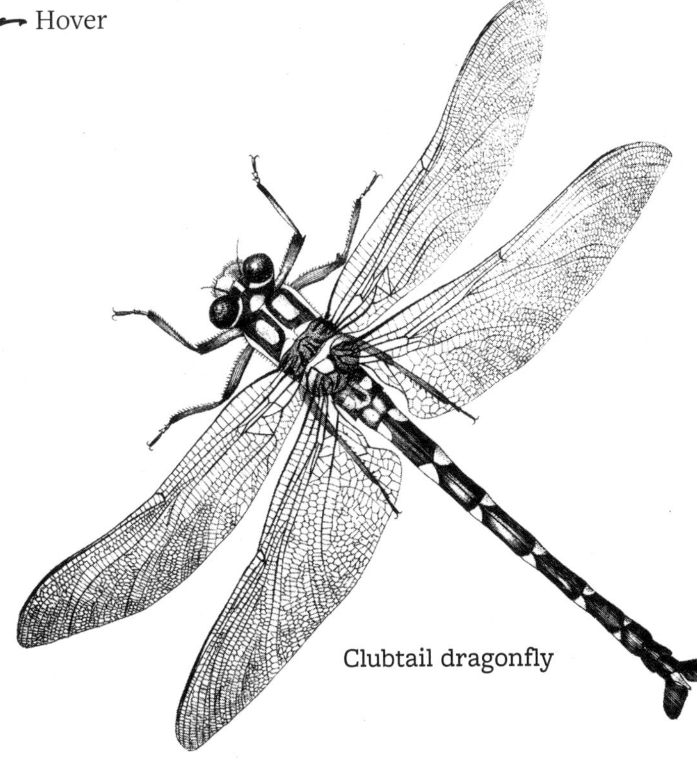

Clubtail dragonfly

Darwin: Looking into the compound eyes of a dragonfly is like looking back deep into time. When dinosaurs grazed along the edges of ancient wetlands 300 million years ago, dragonflies were already there, catching the insects the dinosaurs scared up. In fact, dragonflies were already around millions of years *before* dinosaurs appeared on Earth.

• **Try this:** The next time you see dragonflies, crush a soda cracker into fine pieces in the palm of your hands. Toss some of the crumbs high into the air. If dragonflies are near enough they'll zoom in, thinking it is an insect. Watch them scoop up your crumbs with amazing speed and dexterity.

Activity 23 Fun with Fireflies

• **You'll learn:** How to attract fireflies and make a natural night light.

• **You'll need:** Flashlight, glass jar, ice cream tub with lid.

• **Background:** The firefly is a beetle with a special organ in its abdomen capable of mixing oxygen, a pigment called luciferin and the enzyme luciferase. When the insect flies upward, these chemicals mingle and create a flash. As the insect descends, the flash turns off. When a female of the same species sees the flash, she responds with her own light signal. Eventually the male and female fireflies find each other and mate.

• **What to do:** On a summer evening, just as dusk fades into night, visit a meadow where there are fireflies. If you have a flashlight or a wristwatch that glows in the dark, try reproducing the pattern of flashes. Different species of fireflies flash at different rates. Like Morse code, each pulse of light communicates a special message to the opposite sex. Can you attract a firefly by imitating the sequence?

Make a "night light" for your bedroom. Catch several fireflies in a plastic ice cream tub and transfer them to a glass jar. Add a few leaves and a drop or two of water. Lie in bed and fall asleep to their lovely star-like flashes. Let them go in the morning.

Fireflies

Darwin: Biologists at Tufts University have discovered that there is a dark side to being too flashy. As it turns out, flashier males are more likely to catch the attention of predatory fireflies. For example, the female Photuris or "femme fatale" firefly mimics the flashes of other firefly species, which attracts them to her. She then kills and eats the unsuspecting, lovestruck males. So even though flashier males get to mate more often, they also live dangerously. These predators may affect firefly evolution by limiting how flashy—and conspicuous—a firefly can get.

Activity 24 Calling All Water Striders

• **You'll learn:** How to attract a water strider.

• **You'll need:** Two small twigs, a pond, lake or stream with water striders.

• **Background:** Skating on ice is one thing, but skating on water? How cool would that be! Well, there is an insect that can glide over the surface of ponds, rivers and lakes during the warm summer months. It is called a water strider (not a spider, for it only has six legs—not eight). Water striders take advantage of surface tension to "row" across the water, using their paired legs. They also have small hairs that can both repel water and absorb air. Water striders are predators. When they feel the surface of the water being disturbed, they immediately scoot over to investigate—hoping to find an insect in distress to make a tasty meal.

• **Procedure:** You can attract a water strider by placing two thin twigs in the water. Hold the first halfway under the surface of the water—don't move this twig. Place the other twig beside the first, but don't let them touch. Move this twig up and down like a sewing needle. Your movements will create ripples that simulate a struggling insect. Don't be surprised if a water strider or two glides over and grabs your twig!

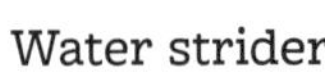

Water strider

Activity 25 A Simple Pond or Stream Study

• **You'll learn:** Some of the intriguing invertebrates that live in ponds.

• **You'll need:** Pail (preferably with a lid), small aquarium (or large glass bottle), small plastic viewing jars, fine-meshed nets, shoes you can get wet, hand lens, field guide or app.

• **Background:** Some of the common invertebrates found in ponds, swamps or streams include stonefly larvae, mayfly larvae, caddisfly larvae (usually in cases of plant material), damselfly nymphs, dragonfly nymphs, water penny larvae, predaceous diving beetles, whirligig beetles, water scorpions, giant water bugs, water striders, water boatmen, backswimmers, mosquito larvae, black fly larvae, leeches and crayfish. Tadpoles, frogs and aquatic salamanders may live here, too. All are easy to catch.

• **What to do:** Take your pail, plastic containers and net to a nearby pond, swamp or shallow stream. Either from the edge or by wading out into the water (no more than knee-deep), dip your net down into the dense aquatic vegetation where a lot of creatures hang out. When you catch something like a "wiggling bug," put it in your pail. Add a little aquatic vegetation to the pail, too. Continue until you have a variety of different creatures. Try different parts of the pond, including the muddy bottom. Don't pour mud into the pail, however. If you are catching creatures in a stream, many will be attached to the underside of rocks. Gently push them off the rock and into the pail. Don't be afraid to hold the creatures briefly in your hand.

When you have caught a nice variety of different invertebrates, transfer a few to viewing jars for close-up looks and identification. You can then either let them go or take some home to keep for a while in an aquarium or a large glass bottle. Pour the water and creatures into the aquarium and set it on a white sheet away from direct sunlight. If you haven't done so already, take some time to view and identify each of the different creatures with a hand lens by placing them briefly in a small plastic bottle. Change about one-third of the water every couple of days with fresh swamp or stream water. Have a look every day at what's going on in the bottle. Have new creatures hatched out of eggs? Have some creatures fallen prey to predators? Be sure to sketch the various species in your nature journal or even photograph them. Include the name. Return the invertebrates to where you caught them after a week or so.

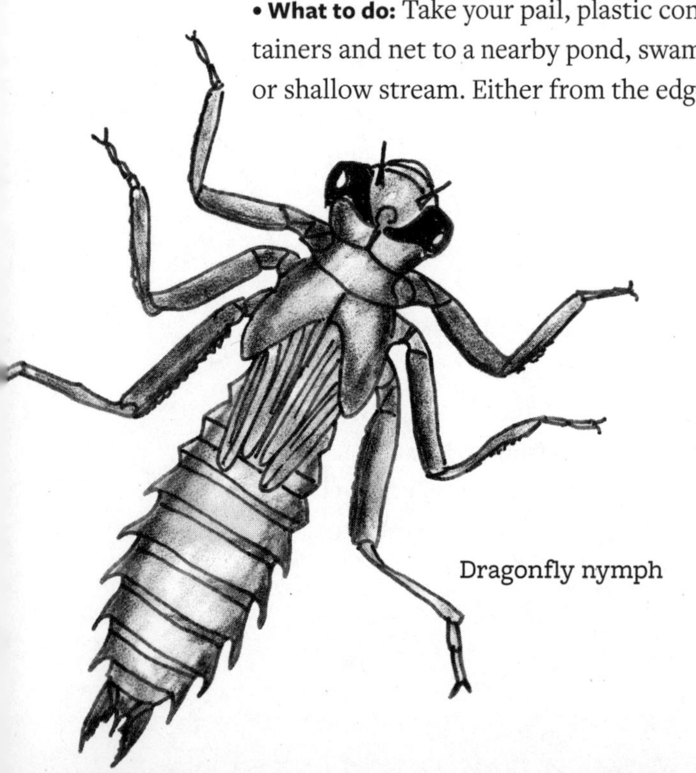

Dragonfly nymph

Questions to ponder

- How do they move? Do they undulate up and down like a mayfly nymph, or move from side to side like a stonefly nymph?
- How do you think they breathe? Diving beetles take a bubble of air down with them like a scuba diver; water scorpions breathe through a tube.
- Look at your critters' jaws. What do you think they eat? Do they have a folding jaw with claspers like a dragonfly nymph or munching mouthparts instead? (See color section, figure 43.)

Catch Invertebrates

- **You'll learn:** The diversity of summer invertebrates.
- **You'll need:** Insect nets and/or small containers with lids, white sheet, viewers (e.g., magnifying boxes, small clear plastic containers), hand lens, camera.
- **Procedure:** Visit a field or roadside with a variety of wildflowers (e.g., goldenrod, milkweed) as well as shrubs or small trees. Many insects can be easily caught directly off the leaves and blooms by easing your container over them and quickly putting on the lid. Using an insect net, however, is sometimes more effective and lots of fun. Sweep your net back and forth along the tops of blooms and through the grass. Place your container over any insects you've caught in the net. Be careful with bees and wasps!

Another technique is to use a white bed sheet. Lay the sheet down near a bush or small tree and gently shake the branches. You will be amazed at how many small invertebrates will tumble onto the sheet. Quickly ease these into your viewers. Collect enough insects so you have at least a few in each viewer. Have everyone sit in a circle holding one viewer with the insects visible. Explain that every time you say "Click," children will pass their insects in the same direction, like you're watching a slideshow. While children are studying what they've found, ask some simple questions like the ones below, one for every click. This is a way for children to share their discoveries without everyone struggling to look into the same container.

- How does your insect move? Does it walk, fly, crawl? If it walks, what is the sequence of legs moving? (click)
- How does your insect breathe? (Check out the abdomen to see if it expands and contracts)—Can you notice the spiracles or breathing holes? (click)
- Does your insect have antennae? What do you think it might use these for? (smelling, feeling) (click)
- Is your insect camouflaged (think about where you found it)? If not, what could its bright colors be saying to potential predators? (click)
- Study the mouthparts. What do you think your insect eats? Does it have sponge-like mouthparts for slurping (like a fly), or piercing mouthparts for sucking (like a mosquito), or chomping mouthparts (like a grasshopper) or drilling mouthparts like a weevil. (click)

Citizen Science Suggestions

Bumblebee Watch: Help track and conserve North America's bumblebees by taking and submitting photos of bees near you. Your work will help researchers determine the status and conservation needs of bumblebees. Find out more at **bumblebeewatch.org.**

- Is your bug an insect? (insects have three body parts, six legs, compound eyes, an exoskeleton, zero, two or four wings and antennae)
- The children may want to photograph some of the insects or draw them in their nature journal. If you can, catch a praying mantis. They make intriguing pets as they catch live insects you feed them.

Activity 27 Identify Insects by Call

• **You'll learn:** How to identify common insects by their song and possibly see and catch them.

• **You'll need:** "The Songs of Insects" by Lang Elliott and Wil Hershberger is a great resource for this activity. It includes a CD. You can also visit their website at songsofinsects.com to hear many of the calls and learn more about the insects.

• **Background:** Like frogs and birds, some insects use sound to attract mates. For instance, crickets and grasshoppers stridulate (see Activity 24, page 123). Knowing what species are calling adds a great deal to the pleasure of a summer evening. For example, the snowy tree cricket makes a soft, rhythmic *treet, treet*. This is the sound you typically hear in westerns when the cowboys are all sitting around the fire at night. Most species call from about July to October.

• **Procedure:** Try learning the most familiar insect calls in your neighborhood by matching recordings of the calls with what you are hearing. Start with the species in the chart opposite, nearly all of which can be found throughout most of the U.S. and southern Canada. At some point, you might also want to see and photograph

Male field cricket

Insect Sounds

Species	Time of call	Description
Four-spotted tree cricket	Day and night	High, non-stop mechanical trill
Snowy tree cricket	Evening and night	Soft, rich, evenly-spaced chirps: *treet... treet... treet...*
Fall field cricket	Day and night	Clear, loud chirps given at one per second
Carolina ground cricket	Day and night	Rapid, faint, buzzy trill with sputtering quality
Broad-winged bush katydid (central and eastern N.A. only)	Day and night	"Counts" from 2–3 buzzes (pause); 4–5 buzzes (pause) etc. to 9 buzzes
Dog-day cicada	Day and evening	High-pitched, sustained buzz or whine; starts soft but gets louder

the songsters in action. Although finding singing insects is challenging, it can be fun. First of all, home in on the general area the song is coming from. Cup your ears to be more precise as to the exact direction, then approach slowly. A technique to use at night is triangulation: two people approach the singer from different directions, then shine their flashlights at the same time at where the sound is coming from—(with luck) they will find the insect where the two flashlight beams cross.

If you locate an insect, wait until it starts singing again. Be sure to observe the movement of the wings. You can even

Darwin: Evolution is happening right before our eyes on the islands of Hawaii. Some crickets living on these islands have lost their ability to make music. This arose because of a mutation in a wing gene. The silent male crickets have "mutant" wings that are more like those of female crickets. This allows them to avoid parasitoid flies that recently invaded Hawaii from North America and are attracted to male cricket song. Quiet crickets avoid those deadly flies but still manage to mate by placing themselves near males that still do sing and intercepting the females when they show up!

try catching the singer. If the call seems to be coming from a small tree or some low branches, lay a white sheet out below the tree and shake it vigorously. If the insect falls to the ground, grab it. Crickets and katydids do well in a simple screened cage and a diet of iceberg lettuce. You'll be able to enjoy your own insect orchestra!

Activity 28 Cricket Thermometer

• **You'll learn:** How to tell the temperature using the sound of the snowy tree cricket.
• **You'll need:** A watch or phone that shows seconds.
• **Background:** Nature has thermometers, too. Snowy tree crickets are known for their rhythmic, precisely timed chirrups. In fact, you can calculate the approximate air temperature based on how fast the cricket is calling; the warmer the temperature, the faster he calls. Snowy tree crickets look a bit like grasshoppers but have long antennae and slender, pale green bodies. Learn the song by listening to a recording (see Activity 27).
• **What to do:** While it's still warm, head out to the woods or a park with trees and listen for snowy tree crickets calling. To calculate the temperature in degrees Fahrenheit, count the chirps over a 14-second period and then add 40; for example, if a cricket sang 15 times in 14 seconds, the temperature would be 55°F; 40 + 15 = 55. (In Celsius, count the number of chirps over 8 seconds and add 5.)

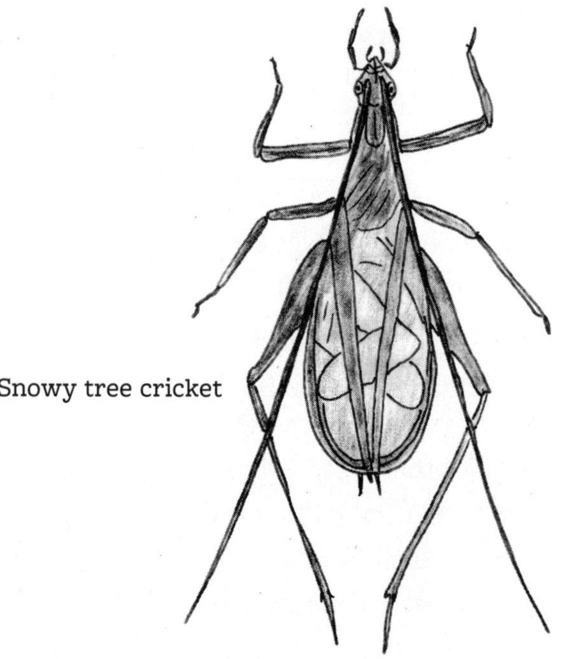
Snowy tree cricket

Plants

Activity 29 My Adopted Tree

• **Procedure:** As explained in the Fall chapter (see Activity 30, page 129), complete the summer section of "My Adopted Tree" in the Appendix on page 341.

Activity 30 Pressing Flowers

• **You'll learn:** How to preserve summer flowers for year-long enjoyment.
• **You'll need:** Blotter or printer paper, flowers, heavy books.

• **Background:** Pressing flowers is a wonderful way to hold onto summer, or any other season when flowers are blooming. Dried flowers can last for years. The best flowers for pressing are those that lie flat and lack thick fleshy parts. Good ones to try include daisies, asters, violets, cosmos, Queen Anne's lace, California poppies, verbenas, larkspurs and pansies. Don't hesitate to try other species, too. You can leave a section of the stem on the flower if desired. You may wish to group the flowers by shape, color, family (e.g., composites), habitat (e.g., roadside, wetland, garden), etc. You can also dry ferns, leaves, grasses, etc. using the method explained below.

• **Procedure:** Pick the flowers when they are in full bloom and any dew on them has dried. Open a large book like an atlas and place a sheet of paper over one of the pages. Lay the flowers face down, making sure they are not touching. Make yourself a note of the date and what species are on the sheet. Lay another piece of paper on top of the blossoms and then close the book. The two sheets of paper will absorb any moisture in the flowers. Stack some heavy books on top and leave undisturbed (no peeking!) for at least a month. Once the flowers are dry, you can glue them in your nature journal with their name and date collected (maybe covering them with clear plastic film for protection), use them to make bookmarks or gift tags, or even make them into a nice arrangement to be framed.

Activity 31 Twig/Wildflower Weaving

• **You'll learn:** To create inspiring art by using the vibrant colors of summer.

• **You'll need:** A forked branch, string or wool, flowers, leaves, grasses, evergreen boughs.

• **What to do:** Bring the vibrant colors of summer home by encouraging your children to engage in a simple weaving exercise. Find a sturdy forked stick about as wide as your thumb width and 20–28 in. (50–70 cm) long. Wrap string or raffia between the forks approximately every inch (2 cm). Harvest colorful flowers, grasses and leaves, and some snippets of evergreen as well. Be careful to harvest only a few plants from any one spot. Now weave each plant through the crisscrossing string. You'll be amazed at the color, texture and form of your creation.

• **Try this:** Collect natural objects (e.g., leaves of various shapes, sizes and colors; twigs; seeds; acorn caps; evergreen needles; berries; shells) and use them as building blocks to make caterpillars, leaf bugs, flowers, spiders and more. Use your imagination! (See color section, figure 44.)

Activity 32 Fir Resin Motor Boat

• **You'll learn:** That fir resin repels or pushes away water.

• **You'll need:** A fir twig and resin, a body of water.

• **Background:** Known also as the blister tree, fir is an evergreen with relatively smooth bark. Common species include balsam fir in the east and amabilis fir in the west. However, scattered along the bark at regular intervals are elongated "blisters," tiny pockets full of sticky resin. It is thought that the resin may help the tree defend itself against insects and diseases. Balsam fir sap was traditionally used as an antiseptic that was spread over wounds and infected areas. Dried into a gum, the sap can also be chewed. It contains an oil that is considered hydrophobic ("water hating"). As the sap makes contact with the water, it repels water molecules and moves anything it is attached to forward.

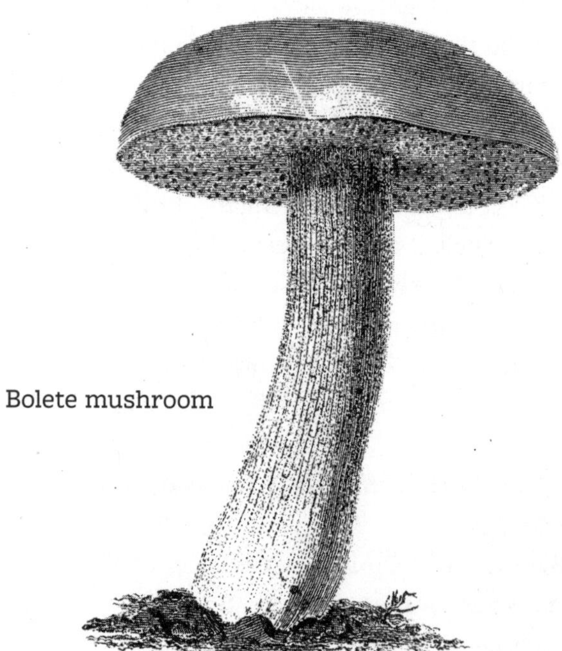

Bolete mushroom

• **What to do:** Take a small, sharp twig about 2 in. (5 cm) long and about as thick as a pencil lead. Burst one blister with your twig and make sure there is a nice globule of sap attached to the twig. Carefully bring the twig and sap to a nearby pond (or quiet water source) and place the twig on the water. Watch in amazement as the twig takes off like a motorboat, making twists and turns as it zooms along the surface of the water.

Fungi

Activity 33 Fungus Scavenger Hunt

• **You'll learn:** The amazing diversity of fungi, even in a small area.

• **You'll need:** A fungus scavenger hunt sheet (see Appendix, page 321), location rich in fungi, camera.

• **Procedure:** Make up a sheet of search items such as those listed below. See how many fungi on the list you can find. You may also want to use tubs or buckets to collect one of each different fungus and bring them back to share with the whole group. An impressive example of biodiversity can be had by gathering all of the different fungi together for a picture or sketch (see below). Alternatively, you could simply take a picture of each fungus as you find it instead of picking it.

Darwin: Believe it or not, fungi are more closely related to animals than to plants. In other words, the common ancestor you share with fungi is not as old as the common ancestor you share with plants. So what do we, as animals, have in common with fungi? Well, here are two examples: fungal cell walls are made of chitin, a substance found in animals (e.g., insect carapaces) but nowhere in the plant world. And the proteins found in fungi are more animal-like than plant-like. Now, there's something to think about while you enjoy your next pepperoni and mushroom pizza!

Weather

Activity 34 Make Your Own Thunderstorm

• **You'll learn:** How to recreate the sound of a thunderstorm.

• **You'll need:** Works best with 12 or more participants.

• **Background:** During the summer, at any given time, there can be as many as 1,800 thunderstorms happening around the world. A thunderstorm occurs when hot moist air rises quickly. On a hot summer's day, sunlight pours down onto the surface of the Earth, creating a column of warm air. Sometimes warm, moist air bumps into colder, drier air. This causes convection, a rapidly rising column of air. As the warm air rises it cools and the water vapor in it condenses, forming a cloud. The cloud will continue to grow as long as the air continues to rise, piling right up into the freezing air above it. Water turns into ice particles that are super-cooled. Ice particles can bounce off of each other and create small electric charges. When lots of ice particles interact (picture a whole bunch of bumper cars), large regions of charged particles can generate a bolt of lightning. Lightning is a high-current surge of electrons that can super-heat the air around it. When this rapid heating is followed by a sudden cooling, sound waves are generated. We recognize these sound waves as thunder.

• **What to do:** Designate one person to be the leader. As soon as the leader begins an action, the rest of the group follows. Use the following sequence and continue until the storm is over:

- Rub hands together to emulate a fine sprinkle of rain.
- Tap two fingers against the palm of your hand to conjure up the first raindrops.
- Snap your fingers gently to increase the intensity of the rain.
- Have some people cup their hands and blow into them. By expanding and contracting their hands they create the sounds of the wind.
- Slap your hands against your thighs quickly—now the rain is falling in sheets.
- Clap your hands quickly together. You have a full-on rainstorm!
- Intensify the wind.
- Stomp your feet hard on the ground while clapping to show thunder.
- Turn lights on and off quickly if you are in a room to simulate lightning.
- You now have a full-on thunderstorm.
- Work backwards through the sequence to ease off: stomping feet, clapping hands, slapping hands against thighs, snapping fingers, tapping two fingers against the palm, rubbing hands and finally stopping. The storm has passed!

Activity 35 Adventures in the Night

• **You'll learn:** To explore and enjoy the natural world at night.

• **You'll need:** Flashlight, blindfolds, wintergreen Lifesavers, pieces of paper of three or four different colors, first aid kit, leaves to smell, candle and matches.

• **Background:** Take advantage of the warm summer weather to discover the natural world after dark. We humans often go into the night with light, but when we do this we bring a touch of daylight into our nighttime experience. To give children a true sense of the magic of the night, try a light-free night hike. This means going into the fields and forests without a flashlight and with all your senses primed. We humans are visual creatures who get 90 percent of our information about the world through our eyes. The darkness of the night may dim our sight, but our other senses take over—we become more tuned into our hearing, smelling and feeling. When done well, a night hike can create powerful memories and a heightened sense of wonder for the natural world.

• **Procedure:**

1. A day or two before the hike, practice identifying some common night sounds such as any common owls in the area, snowy tree crickets, ground crickets, field crickets, whip-poor-wills, coyotes, tree frogs, etc. These sounds are all readily available online. Also take some time to review the main summer constellations—e.g., Ursa Major, Ursa Minor (including Polaris), Cassiopeia, the constellations of the Summer Triangle—and the phases of the Moon. Consider any planets that may be present. Be sure to allow everyone to share their feelings about the night, including any fears they may have. Reassure participants that this will be a fun and safe experience.

2. It is always a good idea to walk the route yourself in daylight. Have a rough idea of what activities you will do where (for example, those that lend themselves to an open area). Think about some activities you could give the group to do as they walk between activity stations. (See list on page 304.)

3. Establish a few ground rules in advance: no flashlights, no practical jokes or scaring each other; the importance of walking quietly and slowly, lifting one's feet a little higher than usual to avoid tripping; no conversation during designated quiet times, so that you can focus on the sounds of the night.

4. Make sure there are two leaders: one at the front of the line and a "sweeper" at the back. Carry an emergency flashlight in your pack as a safety measure.

5. For younger children, extend a rope from the front leader to the sweeper. Each child holds the rope with one hand.

> To go in the dark with a light is to know the light. To know the dark, go dark. Go without sight, and find that the dark, too, blooms and sings, and is traveled by dark feet and dark wings.
>
> —WENDELL BERRY

Here are some night hike activity options

• **Sound:** Use your Deer Ears (see Activity 2, page 270) and conduct a brief sound inventory. Stand perfectly still for one to two minutes and raise one finger in the air for every new night sound you hear. Swivel your ears in the direction of the sound. Afterwards, quietly share what you heard. Talk briefly about how bats use sound to catch moths and how moths have evolved to recognize these sounds and avoid being caught. Play a game of Bat and Moth (see Activity 8, page 274).

• **Smell:** Direct the group to smell the night air and to try to identify what they are smelling. Pass around any strongly scented leaves of plants that grow in the area (e.g., balsam poplar, black poplar) and have everyone rub and smell them. Play a round of scent trails (see Activity 15, page 227).

• **Sight:** *Color in the Night:* Your eyes have special photoreceptor cells called rods

Great gray owl

that do most of the work in dim light conditions. However, rods can't show us color. The other photoreceptors in your eye, called cones, are the ones that are used for seeing color, but they require fairly bright light. When it is dark enough that you can barely see, give each participant four pieces of colored paper. Have them write on each piece of paper the color they think it is. They can keep the paper in their pocket and check the colors when they get back. Did everyone in your group mix up the same color or did everyone get the colors right? Ask the group why some animals see better at night than humans.

• **Night sky:** In an open area, ask the group to try to find the Summer Triangle and the north sky constellations. Can they see Polaris, the North Star? This star allows you to determine the cardinal directions. Food for thought: *"there are more stars in the universe than there are grains of sand on all the beaches of the entire world."* Ask everyone to point to the south, east and west. Point out any planets that are visible. If the Moon is up, ask them what phase it is in and whether it is waxing or waning. If you have time, tell the story of Big History found on page 78 in Key Nature Concepts for Children to Learn.

• **Solo hike/sit:** Place people along the trail—maybe 20 ft. (6 m) apart depending on age and how dark it is—so they can experience the night alone. After five minutes or so, pick them up again. Another option is to have them walk a section of the trail alone, with a leader at each end.

Here are some things to focus on while walking between stations

⟶ Pay special attention to the terrain underfoot (rocks, dips, rises, etc.). Ask them to occasionally step off the path to compare how the ground feels.

⟶ Pay attention to any subtle changes in temperature between two stations (e.g., when entering a forest).

⟶ Focus on the smell of the air and if it changes along the path.

⟶ Focus on sounds by keeping a mental checklist of how many different sounds you hear between stations.

• **Wrap-up story:** At the final station, tell a story that involves the discovery of a magical substance that creates its own light (there is a sample story if you search Upham Woods Outdoor Learning Center Night Hike). Tell the group you have some of that magic with you tonight. Pass around some broken pieces of wintergreen Lifesavers. In pairs facing one another, instruct the group to chew the magic substance with an open mouth, while observing the partner's mouth. Tell them to try not to wet the substance with saliva too much. Ask them what they think creates the blue-green glow when broken by the teeth (or even a pair of pliers)? Explain that the phenomenon is called triboluminescence. Light is released when the chemical bonds of the sugar molecules in the wintergreen oil are broken in the presence of nitrogen in the air.

Save these vision activities for the end of the hike. You'll lose your night vision, so walk carefully!

• **Night vision:** Ask the group to cover one eye with their hand and to stare with their open eye at a lit candle. Extinguish the candle and have participants look around with each eye separately to see if they notice a difference between the two eyes. The difference should be quite dramatic. The pupil in the uncovered eye contracts because of the bright light, while the pupil in the covered eye, which has gained night vision, remains wide open (dilated).

• **Afterimage:** Tell the group to watch as you light a match and move it in a circular pattern. Ask them to quickly close their eyes to try to see an afterimage. Do the same with a flashlight. The image created by the brain remains briefly after the source disappears.

When you get back, discuss what activities everyone liked most, what they learned and if their feelings toward the night have changed.

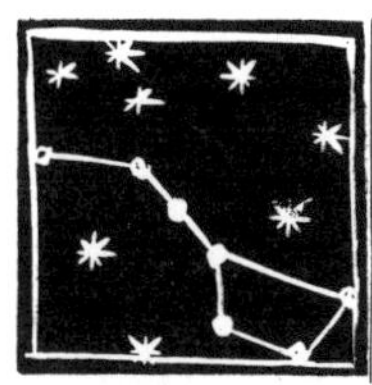

The Sky

Activity 36 Record Sunrise and Sunset locations

• **You'll learn:** To record sunrise and sunset locations on or near the summer solstice.

• **Procedure:** As in the fall (see page 135), winter and spring, take note of exactly where the Sun rises and sets in relation to landmarks on the eastern and western horizons.

Path of the Sun through the Seasons

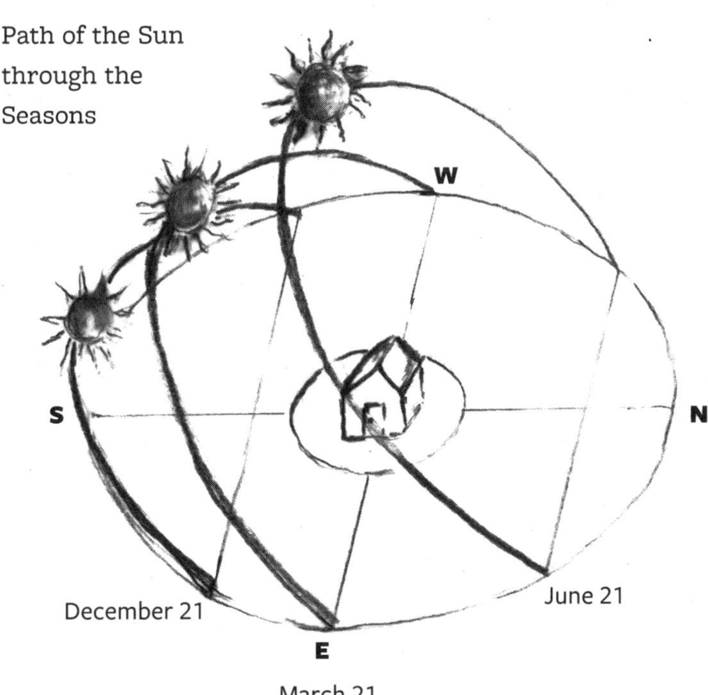

Sagan: Light is something we rarely stop to think about. It actually consists of tiny particles called photons and always moves at the same speed: 186,000 mi. (298 km) a second or 700 million mi. (1.1 billion km) an hour. If you boarded a plane that could fly as fast as these photons, you could travel around the Earth's equator 7.5 times every second! It takes these same photons eight minutes to travel from the Sun to your eyeball on Earth, which allows you to see them. When you look at the Sun, you are, therefore, seeing it as it was eight minutes ago. If the Sun were suddenly to go dark, it would take eight minutes for us to notice. Looking at the heavens is nothing short of looking into a giant time machine. How cool is that!

Activity 37 Measure Your Shadow

• **Procedure:** As you did in September (page 135), December and March, go outside at noon and measure the length of your shadow.

Activity 38 A Swan Flying over a River of Stars

• **You'll learn:** To identify the Summer Triangle.

• **You'll need:** Sky chart or app (optional).

• **Background:** One of the main features of the summer sky is an asterism known as the Summer Triangle. It is not a constellation itself but is made up of the brightest stars of three separate summer constellations: Vega (in the constellation Lyra), Deneb (in the constellation Cygnus) and Altair (in the constellation Aquila). Joining these stars together forms a giant, easy-to-see triangle. A star-rich swath of the Milky Way runs through the Summer Triangle and continues to the horizon in both directions.

Looking like a dimly glowing band arching across the heavens, the Milky Way is the most beautiful feature of the night sky. This is our home galaxy. It is shaped like a spiral wheel, but appears to us as a band because we are viewing its spiral structure from within. Our solar system is on one of the spiral arms about two-thirds of the way—or 25,000 light years—from

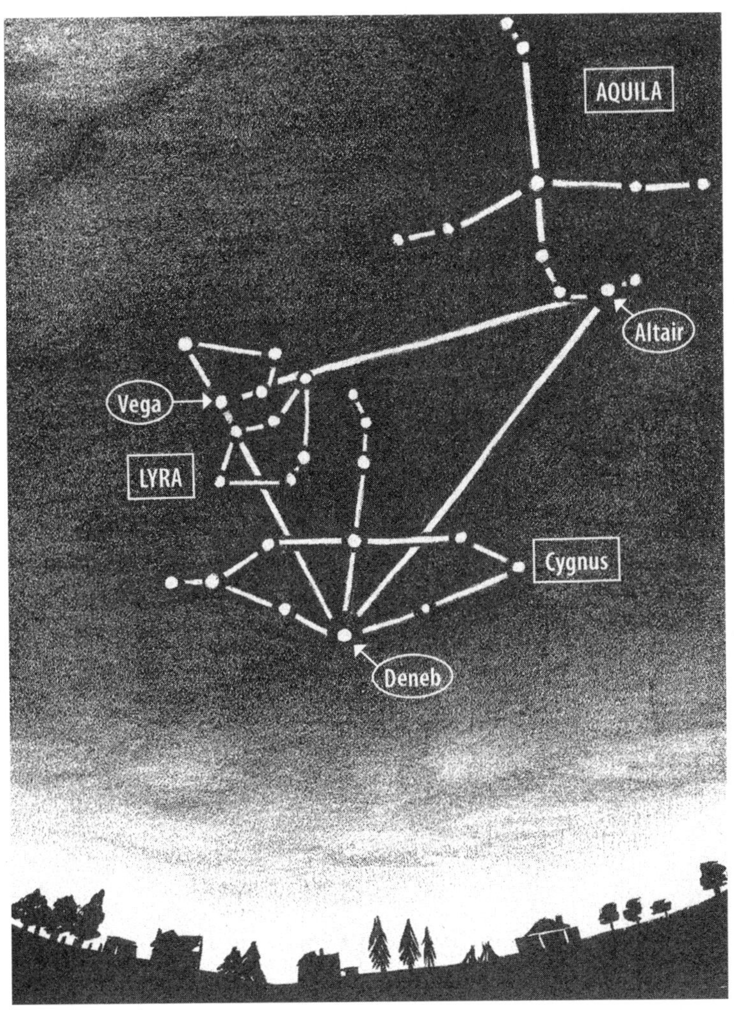

Summer Triangle

the center. Astronomers estimate that the Milky Way consists of some 200 to 400 billion stars!

• **Procedure:** *Summer Triangle*: Find the Big Dipper, high in the northwest. The two stars that form the end of the Dipper's bowl closest to the handle point almost directly to Vega, the brightest star of the Triangle. The other two stars in the Triangle are Deneb and Altair. Deneb marks the tail of Cygnus, the Swan, an easily recognizable constellation. Try to imagine the big bird, wings outstretched, flying down the Milky Way as it heads south. (This image is especially strong in late summer and early fall, when fall migration is underway and you may hear the contact calls of birds passing overhead in the night sky.) Vega, too, deserves special attention. Although it is located in a rather small, unremarkable constellation (Lyra), it is the brightest star of the Summer Triangle

NEIL DEGRASSE TYSON: In July 2015, NASA scientists announced the discovery of Kepler-452b—the most Earth-like alien planet yet discovered. It is located some 1,400 light-years from Earth in the constellation Cygnus. This planet is larger than Earth and its star is older, but the length of its year is almost the same as ours. Its sun would even look and feel quite similar to ours in the sky. Kepler-452b is the first planet to be found in a comparable "habitable zone" to Earth's in terms of its distance from its star. It could, therefore, have liquid water on its surface. It is also older than Earth, which means there has been lots of time for life to arise there. So when you are looking at the Summer Triangle, pay special attention to the Cygnus constellation and think to yourself that there is a planet out there that might very well contain life. Who knows? Maybe they are staring back at us at this very moment!

and the second brightest star in the summer sky. Only Arcturus, which is now high overhead, is brighter.

Milky Way: For optimal viewing, try to choose a cool, clear, moonless night; warm, humid nights tend to produce a lot of haze. A pair of binoculars will transform the gauzy "river of milk" seen by the naked eye into countless thousands of individual stars. Begin by finding the Summer Triangle. If the sky is dark enough, you should be able to see a dazzling section of the Milky Way in the Cygnus constellation. The galaxy is brightest, however, in the area of the constellation Sagittarius, which lies in the southeast. This is because the center of the Milky Way is actually located behind the stars of Sagittarius.

Nature's Fireworks

- **You'll learn:** To see the amazing Perseid meteor shower.
- **You'll need:** Reclining lawn chairs, blankets, snacks (all optional).
- **Background:** A meteor shower occurs when the Earth passes through a stream of debris left behind by a comet. The "shooting stars" in the Perseids, the year's best meteor shower, originate from debris left by the comet Swift-Tuttle. Most of the fragments are particles the size of grains of sand that burn up and emit beautiful streaks of light as they speed through our atmosphere at up to 100,000 mph (160,000 km/h). Meteor showers are best viewed from a dark, open location far

from city lights. However, it's still possible to see at least some from a suburban backyard. Most of us are quite happy even if we just see one every few minutes or so. Viewing is also best when there is little or no moonlight, but even with a bright Moon, you should still see a few. You will also see more meteors after midnight than before; they are usually most abundant in the wee hours before dawn.

• **Procedure:** August 12 is usually the peak date for the Perseids, but viewing can also be good a few nights before this date and up to a week after. Allow for at least an hour of viewing time, because meteors come in spurts. Remember, too, that your eyes can take up to 20 minutes to adjust to the darkness. The Perseid shower originates in the Perseus constellation, low in the northeastern sky just below Cassiopeia. However, as the night progresses, Perseus climbs higher in the sky and is nearly overhead by dawn. At that point, the meteors streak down in all directions toward the horizon. You don't need to know the constellations, however, to watch this or any meteor shower. Just scan the sky—preferably from a reclining lawn chair—because meteors can appear from most any angle. Try to involve the kids, too, since it is still summer vacation. Children are always thrilled to see meteors, especially if it means getting woken up after midnight and lying outside wrapped in a blanket while shooting stars streak by overhead. Snacks and something to drink make the event even more memorable. Just be sure to check the sky conditions before waking them up!

Honoring the Season

Summer Solstice / Midsummer (June 21)

In ancient times, Midsummer celebrations in Sweden were held to welcome summertime and the season of fertility. Ever since the 6th century CE, Midsummer bonfires have been lit all around Europe and southern Sweden. Midsummer night is the shortest of the year and was long considered a magical night and the best time for telling people's futures. You could also discover treasures, for example, by studying how moonbeams fell. It was even said that water was turned into wine and ferns into flowers on Midsummer night. Many plants were believed to acquire healing powers on that one night of the year. In Sweden, it was even said that on their way home from a Midsummer celebration, girls and young women should pick seven different species of flowers and lay them under their pillows. At night, their future husbands would appear to them in a dream.

What you can do

⟵ On the day (or close to the day) of the solstice, watch the sunrise and/or sunset and how the Sun is at its highest northern point in the sky at noon. Sometimes local astronomy groups will hold special events on that day. At the very least, they will be able to suggest a height of land or the top of a building affording an unobstructed view of the rising and setting sun.

⊸ Make a solstice T-shirt with tie-dye, a homemade sun stencil and fabric crayons.

⊸ Make an egg carton sun crown using two egg cartons with a spiky row in the middle, scissors, string, yellow or gold paint and a paintbrush. First, cut out the middle row of spikes from each carton. Paint and let dry, using the lid of the carton as a drying surface. Use the scissors (or a pen/pencil) to carefully poke holes in both ends of each of the spike rows. String the two spike rows together. Measure the sun crown around your child's head to determine the length of the string for connecting in the back. You can also decorate it with greenery, wildflowers, etc. This sun crown is also appropriate for winter solstice. (From Ozark Pagan Mamma June 5 tressabelle.wordpress.com/2011/06/05/kids-activities-for-midsummer-summer-solstice.)

⊸ Make sun cookies for a treasure hunt. Make the kids' favorite cookies, colored with a sun-yellow food dye. Hide them in the backyard and let the kids look for them. Make sure they are shared equally among all participants before anyone starts eating.

⊸ Make a backyard maypole. Materials: 8′ (2.5 m) × 1¼″ (12 mm) PVC pipe, 1½″ (15 mm) PVC cap, heavy umbrella stand, acrylic paint, sandpiper, ten different colored 10′ (3 m) × 1½″ (15 mm) colored cloth ribbons, glue gun. Working outside, sand the PVC pole until its surface is dull. Paint it any color you wish—sun-yellow?—with the acrylic paint. Kids will love painting. Paint the cap, too. Let dry. Hot glue the ribbons inside the cap by gluing down five ends—evenly spaced, and then the remaining five on top, alternating so you get evenly placed ribbons. Make sure your shiny side is out! Then put your cap on the top of the pole and hammer down gently with a mallet or a hammer and cloth. Stick the finished maypole in the umbrella stand. Then explore different ways to dance around it. Just having each child hold a ribbon and walk around in a circle will create a beautiful twisted pattern. (By Jessica Begum, modernmom.com.)

⊸ Make a sun mandala. A mandala is a circular symbol, often seen in Hinduism and Buddhism, which represents the universe. It can be used as a focus for meditation. Just making a mandala is a very calming activity. Gather a selection of small leaves, petals or flower heads. Using

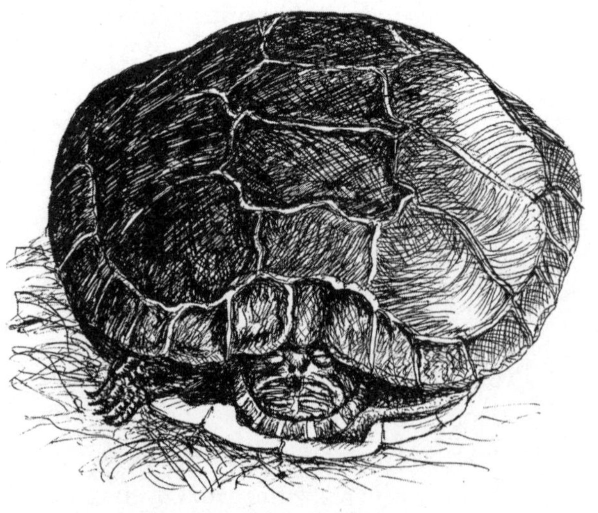
Midland painted turtle

Quotes on summer for contemplation

Nothing is more memorable than a smell. One scent can be unexpected, momentary and fleeting, yet conjure up a childhood summer beside a lake in the mountains...

—**Diane Ackerman**

The hum of bees is the voice of the garden.

—**Elizabeth Lawrence**

Deep summer is when laziness finds respectability.

—**Sam Keen**

Do what we can, summer will have its flies.

—**Ralph Waldo Emerson**

I wonder what it would be like to live in a world where it was always June.

—**L. M. Montgomery**

outdoor chalk, choose colors that match or contrast with the leaves and petals. Working on the driveway or other stone or concrete surface, draw out a simple mandala wheel. You may wish to make it more sun-like by adding rays around the perimeter. Within the mandala, make repeating patterns such as concentric circles of the colors you have chosen. Place the petals and leaves on the appropriate colors in the mandala. Take a picture! If you want your mandala to last a while, use paint instead.

- Make a flower chain. Collect a bunch of long-stemmed wildflowers. Daisies and even dandelions work well. You'll need about 15 to 20 of these. Cross over the flowers about an inch (2.5 cm) or so from the head of the flower. Create a loop so that you go over and under the stem of the first flower. Pull gently until you have a knot. Keep adding more flowers until you have a long chain. You can tie the ends together to make a crown. Use shorter chains to make bracelets and necklaces.

Appendix

Cards for Song Ensemble and Listen for Your Mate

American robin *Cheer-a-lee, cheer-up, cheer-a-lee* (happy!) 4:00 AM–11:00 AM / 3:00 PM–9:00 PM 	American bittern *Gulp-a-pump* (very deep) 4:00 AM–8:00 AM / 8:00 PM–10:00 PM 
Red-winged blackbird *Konk-er-ee* (tinny) 6:00 AM–10:00 AM / 7:00 PM–9:00 PM 	Common yellowthroat *Witchity-witchity-witchity-witch* (rolling) 4:00 AM–8:00 AM / 6:00 PM–8:00 PM 
Mourning dove *There's nothing-do…* (slow, deep) 6:00 AM–12:00 AM / 2:00 PM–5:00 PM 	White-breasted nuthatch *Wee-wee-wee-wee-wee-wee* (nasal, 1 pitch) 6:00 AM–10:00 AM / 4:00 PM–7:00 PM 

Yellow warbler *Sweet-sweet-sweet-I'm so so sweet* (fast) 5:00 AM–9:00 AM / 6:00 PM–8:00 PM 	Song sparrow *Maids-maids-maids-put-on-your-tea-kettle-ettle-ettle* 5:00 AM–9:00 AM / 3:00 PM–6:00 PM 
Black-capped chickadee *Hi Sweetie* or *Fee-bee-bee* 5:00 AM–9:00 AM / 7:00 PM–9:00 PM 	Hermit thrush *Veer-veer-veer-veer* (change pitch each time) 5:00 AM–9:00 AM / 8:00 PM–10:00 PM 
American goldfinch *Pa-chip-chip-chip per-chick-a-ree* (bright) 6:00 AM–10:00 AM / 2:00 PM–5:00 PM 	Great horned owl *Who's awake? Me too* (deep) 4:00 AM–5:00 AM / 10:00 PM (continues) 

Leaf Adaptations Scavenger Hunt

A leaf from the tallest tree in the area (take from the ground) 	Two different species of leaves that both end in a point 	Two different leaves with tiny teeth around the edge 
Two different leaves with big teeth around the edges 	Two different leaves with smooth edges 	Two different leaves with wavy edges 
Two different compound leaves with small leaflets 	Two different simple leaves that are very large 	Two different brown leaves lying on the ground 

Two different leaves with a strong smell when you rub them 	A leaf with tiny thorns like a thistle 	Two different evergreen leaves (or needles) 
Two different leaves that are dark green 	Two different leaves that are light green 	Two different leaves that are orange, red or purple 
Two different leaves that feel thick and leathery 	Your own leaf adaptation discovery	Your own leaf adaptation discovery

Adaptations to Winter Scavenger Hunt

<table>
<tr>
<td>5 kinds of shed leaves on the ground (by shedding leaves, trees minimize water loss)
</td>
<td>An evergreen shaped like a cone (easier to shed snow)
</td>
<td>Gall on a goldenrod plant (safe, sheltered site for an insect to overwinter)
</td>
</tr>
<tr>
<td>Small, thick, leathery leaves (ensure plants do not lose too much moisture)
</td>
<td>A conifer branch bending down with the weight of snow (bend, don't break, under weight of snow)
</td>
<td>Insect eggs (a natural antifreeze in the eggs stops them from freezing)
</td>
</tr>
<tr>
<td>Thick, waxy conifer needles (water loss is greatly reduced)
</td>
<td>A plant like a cattail or grass that appears to be dead (adaptation?)
</td>
<td>Birds at a feeder or eating seeds in a tree or field (adaptation?)
</td>
</tr>
</table>

Ducks swimming or feeding in frigid water (adaptation?) 	A squirrel (some mammals are able to store or find food in winter) 	A squirrel's nest (*drey*) (adaptation?) 
A cocoon on a twig, under loose bark, etc. (adaptation?) 	A bird's nest (why is it empty?) 	Wild mammal tracks on the snow (adaptation?) 
A bird with feathers fluffed up (adaptation?) 	Holes in a tree made by a woodpecker (adaptation?) 	Twig or bark chewed by a mammal (adaptation?) 

Draw or write your own discoveries of winter adaptations:

Adaptations for Reproduction Scavenger Hunt

2 brightly colored male birds such as a cardinal or mallard (females prefer to mate with the brightest males) 	2 drably colored female birds such as a female cardinal or mallard duck (dull color makes them less visible when sitting on the nest) 	3 different kinds of birds repeatedly singing (song attracts and keeps a mate; shows ownership of territory) 
A bird doing a special "dance" or other behavior, such as puffing up its feathers in front of female (adaptation?) 	A bird chasing away another bird (adaptation?) 	Frogs or toads calling (adaptation?) 
A spring field cricket calling (adaptation?) 	A swarm of insects such as midges over a tree (insects find a mate in swarms) 	2 kinds of flowers hanging from twigs and swinging in the breeze (pollen is carried away by the wind) 

<table>
<tr>
<td>2 kinds of flowers with a "bull's eye," such as a dark center surrounded by light-colored petals. (adaptation?)
</td>
<td>2 kinds of flowers with large petals (adaptation?)
</td>
<td>2 kinds of flowers with a distinct odor (odors helps to attract pollinators, especially bees and moths)
</td>
</tr>
<tr>
<td>2 kinds of flowers with nectar guides, lines or spots radiating from the middle (guide pollinators to the nectar and/or pollen)
</td>
<td>A flower with a long stigma and short stamens (helps to prevent self-pollination)
</td>
<td>A red flower (hummingbirds often prefer red flowers)
</td>
</tr>
<tr>
<td>A blue flower (bees prefer blue flowers)
</td>
<td>Flowers with a red/yellow pattern (attract butterflies in particular)
</td>
<td>White flowers with a strong scent, especially at night (moths can easily find them)
</td>
</tr>
<tr>
<td colspan="3">Draw or write your own discoveries of adaptations for reproduction:</td>
</tr>
</table>

Fungus Scavenger Hunt

Fungus with gills	Fungus growing on the trunk of a standing tree	Fungus growing on wood on the ground

Fungus growing out of the soil	Fungus with a ring or skirt on its stem	Fungus with bumps on top

Fungus that looks like Jell-O	Fungus that is O-shaped or shaped like a ball	Fungus that is coral-shaped with fingers going up or down

A fungus with bands of different colors
A white fungus
A brown fungus
A pink fungus
A fungus of another color
A fungus smaller than a penny
A fungus bigger than your hand
Your own discovery
Your own discovery

Non-identification Bird Walk Checklist: *Check all that you see*

Movement	
A bird walking	
A bird hopping	
A bird soaring (almost no flapping)	
A bird flying in a straight line	
A bird flying up and down like a roller-coaster	
Other?	
Location	
A bird perched on a tree	
A bird feeding on the ground	
A bird on a wire	
A bird on a post or fence	
Other?	
Size and color	
A mostly black bird	
A mostly white bird	
A mostly brown bird	
A sparrow-sized bird (6 in. / 15 cm or smaller)	
A robin-sized bird (10 in. / 25 cm)	
A crow-sized bird (18 in. /45 cm)	
Other?	
Communication	
A bird calling (short, simple, one or two notes) or singing	
A pair of birds flying together	
A flock of three or more birds	
Other?	
A few common species to identify — How many can you find?	
European starlings	
Gulls	
Rock pigeons	
American crows	
American robins	
Other?	

Pictures for Imagining Your Ancestors

Oscar Monkman	His father	His grandfather

His great-grandfather	His great-great-grandfather	His great-great-great-grandfather

Long-haired, bearded ancestor	Human with thicker skull under eyebrows	Model of *Homo erectus*

Chimpanzee-like common ancestor 	Lemur-like ancestor 	Shrew-like ancestor 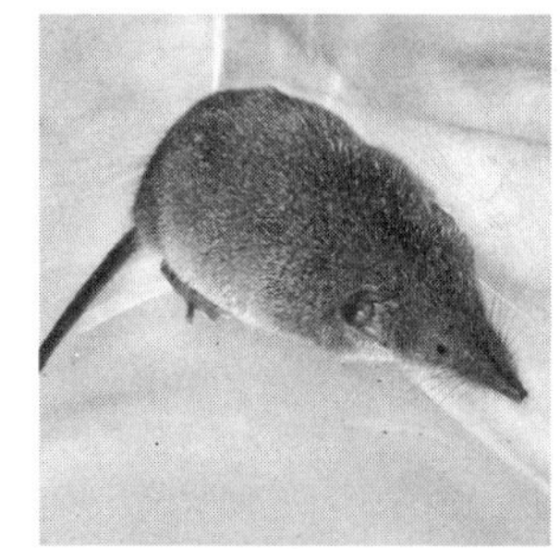
Lizard-like ancestor 	Tiktaalik amphibian-like ancestor 	Fish-like ancestor 
Blue-green algae 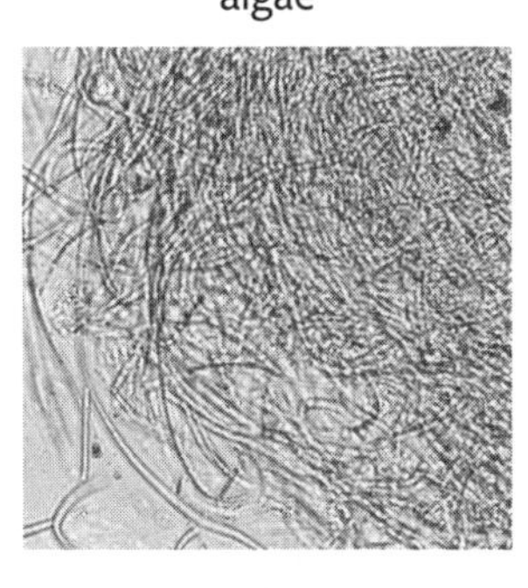		

Fall Phenology Chart
(September, October, November)

Location: ______________________ Year: ________

Instructions

- Gather information from sources such as personal observations, the Internet, newspapers or speaking with seniors.
- Try to be sure the dates are as accurate as possible.
- Feel free to tailor the charts to best fit your region, especially with regard to species.
- Include units (either imperial or metric).
- Discuss any trends you see such as big differences from the long-term averages, and speculate on how these trends may affect the dates for plant and animal events.

Description of sunrise / sunset locations at fall equinox

(Be sure to stand in exactly the same spot each season.)

On or about Sept. 21, the Sun rises (describe where) ______________________

____

On or about Sept. 21, the Sun sets (describe where) ______________________

____

Sketch of sunrise position on eastern horizon showing key landmarks.	Sketch of sunset position on western horizon showing key landmarks.

Sunlight

1. Photoperiod (daylight) on the following days
   - September 22 (fall equinox) ______ hours and ______ minutes
   - October 22 ______ hours and ______ minutes
   - November 22 ______ hours and ______ minutes

2. Length of shadow at noon on September 21 (or closest date possible; measure same person or object each season).
   - September 21 ______

Temperature and precipitation

1. Daily temperatures
   - September 22 High ________ Low ________ Average ________
   - October 22 High ________ Low ________ Average ________
   - November 22 High ________ Low ________ Average ________

2. Dates of temperature "firsts":
   First 20°F (–6°C) ____________________
   10°F (–12°C) ____________________
   0°F (–17°C) ____________________
   below 0°F (–17°C) ____________________

3. Dates of temperature "lasts":
   Last 70°F (21°C) ____________________
   60°F (15°C) ____________________
   50°F (10°C) ____________________

4. Monthly mean temperatures
   - September ________ Long-term September mean ________
   - October ________ Long-term October mean ________
   - November ________ Long-term November mean ________

5. Precipitation
   - Total precipitation for September ________ Long-term September average ________
   - Total precipitation for October ________ Long-term October average ________
   - Total precipitation for November ________ Long-term November average ________

6. Frost, snow and ice
   - First frost ____________ Long-term average date ____________________
   - First snow flurries ____________________
   - First snow flurries of 4 in./10 cm or more ____________________
   - First ice covering birdbath (or puddle) ____________________
   - Lasting snow cover began ____________________

Plants

- Peak leaf color ____________ Species ____________
- Peak leaf color ____________ Species ____________
- Most leaves off native deciduous trees ____________
- Most leaves off non-native deciduous trees (e.g., Norway maple) ____________
- Last field or roadside flower still in bloom: ____________ Species ____________

Animals

- First long-distance migrating geese (not local geese) ____________
- First southbound migrant at feeder (e.g., white-throated sparrow) ____________
- Last monarch ____________
- Last robin ____________
- Last hummingbird ____________
- Last snake ____________
- Last frog ____________
- Last butterfly ____________
- Last dragonfly ____________
- Last chipmunk ____________
- Last cricket heard calling ____________
- Last ____________
- Last ____________

Winter Phenology Chart
(December, January, February)

Location: ______________________ Year: __________

Instructions

- Gather information from sources such as personal observations, the Internet, newspapers or speaking with seniors.
- Try to be sure the dates are as accurate as possible.
- Feel free to tailor the charts to best fit your region, especially with regard to species.
- Include units (either imperial or metric)
- Discuss any trends you see such as big differences from the long-term averages, and speculate on how these trends may affect the dates for plant and animal events.

Description of sunrise / sunset locations at winter solstice

(Be sure to stand in exactly the same spot each season.)

On or about Sept. 21, the Sun rises (describe where) ______________________

____

On or about Sept. 21, the Sun sets (describe where) ______________________

____

Sketch of sunrise position on eastern horizon showing key landmarks. Show fall equinox sunrise position as well.	Sketch of sunset position on western horizon showing key landmarks. Show fall equinox sunset position as well.

Sunlight

1. Photoperiod (daylight) on the following days
   - December 21 (winter solstice) ______ hours and ______ minutes
   - January 21 ______ hours and ______ minutes
   - February 21 ______ hours and ______ minutes

2. Length of shadow at noon on December 21 (or closest day possible; be sure to measure the shadow of the same person or object as in September).
   - December 21 ______ September 21 ______

Temperature and precipitation

1. Daily temperatures
   - December 21 High __________ Low __________ Average __________
   - January 21 High __________ Low __________ Average __________
   - February 21 High __________ Low __________ Average __________

2. Coldest day/night of winter ____________ Temperature ____________

3. Mildest day/night of winter ____________ Temperature ____________

4. Monthly mean temperatures
   - December __________ Long-term December mean __________
   - January __________ Long-term January mean __________
   - February __________ Long-term February mean __________

5. Precipitation
   - Total precipitation for December ________ Long-term December average ____________
   - Total precipitation for January ________ Long-term January average ____________
   - Total precipitation for February ________ Long-term February average ____________

6. Frost and ice
   - First snow flurries of 4 inches/10 cm or more____________________
   - First ice covering birdbath (or puddle) ____________________
   - Ice covering (name water body)________ Long-term average date ____________
   - Ice covering (name water body)________ Long-term average date ____________
   - First ice-fishing permitted ____________ Long-term average date ____________
   - Lasting snow cover began ____________________

Plants

- First skunk cabbage to poke through snow ____________________
- First sugar maple sap to run____________________
- First ____________________ to bloom ____________________
- First ____________________ to bloom ____________________
- First ____________________ to bloom ____________________

Animals

- Last chipmunk
- Last skunk or raccoon ______________________________
- First red-winged blackbird to return ______________________________
- First skunk odor
- First bird song ____________________ Species ______________________________
- First ______________________________
- First ______________________________
- First ______________________________

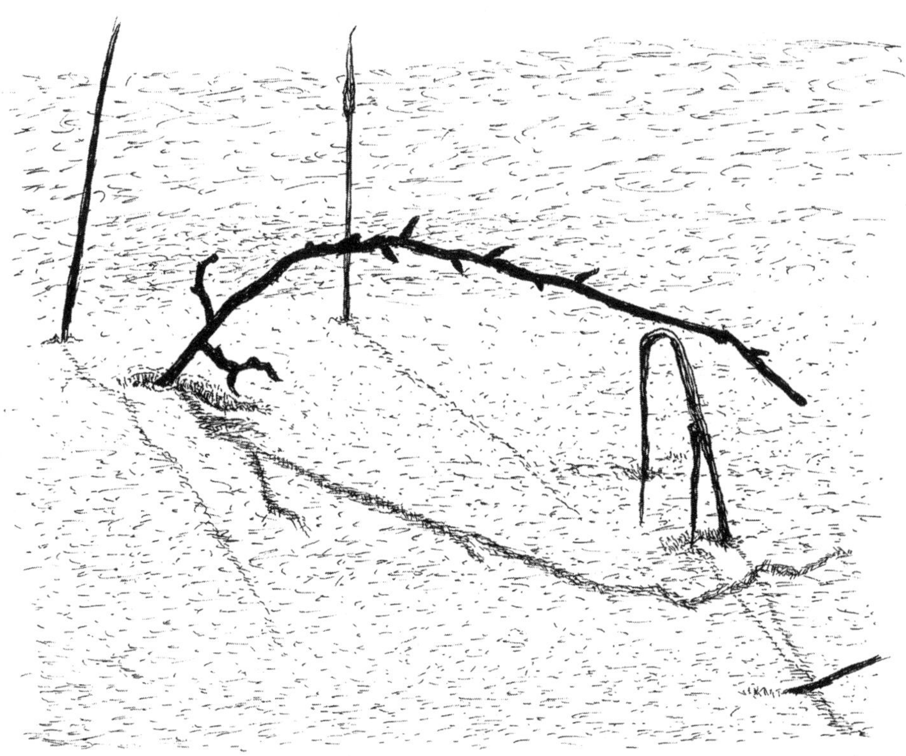

Spring Phenology Chart
(March, April, May)

Location: ______________________________ Year: __________

Instructions

- Gather information from sources such as personal observations, the Internet, newspapers or speaking with seniors.
- Try to be sure the dates are as accurate as possible.
- Feel free to tailor the charts to best fit your region, especially with regard to species.
- Include units (either imperial or metric)
- Discuss any trends you see such as big differences from the long-term averages, and speculate on how these trends may affect the dates for plant and animal events.

Description of sunrise / sunset locations at spring equinox

(Be sure to stand in exactly the same spot each season.)

On or about March 21, the Sun rises (describe where) ______________________________

____

On or about March 21, the Sun sets (describe where)______________________________

____

Sketch of sunrise position on eastern horizon showing key landmarks. Show fall equinox and winter solstice sunrise positions as well.	Sketch of sunset position on western horizon showing key landmarks. Show fall equinox and winter solstice sunset positions as well.

Sunlight

1. Photoperiod (daylight) on the following days
   - March 21 (spring equinox) ______ hours and ______ minutes
   - April 21 ______ hours and ______ minutes
   - May 21 ______ hours and ______ minutes

2. Length of shadow at noon on March 21 (or closest day possible; be sure to measure the shadow of the same person or object as in September and December).
   - March 21 __________ December 21 __________ September 21 __________

Temperature and precipitation

1. Daily temperatures
   - March 21 High __________ Low __________ Average __________
   - April 21 High __________ Low __________ Average __________
   - May 21 High __________ Low __________ Average __________

2. Dates of temperature "firsts":
   First 50°F (10°C) ______________________________
   60°F (15°C) ______________________________
   70°F (21°C) ______________________________
   80°F (27°C) ______________________________
   90°F (32°C) ______________________________

3. Dates of temperature "lasts":
   Last 0°F (–17°C) ______________________________
   10°F (–12°C) ______________________________
   20°F (–6°C) ______________________________
   32°F (0°C) ______________________________
   90°F (32°C) or below ______________________

4. Monthly mean temperatures
   - March _______________ Long-term March mean _______________
   - April _______________ Long-term April mean _______________
   - May _______________ Long-term May mean _______________

5. Precipitation:
   - Total precipitation for March _______________ Long-term March average _______________
   - Total precipitation for April _______________ Long-term April average _______________
   - Total precipitation for May _______________ Long-term May average _______________

6. Frost, snow and ice
   - Last snowfall ____
   - Last old snow to melt _______________ Long-term average date ______________________
   - First spring rain ____
   - Ice out of lake (name) ___________: ___________ Long-term average date ___________
   - Ice out of lake (name) ___________: ___________ Long-term average date ___________
   - Last date ice-fishing permitted _______________ Long-term average date ___________

Plants

- First skunk cabbage to poke through snow ______
- First crocus to bloom ______
- First tulip to bloom ______
- First dandelion to bloom ______
- First lilac to bloom ______
- First marsh marigold to bloom ______
- First leaves on deciduous tree ______ Species ______
- First flowers on deciduous tree ______ Species ______
- All deciduous trees fully in leaf ______
- First pollen cones on conifers ______
- First ______ ______
- First ______ ______
- First ______ ______

Animals

- First chipmunk ______
- First skunk (animal or odor) or raccoon ______
- First bird song ______ Species ______
- First robin ______
- First robin song ______
- First robin nesting ______
- First red-winged blackbird ______
- First tree swallow ______
- First killdeer ______
- First northbound geese ______
- First hummingbird ______
- First bat ______
- First baby mammal ______ Species ______
- First snake ______
- First turtle ______
- First frogs calling ______ Species ______
- First biting mosquito ______
- First butterfly ______ Species ______
- First monarch ______
- First dragonfly ______
- First bumble bee ______
- First ______ ______
- First ______ ______

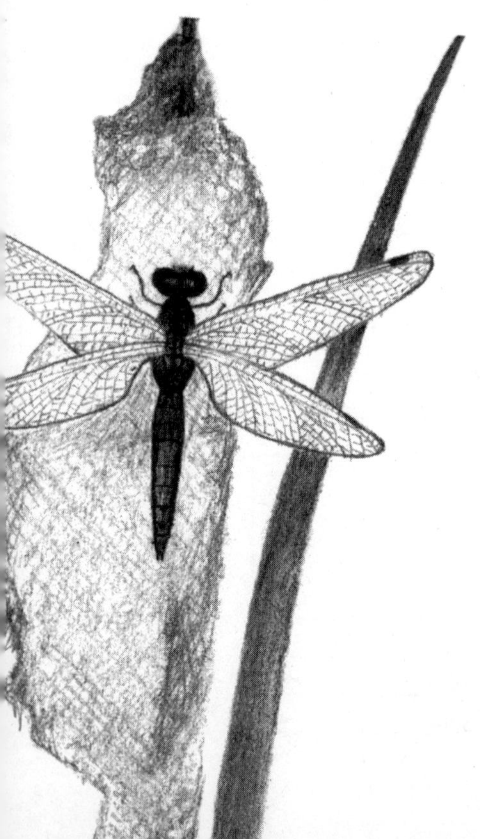

Summer Phenology Chart
(June, July, August)

Location: ______________________________ Year: __________

Instructions

- Gather information from sources such as personal observations, the Internet, newspapers or speaking with seniors.
- Try to be sure the dates are as accurate as possible.
- Feel free to tailor the charts to best fit your region, especially with regard to species.
- Include units (either imperial or metric).
- Discuss any trends you see such as big differences from the long-term averages, and speculate on how these trends may affect the dates for plant and animal events.

Description of sunrise / sunset locations at summer solstice

(Be sure to stand in exactly the same spot as in the other seasons.)

On or about June 21, the Sun rises (describe where) ______________________________

____

On or about June 21, the Sun sets (describe where) ______________________________

____

Sketch of sunrise position on eastern horizon showing key landmarks. Show sunrise positions at the fall equinox, winter solstice and spring equinox as well.	Sketch of sunset position on western horizon showing key landmarks. Show sunset positions at the fall equinox, winter solstice and spring equinox as well.

Sunlight

1. Photoperiod (daylight) on the following days
   - June 21 (summer soltice) ______ hours and ______ minutes
   - July 21 ______ hours and ______ minutes
   - August 21 ______ hours and ______ minutes
2. Length of shadow at noon on June 21 (or closest day possible; be sure to measure the shadow of the same person or object as in March, December and September).

June 21 __________ March 21 __________ December 21 __________ September 21 __________

Temperature and precipitation

1. Daily temperatures
   - June 21 High __________ Low __________ Average __________
   - July 21 High __________ Low __________ Average __________
   - August 21 High __________ Low __________ Average __________
2. Coolest day/night of summer __________ Temperature __________
3. Warmest day/night of summer __________ Temperature __________
4. Monthly mean temperatures
   - June ______________ Long-term June mean ______________
   - July ______________ Long-term July mean ______________
   - August ______________ Long-term August mean ______________
5. Precipitation
   - Total precipitation for June ______________ Long-term June average ______________
   - Total precipitation for July ______________ Long-term July average ______________
   - Total precipitation for August ______________ Long-term August average ______________

Plants

- First milkweed in bloom ______________________________
- First hayfield cut ______________________________
- First oxeye daisies in bloom on roadsides ______________________________
- Peak pollen on cars and other surfaces ______________________________
- First Queen Anne's lace in bloom ______________________________
- First local strawberries ripen ______________________________
- First serviceberries (Saskatoons) ripen ______________________________
- First tomatoes ripen ______________________________
- First sweet corn ripen ______________________________
- First goldenrod flowers ______________________________
- First aster flowers ______________________________
- First fall colors on tree, vine or shrub ______________ Species ______________
- First ______________________ ______________________
- First ______________________ ______________________
- First ______________________ ______________________

Animals

- First monarch__________
- Last northbound Arctic shorebirds pass through__________
- First fawn __________
- First turtle laying eggs__________
- First bass spawning __________
- First giant silk moth (e.g., Cecropia) __________
- First flocks of blackbirds__________
- First swallow flocks congregating on wires __________
- First southbound Arctic shorebirds arrive__________
- First baby frogs or toads leave natal ponds __________
- First cicada calling __________ Species __________
- First field or ground cricket calling __________ Species __________
- First tree cricket calling __________ Species __________
- First katydid calling __________ Species __________
- First baby turtles hatch__________
- Last bullfrog call__________
- Last robin song__________
- First/last __________ __________
- First/last __________ __________

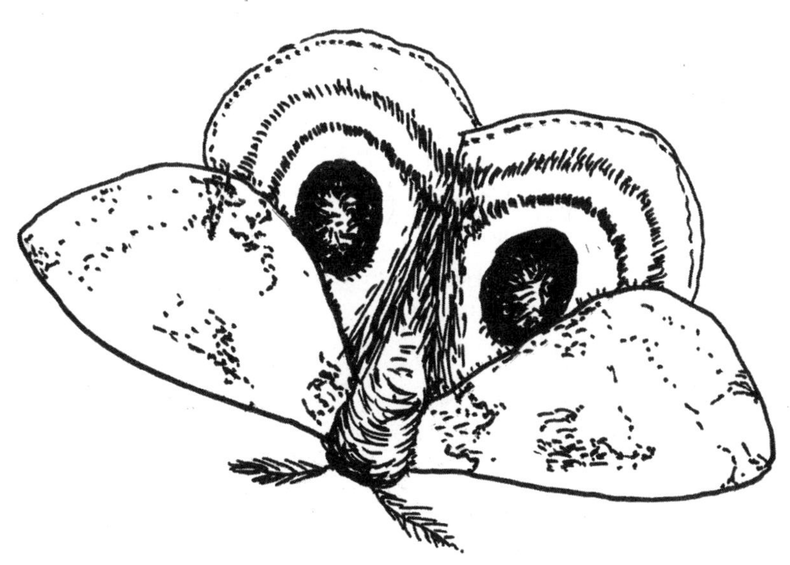

My Adopted Tree
(Fall)

Initial visit: ______________________________ Date: ______________

- Height: _____ feet (meters), or about ____ times my own height
- Trunk circumference: ______ inches (centimeters), or about _____ of my hands
- Bark: color and shade ______________ Texture ______________
- What else do you notice? (e.g., moss? holes?) ______________
- Leaves: color and shade ______________ Measurements ____ in. (cm) by ____ in. (cm)
- Leaf type: ____________ (simple or composite) Arrangement: ______________ (opposite or alternate)
- Rub a leaf. It smells like ______________
- Are there any signs of insect activity or use by birds and/or mammals? ______________
- Describe them ______________
- Are there any fruits or seeds present?_______ Describe them ______________
- How do you think the fruits or seeds dispersed? ______________
____
- Based on your description, give your tree a fun name (e.g., "Rough Roy") ______________
____
- What species is your tree? ______________
- Why did you choose this particular tree? ______________
____
____
- Draw or photograph the tree as a whole, a leaf, a seed or fruit, the twig where two leaves are attached. (Use back of sheet.)
- Write in your nature journal about your tree. For example, you could write about some experiences it may have had since it was a seedling. Write in the first person, as if the tree is talking.
- Press a couple of leaves and include them in your natural journal or on a bulletin board. Alternatively, include some leaf prints.

Follow-up fall visits

- When did the leaves start to change color? ______________
- What color(s) did the leaves become? ______________
- When did the tree reach its peak color? ______________
- When did leaves start to fall? ______________
- When had all (or nearly all) of the leaves fallen off? ______________
- What does a fallen leaf from the tree smell like? ______________
- Drawings and/or photographs (use back of sheet)

My Adopted Tree
(Winter)

1. Find a twig where last year's leaves were attached. What color is it? __________
   What color are the larger branches? ________________

2. Look to see if there are buds on the twig.
   - Are they opposite ___ or alternate ___?
   - Is there a bud(s) at the very end of the twig? ____ Is it different from the side buds? _____
     If so, how is it different? _______________
   - What color are the buds? _________ How long is the average bud? _________ in./cm
   - Using a hand lens, look to see if there are any scales on the bud. If so, how many? _______
   - Just below the bud, try to see where last year's leaf was attached. The attachment point is called a leaf scar. (Use back of sheet.)
   - Tie a small piece of string or masking tape just below a healthy-looking side bud (Bud A) and another piece below a large end bud (Bud B). Draw or photograph them before they begin to swell and open in spring. You will come back in the spring to see what comes out of each bud (leaves? flowers? both?).

3. What else do you notice?
   - Are there any signs a bird, mammal or insect has been using this tree, such as tracks in snow, insect egg mass, old nest in branches, etc.? ______________________________
   - Look for fallen leaves on the ground under the tree. Describe them and explain how they have changed since they have fallen. ______________________________
     ____

4. Drawings or photos (use back of sheet). Draw a section of a twig showing a bud and leaf scar; draw whole tree.

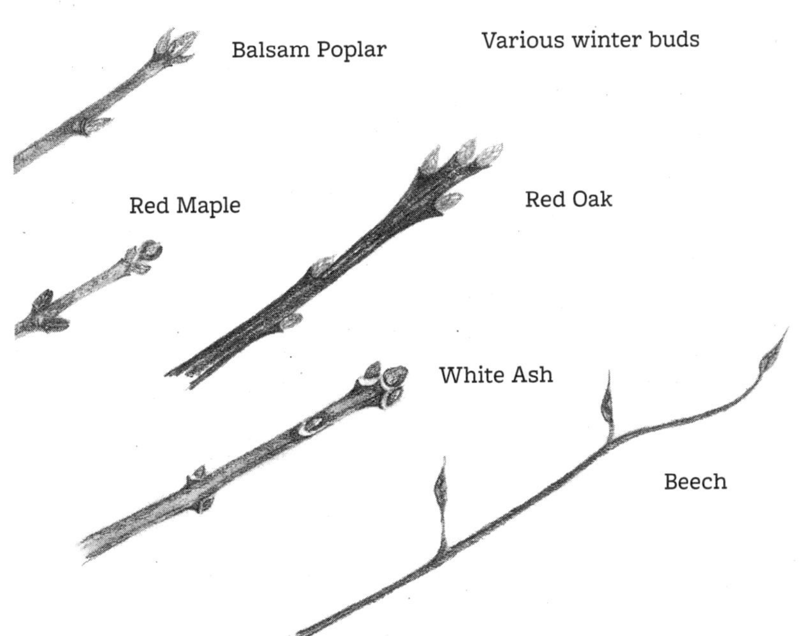

My Adopted Tree
(Spring)

1. Take a picture of your tree every week or so, and more often when change is happening fast. Always stand in the same spot to take the picture. Put the pictures in your nature journal or on back of sheet.

2. Look carefully at the two buds you have identified with ribbon or tape.
   - When did the buds start to open?
     Bud A ____________________ Bud B ____________________
   - What came out of each bud?
     Bud A: ____________________
     Bud B: ____________________
   - Take a photograph or sketch of each bud, showing all the growth that has emerged.
   - When did the first flowers appear? ____________________
   - When did the first leaves appear? ____________________
   - What shade of green are they? ____________ What do they smell like? ________
   - What color are the flowers? What do they smell like? ____________________
     What kind of insects are visiting the flowers (if any)? ____________________
   - Make a detailed sketch of a flower. Try to show all of the parts (e.g., pistil, stamen, etc.). (Use back of sheet.)
   - Take a picture or make a sketch of a leaf and a flower and place on back of sheet.
   - When had all of the leaves fully emerged? ____________________
   - Are any animals using the tree, such as birds, insects, spiders, etc.? Can you identify them?
     ____

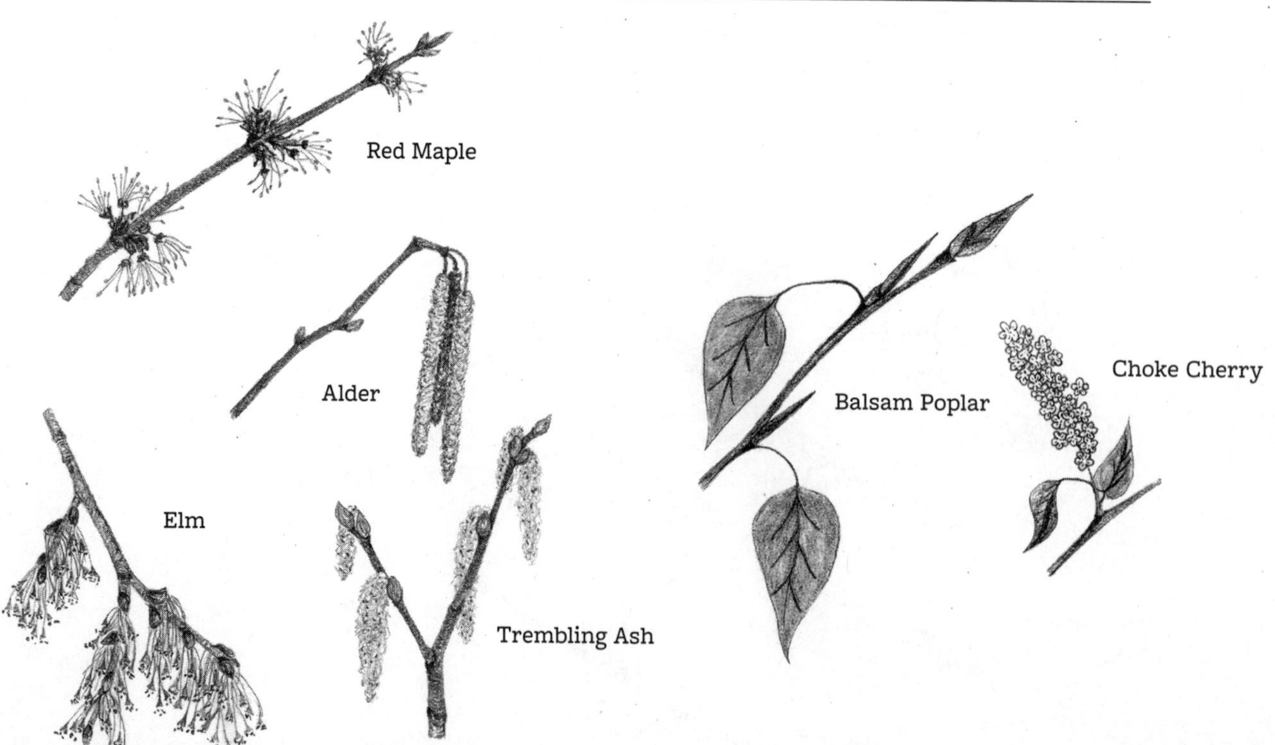

My Adopted Tree
(Summer)

1. Early summer visit: ______________________________ Date: ____________________
 • Are the leaves being eaten by insects? _____ If so, what kind? ____________________
 • Describe the damage to the leaves ____
 • Are there any fruit or seeds on the tree? _____ When did they appear? ______________
 • Check all of the new growth that has come out of each of the two buds you marked.
 Bud A: How many leaves ____, flowers____, fruit/seeds____ ? Measure the length of new growth from original bud to tip of furthest leaf _______ in. (cm)
 Bud B: How many leaves ____, flowers____, fruit/seeds____ ? Measure the length of new growth from original bud to tip of furthest leaf _______ in. (cm)
 Comments ____
 • As you did in the spring, take a photograph or sketch of all the growth that has emerged from each bud. (Use back of sheet.)

2. Late summer visit: ______________________________ Date: ____________________
 • Check again all of the new growth that has come out of each of the two buds you marked.
 Bud A: How many leaves ____, fruit/seeds____ ? Measure the length of new growth from original bud to tip of furthest leaf _______ in. (cm)
 Bud B: How many leaves ____, fruit/seeds____ ? Measure the length of new growth from original bud to tip of furthest leaf _______ in. (cm)
 • Comments ____
 • Is your tree is suffering from any kind of stress (e.g., drought, insects, fungi, etc.)? If so, what? ____
 • Sit in the shade under the tree. How does the temperature compare?________________
 ____
 • Other comments? ____

What's Wrong with the Scenario? — Answer Key

Corrections for Fall (p. 94)

1. Sun rises in east.
2. Birch leaves are yellow in the fall.
3. Apples blossom in the spring.
4. Geese fly south in the fall.
5. Geese don't whistle; they honk.
6. Robins don't sing in the fall.
7. Black bears give birth to newborns in the winter.

Corrections for Winter (p. 153)

1. Sun should be low in southern sky.
2. Birds don't sing in early winter.
3. Birds don't nest in early winter, either.
4. Chickadees don't eat together at a feeder; they come in one at a time.
5. Gray squirrels don't turn white in the winter.
6. The buds have been on the twigs since last summer.

Corrections for Spring (p. 210)

1. Swallows don't build a nest on branches.
2. Swallows don't eat seeds.
3. Goldenrod and aster don't bloom in the spring.
4. Big Dipper should be in northern sky.
5. Bullfrogs don't whistle; they make a garrumph.
6. Bucks shed their antlers during the winter and start growing new ones in the spring.

Corrections for Summer (p. 267)

1. Monarch caterpillars only eat milkweed.
2. Dragonflies don't drink nectar; they eat other insects.
3. People aren't allergic to goldenrod pollen; it is too heavy to float in the air.
4. By summer, young crows are as big as their parents.
5. Cicadas make a harsh buzz, not a cheery whistle.
6. Leo the Lion is seen in the spring, not in the fall.

Artists' and Photographers' Credits

Drawings

- Kady MacDonald Denton: Cartoons of Charles Darwin, Carl Sagan and Neil DeGrasse Tyson
- Judy Hyland: All species and activity icons; Pages 1, 2, 3, 4, 6, 14, 19, 20, 23, 25, 27 (top), 29, 39, 48, 56, 63, 71, 73 (bottom), 74, 76, 77, 78, 79 (both), 82, 88, 89 (top), 90, 91 (top), 92, 100, 118, 120, 124, 128 (right), 132, 135, 136, 149, 151, 154, 158, 164, 182, 184, 190, 194, 200, 201, 204, 205, 207 (top), 234, 242, 250, 251, 258 (bottom), 260, 261, 262, 267, 274, 276, 279, 284, 288, 289, 296, 305
- Kim Caldwell: Pages 15, 17, 61, 64, 67, 93, 98, 104, 111, 114, 116, 125, 177, 202, 230, 235, 259, 268, 277, 292, 328, 334, 335, 339, 340
- Doug Sadler: 5, 11, 13, 21, 32, 34, 35, 36, 37, 44, 46, 51, 55, 62, 66, 73 (top), 83 (both), 85, 89 (bottom), 91 (bottom), 94, 97, 101, 103, 106, 107, 108, 128 (left), 141, 147, 150, 163, 166,174, 180, 186, 196, 198, 199, 203, 207 (bottom), 208, 209, 212, 216, 221, 224, 253, 263, 264, 265, 266, 280, 303, 310, 326, 329, 331, 332, 337, 338 (both), 341
- Jean-Paul Efford: 42, 192, 244, 307
- Jacob Rodenburg: 27 (bottom), 28, 40, 52, 55, 122, 133, 168, 170, 172, 218, 228, 232, 237, 248, 258 (top), 271, 286, 290, 293, 294, 298
- Hannah Palmer: 49
- iStock: 22, 38, 77, 113, 220, 226, 273, 281, 291, 300, 339
- Pixabay: 33, 60
- Other: 69 (from Origin of Species, Wikimedia), 139 (Andonee, Wikimedia)

Photographs

Color Insert

- Jay Fitzgerald: Number 19
- Drew Monkman: Numbers 1, 3, 5, 9, 13, 17, 21, 24, 26, 30, 31, 38, 40, 43
- Jacob Rodenburg: Numbers 4, 7, 11, 12, 14, 15, 20, 22, 28, 33, 35, 36, 37, 42, 44, 45
- iStock: Numbers 16, 46, 47

- Pixabay: Numbers 2, 6, 8, 18, 23, 27, 29, 34, 41, 48
- Other: Numbers 25 (Opuntia, Wikimedia), 32 (George Chernilevsky, Wikimedia), 39 (ALLIOT Brigitte, Wikimedia)

Appendix:

- Song Ensemble: Karl Egressy (red-winged blackbird, mourning dove, common yellowthroat, white-breasted nuthatch, yellow warbler, song sparrow, black-capped chickadee and American goldfinch; Drew Monkman (great horned owl and American robin), Nima Taghaboni (American bittern),William H. Majoros, Wikimedia (Hermit thrush)
- Leaf Adaptations: Pixabay
- Adaptations to Winter: Karl Egressy (goldeneye duck); Drew Monkman (birds at feeder, squirrel's nest, gall); Jeff Keller (black-capped chickadee)
- Adaptations for reproduction: All iStock and Pixabay except: Karl Egressy (song sparrow singing); Drew Monkman (flowers hanging from twigs)
- Fungus scavenger hunt: All Pixabay
- Imagining Your Ancestors: Drew Monkman (Monkman family pictures); Michelle Monkman (lizard-like ancestor); Tim Evanson, Wikimedia (long-haired ancestor); Museum für Naturkunde, Wikimedia (thick skulled ancestor); Cicero Moraes, Wikimedia (Homo erectus); Kabir Bakie, Wikimedia (chimp); Emmanuel Faivre, Wikimedia (lemur); Sjonge, Wikimedia (shrew); National Science Foundation, Wikimedia (Tiktaalik); James St. John, Wikimedia (primitive fish); Willem van Aken, Wikimedia (alga)

Others:

- Hannah Palmer: Page 49
- Drew Monkman: Pages 50, 58, 215
- iStock: Page 75, 189

Index

About the Authors

Jacob Rodenburg is the executive director of Camp Kawartha, an award-winning summer camp and outdoor education centre that uses music, drama, hands-on exploration, games and other activities to inspire awe and wonder for the local environment. He teaches part-time at Trent University, where he spearheaded the development of an "Eco Mentor" certificate program for teacher candidates that was subsequently adopted by several other universities. Jacob also conceived and helped to establish one of Canada's most sustainable buildings, the Camp Kawartha Environment Centre. Jacob has worked in the field of outdoor education for 25 years and has published numerous articles on children, nature and the environment. He recently received the Ontario Society of Environmental Educators Award for "Leadership in Environmental Education."

Drew Monkman is an award-winning naturalist, nature writer, environmental advocate and retired teacher. Drew's interest in integrating environmental education into all areas of the curriculum inspired him to oversee the development of a schoolyard naturalization area and outdoor classroom, which went on to become a model for many similar projects. His popular nature column "Our Changing Seasons" appears weekly in the *Peterborough Examiner*. Drew is also the author of two books outlining events in nature through the 12 months of the year, including *Nature's Year: Changing Seasons in Central and Eastern Ontario*. In June 2016, he was awarded an honorary Doctor of Science degree by Trent University. Visit Drew's website (drewmonkman.com) to see past columns, his Twitter feed, local nature sightings and information on climate change in central Ontario.

If you have enjoyed *The Big Book of Nature Activities*, you might also enjoy other

Books to Build a New Society

Our books provide positive solutions for people who want to make a difference. We specialize in:

Climate Change ◆ Conscious Community
Conservation & Ecology ◆ Cultural Critique
Education & Parenting ◆ Energy ◆ Food & Gardening
Health & Wellness ◆ Modern Homesteading & Farming
New Economies ◆ Progressive Leadership ◆ Resilience
Social Responsibility ◆ Sustainable Building & Design

New Society Publishers

ENVIRONMENTAL BENEFITS STATEMENT

New Society Publishers has chosen to produce this book on recycled paper made with 100% post consumer waste, processed chlorine free, and old growth free.

For every 5,000 books printed, New Society saves the following resources:[1]

50	Trees
4,513	Pounds of Solid Waste
4,966	Gallons of Water
6,477	Kilowatt Hours of Electricity
8,204	Pounds of Greenhouse Gases
35	Pounds of HAPs, VOCs, and AOX Combined
12	Cubic Yards of Landfill Space

[1] Environmental benefits are calculated based on research done by the Environmental Defense Fund and other members of the Paper Task Force who study the environmental impacts of the paper industry.

For a full list of NSP's titles, please call 1-800-567-6772 *or check out our web site at:*

www.newsociety.com